General 'Boy'

There was one, however, who towered above all …
I refer to Lieutenant-General Sir Frederick Browning,
known to us all as General 'Boy'.

General Sir Richard Gale, *With the Sixth Airborne Division in Normandy*

General 'Boy'

The Life of Lieutenant General Sir Frederick Browning

GCVO, KBE, CB, DSO, DL

Richard Mead

Foreword by
HRH The Duke of Edinburgh

Pen & Sword
MILITARY

First published in Great Britain in 2010
and reprinted in this format in 2017 by
PEN & SWORD MILITARY
An imprint of
Pen & Sword Books Ltd
47 Church Street
Barnsley
South Yorkshire, S70 2AS

ISBN 978 1 47389 899 8

A CIP catalogue record for this book is
available from the British Library.

Typeset in 10pt Palatino by Mac Style Ltd, Bridlington, East Yorkshire

Printed and bound in Malta by
Gutenberg Press Ltd

Pen & Sword Books Ltd incorporates the Imprints of Pen & Sword
Archaeology, Atlas, Aviation, Battleground, Discovery, Family History,
History, Maritime, Military, Naval, Politics, Railways, Select, Transport,
True Crime, Fiction, Frontline Books, Leo Cooper, Praetorian Press,
Seaforth Publishing, Wharncliffe and White Owl.

For a complete list of Pen & Sword titles please contact
PEN & SWORD BOOKS LIMITED
47 Church Street, Barnsley, South Yorkshire, S70 2AS, England
E-mail: enquiries@pen-and-sword.co.uk
Website: www.pen-and-sword.co.uk

Contents

List of Maps

Foreword by HRH The Duke of Edinburgh

BUCKINGHAM PALACE

I am delighted that Richard Mead decided to write a biography of General Sir Frederick 'Boy' Browning. He was a very remarkable man with huge ability and great charm. He was a member of a generation which had to face the traumas of active service in two world wars; in front-line service in the first, and with all the heavy responsibilities, and risks, of higher command in the second.

Although I did meet him while he was serving as Chief of Staff to my uncle – Dickie Mountbatten – as Supreme Allied Commander in South East Asia, it was only when he came to us as Comptroller and Treasurer that I got to know him well. As I was still serving with the Navy, and expected to go on doing so for many years, I was inevitably away from home for much of that time. His seniority in the Army, his connection with the Grenadier Guards and his wide circle of friends in positions of responsibility, were immensely valuable to the Queen and myself in the early years after our marriage.

Even though we were in different age groups, and with different service backgrounds, we did have one great interest in common. We both enjoyed boats and yachting. It was in his converted MFV *Fanny Rosa* that I stayed during my first visit to Cowes Regatta in 1948.

His last years were sad, but they were only a very small part of his long, active and distinguished career.

Philip

Introduction

In selecting a British general of the Second World War for a new biography, I had a short list of eight, the only qualification for inclusion being that no such work already existed. The list comprised senior officers of distinction, some of whom had led large formations in the field, whilst others had exercised considerable influence from behind the scenes. One name stood out, however, a man whose military career had not matched those of some of the other contenders, but who was in every other way more interesting. Lieutenant General Sir Frederick Browning – called 'Boy' in this book from the time he received the nickname, prior to which he is 'Tommy', his name in the family – has long been of some interest to military historians as a result of his close association with Great Britain's airborne forces during the Second World War. Their interest has focused on his involvement in Operation 'Market Garden' and the disaster at Arnhem, in connection with which he allegedly gave a now much-used expression to the English language – 'a bridge too far'. However, it is also generally recognized that he was decorated for bravery in the Great War, represented his country at two sports, initiated a tradition at Sandhurst which persists to this day and served as a senior member of the Royal Household. To cap it all, he was married to one of the most enduringly popular novelists of the twentieth century, Daphne du Maurier. Why, then, had no biography appeared many years before?

Boy himself discouraged any such work in his lifetime, indeed he went so far as to obtain undertakings from some of those who served on his staff at South-East Asia Command that they would not cooperate with any potential biographer. After his death the members of his family were approached on more than one occasion by a would-be author but were unenthusiastic, whilst Daphne herself refused to write about him. Subsequently Boy did not come out well from the works of some historians, and indeed film directors, who covered 'Market Garden', but nobody appeared to have researched his role or his background in any depth, his detractors at best repeating the charges made by others, at worst resorting to little short of character assassination. It was time for a closer look.

Quite why Arnhem continues to exert such fascination is something of a mystery, although it probably has something to do with the British love of heroic failure: Sir John Moore's retreat to Corunna, the Charge of the Light Brigade and the evacuation of the BEF from Dunkirk would be other good examples. The flow of books on the subject seems never-ending, notwithstanding that little in the way of new information has emerged over the last twenty years. British authors have, for the most part, concentrated on the exploits of 1 Airborne Division and the attempts of Horrocks's 'cavalry' to relieve them. The deeds of the two American airborne divisions, other than in the crossing of the Waal at Nijmegen, have had much less prominence, whilst the actions of VIII and XII Corps have largely been ignored.

The criticisms of Boy have thus tended to be from the perspective of those concerned with Arnhem itself, which was not just a failure, but a disaster. This also explains something which I had not hitherto realized, which was that Boy has been far from popular with some of the veterans of 1 Airborne, who attach much of the blame for the debacle to him, compounding this with his subsequent treatment of the Polish General Sosabowski, who to many of them was a hero. This contrasts completely with the views of those who served under him at other times, who have by and large been great admirers.

Although almost every book on Arnhem, or on 'Market Garden' as a whole, refers to Boy, his appearance has been episodic, none of them following him closely through either the planning or the execution of the operation. I have tried to put him more firmly in context and the result produces alternative explanations for some of his decisions and actions to those which have become widely accepted, although a number of the criticisms continue to stick. Because I have decided to look at 'Market Garden' from Boy's perspective, trying to focus on what he did and what he knew, I have written relatively little on the battle at Arnhem itself. It is more than just background noise, a description which might apply for the most part to the operations of VIII and XII Corps and, to some extent, of the US 101 Airborne Division, but it is not detailed, because Boy was largely unaware of events there, a fact which has, rightly or wrongly, led to much criticism of his role. However, the reader has a wide choice of literature should he wish to know more – indeed one is led to wonder if the world can really take much more on the subject.

As 'Market Garden' provided the only occasion bar the Japanese surrender in 1945 on which Boy can be said to have been at the centre of events of world importance, and as it represented the summit of his military career, it takes up a disproportionate part of this book. In reality it occupied a tiny part of his life: from the time of its conception to the withdrawal of the Airborne Corps HQ from Holland was a period one day short of a month. There were sixty-eight more years to research.

One of the major difficulties was the absence of a paper trail. Boy never kept a diary and relatively few of his letters have survived. The majority of those that have, written to Daphne in pencil whenever he could find a moment, on anything which came to hand if no proper writing paper was available, cover a short but fascinating period, from just before the invasion of Normandy to his departure from SEAC in July 1946. Surprisingly, hardly any of them seem to have passed through the hands of the censor, but he was in any event quite discreet, offering for the most part little for the military historian, though a great deal for the biographer. Every now and then, however, his enthusiasm for or frustration with military matters bursts through.

The letters to Daphne are not easy to read, as they are written in the private language used by the two of them, with much inversion of pronouns, for instance 'me' for 'I' and vice-versa, 'ee' for 'you' (possibly a reflection of Cornish dialect), some occasionally strange syntax and the frequent use of codewords. By way of example, the letters all end with the same words: 'With all the love in a man's heart to him own beloved Mumpty and God bless 'ee, the Bumps and small Tiny. Your own devoted Tim'. This may seem childish to some, but I find it rather endearing and reading the letters helps to add substance to Boy's complex character.

There exist a scattering of other letters to Daphne from the late 1940s and early 50s, a small number to his sister and his Aunt Helen and some more formal letters written whilst at Buckingham Palace, but not on palace business. A handful of other documents have survived, notably the journal of the cruise to Fowey on which he first saw Daphne and the manuscript of his unperformed ballet *Jeanne d'Arc*. Otherwise there is nothing from him at all. Boy did, however, leave his mark through the writings of others, not just in military histories, but in personal reminiscences. He features in a number of published autobiographies and collections of private papers.

As far as Boy's relationship with Daphne was concerned, I found that much of the work had been done for me. I had read Margaret Forster's excellent biography of Daphne soon after its publication in 1993 and was pleased to hear from the family that it was very accurate, their only significant criticism being that it had failed to bring out sufficiently a sense of fun which she shared with Boy. Daphne herself could certainly not be charged with any failure to leave a paper trail, most of which is housed in the archives at Exeter University.

The most uneventful time of Boy's professional life as far as a researcher is concerned is the inter-war period during which, except for the four years at Sandhurst, he was on regimental duty. There are virtually no living witnesses of this period, apart from members of the family who were very young, and little of moment took place other than a relatively brief episode when he commanded a battalion in Egypt. Thanks to the good offices of his elder daughter, Tessa, I was able to obtain all Boy's confidential reports, which provided some background to the trajectory of his career.

As far as Boy's post-war career and private life are concerned, we move on to much firmer ground, as there are many who still remember him. This period will not prove so interesting to the military enthusiasts, but it throws yet more light on the personality of the man, which was much more complex than has ever been recognized by military historians. The side of his character which Boy showed to the world, even to those with whom he worked closely, was quite different from that which his family and close friends knew.

During my research I spoke to a number of people who knew Boy well, others who knew him only slightly and a few who knew him not at all, but were still relevant to his story. All had views to offer, both positive and negative, and nobody was indifferent to him, which confirmed me in my view that he would be an interesting subject. A *sine qua non* of the project was the cooperation of Boy's children, but happily for me they also felt that it was high time the record was put straight.

Note on nomenclature

I have described military units and formations in the following way, which may not conform to strict practice, but is at least consistent: 21st Army Group, Second Army, XXX Corps, 1 Division, 2 Brigade, 3rd Battalion. If the formation is specialized, for instance Armoured or Airborne, I say so. There are occasions when I discard the word 'Division', using for instance just '1 Airborne' when its repetition would make the text somewhat laboured, but the context should be clear.

Prologue

The biting wind drove gusts of rain across the bleak countryside, which stretched as far as the eye could see, its horizon broken only by the occasional farm building and a few lines of trees along the muddy roads and innumerable intersecting ditches. The man in the Airborne smock and the maroon beret stood by his jeep, waiting for his colleague to join him. He felt as bleak as his surroundings and desperately worried. The operation on the previous night had been a complete disaster, extinguishing any hope for a miraculous deliverance.

In the distance another jeep appeared, driving fast towards him. It drew up alongside and a man in a peaked cap and a smock with a sheepskin collar stepped out. He looked tired, as well he might, not least because he had just experienced a hair-raising drive through enemy lines. After greeting him, the first man asked the only questions which mattered:

'What did Bimbo say, Jorrocks?'
'He said that he'll support whatever we decide. Monty agrees.'
'And what do you think?'
'I'm sorry, Boy, but I think we've had it.'
'You know I do, so let's get them out tonight.'

For the man in the peaked cap, it was the end of his hopes. For the man in the maroon beret, it was also the end of his dreams.

Chapter 1

Family (1335–1896)

If the family genealogists are to be believed, the Browning family is of some antiquity. One of them has traced its origins back to the second son of the chieftain of the Celtic tribe known as the Brunii, who were settled in what is now Belgium at the end of the first century BC. The story goes that this son refused to bow to Julius Caesar and sailed north, settling first in the Frisian Islands and then on the south side of Bukken Fjord in Norway. One of his descendants travelled to England in the fifth century, as legend has it to assist King Vortigern in his campaign against the Picts, decided to stay on and eventually put down roots in Wessex.

The descent from these early Brunings is highly questionable and the various family trees are inconsistent and contradictory, but there is common ground with Sir John Bruning or Browning, born in 1335 in Leigh, Gloucestershire, who married Alice, the daughter and heiress of Sir John and Lady Maltravers of Melbury Sampford in Dorset. In the church at Melbury Sampford can still be seen two alabaster effigies of family members. His son, also Sir John, married the daughter of Sir Thomas FitzNicholl, a kinsman of the Hardings of Berkeley Castle. Through this connection he obtained the manor of Coaley in Gloucestershire, where the family residence was Garter Court, long since demolished. It is from this branch that the poet, Robert Browning, was descended. The link to the family with which we are concerned is more tenuous but, from the evidence available, Thomas Browning, who was born in about 1630 and died in 1700, was a cadet member of the Coaley Brownings.

With the descent from Thomas one is on genealogically firm ground. He was a mercer whose wife, Elizabeth, came from Burton Latimer in Northamptonshire, where they both settled. His grandson William moved with his family to the London area, possibly following his uncle, Thomas's fourth son, who had settled in Bermondsey and became in due course the High Sheriff of Surrey. The family remained in the London area and appear to have been solidly middle-class, but of relatively modest means. However, Thomas's great-great grandson, Henry, born in 1796, married well, his wife Anne Bainbridge being a woman of some wealth, and he was able to buy a house in Grosvenor Street, even then in a fashionable area of London.

Henry sent his second son Montague Charles, who was born in 1837, to school at Eton, from where he joined the Army, the first of this branch of the family to enter either of the two services. Montague Charles served in the 87th and 89th Regiments of Foot, seeing action as a young officer in both the Crimean War and the Indian Mutiny and rising in due course to the rank of Captain. In 1862 he married Fanny Hogg, the daughter of the rector of Fornham St Martin, near Bury St Edmunds in Suffolk, and later purchased Brantham Court, near Manningtree in the same county. His financial circumstances bolstered by being a residuary co-legatee of his childless Uncle Thomas, he was recognised as a man of some substance locally, becoming a Justice of the Peace, a colonel in the West Suffolk Militia and a Companion of the Bath.

Montague Charles's eldest son, Montague Edward, born in 1863, became the most distinguished of the line thus far. He entered the Royal Naval College, Dartmouth, in 1876 and was made midshipman in the Royal Navy two years later, establishing himself as a gunnery expert before promotion to commander in 1897 and captain in 1902. He attained flag rank in 1911 and subsequently commanded the 3rd Cruiser Squadron in the Grand Fleet in 1915. In 1916 he was appointed Commander-in Chief of the North American and West Indies station, returning to the Grand Fleet as commander of the 4th Battle Squadron in 1918. Following the end of the Great War he was appointed head of the Allied Naval Armistice Commission and was rigorous in his insistence on adherence to the terms of the Armistice.[1] A spell at the Admiralty as Second Sea Lord was followed by three years as Commander-in-Chief at Devonport. In 1925 he became the First and Principal Naval Aide-de-Camp to King George V and, following his retirement in 1926, was appointed Rear-Admiral of the United Kingdom in 1929 and Vice-Admiral of the United Kingdom in 1939, from which role he only retired in 1945.[2]

Admiral Sir Montague Browning GCB, GCVO, GCMG was clearly an exceptional officer and, by all accounts, a popular one. Called Monty by his family and personal friends, he was known throughout the Navy as 'Hooky', having lost his left hand through an accident early in his career and had it replaced with a hook. In 1930 he applied for a grant of arms for use by himself and all descendants of his father. The arms granted were 'Argent three bars wavy Azure on the quarter of the first a Cross Gules', a direct allusion to those of the Brownings of Coaley 'Azure three bars wavy Argent', in spite of his inability at the time to demonstrate conclusively his descent from the Gloucestershire family.[3] As a crest, he took a pair of silver wings emerging from a gold naval crown. The wings had also been included in the arms of the Brownings of Coaley and apparently alluded to the helmet adornments of their Frisian ancestors.

Montague Charles and Fanny had four other children. The second son, Arthur, born in 1864, joined the Army as an officer in the King's Royal Rifle Corps, but died at the age of 29. The only daughter, Helen, born in 1865, had a serious accident whilst playing leapfrog with her brothers as a child: she fell very badly, injuring her spine and, although she could walk with some difficulty, she spent much of her time in a wheelchair. The third son, Berthold, born in 1867 and known to family and friends as Bertie, obtained a MA at Christ Church, Oxford and then followed his maternal grandfather and a number of other Hogg relatives into the Church of England. In due course he became rector of Pakenham, two villages away from Fornham St Martin.

Frederick Henry, the youngest child, was born in Pakenham on 1 August 1870. Unlike his father, Freddie was sent to school at Wellington College, possibly with a career in the Army in mind, as the school had a reputation in that direction. It is likely that his mother influenced the decision: Fanny's brother had been at Eton and was unhappy there. Freddie did well at Wellington, both in the classroom and on the playing field – indeed he proved himself to be an excellent sportsman, representing the school in the cricket first XI in both 1887 and 1888 and in the rugger first XV in 1888. The sport at which he excelled, however, was rackets, in which he was in the school first pair for three years. When he went up to Magdalen College, Oxford, in 1889, Freddie continued playing rackets at the highest level, gaining his half-blue in the match against Cambridge in 1890. He subsequently went on to win the Amateur Doubles Championship twice, in 1893 and 1895. With a powerful forehand from his preferred position on the right hand side of the court, he was considered by many to be the best amateur of his generation, in a game dominated by amateurs.

Freddie proved to be a good cricketer at Oxford as well and, although he failed to win university honours in the sport, he played for his college in 1890 and 1891. He never rose to the same heights as in rackets, but he continued to participate as a serious amateur, playing for the MCC until his late thirties and going on tour with the club's team to America in 1909. He was elected to the MCC committee in 1920 and, prior to the Great War, also became a committee member of both the two great 'nomadic' amateur cricket clubs, I Zingari and the Free Foresters.

When Freddie came down from Oxford, having decided not to take his degree, he did not follow his two brothers who had joined the services or the one who had taken holy orders, but chose rather to go into the wine trade. A short time later he joined the family firm of Twiss & Brownings, whose main business was the importation of Hennessy brandy, having acquired the sole agency in 1840. The partners were his father, two of his uncles and two of his cousins, most of whom did not actually work in the business. Freddie, who became the senior partner of Twiss & Brownings in 1905, formed a close friendship with the Hennessy family, which was continued by subsequent generations.

The wine trade suited Freddie's character well. Sir Samuel Hoare, writing of him in *The Times* after his death, said 'Friendship was the very essence of his life. No trouble that he would not take for a friend, no sacrifice that he would not make. You just had to ask him for his help and advice and it was yours in all its value and profusion.' Another unnamed correspondent described his character: 'Gay, witty, with an acute sense of humour, "la joie de vivre" was in his blood and he made everyone round feel as he did. Shrewd and gifted with great common sense, he was above all things human, and though gay and debonair he sympathised with the troubles of others as if they were his very own.' There may be some hyperbole in such sentiments, but Freddie was clearly both genuinely popular with and much valued by his friends.

One such friend was Rupert, the son of Richard D'Oyly Carte, who had brought together W. S. Gilbert and Arthur Sullivan to create the Savoy Operas. Richard had also built the Savoy Hotel, which was opened in 1889, and in 1903, two years after his father's death, Rupert became chairman of the hotel company. Freddie was invited to join the board and in due course also the boards of the sister companies owning and managing the Berkeley and Claridges hotels. He used to lunch or dine regularly at the Savoy, where he was able to entertain his wide circle of friends.

Notwithstanding his very recent start in business and his busy social and sporting life, Freddie also found time to get married, on 1 March 1894 at St Mary Abbots, Kensington, to Anne Alt. Always known as Nancy, his bride was the daughter of Colonel William Alt and his wife Elisabeth. Elisabeth's father, George Earl, was a scientist, author, ethnologist, traveller and linguist of some distinction. In 1830, at the age of fifteen, he sailed for Australia, where he interested himself in the affairs of the aboriginal peoples. He accompanied Darwin in the *Beagle*, acting as an interpreter of the various native languages in which he had become proficient, and was a friend of Rajah Brooke of Sarawak. His travel books were best sellers of their day. He eventually became Assistant Resident Councillor and Police Magistrate of the Straits Settlements, where he died in 1865.

William Alt's own background was as interesting as that of his father-in-law. Born in 1840, his father died when he was very young, leaving his mother nearly penniless, so he entered the merchant navy at the age of twelve, transferring to the China Customs Service seven years later. He left China for Nagasaki almost immediately, when that port was opened for the first time to foreigners other than the Chinese and the Dutch, registering with the British consulate as a general commission agent. In his first decade there he amassed a considerable fortune, which allowed him to build a 60-foot yacht named *Phantom* for his personal use and to build a very substantial house on the southern slopes of a mountain overlooking the city.[4] William became a prominent figure in the local community, being elected in 1861 as one of the initial committee of the Chamber of Commerce and in 1862 to the newly formed Municipal Council.

On his way back to England on business in 1863, William met and fell in love with Elisabeth Earl in Province Wellesley, where her father was the Magistrate. On his return he accompanied Elisabeth and her parents to Australia and they were married in Adelaide. They returned to Nagasaki, before moving on to Osaka, when that city too was opened to foreign trade in 1868 and then to Yokohama eighteen months later. In 1871, William's poor health required him to return to England permanently and he and his wife settled first in Surrey and then in Kensington, at the same time acquiring a villa at Rapallo in Italy, where they used to spend the winter. He became an officer in the 22nd Middlesex Rifle Volunteer Corps, usually called The Rangers, becoming in due course its Colonel and receiving the Volunteer Officers' Decoration. Appointed a Companion of the Bath for his contribution to British interests in Japan, he donated much of his fine collection of Japanese art to the Victoria and Albert Museum.

Nancy was the fifth child and fourth daughter of William and Elisabeth Alt. She was born in 1872 after the couple's return to England and was followed by two more sisters and another brother. She was by all accounts a charming young woman at the time of her meeting with Freddie Browning, when she was twenty-two and he was twenty-three, and Freddie's parents were delighted with her. As far as the marriage was concerned, it was certainly happy enough initially, though Nancy had to fit in with Freddie, whose sporting and social activities remained very important to him.

The couple bought the lease of a house at 31 Hans Road, just off Brompton Road, and lost no time in starting a family. Helen Grace Browning, always called by her second name, was born at the family home on 7 March 1895 and Frederick Arthur Montague Browning on 20 December 1896.

Chapter 2

Tommy (1896–1914)

Although he was christened after his father and two of his uncles, virtually nobody ever called the young Browning by any of his given names, except the first on formal occasions. To the family and to close family friends, he was always Tommy. This was apparently the name of a toy monkey to which he became much attached as a baby and which he may well have resembled. Whatever the case, the name stuck to him.

In later life Tommy used to say that he was born in the piano department of Harrods, the side of Hans Road on which the family house stood having by then been torn down to make room for the expansion of the department store. Number 31 was to be his home for much of his childhood, although Freddie and Nancy subsequently moved to 44 Lowndes Street, a few hundred yards away.

A member of a very large family herself, Nancy would have loved to have had more children. Freddie, on the other hand, considered that he had done his bit and that to enlarge the family would require him to sacrifice some of his other activities, notably the sporting ones, which he was not prepared to do. Conjugal relations therefore came to an end after Tommy was born and Nancy turned increasingly to religion. In this she was doubtless encouraged by the numerous clerics on the Browning side and particularly by her parents-in-law, who were both devout Christians. The strong faith of his mother and his paternal grandparents did have an impact on Tommy himself. He became a regular churchgoer from childhood onwards and, whilst he never wore his religion on his sleeve, he regarded it as a central tenet of his life and conducted himself according to a moral code which was very much based on Christian ethics.

One other aspect of Tommy's childhood would return throughout his life and it concerned his health. From time to time, generally when he was overtired, he would be afflicted by severe stomach pains, which when he was young could only be relieved by his mother gently rubbing the spot. Known in the family as 'Tommy's tum' and to himself as 'me tum', this ailment was never satisfactorily diagnosed. It could be brought on by strenuous unaccustomed exercise, but was possibly more nervous in its origin. Over time he learnt how to control it, but when it struck it was generally quite debilitating and would effectively put him out of action for anything between a few hours and some days. His cousin, Hubert Browning, who witnessed an attack whilst staying with their mutual grandparents when Tommy was in his early teens, certainly felt that it was as much psychological as physical, but saw that he was in quite considerable pain. It was a harbinger of health problems which would plague him all his life and even have an impact on his career.

This apart, Tommy had a happy childhood. He adored his mother, whom he always called 'Mumbo', and had a good relationship with his father. Freddie was unquestionably a loving parent to both his children, writing the most affectionate letters whenever they were away, but he never allowed them to interfere with his many activities. Partly as a result of this, as Tommy and Grace grew older, they spent more and more time away from London, usually with their two sets of grandparents. The senior Brownings still lived at Brantham Court when the children were young, but moved later to Bramfield House, Hertford. Tommy's aunt, Helen Browning, who was mostly confined to a wheelchair, lived with them and Tommy became extremely fond of her as well.

Perhaps more surprisingly, once they had reached the ages of about five and six, Tommy and Grace spent time with their Alt grandparents at Rapallo on the Ligurian coast and, on at least one visit, the two of them were there for nearly nine months. By this time William Alt liked to spend the autumn, winter and spring in Italy, as the mild climate helped to alleviate his bronchitis and the children would go out by boat with their nanny to join him and Elisabeth. The Alts also had a house in Airlie Gardens, between Holland Park and Church Street, Kensington, which was supposedly high enough to avoid the fogs and smogs that plagued London at this time and which affected William's chest so badly. In November 1908, on the one occasion when William either decided not to go to Rapallo or planned to go later than usual, he contracted pneumonia and died at the relatively young age of sixty-eight. The villa was sold soon afterwards, but Elisabeth continued to live in London with her two unmarried daughters until she herself died in 1923.

As Tommy grew older it became clear that he was developing an assertive character, indeed he became increasingly boisterous and at times disruptive, to an extent that his mother, the normally gentle 'Mumbo', often lost her temper with him. Notwithstanding the fact that she was some twenty-one months older, he tended to dominate his sister Grace, who was inherently rather lazy and would have preferred to stick to her books, but was invariably co-opted into his games in a subservient role. If she declined to participate he would pull her hair until she begged for mercy. He also delighted in breaking all the glass in the greenhouses and, on occasion, throwing stones at the gardeners. Freddie decided that the only course of action was be to send him to boarding school as early as possible and in September 1905, three months before his ninth birthday, he was despatched to West Downs School, Winchester.

Exactly why Freddie chose West Downs for his son is not recorded. It was at the time a relatively new school, having been founded in 1897. The founder and headmaster, Lionel Helbert, was a remarkable man. He had had a brilliant academic career at Winchester and at Oxford, where he was a contemporary of Freddie's, and it is possible that they knew one another, although they were at different colleges. They might also have met in the years after coming down from university, as both had wide circles of friends, although Helbert was in a very different *milieu* as a Clerk to the House of Commons. He had, however, long been attracted to schoolmastering and decided to start his own prep school. With his sister, Lady Goodrich, he found some defunct school buildings on the hill leading west out of Winchester, refurbished them and opened West Downs with just three pupils.

By the time Tommy arrived the number had been built up, very largely as a result of the connections Helbert had made from his time at the House of Commons, and was in the region of sixty-five. Helbert was in many ways years ahead of his time. He took a very personal interest in all the boys, not only from an academic but also from an extra-curricular perspective, and took the trouble to get to know their parents as well. On certain days, notably his own birthday and Trafalgar Day, he would take the whole school up on the South Downs for a picnic. His selfless interest in the boys was displayed on one occasion on behalf of Tommy. The boy contracted chickenpox just before the start of one Christmas holiday and Freddie refused to have him home. He spent the whole holiday in the school sanatorium, being ministered to by such of the staff as remained and by Helbert himself.

Sport played a big part at West Downs and here Tommy began to show that he was his father's son. The school was small and it was probably not difficult to get into the teams, but for two consecutive years Tommy kept wicket for the First XI at cricket and was awarded his colours. In the first of these, 1909, another member of the team was Oswald Mosley. Tommy also played for the First XI at football and won a number of cups and badges for diving. This last would have surprised those who knew him later in life, as he professed a lifelong aversion to swimming, but it was possibly the activity which allowed him out of the pool as fast as possible.

It does not seem that he was particularly distinguished academically, as he left as late as his age permitted, not much short of his fourteenth birthday. However, he enjoyed his time at West Downs, so much so that he had no hesitation in sending his own son there. Both Freddie – to whom Helbert used to write addressing him as 'My dear ole [sic] man' – and Tommy remained devoted to Lionel Helbert until he died in 1919 after a brief illness, exacerbated it was said by his horror at the slaughter of the Great War, in which so many of his former pupils had died: they included 25 per cent of Tommy's 1905 intake.

Tommy did not follow his father to Wellington, but rather his grandfather to Eton, where he arrived as a new boy at the beginning of the Michaelmas Half in September 1910. The Headmaster of the day, Edward Lyttleton, was known as a sportsman rather than a scholar and his regime probably suited boys like Tommy well. He was placed in Somerville's House[1] situated in Keats Lane in Coleridge House. His housemaster, Annesley Somerville, was well regarded and the house was a successful one at the time.

Although he enjoyed himself there, Tommy did not have a notably sparkling career at Eton. Scholastically he was average, finding himself in the Middle Division as he reached the Fifth Form in September 1913. Shortly afterwards he moved to the Army Class for the remainder of his school career, joining those who were destined for a regular commission in the Army via the Royal Military College at Sandhurst or the Royal Military Academy at Woolwich. Quite when he made this decision it is impossible to say,[2] but Army Class II, in which he sat, was under the superintendence of Somerville, who doubtless saw the boy's potential in this direction. Tommy had in any event joined the Officers Training Corps (OTC) in May 1912 at the age of fifteen. The OTC was and remained an entirely voluntary activity and only a relatively small minority joined it until late 1914, when there was an understandably enormous expansion, so his early participation was an indication of real interest, although he never progressed beyond the rank of private. Entrance to the Army Class required a certain standard in both Maths and German in the School Trials (internal exams), but Tommy had taken German rather than Greek at School Certificate level so was well placed in that direction. Once there, the objective was no longer to pass the Higher School Certificate, but rather the Army Entrance exam.

Perhaps surprisingly in the light of his later athletic success, Tommy never represented the school in any sport. He continued to play cricket initially, but moved from 'dry-bob' to 'wet-bob' in his last year, when he rowed for his house in the Junior House Fours in the bumping races of 1914. The boat had some success, bumping up two places and moving from the second to the first division. More importantly, he and R. G. Barker won the Novice Pulling (Pairs) in the same year. Tommy also played at a senior level one of the two uniquely Etonian games, the Field Game, and was in the Somerville's team which narrowly lost the House Cup Final at the end of his last term. Otherwise, the only sporting activity recorded was one which he would take up much more seriously some years later and at which he would eventually excel. On 28 March 1914 he ran in the finals of the hurdles at the Sports Day, coming in third.

It was probably on the social side that Tommy shone brightest, once again emulating his father. Eton had no prefects appointed by the Headmaster, so the authority of the boys was wielded through other means. In the individual house, this was through the House Debating Societies and the House Library, membership of both of which was by election, the voters being the existing members. Tommy was elected to the Somerville's Debating Society in the Michaelmas Half of 1913, over a year before he left. The first debate at which he spoke came shortly afterwards and concerned 'The advantages and disadvantages of a Channel Tunnel', an issue which had exercised the nation since the days of Napoleon and was to continue to do so for a further seventy-five years. In the debate Tommy proposed the advantages, on the grounds that it would benefit trade and improve relations between France and Great Britain. He suggested that any objection could only be founded on the assumption that France was held by an enemy of Great Britain, but that in any event, a tunnel would be easy to defend and, if necessary, to destroy. The argument carried the day.

Tommy was also elected as a member of the House Library, which effectively comprised the house prefects, in the Michaelmas Half of 1914. As in gentlemen's clubs, the election method involved the use of white and black balls, but he received none of the latter on this occasion. The same cannot be said of his election to Pop, the Eton Society,[3] whose members are the nearest thing to school prefects and who are distinguished by their dress, which includes checked trousers and coloured waistcoats. Pop, to an even greater extent than the house equivalents, was and is a self-perpetuating oligarchy, as only those who find favour with a substantial majority of the incumbent members can enter. It requires four black balls to be rejected: Tommy received three!

In Tommy's day, most of the twenty-three members of Pop were the school's top athletes, although a few had achieved popularity for other reasons. Many of them were to feature subsequently in his life, although the coming conflict would reduce their numbers seriously. There were five debates during the period of Tommy's membership, the first of which was 'Whether the annihilation of Prussia is desirable', a motion which was rejected by twelve votes to ten, a surprisingly mature outcome in the light of the jingoistic mood of the nation at the time.

The Old Etonian network has always been extraordinarily influential and the connections which Tommy established during his time at the school, particularly through membership of Pop, were to be of benefit throughout his life. Even if he had not been particularly friendly with another old boy of the same vintage, the very fact that they had attended the school at the same time would give them common ground. His contemporaries included a future Prime Minister, Anthony Eden, and a number of other future politicians, including Oliver Stanley, Eden's predecessor as Secretary of State for War and later Colonial Secretary in Churchill's wartime Government, and Oliver Lyttleton,[4] the Minister for Production in the same Government.

As for future army officers, there were a large number who would enter, but not survive the Great War. Of those who did, the most successful were Richard McCreery, the last commander of Eighth Army in Italy, and his predecessor in that role, Oliver Leese. McCreery was also in the Army Class, always destined to be a professional soldier, though his career and Tommy's would hardly cross subsequently. Leese, on the other hand, would feature large in Tommy's life thirty years later. Leese was about two years older, but stayed on at school until he was nearly twenty. Partly because of his long career there, he became a member of Pop in 1913 and was one of relatively few members of the Sixth Form. He was also a notable cricketer, although, to his lasting regret, he was Twelfth Man for the annual match at Lords in 1914 against Harrow. Confident and ebullient, he stood head and shoulders above most of his contemporaries and would go on to have an outstanding military career, but it was to end in controversy in circumstances in which Tommy was to be intimately involved.

Tommy sat the Sandhurst entrance exam on 24 November 1914. In common with a large number of other candidates he failed to achieve the required marks in some of the compulsory papers. He passed English and French comfortably, but fell short in the joint History & Geography paper and did very badly in Mathematics. All was not lost, however, as there was a provision in the Regulations for Admission to the Royal Military College whereby the headmasters of certain schools, including Eton, could recommend candidates for nomination by the Army Council. Lyttleton obliged and the Army Council, probably concerned by the already significant losses of officers on the Western Front, made the required nomination.

Chapter 3

Boy (1914–1916)

After a brief Christmas holiday, Tommy entered Sandhurst on 27 December 1914. The Great War was less than five months old, but it was already apparent that it would not be the quick affair many had expected. The war of movement of the first two months, in which the British Expeditionary Force (BEF) had first been forced to retreat from Mons and had then struck back with the French in the 'miracle of the Marne', was followed by the inconclusive First Battle of the Aisne and the 'race to the sea', in which each side had attempted to outflank the other until the Allies reached Nieuport, north of Dunkirk, in early October. With a stalemate in place, the BEF was positioned around the town of Ypres, where a battle raged for four weeks from 30 October to 24 November. Although the town was held, with a salient to the east, the First Battle of Ypres was an unmitigated disaster for the Regular British Army, which was effectively destroyed as a fighting force. Replacement could only come from the Territorial Force, up until then essentially a home defence organization, and from Lord Kitchener's New Army, which was in the early stages of its formation.[1]

Tommy could thus afford to take the time required by the Sandhurst wartime course without fear of missing the boat. Unlike during the Second World War, the Royal Military College and the Royal Military Academy at Woolwich remained open and continued to prepare gentlemen cadets for regular commissions,[2] although much the larger proportion of those who became officers during the Great War did so by other routes, usually through being commissioned in the Special Reserve or by promotion from the ranks. Upwards of twenty thousand officers were commissioned purely on the strength of their experience in the OTC.

Sandhurst had already expanded in the immediate pre-war years. In 1912, the completion of the New College allowed the formation of additional companies, and these were increased in number from eight to ten during the Great War. Additional accommodation was found by doubling up in rooms and by taking over the nearby Staff College and the course was reduced from a year initially to three months, but later extended to six in Tommy's time, to eight in 1916, to ten in 1917 and back to twelve months with three terms in 1918. The curriculum was truncated accordingly, but drill and musketry retained their prominence.

In contrast to his modest achievements in both the OTC and the entrance exam, Tommy did well at Sandhurst, rising to Under-Officer in H Company. His contemporary, Collie Knox, later wrote that, on returning late from an evening in London, 'None of us were too anxious to be caught by our Cadet Under-Officer.

We all liked him, we all admired him, but we had a wholesome respect for him.'[3] Knox went on to say that the Company Staff Sergeant, Bill Harley, stood in some awe of Tommy, whilst it was rumoured that even the College Sergeant Major, Mr Wombwell, had hushed his mighty voice in his presence.

Tommy graduated from Sandhurst and was gazetted a Second Lieutenant in the Grenadier Guards on 16 June 1915. This was one of the most prestigious regiments in the British Army and, although he was interviewed successfully by the Lieutenant Colonel commanding the regiment, Colonel Sir Henry Streatfeild, a personal introduction would have been required for him to be accepted, even at a time of national emergency. This can only have come from one or more of the connections which Tommy's father had been steadily building during the years leading up to the War.

Freddie had actually been in France himself during the autumn of 1914 as a result of his membership of an organization with which he had become involved many years earlier. The National Service League (NSL) had been founded by the 4th Duke of Wellington in 1902 to campaign for compulsory military training. Its President was Field Marshal Earl Roberts of Kandahar, who had taken on the role in 1905, not long after he retired from the Army. The NSL was an unashamedly patriotic organization which had been formed in the aftermath of the South African War. That war had started very badly and was only rescued from disaster by Roberts during the first nine months of 1900, by which time it had exposed serious failings in the direction of the Army. It was partly in response to this and partly because of the growing threat of German militarism that a number of leading politicians and businessmen had formed the NSL.

At the time Great Britain and the United States were the only major powers not to have large conscript armies. The former had always relied on naval supremacy, but many thought, correctly as it turned out, that another major conflict in Europe would require a much larger army than one primarily designed for colonial wars and which had shown itself ill-equipped to fight even an amateur European foe in South Africa. The NSL did not propose full-time conscription, because it realized that it would be deeply unpopular, but instead advocated a requirement for all men in a certain age group to undergo two months of initial training, followed by annual periods of training for three years. Although opposed by most in the governing Liberal Party, it attracted a number of influential members, including Rudyard Kipling and Field Marshal Viscount Wolseley, Roberts's predecessor as Commander-in-Chief.

Freddie was one of a number of businessmen who joined and he became exceptionally close to Roberts at the centre of the NSL's activities. Early in 1914 he used an I Zingari cricket tour to Egypt to canvas Field Marshal Viscount Kitchener, the British Agent, Consul-General and Plenipotentiary, and effective ruler of the country, for his support. Kitchener, although himself a Tory by personal persuasion like most supporters of National Service, had held himself aloof from the campaign. However, sitting next to Freddie at dinner, he agreed that he was broadly in favour and would come out in support at the right time. In the event he was never to do so as events supervened, notably his own appointment as Secretary of State for War in August 1914.

Roberts was appointed Colonel-in-Chief of the Empire Troops in France at the beginning of the Great War and selected Freddie to accompany him to the front as his ADC in the autumn of 1914. Roberts, however, having discovered on a visit to Ypres that the Indian sepoys lacked winter greatcoats, declined to wear his own, contracted pneumonia and died in St Omer on 14 November. Although this meant an end to his patronage, Freddie had by that time built up an impressive list of powerful contacts throughout British society, including a number of serving and retired army officers. He was thus in a good position to see his son into the best possible regiment.

The Grenadier Guards, in which Tommy was to serve for twenty-four years, was not the oldest regiment in the British Army, but it was possibly the most celebrated. Formed by the future King Charles II in 1657 during his exile, it became the First Regiment of Foot Guards in about 1685 and the Grenadier Guards in 1815, after it had defeated Napoleon's Imperial Guard at Waterloo, in further recognition of which it adopted the bearskin as a mark of distinction. Its former members include the great Duke of Marlborough and numerous Field Marshals, its Colonel-in-Chief is invariably the monarch and its Colonel is as often as not a member of the Royal Family: in 1915 he was King George V's uncle, the Duke of Connaught.

On the outbreak of the Great War there were three regular battalions of the Grenadiers, two of which, the 1st and 2nd, joined the BEF in 1914. Tommy was initially posted to the 4th Battalion, which had recently been formed out of the former Reserve Battalion and which had moved out of London to Bovingdon Camp, near Marlow, to carry out field exercises. This was the first time in the history of the regiment that a battalion of this number had been formed, the reason lying in Lord Kitchener's decision to form a Guards Division, the completion of which required this additional unit. Both the 3rd and 4th Battalions left for France to join the new division in the summer of 1915, the latter in mid-August. The remaining unit was designated the 5th (Reserve) Battalion and acted thenceforward as the training battalion for new recruits, the receiving battalion for the sick and wounded from France and the provider of guards for duties at St James's and Buckingham Palaces, the Tower of London, Windsor Castle and the Bank of England.

Tommy was still considered too young and inexperienced to accompany the 4th Battalion to France and was transferred to the 5th. With the departure of the active service battalions, most of the remaining officers were relatively elderly Reservists, many of whom had served in the Boer War. They were, however, supported to a substantial extent by regular NCOs, who continued to run the training, which focused initially as much on traditional drill as on the more appropriate courses in musketry, machine guns, hand grenades and gas. As far as drill was concerned, Tommy was in his element, seeing it as an essential part of discipline. He was already establishing a reputation as an exceptionally well turned out officer, but he also showed signs of being an excellent shot.

It was almost certainly early in his military career that Tommy received the nickname which was to stick to him throughout his life. For a regiment widely perceived by others to be the epitome of strict discipline and military precision, the Grenadiers have a relaxed attitude to personal forms of address. It is customary for all officers up to the rank of major, and even lieutenant colonels if they have not yet commanded a battalion of the regiment, to address each other by their Christian names. Moreover, the regiment at this time was notoriously fond of nicknames, which were often used in preference to given names. In many cases these suggested the opposite of the bearer's physical characteristics, examples being 'Fatty' Cavan, 'Fatboy' Gort and 'Bulgy' Thorne, all of whom were noticeably trim in figure, and 'Tiny' Freyberg, who was very tall.[4]

In the case of Second Lieutenant Browning, the nickname was much more apposite. 'Boy' could, of course, have originated simply from his initial juniority, but it was also an expression of a side to his character which he was never really to lose. Brian Urquhart, who served under him for three years from 1941, when Boy became forty-five, said later that it was surprisingly accurate: 'In his dashing appearance, his perfectly harmless vanity, his enthusiasm and hyperactivity there certainly was an element of never having quite grown up.'[5]

There are two other possible explanations, although both are conjecture. The first is that it was to distinguish him from his father, another Frederick, who held a temporary commission throughout the Great War. The second is even more tenuous, but equally plausible. An able and popular member of the regiment was the then Major Bertram Sergison-Brooke, who would have been known to many of the officers in the 4th and 5th Battalions and who also bore the longstanding nickname of 'Boy'. 'Boy' Brooke bore some similarity to 'Boy' Browning in looks and had the same penetrating gaze, and it is quite possible that the younger man showed other traits of character reminiscent of his superior officer. Whatever its origins, the nickname, initially confined to the regiment, was increasingly used by all others to address him familiarly or to refer to him from afar, whether in the Army or outside. The family and close family friends continued to call him 'Tommy', but to the rest of the world he was now 'Boy'.

Boy did not have to wait for very long before joining one of the active service battalions. On 13 October he left the barracks at Chelsea for France in charge of a reinforcement draft, reporting for duty at the 2nd Battalion three days later. The battalion had been one of the original units of the BEF, in which it had formed part of 4 Guards Brigade in 2 Division. As such it was drawn into the retreat from Mons, fighting hard before retiring exhausted to a position east of Paris. It then joined the successful counter-attack on the Marne, crossing first that river and then the Aisne in mid-September 1914. Exactly a month later, as the BEF was hurriedly moved to counter the German threat on the left of the Allied line, it was drawn back through Paris and then north to Hazebrouck. With a former Grenadier, the Earl of Cavan, now in command of 4 Guards Brigade, the battalion moved up to Ypres on 20 October.

The Regular 2nd Battalion perished at Ypres. From 21 October to 19 November it was in action on the front line almost continuously, hanging on desperately to its positions south-west of the town, often against an enemy in greater numbers. Of the twenty-three officers in the battalion at the beginning of the battle, eight were killed and six wounded, whilst the attrition in other ranks was nearly as bad, the total loss amounting to over half the battalion. It was eventually relieved on 19 November and was in no condition to re-enter the line for another month. This, however, marked the end of the German attempt to achieve a major breakthrough in 1914 and the front became static.

1915 was a difficult but less disastrous year for the 2nd Battalion. Reconstituted largely with drafts from the 3rd Battalion, it participated in May in the Battle of Festubert, an abortive attempt to gain ground further south, in the course of which its original Commanding Officer, Lieutenant Colonel Abel-Smith, was killed and his place filled by the second-in-command, George Jeffreys. There were further losses of both officers and men, albeit at nothing like the level experienced at Ypres. In September, with the formation of the Guards Division under Lord Cavan, the battalion was transferred to 1 Guards Brigade, in which it was to remain for the rest of the war. The new division's first battle came at Loos in September 1915, but the 2nd Battalion only played a minor supporting role.

By the time Boy arrived in the second half of October 1915, the battalion had settled down to trench warfare in the area of the Hohenzollern Redoubt north of Loos, coming in and out of the line, engaging in patrolling and larger company actions and being subjected to constant shelling, which continued to cause casualties. Not a single officer remained who had gone with the battalion to France in August 1914. The longest serving officer was Jeffreys, who had joined the battalion just after its arrival on the Continent and who would prove to be one of the most successful Grenadier officers of the war. Descended from the brother of the notorious seventeenth-century figure 'Hanging' Judge Jeffreys and popularly known as 'Ma' (apparently, for some obscure reason, after the Madam of a brothel in Kensington), he was much admired by those under his command. As second-in-command, he had played a key role in the retreat from Mons and the battles on the Marne and the Aisne. He was in many ways a model for the young second lieutenant who had just reported to him, as an officer who was regarded as firm but fair, a stickler for discipline but also an inspiring battlefield commander, a demanding superior officer but one with a dry sense of humour.

Boy was immediately thrust into the dangerous life of a subaltern on the Western Front, taking command of a platoon of soldiers. A few days after his arrival, the shelling became so intense that it was feared that a major enemy attack was about to be launched, but it never materialized. Shortly afterwards the battalion was withdrawn into billets behind the lines for a brief rest, before returning to take over a line of trenches which were in particularly poor condition, being flooded and with crumbling breastworks and parapets which were far from bullet proof. Considerable work had to be done to put them back into a serviceable state, a miserable task made worse by the very cold weather, with early snow from time to time. On 20 November another new officer arrived, a man who would play an important part in Boy's career two-and-a-half decades later. Major the Right Honourable Winston Churchill MP joined the battalion on temporary attachment, pending his posting to another unit as commanding officer.

Churchill was in political eclipse. As First Lord of the Admiralty at the beginning of the war, he had been in a powerful position in Asquith's cabinet. The Royal Navy, however, had had a poor start with losses at Coronel and in the North Sea, only partially redeemed by successes at the Falklands and the Dogger Bank, whilst the Royal Naval Division failed to hold Antwerp. Events went from bad to very much worse with the fiasco of Gallipoli, where the campaign, a brainchild of Churchill's, foundered completely, with huge Allied losses both in ships and – more disastrous in human and political terms – in the men of the British and Anzac forces. Churchill's choice as First Sea Lord, the ageing Jackie Fisher, resigned and the decision by Asquith to invite the Conservatives into a coalition government in May 1915 meant the beginning of the end for Churchill; they were still fuming about his defection from the party in 1904 and named his removal from the Admiralty as the price of their cooperation. Appointed Chancellor of the Duchy of Lancaster, an impotent position, he was compelled to resign six months later by the cabinet's decision to withdraw from Gallipoli against his wishes.

Churchill had begun his adult life in the Army, seeing action on the North-West Frontier, in the Sudan and in South Africa, and ever after believed himself to be an expert in military matters. Moreover, he was genuinely anxious to be close to the action. He therefore obtained an undertaking from Sir John French, who was then in command of the BEF, that he would be given a brigade as soon as one became available. Much to his dismay, Asquith barred his promotion to brigadier general, but allowed him to take command of a battalion. It was decided, however, that he would spend time in the trenches with another unit in order to learn as much as possible about conditions and modern military methods before proceeding to his new command. The unit chosen was the 2nd Battalion Grenadier Guards.

Jeffreys was not pleased. When Churchill reported for duty, he told him very bluntly that he had certainly not asked for him and indeed had not even been consulted on the attachment, leaving the former minister in no doubt as to his feelings. Nevertheless, Jeffreys was a pragmatist and resolved to make the best of it as, to his credit, did Churchill.[6] The ex-minister found himself in the same company as Boy, who was detailed to accompany him round the trenches. Churchill had not arrived well equipped and, in particular, lacked a greatcoat, a vital garment in the bitterly cold weather. Without hesitation, Boy lent him his own and Churchill never forgot the young officer.[7] Already forty years old, Churchill was exhausted at the end of his first day and spent the next one in bed, but he quickly recovered his energy and enthusiasm and threw himself into the role, dispelling the initial hostility with which he had been met and gradually gaining the respect of the battalion. By the time he left to take command of the 6th Battalion Royal Scots Fusiliers in January 1916, he and the Grenadiers had developed a mutual admiration.[8]

Boy's career now took what must have seemed at the time like a serious reverse, but in retrospect was almost certainly a blessing in disguise. On 6 January 1916 he was invalided back to England and admitted to hospital. Exactly what he was suffering from is uncertain, although it was not simply 'me tum' which, whilst debilitating, never required hospitalization and tended to be over in days, although this may have been an additional symptom. Many years later it was reported to be a combination of trench fever and conjunctivitis, which certainly has the ring of truth. Trench fever was endemic in all the armies of the Great War, accounting for about a quarter of all British troops reporting ill and far outweighing battle casualties. Until close to the end of the war it baffled the medical profession, but it was found in 1918 to be a disease transmitted by a bite from or contact with the excretions of the ubiquitous body louse. The symptoms were high fever, severe headaches, skin rashes, leg pains and (consistent with conjunctivitis) inflamed eyes. Some patients recovered after five to six days, but prolonged hospitalization was common, with relapses being reported in many cases. It was rarely fatal, although it could lead to complications.

Boy's malady was less likely to have been that other common complaint of those in battle, shell shock, if only because he had been at the front for a short and relatively uneventful time. The symptoms of this were severe fatigue, irritability, the inability to take decisions and, in some cases, a nervous breakdown. Although recognized even at the time as a genuine illness, it was difficult to distinguish in some cases from malingering. For this reason there was a lack of sympathy among senior officers for the sufferers, who would often find their careers blighted as a result. This certainly did not happen to Boy. Nevertheless, he did fall ill with nervous exhaustion from time to time throughout his life, usually as a result of either overwork or emotional stress, and it is possible that something of this nature contributed to the relatively long period before he was fully fit.

Boy was in hospital for just under four weeks, which would be quite typical of trench fever, and was then sent on sick leave for a further two months. By mid-April he was judged well enough to undertake light duties and was initially posted to the 5th Reserve Battalion, but two weeks later he was sent on attachment to the Guards Depot at Caterham. Every month he had to attend a medical board at Caxton Hall and for seven months in succession he failed to be passed fit for active service, until on 20 September he at last convinced the doctors that he had completely recovered. Just after the end of the month he returned to France.

Chapter 4

Trenches (1916–1918)

On 6 October Boy reported back for duty at the 2nd Battalion. The first eight months of 1916 had been a relatively quiet time for the battalion, at least by the standards of the Great War, with no involvement in major battles. In February it moved back to the Ypres sector, but at the end of July the Guards Division began its move to the Somme, concentrating there early in the following month. The Somme offensive, which was launched on 1 July and was designed to take the pressure off the French at Verdun, had thus far not achieved any of the objectives of the new Commander-in-Chief of the BEF, Sir Douglas Haig, who had replaced Sir John French in February.

Although in many ways the Somme was the finest hour of the Guards Division, for the 2nd Battalion it was nearly as disastrous as First Ypres. The division's attack on Ginchy on 15 September failed to reach its final objective, but only because the failure by the flanking divisions to conform to the line left the Guards unsupported. Ten days later it tried again and this time took Lesboeufs successfully, but the price was very high. The initial attack cost the 2nd Battalion 365 casualties, with three officers killed and nine wounded, the latter including a future Prime Minister, Lieutenant Harold Macmillan. By the end of the subsequent advance the casualties numbered a further 342 with four more officers killed and five wounded. The battalion was withdrawn to recover at Aumont, which is where Boy rejoined it.

He had been fortunate in his timing for had he remained he would almost certainly have been killed or injured at the Somme. There were only three officers left from those who had been in the battalion at the time he fell sick and a mere six other ranks whom he knew by name. Most importantly there was a new Commanding Officer, as Jeffreys had been given a brigade. Lieutenant Colonel C. R. Champion de Crespigny, known as 'Crawley', was out of a different mould to that of his predecessor. He was much more free and easy in his manner, and his interests, other than soldiering, were hunting, shooting and gambling. He was never known to pick up a book. He was every inch a Guards officer in his dress – at a time when the high attrition of officers had led to orders to abandon the Guards' gold-braided peaked caps in favour of their service dress equivalent, de Crespigny insisted on continuing to wear the former, accompanied at the other end by boots and spurs – and he maintained the strong discipline that Jeffreys had instilled. He had a cheerful disregard, however, for those in authority. Macmillan later told the story of a dictum being received from the brigade to produce a return of the number of rats in the trenches, following questions being asked in Parliament. De Crespigny organized a huge rat hunt, had the victims put into bags and, after a suitable time for them to mature, had them deposited at dead of night outside the brigade HQ!

The 2nd Battalion did not return to the line until mid-November, after which it was in and out on a regular basis, without any major action being fought. For Boy, there were no repercussions from his absence, but the war now became a time of deep frustration. In the line there was constant danger but little real achievement: out of the line there was only boredom. He now commanded a platoon in Captain 'Tiny' Buchanan's No. 1 Company, and began to develop a reputation among his soldiers as a good officer. The only contemporary recollections of this part of Boy's life are those of one member of his platoon, Private Frank Whitehouse. Whitehouse recalled Boy during one German attack, like the other officers armed only with a pistol, borrowing a rifle from one of his men and standing on the fire-step, blazing away at the advancing enemy, while the rifle's owner handed him up clip after clip until his pouches were empty. The attack failed and Boy, his face blackened, handed back the rifle with evident satisfaction and thanks to its owner.

On another occasion Whitehouse was ordered to take food out to two men occupying a sap ahead of the front-line trench. Not knowing how to get there, he asked for volunteers to show him, but no one came forward. Boy then appeared and, on finding out the situation, said that he would guide the soldier across himself. Just after they got through the wire a flare went up from the German trenches and a machine gun began to traverse towards them. Both men hit the ground, the lid of the food container burst open, and stew poured down Whitehouse. Boy helped him up and asked if he was all right. 'Sir,' came the reply 'except for bits of carrot and onion in the arse of me trousers', which caused the young officer considerable mirth.

He developed something of a reputation for the welfare of his men, expressed on one occasion by his insistence that a rum ration should continue to be shared round until it was completely finished, much to the annoyance of the quartermaster sergeant, who had designs on the leftovers. He gave prizes for the best billets and ensured that work was shared out evenly and that those who slacked had to make up time on their more diligent colleagues.

Whitehouse's admiration was probably enhanced by Boy almost certainly saving his life. During an advance, the platoon had to leave the end of a sap over ground which was on a forward slope covered by machine gun fire. A newly-joined subaltern, together with his sergeant, ordered a Lewis gun team over the top, where they were immediately killed. A second team was then ordered over, meeting the same fate. Whitehouse's own team was next in line but refused to go. Just as this happened, Boy arrived on the scene to see what was holding up the advance, listened to Whitehouse's explanation and immediately accepted it, saving him from the choice of either certain death or a court-martial, followed in all probability by a firing squad. Boy could already understand when to put military common sense before blind obedience to duty. As a postscript, the officer concerned then made Whitehouse's life generally unpleasant and had him framed on a charge of sleeping on sentry duty, for which the penalty was death. After hearing the flimsy evidence, Boy had the charge dropped.

Like many other officers, Boy suffered most from boredom. The static nature of the war contributed to this, with the lack of any major offensive from either side in the battalion's sector resulting in longer periods out of the forward trenches, but little in the way of recreation or entertainment. There were few and all too short periods of leave, some of which Boy spent enjoying the hospitality of the Hennessy family in Paris. The newspapers arrived promptly, there were supplements to rations sent out either from the regiment or the family, and on certain occasions the Quartermaster was able to produce some wine, but life on the whole was drab at best and more often extremely uncomfortable. Boy amused himself by reading, not only books, but also magazines and catalogues – he was particularly keen on those for cars, the more expensive the better – which were sent to him by Grace, as were a gramophone, a selection of records and various luxury foods. He also developed an addiction to cigarettes which was to last a lifetime.

During June 1917 the Guards Division returned to Ypres and on 2 July the 2nd Battalion relieved 3rd Battalion Coldstream Guards in the Boesinghe sector north of the town along the Ypres–Yser Canal. Preparations were made for the next great offensive, Haig's plan to drive forward from the salient, capture the strategic railway which ran north to Ostend and establish the Allies along a line from Courtrai to Bruges and then on to Zeebrugge. This would become known as the Third Battle of Ypres, or more popularly Passchendaele, and was to last for more than three months.

1 Guards Brigade was now commanded by Jeffreys. Its role was to hold back until the other two brigades in the division had captured the first three objectives and then pass through to take the fourth. The attack began before dark on 31 July and was highly successful. Notwithstanding the driving rain turning the ground into a morass, the first three objectives were taken and 2nd Grenadiers duly passed through with the rest of the brigade to take the fourth objective, some one and three-quarters of a mile from the start point. Resistance intensified and casualties mounted, but the new line was held. Only seventeen out of twenty-eight officers in the battalion participated in this part of the battle and Boy was not among them.[1] Two officers were killed and four wounded, a relatively modest casualty list by the standards of the war. On 2 August the battalion was relieved and moved back into reserve.

The battalion spent much of August training for the next major attack and by the end of the month was employed carrying material up to the front, suffering a number of casualties from shelling. During September it came back into the line again in a notoriously marshy section overlooked by the enemy, before reverting to its tiresome duty of providing human pack animals. At the end September Jeffreys was appointed to command 19 Division and was succeeded by de Crespigny at 1 Guards Brigade. A new Commanding Officer arrived at 2nd Battalion in the shape of Lieutenant Colonel Guy Rasch, who was to take it through to the Armistice.

As Adjutant of the 1st Battalion Rasch had fought at First Ypres, from which he had emerged as the only captain alive and unwounded, with one lieutenant, two second lieutenants and one hundred men, who were reconstituted temporarily as a single company. With a DSO and promotion to major he had been posted to the 3rd Battalion as second-in-command in 1916, serving on the Somme and in the first part of Third Ypres, prior to his transfer to the 2nd Battalion.

The next attack by the Guards Division took it forward along an extension of the same axis of advance from Boesinghe, with the objectives of crossing a marshy stream called the Broembeek and then taking and holding the southern edge of the Houlthurst Forest. This time 1 Guards Brigade shared the lead, with the 2nd Grenadiers in the van and Boy accompanying Rasch as Acting Adjutant. The attack began at 0520 hrs on 9 October. The condition of the Broembeek gave grounds for concern after heavy overnight rain, but patrols found it fordable and it was crossed with less difficulty than anticipated. The Germans were initially taken by surprise and their defences overrun, but the attacking companies were now exposed and heavy shelling caused casualties, although their objective was reached. The advance was deeply unpleasant for the troops because of the nature of the ground, deep in viscous mud after further heavy rain and pitted with shell holes, but it was a successful operation in a battle which advanced the front line by a meagre four miles. A further bulge was created at Passchendaele itself, where the rate of attrition had been appalling, but this did not result in the major breakthrough for which Haig had hoped.

After its relative success, the Guards Division had a month's respite and the 2nd Battalion was sent to the area between St Omer and Calais, where it trained extensively. On November 11 the whole division began to move south to join what would be the BEF's next major operation, a surprise attack towards Cambrai, with the objective of disrupting a major centre of German communications. For the first time, tanks would be used in quantity[2]. The surprise worked and Sir Julian Byng's Third Army poured forward on 20 November, the tanks in the van, overrunning the German lines and forcing the enemy back in confusion. Within two days a salient had been created, ten miles wide and six deep, but there was still no decisive breakthrough.

The Guards had been given a follow-up role and it was 23 November before the 2nd Battalion entered the line at the furthest point of the advance near Camaing. Following an abortive advance by 2 Guards Brigade, it was relieved on 28 November and marched back to new billets in the village of Metz. Two days later the Germans launched a major counter-attack, both on the salient and further south. Shortly after 0900 hrs on 30 November Rasch was ordered by de Crespigny to move at short notice with the rest of the brigade towards Gouzeaucourt, south of the salient, which was reported to be in the hands of the Germans. As the guardsmen advanced, their movements were hampered for a while by retreating British soldiers who had given up their positions. The 2nd Battalion acted as the brigade reserve and was not required in an action which saw Gouzeaucourt successfully recaptured, but early on the following morning it was given new orders, to take the strategically important feature of Gauche Wood, south-east of the village.

The four companies assembled on a sunken track behind a railway embankment on the outskirts of Gouzeaucourt. At 0640 hrs they advanced in two lines of two platoons each, with No. 1 and No. 3 Companies in the van, followed at a distance of 250 yards by No. 2 under Boy and No. 4 under Lieutenant Guy Westmacott. Twenty tanks had been allocated to the brigade, but these failed to appear and the attack went in without them. The plan was simply to rush the wood over the open grassland in front, and in the first minutes it worked well, with enemy machine gun fire largely going overhead. Once the Grenadiers had reached the wood, however, casualties began to mount very fast, largely from snipers concealed amongst the trees. Although the enemy machine-gun positions were captured and the Germans forced back through the wood in hand-to-hand bayonet fighting, one officer was killed and seven wounded, one of whom later died, the casualties including the commanders of the two leading companies. This left Westmacott and Boy responsible for the whole battalion front.

Westmacott took the right flank, moving out of the wood with his own company and two platoons of No. 2 Company in order to dominate the small valley that lay between it and the village of Villers Guislain and to fend off the German counter-attacks which were now mounted from that direction. As the senior officer, Westmacott ordered Boy to reorganize the remainder of the force, which was still in the wood and engaged at close quarters with the Germans. Shortly afterwards another officer was wounded and only three remained of the twelve who set out: Boy on his own in the wood, and Westmacott with Lieutenant Loftus on the flank. Westmacott and Boy then agreed that the latter should take up a position just beyond the forward edge of the wood, which proved a wise move as shortly afterwards the Germans shelled it intensively.

The two officers got their positions thoroughly dug in, placing seventy men in reserve to strengthen whichever of them required it. During the course of the day the Grenadiers became intermingled with the dismounted cavalry of the 18th Bengal Lancers,[3] who had joined the front from the right and were now able to bolster the line of defence alongside the guardsmen, together with some Lewis gunners from the missing tanks, all of which had been knocked out on their way forward. Although the wood itself continued to be heavily shelled, the position was now stable and further reinforcements began to appear during the afternoon in the shape of a company of 2nd Battalion Coldstream Guards, who brought with them extra ammunition, and a detachment from the Canadian cavalry regiment, Lord Strathcona's Horse. During the night the battalion was eventually relieved by a company of the 3rd Battalion Grenadier Guards and the survivors moved back exhausted to Gouzeaucourt. In addition to the officers, 151 NCOs and other ranks were killed, wounded and missing.

Gauche Wood was an important engagement for the Grenadiers, generally regarded as a heroic achievement against the odds, the GOC III Corps describing it as a 'very fine attack … worthy of the highest traditions of the Guards.' It established a reputation for Boy within the regiment as a fighting soldier which was to last his entire life. It also earned both him and Westmacott[4] the Distinguished Service Order, an unusual, albeit by no means unprecedented, award for those of the rank of lieutenant. Boy's citation in the *London Gazette* read:

> For conspicuous gallantry and devotion to duty. He took command of three companies whose officers had all become casualties, reorganized them, and proceeded to consolidate. Exposing himself to very heavy machine-gun and rifle fire, in two hours he had placed the front line in a strong state of defence. The conduct of this officer, both in the assault and more especially afterwards, was beyond all praise, and the successful handing over of the front to the relieving unit as an entrenched and strongly fortified position was entirely due to his energy and skill.

Congratulations on the award were received by Freddie and Nancy from many friends and acquaintances and one letter in particular gave a great deal of pleasure. It came from Clive Wigram,[5] the Assistant Private Secretary to King George V and a personal friend of both Freddie and his brother Monty:

York Cottage
Sandringham
Norfolk
3rd January 1918

My dear Freddie

In a submission that came to the King this morning, containing the names of Officers who have been given 'immediate awards' in the field, is included the name of your son for the DSO.

His Majesty was delighted to see how well your son had done, and heartily congratulates you and Mrs Browning on his fine achievement, a statement of which I enclose.

It is a good performance for a Lieutenant in these days to get a DSO, as this decoration is only given to the Junior Ranks for very special services; in fact it would have been a VC in any other campaign.

I am so glad to see that my Regiment, the 18th Lancers, was with him, I believe that they did very well, two boys in one Squadron were decorated, one with the DSO and one with the Military Cross.

Yours ever
Clive Wigram

For Boy the war continued as before, but he had been profoundly changed by the experience of Gauche Wood. Although he had by that time been on active service for a total of seventeen months and had seen a lot of fighting, this was the first time he had been so exposed at close quarters in such a tense situation, where all depended on him. The confusion and carnage of this battle stayed with him for the rest of his life in the shape of recurrent nightmares, from which he would wake up shouting. For the time being, however, there was nothing for it but to get on with the job.

Less than a month after Gauche Wood he was promoted to acting captain and confirmed in command of No. 1 Company. Early in the New Year there was a reorganization which resulted in the creation of a fourth Guards brigade to serve outside the Guards Division, with the result that that each existing brigade was reduced to three battalions. A system was established where at any moment one battalion would be in the front line, one in support and one in reserve. 1 Guards Brigade's frontage was now astride the River Scarpe, with the rear battalion in Arras. Down by the river the trenches were particularly difficult to dig as the water table was encountered after a few feet, making the line itself distinctly unpleasant at that point. Other than the occasional raid, at which Boy was by now an old hand, nothing of great significance happened until the last week of March 1918.

On 21 March, General Ludendorff launched a massive attack in heavy fog on the British positions on either side of the Somme, with the objective of breaking through to the Channel coast and separating the BEF from the French Armies to the south. Against the twenty-six divisions of Byng's Third and Sir Hubert Gough's Fifth Armies he mustered a total of sixty-three divisions. In the face of such unequal odds the line gave way and a retreat began. By 25 March, it seemed that a total collapse was imminent as Bapaume and Peronne fell and by the end of the month Amiens was threatened. Foch was placed in supreme command of the Allied forces, with a mandate to coordinate operations, and French reinforcements were rushed to the front. By 5 April it was clear that Foch's actions had succeeded in stabilizing the position and that the immediate crisis was at an end. The German offensive petered out, but an enormous amount of territory had been lost.

Rumours of the German offensive reached the 2nd Battalion on the first day, but it was only three days later that it received orders to move, taking up position south of Arras with the rest of the Guards Division and covering the withdrawal of battalions from 31 Division. The 2nd Battalion was positioned astride the Arras to Albert railway, with Boy's No. 1 Company and No. 2 Company on the east side and the other two companies on the west. The first German troops appeared on 27 March, advancing in twos and threes rather than their customary close formation, which made them more difficult to pick off. Nevertheless, they were held by steady and accurate rifle and machine-gun fire, with Boy's company managing to enfilade the advancing troops as they moved across the British front, wreaking significant damage.

The first attack was thwarted, but the Germans tried again the following day, with the two companies east of the railway being singled out for especially heavy shelling prior to the infantry advance. Once again the defence was solid and the Germans abandoned their efforts in favour of concentrating further south. As the Grenadiers would learn later, they were positioned on the far right flank of the German offensive, with the heaviest fighting taking place twenty or more miles away as the Germans attempted to reach Amiens. On 31 March the 2nd Battalion was relieved and went into reserve.

In early April Ludendorff switched his attention to Flanders, with an initially successful attack south of Armentières, some way from the Guards Division's position in the new line of trenches which had been formed between Arras and Compiègne. The pressure off, a routine was established for the individual battalions of five days in the front line and two in reserve. Intensive shelling continued, but no further attacks were mounted by the Germans, although they were expected every day. By 6 June,[6] the situation had relaxed sufficiently for the battalion to leave the line completely for three weeks training, during which Rasch instituted a platoon competition in activities such as grenade throwing, bayonet fighting and musketry and there was even time for a divisional horse show on 22 June, at which the battalion won the cup.

On 29 June Boy took a party of men in buses to Hesdin, the HQ of Third Army, where they mounted a Guard of Honour for their Colonel, the Duke of Connaught, on the following day. Boy's own standards were by now extremely high and the onlookers refused to believe that the soldiers had just come out of the line and had not been brought over from England specifically for the purpose. General Byng sent a message that their turnout, bearing, marching and handling of arms were beyond all criticism. For the Grenadiers, this was an indication of things to come from the young officer.

In early July the 2nd Battalion returned to the same area of the line. The only change to the normal routine was the arrival of a number of American officers and men, who were attached to obtain experience, prior to moving on to join their country's forces in the Meuse-Argonne sector. At the end of August the battalion participated in one of a number of actions which had begun earlier that month on what Ludendorff described as 'the Black Day of the German Army', when the outer defence line of Amiens was retaken for the first time since early April. This was a prelude to the series of operations which began in late September and which were to bring an end to the war. Boy was to be intimately involved, but at a level far removed from that of an infantry company.

From June 1915 to August 1939, Boy spent his entire career on regimental duty with the Grenadiers, with only two postings away from the regiment. The second and longer of these was the four years at Sandhurst in the 1920s. The first and much shorter was from September to November 1918, when he was detached to act as ADC to the GOC-in-C Fourth Army, Sir Henry Rawlinson. Rawlinson had experienced mixed fortunes during the war. He commanded IV Corps at the First Battle of Ypres in 1914 and then at Neuve Chapelle and Loos in 1915. Never on good terms with Sir John French, he was pleased when the latter was replaced by

Haig, a move which saw Rawlinson placed in command of Fourth Army for the Somme battle. The disaster there, however, did his standing no good and he was sidelined for nearly eighteen months.

At the end of March 1918 Rawlinson was brought back in haste to organize the reinforcements which were assembled to prevent Ludendorff's breakthrough at Amiens. His role in stopping the German advance rehabilitated his reputation and it was the attack by his Fourth Army on 8 August which caused Ludendorff's 'Black Day'. For the rest of August and throughout September he kept pressing, making some ground every time he attacked, but saving his main strength for the concerted Allied offensive which would be mounted at the end of the month. This involved four major operations, which kicked off on consecutive days. On 26 September the US First Army and French Fourth Army attacked in the Meuse-Argonne sector. On 27 September the British First and Third Armies began their push between Epéhy and Lens, south of Arras. On 28 September the British Second Army, the French Sixth Army and the Belgian Army launched their divisions along the front from Armentières to the sea. Finally on 29 September the French First Army and Rawlinson's Fourth Army, reinforced by two American divisions, drove forward from the Somme.

Boy reported to Rawlinson on 12 September, remaining with him until 4 November, by which time it was abundantly clear that the war was won. Quite why he had been selected for the role is not known, but it may be significant that Rawlinson was both an Old Etonian and a former Guards officer, having transferred to the Coldstream from the King's Royal Rifle Corps in 1889. He had also been a protégé of Roberts, on whose staff he had served in South Africa and may have known Freddie. Like most field commanders, he preferred ADCs who had seen action and Boy, whose background was similar to his own and who by this time was already showing a capacity for organization, would probably have suited him very well. It was a very short term appointment, however, and Boy was more than likely filling in for another officer who was sick or wounded. He wrote to Grace: 'My new job is very comfortable, but no use for a soldier, but its doing me good to be away from things for a bit.'[7]

For the first time since 1914, the war on the Western Front became one of forward movement as each of the Allied attacks pushed back the exhausted and demoralized Germans. On the Fourth Army front the Hindenburg Line was penetrated almost immediately and Rawlinson's divisions drove east towards the Belgian border. Boy would never forget the exhilaration of these weeks, as the enemy was repeatedly placed on the back foot due to the aggressive tactics of the Allies, and it would strongly influence his thinking and that of many other senior British officers in the late summer of 1944, at which time the Germans were again apparently on the run. By early November, with its army in a state of near mutiny, Germany sued for peace, by which time Boy had been released back to his regiment.

On 4 November Boy reported not to the 2nd Battalion, but to the 1st as Adjutant. The Commanding Officer was Lieutenant Colonel the Hon. W. R. Bailey,[8] whom

Boy knew well. Bill Bailey had had a remarkable record of service in the 2nd Battalion, of which he was Adjutant when Boy first joined in October 1915 and second-in-command to Rasch when he returned from sick leave nearly a year later, one of the three officers who had survived the Somme intact. Bailey had only taken command of the 1st Battalion a month previously, after Lord Gort had been seriously wounded during the initial attack on the Hindenburg Line,[9] although he had stood in for Gort on a temporary basis during the summer and had been slightly wounded himself during one of the advances in August. It is quite possible that he had asked for Boy, as he characterized him in a subsequent report as 'a born leader'. The war by this time was in its last days, but the 1st Battalion was in action with the Guards Division right up to 7 November, the rapid advance culminating in the capture of Maubeuge, a fortress town and railway junction south of Mons.

Chapter 5

Peace (1918–1924)

Exactly a week after the Armistice, the four Grenadier battalions left Maubeuge on foot for Cologne, where the Guards Division was temporarily to join the occupation forces. The 1st Battalion took a route past Charleroi and Namur and through the Ardennes, being received for the most part with great enthusiasm by the Belgians. Once into Germany the soldiers were surprised at the lack of hostility shown by the local population. On 20 December, after a month on the road, they arrived in Cologne, where they were actually welcomed as protectors against the anarchy which was springing up in the defeated country. In January a party from each battalion was sent to bring the colours out and in late February orders were at last received to return to England.

On 9 March Boy left France, arriving back in plenty of time to participate in the great parade of the Guards Division and the Household Cavalry from Buckingham Palace to the City of London. The procession was led by the Earl of Cavan, the division's first commander, with the Prince of Wales, also a serving Grenadier during the Great War, riding alongside him, closely followed by Major General Feilding, who had led the division since before the battle of the Somme, and his staff. Most of those who had commanded Guards brigades were present as were many former commanding officers, each one riding at the head of the battalion he had once commanded, next to the incumbent, whilst demobilized soldiers followed their battalions in plain clothes.

Boy had had a 'good' war. He had come out physically unscathed, a remarkable achievement for one who had spent nearly two and a half years as a junior infantry officer on the Western Front. In addition to his DSO, he had a French Croix de Guerre to his name and had been mentioned in despatches. Because of the close contacts established between the officers of the Guards Division, he was widely known in all the regiments of the Brigade of Guards, although his acquaintances in the wider Army were more limited. He was still only twenty-two and now had to decide, like most of the other officers, whether or not he wanted to stay on. As he held a regular commission, to do so would not have been difficult, but the attractions of peacetime soldiering had to be weighed up against the alternatives.

Boy's father had also had a good war. Following the death of Lord Roberts in 1914, Freddie had left Twiss & Brownings in the hands of its managers and volunteered his services to the Government. In February 1915 he was made Comptroller of the Trade Clearing House, moving on to be head of the War Trade Intelligence Department. At the beginning of 1916 he was invited by Captain Mansfield

Cumming RN to join the Secret Service Bureau, also called the Secret Intelligence Service. Cumming had joined this organization in 1909 as head of its foreign section and between then and 1914 had created a substantial network of agents, all of them being directed against Germany. From his habit of initialling all his letters 'C' in green ink, he became known by this initial, which was subsequently used for all his successors in the SIS, or MI6, as it became more popularly known.

With a temporary commission as a lieutenant colonel, Freddie was just the man Cumming needed to provide the right connections and the two of them got on very well together. He became, in effect, Cumming's 'fixer', the man who would find a way to achieve a goal by routes apparently unavailable to the other members of the organization and the one who could introduce 'C' and the other key intelligence officers to all the people who mattered. In addition he assumed responsibility for economic intelligence, leaving the political and military sides to others better qualified.

At the end of the war Freddie stood down from his job at the Secret Service Bureau and reverted to civilian life, taking with him the honorary rank of lieutenant colonel and a CBE.[1] Now approaching fifty and having been for some time the senior partner of Twiss & Brownings, he suggested to Boy that he might like to join the firm, as by this time no other member of the family was actively involved. Not for the last time, Boy thought seriously about it, but the decision was easy to make. He believed that the Army, and particularly the Grenadiers, would provide a much more satisfying life than the wine trade. It was a considerable disadvantage that he had no independent means, unlike most of his fellow officers, and money concerns would be a continuing theme of his life, but at least Freddie was a wealthy man and Boy might look for an inheritance in due course. In the meantime he would have to live on his army pay.

In any event, although no less sociable than Freddie, and in due course no less well connected, his character was more suited to the Army than to business. He knew from his experience of the last three years that he possessed the power of command. He responded instinctively to the discipline and high personal standards demanded by the Army, which he sought at every opportunity to convey to others, and he enjoyed the comradeship which was inherent at all levels in a good regiment. There was little that the wine trade could deliver to him other than a comfortable life, which was certainly not at the top of his list of priorities.

He was also well regarded by a number of more senior officers who would have a great impact on the Grenadier Guards over the next twenty years and, in some cases, prove to be influential beyond the regiment. As Adjutant of the 1st Battalion, he had retained the rank of acting captain on his return to England and he was recommended for promotion to the substantive rank in the summer of 1920 by the Commanding Officer, Claude Hamilton, a recommendation strongly endorsed by George Jeffreys, who was now the Major General Commanding London District.

Peacetime soldiering was very different from Boy's previous experience. The mass demobilization which took place in the two years after the War meant that the battalions, now reduced again to three, were substantially manned by recent recruits, both subalterns and other ranks, although the senior NCOs had all seen active service. The objective was to get each battalion back to the pre-war level of efficiency, which had been very high, and in this Boy excelled. He began to develop a name with his superiors as a smart and energetic officer who could be counted on to instil the highest standards in those under his command, and with his subordinates as a strict disciplinarian with an occasionally explosive temper, albeit one which was never long-lasting.

The life of the average Guards officer was by no means demanding. As the 'war to end all wars' was now over, the Government accorded very little priority to the armed services, implementing the 'Ten Year Rule' – a doctrine which made the presumption that there would be no major war for ten years and which in 1928 was permanently extended on a rolling basis. The Army was, if anything, a Cinderella organization compared to the Royal Navy, good for imperial policing, but otherwise not worth devoting resources to. As far as the Guards were concerned, the public and ceremonial duties reverted to pre-war practice. There was a strong focus, as before, on drill, whilst warlike exercises received less prominence. Much of the training could be safely left to the excellent cadre of warrant officers and NCOs. For the commissioned officers there was plenty of time for both leave and other activities, largely sporting in nature.

The one officer in each battalion who had to work hard was the Adjutant, and for this he received more pay, which would have been an additional attraction to Boy at the time. As the right-hand man of the Commanding Officer, he had to run the organization and administration of the battalion other than its logistical requirements, which were handled by the Quartermaster. He was in particular concerned with discipline, both in general and as it related to individuals. As such, he was by some way the busiest officer in the battalion, with consequently less time for the other activities.

Boy's appointment allowed him to become close to Hamilton's successor as Commanding Officer, who was the man who shared his nickname, 'Boy' Sergison-Brooke. The latter, like many other officers, had taken a reduction in rank from brigadier general and reverted to battalion command. Sergison-Brooke's opinion of Boy was entirely favourable. In his Annual Confidential Report for 1921, he wrote: 'I have never seen a more promising young officer in the Regiment, and cannot speak highly enough of him.' This was echoed by Jeffreys at Horse Guards: 'I regard him as the best Adjutant in the Brigade of Guards.' In June 1921, for the first time since 1914, the King's Birthday Parade was held on Horse Guards Parade in full dress uniform.[2] The 1st Battalion of the Grenadiers formed one of the Guards and Sergison-Brooke commanded the parade as Field Officer in Brigade Waiting, selecting Boy to ride beside him as one of the two officers on his staff.

In November 1921 Boy was appointed the Grenadiers' Resident Captain at the Guards Depot at Caterham, where he had been posted briefly in 1916 whilst unfit for active service. The Depot was where the recruits of all five regiments of Foot

Guards were sent for their primary training. It was housed in rather grim barracks, but had the advantage of extensive grounds. At the time there were fifteen officers on the establishment – the CO, Adjutant and Quartermaster plus three each from the Grenadiers and the Coldstream and two each from the Scots, Irish and Welsh. Most of these commuted daily from London, but Boy lived there alongside his equivalents in the other regiments.

For Boy this was a good posting for two reasons. The more important one was that this was where the process began of turning young and untrained civilians into guardsmen, instilling into them the qualities of discipline, obedience and smartness to which Boy himself now subscribed so wholeheartedly and differentiating them from not only the man in the street, but also their comrades in the wider army. This was the first and best opportunity to create out of unpromising raw material what the Guards believed would be the finest soldiers in the world, and the standard set by the officers and NCOs of the Depot would be those to which the new recruits would aspire.

It was here over the next two years that Boy honed the reputation, among the other ranks in particular, which would follow him through his regimental career, as an officer who would only accept the highest standards and who would lead by example. He was intolerant of slackness in any respect, but particularly in dress, where he expected all to be as immaculate in their turnout as he was. However, he was no petty tyrant. He took great care to understand the men under his command and to inspire rather than browbeat. It is doubtful that he was as popular as other officers who permitted more latitude, but he was admired and even copied.

Drill remained of the utmost importance, not only because this was what guardsmen were supposed to excel at on ceremonial occasions, but also because it was the foundation of obedience to orders. Boy developed a great respect for the drill sergeants of his regiment, whom he regarded as the finest exponents of military discipline. He would use them in the future, even outside the regiment, on occasions when he considered that standards were below the level he demanded. In addition to drill, the recruits were introduced to marksmanship, with instruction being given on the miniature range. Perhaps the most important lesson, however, was on the history and traditions of the regiment, with pride in its achievements being a major ingredient of the glue that bound together a disparate band of individuals into a single unified body.

Boy was particularly concerned with developing the physical fitness of the recruits. Most of them came from the working classes and, in the aftermath of war, were often badly nourished and unused to any sort of regular exercise. This is where Boy excelled, as sport was rapidly becoming the next most important thing in his life after the regiment and the ease with which he could pursue his interest was the second reason why the posting to the Depot, free from the greater demands made on a battalion adjutant and away from the fleshpots of London, was so attractive to him.

In some of his sporting activities Boy followed the conventional preferences of the army officer. He was handy with a shotgun and more than capable as a horseman, although it would be not until some time later that he would ride competitively. He took up three sports, however, which were more unusual for the average army officer. One was archery, which he enjoyed for the rest of his life, but which offered little opportunity for representative honours. In the other two, athletics and bobsleigh, he went on to compete at the highest level.

His focus in athletics was on hurdling, the event which he had taken up with modest success at Eton, although he competed on occasion in both high and long jump. In the United Kingdom there were three standard distances, 120 yards over hurdles of 3' 6" (106.7cm) and 220 yards over hurdles of 2' 6" (76.2cm), known respectively as the high and low hurdles, plus a longer race over 440 yards: Boy would participate in all of these. He was later to write of hurdling: 'It is, in my opinion, the most fascinating of athletic events both to watch and to take part in. In no other event can so much be attained with a minimum of natural ability. All the best times have been made by a few men who have demonstrated the value of intensive application of hurdling science.'[3] Whether or not he had natural ability, he must have been built to what he saw as the physical specifications. 'The best type of hurdler' he wrote 'is found in the tall, loose-jointed individual without too much muscular development, but with a certain amount of natural sprinting ability.'[4]

Against those with whom he was in closest contact, his comrades in the Army, he was soon to show his skill and in July 1921, whilst still Adjutant at the 1st Battalion and before he had started serious training, he came in a close second in the high hurdles at the Guards athletics meeting. There was a grass track at the Depot which he could use at will and that year he also joined the South London Harriers, one of the best athletic clubs in London. He was proposed by Major William 'Babe' Alexander,[5] an officer in the Irish Guards, and by E. J. Holt, the honorary secretary of the club, who was not only a good athlete himself, but who went on to become a leading sports administrator.[6] The club maintained a coach at both Crystal Palace, relatively convenient for Caterham, and at Stamford Bridge, and there would have been opportunities to train with good club athletes.

By the summer of 1923, he was the winner of both high and low hurdles at the Guards Brigade sports, and the high and long jump as well, and later that summer was in the winning Army team in the 200-yard hurdle relay at the Inter-Services Championship.[7] Rather more significantly, he came fourth in the high hurdles in the English AAA Championships in June of that year and, although he failed to qualify for the final of the same event at the British Championships, he came third in the 440 yards hurdles. This brought him to the notice of the wider athletics community and in May 1924 he was selected provisionally to represent Great Britain in both the 100m and 400m hurdles at the Olympic Games to be held that year in Paris.

This was the 'Chariots of Fire' games in which Harold Abrahams and Eric Liddell were to achieve sporting immortality. Although Boy failed to make the cut when the final team was chosen, possibly because he was not fully fit after a serious bobsleigh accident earlier in the year, he would still become a friend of Abrahams and other leading athletes of the day. It was his misfortune to be competing against some other very fine runners in his event, notably Fred Gaby, who was at the peak of his powers in 1924, followed by the much younger David Cecil, Lord Burghley, who achieved selection in 1924 but had to wait until the Amsterdam Games in 1928 to win a gold medal for Great Britain.[8]

Boy's most successful year came in 1925, when he ran third behind Gaby and Burghley in the Kinnaird Trophy low hurdles race that June and second behind Gaby in the English AAA Championships early the following month. Subsequent reports that he won the AAA Championships three years in succession are well wide of the mark, but he did, as claimed, represent England internationally. Other than at the Olympic Games, there were relatively few opportunities for international competition, but Boy was selected for the match against Ireland and Scotland in Dublin on 10 July, coming fourth in the final behind Gaby, an Irishman and a Scotsman.

He was an Olympian, however, in another sport – bobsleighing. This was not something that could be practised at the Guards Depot or anywhere else in the country with any reliability. History does not relate exactly how Boy became involved, but the catalyst may well have been Brigadier General R. J. Kentish, *Chef de Mission* of the British team for the first ever Winter Olympic Games at Chamonix in 1924, as he was also a Vice-President of the South London Harriers. Until relatively recently bobsleighing had been unknown in most countries outside Switzerland, where it had developed from tobogganing and was originally run on normal country roads rather than dedicated tracks, but a purpose-built run had been built before the Great War in St Moritz. It was thought by some to be too dangerous, but Sir Arnold Lunn, the doyen of Alpine sports, had assured the International Olympic Committee that Great Britain would show the way even without much practice and a team was assembled, five of whose members were serving army officers.

The bob itself was very different from the high-tech models used today and consisted of two wooden sleighs attached together, the front one of which could be steered by a wheel or a rope, whilst the rear sleigh had fixed runners. It could carry either a four- or a five-man crew. The riders had the choice of sitting upright as they do now, or lying *ventre à terre*, flat on their stomachs as in the modern skeleton, each crew member on top of and with his head level with the middle of the back of the man in front, the brakeman at the rear with his legs dangling behind. The latter method supposedly created less wind resistance.

The British team gathered in Chamonix in January 1924. It had been decided by the organizers that each of the two representative bobsleighs would carry four riders, but the British were able to draw from twelve potential riders, which turned out to be just as well. Boy was initially selected as the brakeman for the first bob, responsible not only for applying the brakes as appropriate, but also for delivering the final push-off, vital to a good time. In the event, during a practice run on 31 January, things went badly wrong, the bob crashed and Boy was flung out, injuring himself sufficiently not to be able to compete in the Games themselves. It was reported in the press variously that he had broken one leg in two places and that he had broken both legs, but his parents placed a notice in *The Times* a few weeks later to thank those who had inquired after his health and to say that 'reports of his injuries were much exaggerated. The wound in the knee is progressing favourably, and it is hoped that there will be no permanent effect.'

Boy's bob went on to race with a reserve crew member, but was unplaced. The other British bob won the silver medal, being beaten by the well-practised Swiss. This was not the end of Boy's career in bobsleigh: he competed again in the Winter Games of 1928 in St Moritz, but neither of the two British bobs was placed in the medals.

Two months before going out to Chamonix, Boy had left the Guards Depot on a posting to the 2nd Battalion at Chelsea Barracks. With his absence first in France and later on sick leave whilst recovering from his injury, he had hardly time to make an impact before he was instructed to report for duty at the Royal Military College, Sandhurst, where he had been appointed the Adjutant.

Chapter 6

Sandhurst (1924–1928)

Sandhurst came at just the right time for Boy. While he was still at the Guards Depot he had once again questioned his choice of career, discussing a move to civilian life, possibly at Twiss & Brownings, with one of his fellow officers, Eric Mackenzie of the Scots Guards. Like many of his generation, he was probably daunted by the slowness of promotion in the peacetime Army. He was lucky to have been promoted to captain at a relatively early age for peacetime, on the strength of his active service experience and because so many others had either been killed or disabled in the Great War or left the Army soon afterwards. Nevertheless, and notwithstanding the good reports he had received at the Depot, there was little prospect of further promotion for several years and the best he could probably hope for within the regiment was to be second-in-command of a company. It was too early for him to attend Staff College, although Jeffreys had said in his 1923 confidential report that he should certainly go there in due course.

As it turned out, Boy was fated never to pass through the Staff College. Instead it was the four years at Sandhurst which represented the only major opportunity for him to develop a reputation outside the Brigade of Guards. Every single cadet who passed through the Royal Military College during the four years of his appointment would remember him. In many ways the timing could not have been better, as this was an important group of future officers, who would rise to be the lieutenant colonels, colonels and brigadiers of the latter part of the next war. Four of them – James Cassels, Robert Laycock, 'Pip' Roberts and Dudley Ward – would reach the rank of temporary or acting major general before September 1945.

Amongst the staff there were a few friends from the Guards, including 'Babe' Alexander. Others were unknown to Boy and, of these, a number would re-enter his life at much later dates. They included one of the company commanders, Richard O'Connor of the Cameronians, and two captains from the Indian Army, Douglas Gracey of the Gurkhas and Pete Rees of the Rajputana Rifles. Two others would make a more significant impression, one professionally and one personally. Miles Dempsey of the Royal Berkshire Regiment, almost the same age as Boy, would cross his path on a number of occasions, including during the most important single episode of his career. Eric 'Chink' Dorman-Smith of the Royal Northumberland Fusiliers was to be one of the more controversial senior officers of the Second World War, but he did not serve with Boy after Sandhurst. Instead, he became a personal friend of both Boy and his future wife.

On the face of it, Boy and Chink were not at all alike. Admired for his smartness and for his organizational ability, Boy was nevertheless a very conventional soldier and one who was instinctively respectful of authority. Chink was, at least in his thinking, anything but conventional, questioning all the time how the Army functioned and what it had learnt from the Great War, and not hiding his scorn for those who were unable to see that change was required. He was already showing the independence of mind which would lead to clashes with those of a more mundane mentality – unfortunately for him they numbered many of his superiors and peers in the Army – which many years later would blight his career.

What the two men shared was a great desire to lift the quality of the peacetime Army, Boy largely through the training and discipline which he had seen working well in action in the Great War, Chink through the application of military science. Neither had much appetite for the long periods of leisure available, unless they could be used profitably in other activities. Both were keen on fitness and particularly on winter sports. Both were significantly better read than many of their brother officers. During their time together at Sandhurst, Boy and Chink sought out each other's company and the friendship prospered.

Boy's major concern was not with making friends, though this was an attractive by-product of his appointment, but for carrying out his job to the best of his ability, and in that he certainly succeeded. The post of Adjutant at the Royal Military College went back at least to 1805, some three years after gentlemen cadets had been first admitted at Sandhurst, but it had not been continuously filled until after 1910. Since the Second World War, the appointment has always been held by an officer of one of the regiments of Foot Guards, although this was not invariably the case in earlier years. Boy himself took over from another Guards officer, Arthur Smith of the Coldstream, whilst his first Commandant was a member of his own regiment, Charles Corkran. Corkran had had a distinguished career in the Great War, commanding the 1st Battalion at Festubert and then 3 Guards Brigade on the Somme. He and Boy had not served together before, but they knew each other both personally and by reputation and there was immediately a mutual respect.

The role went beyond being the chief staff officer to the Commandant, although that was a vital part of it. It was not exclusively an office job, as the title might suggest, but a high profile position entailing responsibility for the overall conduct of the cadets and to some extent for the reputation of the entire establishment. The first way in which this could be achieved was to set an example, and Boy set out to do just this. He already had a reputation for being immaculately turned out and he expected the cadets to be likewise. He also was a stickler for discipline and demanded absolute adherence to orders, not just from the cadets, but also from the NCOs who acted as instructors. An anonymous cadet noted subsequently that 'he was the most efficient of the Adjutants. Sergeant-Major Brittain was the drill sergeant of my company – No 4. On one memorable battalion parade, after rehearsing the march-past several times, Boy ordered the drill sergeants not to give the step, but from the rear of No 4 came Brittain's stentorian "Left Right LEFT". Then, to the joy of No 4 Company, the Adjutant said "Sergeant-Major Brittain, get off parade".'

Boy had by this time developed a nice sense of how to make the punishment fit the crime. One night as a prank a number of cadets tore from their mountings some of the antique cannons adorning the college, towed them to the lake and threw them into the water. This did not go unnoticed the next day and the Commandant demanded redress. Boy's solution was typical. At 0500 hrs the next morning the cadets were aroused from their deep sleep by the fire alarm and rushed outside in accordance with the rules. Once formed up, they were addressed by Boy, who informed them that they were to salvage the cannons from the lake and replace them exactly as they were before breakfast, which duly happened to the accompaniment of much grumbling.

Adherence to Boy's standards was also demanded of visitors. Mark Henniker, later to serve under Boy, recalled their first meeting, when he visited Sandhurst to play hockey as a member of a team from the rival establishment, the Royal Military Academy, Woolwich: 'We had arrived dressed in plain clothes to find the Sandhurst cadets on parade under the Adjutant. We should have stood up as the companies marched past, but we lay basking in the sunshine on the grass at the side of the parade ground and watched them. The Adjutant gave us a sound lesson in good manners which I expect we all remembered thereafter.'[1]

The appointment brought with it accommodation in the centre of the College. Lake House is sited between the Old College and the New College, overlooking to the front a key road junction across which everyone has to pass at some time each day, an ideal situation for the Adjutant. It was built in 1810, at the same time as the Old College and specifically for the use of the Surgeon. During the Great War it fell into disrepair and was condemned as unfit for human habitation. After being completely renovated, it was given over to the Adjutant. Although attractive in aspect, it looks larger than it is, having only three bedrooms, but it has excellent reception rooms and a basement area covering the full extent of the ground floor, where the servants of Boy's era lived and worked. There is a secluded garden behind the house. For a bachelor it was more than adequate and for one who enjoyed entertaining as much as Boy, it was ideal.

The RMC had been organized from 1903 onwards to resemble an infantry battalion and after the Great War was divided into four companies, each with its own commander and company officers. When the college paraded as a whole, however, it was the Adjutant, mounted on a white horse, who was in command. There were many occasions on which this happened during Boy's posting, an example being the unveiling of the Soldiers' Memorial by the Prince of Wales in June 1927. The most frequent event, however, was the commissioning parade, now known as the Sovereign's Parade. This was the climax of their college career for the cadets in the senior term, who at the end of the parade marched up the steps into the Old College to the strains of 'Auld Lang Syne'.

On 14 July 1926 a new tradition was initiated. In the words of the *RMC Magazine & Record*: 'The Parade concluded in the time-honoured form, though there was one addition, which we do not remember to have seen before. This was no less than the appearance of "the Vicar" bringing up the rear of the battalion as it marched up the steps into the Grand Entrance. The Adjutant was riding "the Vicar" but which of the two was in charge we have no means of saying.'

This feat of equestrianism is one not to be undertaken lightly and other than by a very good horseman. Provided that momentum is achieved, horses will very willingly go up steps, particularly if they know that there is a reward waiting for them, but if they are not urged on there is a danger that they will baulk at the bottom or, worse still, half way up, so some riders prefer to take such an obstacle at the trot rather than the walk. Horses are, moreover, much more reluctant to go down steps and there is a serious risk of slipping, particularly with iron horseshoes on Portland stone. The solution at Sandhurst is to turn right down a corridor in the building, then left towards a back door which, because the Old Building is on a slight slope, is accessed by fewer and shallower steps, over which a ramp can be constructed.

There have been a number of explanations for Boy's feat, which is now performed by the Adjutant at every Sovereign's Parade. According to the Browning family, the first such occasion took place not at the parade itself, but at a rehearsal during which the cadets had executed their drill so badly that an incensed Boy rode up the steps to berate them. There are other, less flattering, versions of the story, notably one in which Boy is supposed to have ridden into the building to take shelter from a sudden rainstorm, which threatened to spoil his immaculate uniform. This seems unlikely, partly because Boy would have put devotion to duty even before attention to dress and partly because 14 July 1926 was a glorious sunny day.

The most convincing explanation comes from another source, Corkran's niece Ruth Farquhar. When she died in 2007, aged 97, the following reminiscence was discovered in her papers:

My father was killed by a German sniper in the closing stages of the Great War. Thereafter my mother's eldest brother, Charles Corkran, played a large part in the upbringing of my three brothers and myself. We Farquhars frequently stayed with him and my Aunt Winnie and when they came to London they stayed with us.

In the nineteen twenties, Charles Corkran was appointed Commandant at Sandhurst, and the added joy of staying there was the early morning ride. My Uncle had two chargers, he rode one and I rode the other. If he was too busy, I sometimes got two rides. Boy Browning was the Adjutant and he often accompanied us on his venerable and much loved Spook, who was pure white.

We used to ride up behind the College onto Barossa Common and there was a short cut up some steps – just long planks cut into the bank. These were no problem to wise old Chargers.

My Mother and I were staying at Government House at one time for a week which culminated in the Commissioning Parade, with Boy in charge and my Uncle on the Platform with whichever VIP had been invited to take the Salute.

Sometimes it was the King or a member of the Family or once, I recall, it was the King of Norway.

One morning in the middle of the week we rode up the planks, through the short cut and across Barossa and Boy was eulogizing the wonders of the Spook – 'You can teach him anything' he said. I said: 'You ought to follow the Cadets who are passing out on Saturday, up the steps into the Old Building.' In the final march-past the leaving Cadets came last and instead of marching off the Parade Ground, it was the custom for them to wheel off and disappear up the steps with the Band playing Auld Lang Syne. Boy said: 'You had better ask the General about that.' The General, with a twinkle in his eye, thought that was a splendid idea.

Boy, with the Riding School Sergeant Major, gave Spook a couple of rehearsals, with a bowl of carrots and oats ready for him in the Old Building and of course he never batted an eyelid; but on the morning I think we all, especially Boy, had rather cold feet.

It was a lovely day and a magnificent Parade and the Cadets duly marched off as scheduled. Then there was an audible gasp from the crowd as the resplendent Adjutant, and his even more resplendent Charger, followed them up and were enfolded in the wide double doors at the top.

This tradition has been followed ever since and continues to this day.[2]

Ruth Farquhar was not quite right about the tradition. It was actually abandoned during the 1930s and reinstituted after the Second World War. However, it does continue to this day. On one aspect she and the Browning family agree, which is that the horse was Spook and not The Vicar. The other notable fact about this particular parade was that the officer taking the salute was General Sir George Milne,[3] then the Chief of the Imperial General Staff, and the cadet receiving the Sword of Honour was Senior Under Officer A. J. H. Cassels,[4] who thirty-nine years later would become one of Milne's successors at the top of the British Army.

Horse riding was now an important part of Boy's life. At the end of 1926 he reached his thirtieth birthday and was past his prime as far as athletics were concerned, although he continued to train the cadets and to participate, and to do well, in regimental and intra-Army events. He was a regular member of the Staff College Drag Hunt, which enabled him to have some useful social contact with the students at the nearby college, although his enthusiasm in the field occasionally provoked strong language from the hunt's Master. Dorman-Smith had gone straight on to Camberley from Sandhurst and was the hunt's Assistant Secretary, whilst Boy's Eton contemporary, Richard McCreery, one of the finest horsemen of the day, was one of the whippers-in.

Boy also rode in point-to-point races and began a short but moderately successful spell as a show-jumper. He won the Officers' Jumping Competition at the Royal Tournament in May 1927 and the jumping class for infantry officers at the Southern Command Horse Show that July. He was good enough to participate in the blue riband event of the sport, the King George V Cup, winning the first pool but failing to lift the trophy itself.

The four years at Sandhurst underpinned Boy's reputation for the next decade or more. Corkran consistently enthused about him, describing him as having a 'great influence for good' at the college with the ability to inculcate his own high standards in others. Corkran's successor, Eric Girdwood went even further in his final report: 'He is gifted with sound common sense, tact and a pleasing personality which has ensured him the wholehearted support of all ranks at the RMC and gained for him the respect and admiration of every GC who has passed through the college during this period. He possesses powers of organization and administration above the average and by his personal example and the sense of discipline and duty which he instilled into the Staff and GCs has produced a military machine of a very high standard.' Even the RMC Magazine & Record went so far as to say that 'when anyone has made a job so peculiarly his own it always seems difficult to imagine anyone else occupying it.'

Boy's last duty was to accompany Girdwood and a party of cadets to the French Military Academy at St Cyr in March 1928. One month later he left the Royal Military College to return to his regiment, his career and his life in general seemingly set fair. As it turned out, he was shortly to suffer three serious setbacks, each of which would make an impact on his future life.

Chapter 7

Hiatus (1928–1931)

Initially all continued to go well for Boy. He was posted to the 3rd Battalion, commanded by another outstanding Grenadier officer, Andrew Thorne. The slowness of peacetime promotion can be illustrated by the fact that 'Bulgy' Thorne had first commanded the same battalion nearly twelve years earlier in September 1916 and taken it through the closing stages of the Somme, followed by Third Ypres, Cambrai and the Ludendorff Offensive. Just before the end of the Great War he had been given command of a brigade, but had been reduced to his substantive rank after the Armistice. He was to remain a lieutenant colonel until 1931, after which he achieved rapid promotion.

For Boy the stars were still shining, as he was promoted to major soon after his arrival at the battalion. Shortly afterwards he was sent off for a refresher course at the Small Arms School, where one of his fellow students was Dempsey, returning from there to settle down to regimental duty, initially at Pirbright and then at Aldershot. All was far from well beneath the surface, however, and the first cause of concern was his health.

Throughout his military career Boy invariably worked at a high tempo, finding it very difficult to give less than everything to the job in hand. For four years at Sandhurst he had held down one of the most demanding jobs in the Army for one of his rank, driven not only by innate enthusiasm, but also by adherence to his own very high standards. When he was off duty, he was devoting similar levels of drive to his sporting interests. The result was that by the end of 1928 he was feeling the effects of exhaustion yet was still unable to compromise in any way in his new role as a company commander.

During the early months of 1929, Boy was frequently compelled to go off on sick leave for short periods and by that summer it was clear that he was running the risk of a more serious breakdown, possibly exacerbated by events in his private and family life. Thorne was totally sympathetic. In his report in September 1929 he wrote: 'His 4 years as Adjutant of the RMC has overtaxed his strength and exhausted his nervous energy, with the result that he has no or little reserve to fall back on. He does everything so energetically and has so many interests that it will be necessary for him to have a complete rest before he can get properly fit.' Sergison-Brooke at 1 Guards Brigade, the immediate parent formation of the battalion, and Lord Henry Seymour, the Lieutenant Colonel commanding the regiment, both agreed, the latter remarking that if Boy repaired his health he would make an excellent commanding officer. He was granted extended leave on the grounds of nervous exhaustion and required to attend a medical board before returning to active duty. It was not until 5 May 1930 that a board at Millbank eventually passed him fit.

Although it had little impact on his regimental reputation, Boy's long period of incapacity had one potentially serious adverse effect on his career. In every single annual report since the Great War he had been recommended for the Staff College course and his name had been placed on the Selected List. Passing through Staff College, whether at Camberley or at Quetta in India, was an essential component of the career of every officer with the ambition to progress to the top of the Army. Without the magical letters *p.s.c.* after his name, an officer could usually expect his promotion ceiling to be set at lieutenant colonel, with command of a battalion being the most senior appointment he might anticipate. Most Staff College graduates, on the other hand, could look forward to new career opportunities, whether on the staff or as field commanders, enhanced by their two years of contact with the best of their peer group and with the members of the directing staff, who were drawn from the most promising officers in the Army.

Boy had effectively held a staff appointment for four years at Sandhurst and it was almost certainly thought that he should return for a spell of regimental duty before going to Camberley. However, at the beginning of 1930 he was clearly in no state to join the rigorous two year course and although he was pronounced fit later that year and Corkran, now commanding London District, thought he was still a most suitable candidate for the Staff College, he had yet to demonstrate that he had recovered his stamina. By the time he had done so in late 1931 he was over the permitted age for entry. This was a potentially critical blow for Boy and meant that he was likely to see out his career in the regiment, unless he proved to be so outstanding that he was considered fit to command larger formations in due course. Even then his lack of knowledge of staff procedure was likely to count against him.

In the meantime, there were also problems in his private life. When Boy returned from Sandhurst he was thirty-one years old and still unmarried. He was unquestionably attractive to women and remained so throughout his life. Physically he was good-looking, with strong features accentuated by a rather hooked nose and a penetrating gaze, and he had an athletic figure. He was naturally charming and highly sociable, with a pronounced sense of humour, and off duty he could be very relaxed, indeed he was quite a different person from the explosively-tempered disciplinarian frequently seen by his subordinates. His interests already extended well beyond the Army and sport. He was well read, enjoyed music, theatre and ballet, liked fast cars and was interested in current affairs. He thus had little difficulty in attracting a succession of girlfriends, including Lady Moira Scott (later Combe), with whom he remained friends for the rest of his life, although nothing more serious came of this relationship. Then, sometime in 1928, he met Jan Ricardo.

Jan was herself the daughter of an army officer, Lieutenant Colonel Wilfred Ricardo. She was dark, glamorous and attractive and Boy fell for her. Their engagement was announced on 25 March 1929, with an accompanying statement that the marriage was to take place at the end of April. The months passed and nothing happened, until a further announcement was made on 26 July that the marriage had been called off. Jan had the reputation of being rather highly-strung, an accusation that was also occasionally levelled at Boy, and it is possible that the relationship was somewhat tempestuous as a result. Whether Boy's state of health at this time contributed to the breakdown or was partially caused by it cannot be said, but it was probably not helped by the strain. There have been competing stories as to who broke off the engagement. It is possible that Boy, always worried by concerns over money, had reached the conclusion that he could not support a wife at this time on his army pay. On the other hand Denys Browning, Boy's cousin, said that Boy was 'rather miserable' when he came down just after the break-up to stay with his Uncle Bertie's family, who were on holiday in Wales, which might suggest that it was Jan who took the decision. Either way they parted, although she, or rather the memory of her, would be resurrected in his life in an unexpected way some years later.[1]

Another sad event was to take place later in 1929. During the 1920s, Freddie had gone from strength to strength. In 1926 an opportunity arose to merge Twiss & Brownings with the old established firm of E. Price Hallowes, which had the exclusive agency for Heidsieck & Co.'s 'Dry Monopole' champagne and also imported port and wines from Bordeaux and Burgundy. Freddie became the chairman of Twiss & Brownings & Hallowes (later called Twiss, Browning & Hallowes) and the combined firm prospered.[2] Whilst retaining the house in Lowndes Street, Freddie took the lease of Flaxley Abbey, a large country house in the Forest of Dean in Gloucestershire, not far from the home of his distant ancestors at Coaley.[3] Nancy moved down there and at weekends Freddie adopted the life of a country gentleman.

He continued with his packed social life, whether in London or the country, indeed it was said of him that he never dined alone and that he drank both champagne and Cointreau every night of his life. Like Boy, his health began to fail, but in Freddie's case it turned out to be much more serious, as he was diagnosed with cirrhosis of the liver. He was still fit enough to attend the Lord Mayor's dinner at the Mansion House for the I Zingari Cricket Club in March 1929, in company with both Boy and his brother Monty, but he went into a decline over the following months. He died on 13 October.

The funeral took place at Flaxley Parish Church four days later, attended by Boy, Grace, Freddie's brothers Monty and Bertie and sister Helen, and a small number of close family friends. On the same day a memorial service was held at St George's, Hanover Square. Nancy, supported by other Browning relatives, was there rather than at the funeral and the church was packed with mourners, who included Rupert D'Oyly Carte, Sam Hoare, Moira Combe and, some three months after the engagement had been called off, Jan Ricardo.

From a financial perspective, Freddie's death could not have been more badly timed. Eleven days later the stock market crashed in Wall Street, triggering similar falls over the following months in London and other markets. Freddie's estate was valued at the pre-crash prices, which were not to be seen again for many years, and

Estate Duty levied accordingly at what was by then a ruinous level. From being wealthy, Nancy suddenly found herself in relatively straitened circumstances. Flaxley had to go, as did Lowndes Street. She moved temporarily to the Dower House at Crawley near Winchester, close to Monty's house, and then to Rousham Old Rectory, near Steeple Aston in Oxfordshire, where she was to live for many years.

For Boy, who was always concerned about money, it removed any hope of an inheritance and left him entirely dependent on his army pay. It was probably as well, for this reason if no other, that he had not married Jan. The shock of Freddie's illness and death probably contributed to Boy's own ill-health and delayed his recovery. Recover he did, nevertheless, and after being passed fit was welcomed back to the battalion, which was now in London. He was too late to take his company through the collective training programme for 1930, but threw himself into other activities, notably the training of the athletics team, with renewed energy. Thorne moved on at the beginning of 1931, to be succeeded by his second-in-command, Lieutenant Colonel W. S. Pilcher, who had commanded the 4th Battalion in heroic circumstances at Hazebrouck during the worst moments of the Hindenburg offensive. By the time Pilcher came to report on him in September 1931, Boy was no longer eligible for Staff College, but his commanding officer recommended that he should attend the Senior Officers School. Lord Gort, now the Lieutenant Colonel commanding the regiment, agreed that Boy would in due course make a good battalion commander, but commented that he should 'be at pains to consider tactical problems involving the employment of other arms and the administrative difficulties involved in all their aspects before coming to decisions, so as to fit himself in all aspects for command.'

Now too old to participate at the top level in athletics or winter sports, Boy developed another passion, this time for sailing, which he would retain for the rest of his life. He learnt to sail competently and participated in the Household Brigade Sailing Regatta at Emsworth Harbour in July 1930, coming fifth in the dinghy race, but his strong preference was for motor boats. He decided to buy a 20-foot Simms-built cabin cruiser, powered by a 10-17 horsepower Thornycroft engine, which he moored near Ryde on the Isle of Wight.

Ygdrasil, familiarly known as 'Yggy', was so named after the ash tree which in Norse mythology spread out over and also supported the world. Whilst small, she was, according to Boy 'an exceptionally staunch little sea boat, although rather quick on her helm in a following sea'. She provided him with a great deal of amusement and some welcome relaxation, mostly pottering up and down the Solent, although he sailed her from London to Chatham and back in the spring of 1931. In September of that year he set out on a much more ambitious voyage and one which was to have momentous consequences.

Chapter 8

Daphne (1931–1932)

Boy's voyage along the South Coast of England in September 1931 was motivated by his desire to visit Fowey, as a result of a book he had just read. *The Loving Spirit* had been published earlier that year, the first full-length work of a young novelist, Daphne du Maurier. Perhaps somewhat strangely for a man of action, this particular tale, a neo-Gothic romance about four generations of a seafaring family, stirred Boy's imagination. He was particularly taken with the description of Plyn, the fictional town in which much of the book is set and which is closely based on Polruan, the small town across the river from Fowey. He was intrigued too by what he had learnt about the 24-year-old author.

For such a relatively long voyage, Boy needed a crew, and he found one in the person of John Prescott, a close friend from the Grenadiers. Prescott was a fellow officer in the 3rd Battalion, in which he was slightly junior to Boy, having been promoted to major a few months before they set off. He had also been a direct contemporary at Eton. He was an attractive companion, not only because they got on well, but also because Prescott was a West Countryman who knew some of the waters they were to sail. Furthermore, he had a series of aunts living at conveniently spaced intervals along the coast, whose hospitality they hoped to enjoy. It was agreed that Boy would be captain and cook, whilst Prescott would be engineer and navigator.

'Yggy', towing a tender two-thirds of her own size, which reduced the speed considerably, left Wootten Creek on the Isle of Wight on 17 September and sailed via Mudeford, Poole Harbour and Lyme Regis to Torquay. Neither the aunts nor the engine proved to be entirely reliable, so it was four days before they arrived at their intermediate destination, whence the two men had to break their journey for a return to London, arriving back again late on 29 September. Their attempt to resume the voyage was foiled by the weather, but after two days sheltering in Torbay they set sail for Salcombe and early in the evening of 3 October they rounded the point into the estuary of the River Fowey where they secured a mooring from George Hunkin, the local boatman.

Their arrival had not gone unnoticed. The author of *The Loving Spirit* was staying at Ferryside, the du Maurier country home in Bodinnick, next to the Fowey ferry, from where her sister Angela had spotted the two men cruising past slowly in 'Yggy' and drawn them to Daphne's attention. Daphne had been immediately attracted by Boy's good looks and soon discovered who he was from the gossip in the town. Boy, for his part, made no attempt to introduce himself, but left the boat in Hunkin's hands for the winter and returned to London.

It was to be six months before they were to meet, although Boy did return on more than one occasion with his batman,[1] Guardsman George Richards, as his crew, before laying the boat up for the winter. In April 1932 he went down to Fowey again to pick up the boat and, hearing that Daphne was convalescing after an operation, asked Mrs Hunkin to take a note to her. 'Dear Miss du Maurier' it read, 'I believe my late father, Freddie Browning, used to know yours, as fellow-members of the Garrick Club. The Hunkins tell me you have had your appendix out and can't do much rowing yet, so I wondered if you would care to come out in my boat. How about tomorrow afternoon?'[2] Daphne, intrigued by what she had learnt of Boy, accepted immediately.

Daphne du Maurier was born on 13 May 1907 and was thus more than ten years younger than Boy. Her background had a strongly artistic flavour. Her father was the actor and theatre manager, Sir Gerald du Maurier, who was himself the son of George du Maurier, the illustrator, *Punch* cartoonist and author of *Trilby*, the book which gave both the eponymous hat and the name Svengali to the English language. Gerald, who was born in 1873, had become an actor not long after leaving Harrow. His career took off as a result of a close association with J. M. Barrie, his role as Ernest Woolley in *The Admirable Crichton* bringing him to the attention of West End audiences for the first time as a leading man. It was during the first run of this play in 1902 that he met Muriel Beaumont, the daughter of a Cambridge solicitor, who was one of the cast. Gerald fell in love with her instantly and they married in April of the following year.

Barrie remained a strong influence on Gerald's career and became a close friend of the family. The five sons of Gerald's sister, Sylvia Llewellyn-Davies, were the inspiration for *Peter Pan*[3] and when the play was first staged in 1904, Gerald played Captain Hook, possibly the best known and best loved villain in British theatre. Barrie's original intention was to have Hook played by Dorothea Baird, who had been cast as Mrs Darling, possibly to add some piquancy to Peter's attitude towards mothers, but Gerald persuaded him to double up the role with that of his own part, Mr Darling, a tradition which has been followed to this day. Gerald had a great enthusiasm for playing strong characters, including the title roles in *Raffles* and *Bulldog Drummond*. He also had an outstanding eye for leading ladies such as Gladys Cooper, Gracie Fields and Gertrude Lawrence, and conducted a number of extra-marital liaisons.

Not long after Daphne was born, Gerald moved into management when he took on Wyndham's Theatre, but he continued to act himself. Not one for Shakespeare and other great classics, he tended towards the lighter end of the theatrical spectrum, but was nevertheless one of the foremost performers of his time, synonymous with the West End over nearly three decades.

Daphne's milieu was thus entirely different from Boy's, the common thread being the vigorous social lives enjoyed by their respective fathers, but whereas Freddie's world was focused on sport, commerce and the services, Gerald's was firmly embedded in all aspects of the arts. It was thus not surprising that Daphne began writing stories and poetry at an early age, encouraged by Gerald and by her governess Maud Waddell, known to all as 'Tod', who joined the household in 1918 when Daphne was eleven. Some twenty years older than Daphne, Tod was to become a great confidante and a considerable influence on her life. She was herself a very strong character, without any formal training for her role as governess, but with a love for great literature and particularly poetry, which she imparted to her receptive young pupil. She left the du Mauriers at the end of 1921, after not much more than three years, but the two women began a regular correspondence which would last until Tod physically re-entered Daphne's life as governess to her own children in 1945.

The only outside education which Daphne received was three terms in 1925 at a finishing school at Camposena, outside Paris, but academically it was not a great success. In the holidays, and after she had left, she concentrated on writing both poetry and short stories, the latter populated with unpleasant men and weak women. She was encouraged by her father, who felt that there was the making of a good writer in her, and she was motivated by a new found enthusiasm, this time for Cornwall. Because of Gerald's work, the family lived in London, in a large and attractive Queen Anne house close to Hampstead Heath called Cannon Hall, but in the summer of 1926 he and Muriel took the family down to Cornwall with a view to buying a holiday home there. They discovered that the house opposite the pub in Bodinnick was for sale and put in an offer which was accepted in time for them to move in that autumn. Ferryside, as it was renamed, had been part of a boatyard and was in ramshackle condition, but it had tremendous character and was beautifully positioned, looking across the river to the brightly painted houses of Fowey, crowding the hillside on the far bank.

Daphne was enchanted by Ferryside, Fowey and the south coast of Cornwall. She knew from the start that she would be able to live very happily there and felt instinctively that this new environment would provide fuel for her creative talent. In the following May, after the necessary renovations had been completed, Muriel moved in with Daphne and her other two daughters, Angela and Jeanne, respectively three years older and four years younger. Daphne immediately immersed herself in her surroundings, going for long walks past Polruan to the cliffs along the coast and through Fowey up into the woods and fields beyond. She also started to sail, learning very quickly how to handle small craft from one of the local boatmen. When Muriel and her sisters returned to London on the day after Daphne's twentieth birthday, she stayed on alone for the first time in her life and loved every moment of it.

Throughout her childhood Daphne had an extraordinarily close relationship with Gerald, partly because Muriel, called 'Mo' by her family, seemed to prefer Angela, and partly because she was closer in temperament to the son Gerald had always wanted but never had. Indeed Daphne went out of her way to behave like a boy, dressing in shorts and shirts rather than dresses and wearing her hair short. She fantasized that she was a boy and behaved accordingly. When it became physically apparent that she was in all respects a girl, she became quite distressed and this confusion was to remain with her for some years and recur intermittently later, although she learnt how to shut the boy side of her 'in a box'. As she entered her late teens, she found other emotions awakening. She developed a crush on Fernande Yvon, one of the teachers at Camposena, and began to suspect that she might have 'Venetian tendencies', du Maurier family code for being lesbian. Although she went on holiday with Ferdy, as she called Mlle Yvon, and it was possible, if not likely, that the two women went beyond simple friendship, no great romance ensued, although Daphne remained in touch with Ferdy for the rest of the latter's life.

It became clear not very long afterwards that Daphne was just as drawn to the opposite sex. In early 1929 she went on a winter sports holiday to Caux in Switzerland, staying with her father's friend, the novelist Edgar Wallace, and his wife Pat. There she met Carol Reed, the illegitimate son of Herbert Beerbohm Tree, an actor-manager like her father, albeit of an older generation.[4] Reed came from the same background and they had a number of friends in common. He was also tall, good-looking and rather Bohemian, which she fancied herself to be at the time. Daphne was immediately attracted to him and they became lovers.

Gerald was not at all happy about the affair despite the fact that Violet Tree, Reed's aunt, was a friend. He was in fact jealous, as Daphne was his favourite daughter and he had become very possessive of her. Muriel was equally hostile and in such circumstances, Daphne reacted in just the way they would not have wished, by consummating the relationship. However, this was no great passion, not least because she became the dominant partner, which she found rather unsatisfying. The affair continued for some two years, but by the summer of 1931 it had petered out, although Daphne and Reed remained good friends.

Part of the reason for her waning interest in Reed was that Daphne had realized that her creative powers were enhanced whenever she was down in Cornwall, so it was necessary to part from him, as he was by now immersed in his career in London and elsewhere. She was given permission by her parents, doubtless anxious to keep the lovers apart, to spend the winter of 1929/30 at Ferryside, provided only that she slept in one of the cottages opposite, working in the house during the day. In May 1929 she had had one of her short stories, 'And now to God the Father', published in *The Bystander* for the first time. This was followed the following month by another story, 'A Difference in Temperament'. She felt, however, that she had the bones of a novel lurking in the back of her mind, and she needed the environment of Cornwall and the seclusion of Ferryside in winter to bring it out.

Whilst learning to sail, Daphne had become intrigued by the hulk of the schooner *Jane Slade*, lying in the Pont inlet between Bodinnick and Polruan, with its figurehead intact. She became even more interested when she learnt from Adams, the boatman, that he was a descendant of the woman after whom the vessel was named. Out of this emerged *The Loving Spirit*, which told the tale of four generations of the Coombe family starting with Janet, loosely based on Jane Slade herself, and moving on to her adored son, Joseph, grandson Christopher and great-granddaughter Jennifer and centred on the fictional town of Plyn. Daphne had written the first three parts of the novel by Christmas 1929 and completed the last part by the end of March in the following year. It was published by Heinemann in February 1931, to critical and public acclaim. Boy read it soon after publication.

On the face of it, Boy and Daphne were not obviously suited to one another. He was every inch the army officer, disciplined, smart, practical, organized and self-confident. If there was one trait for which he failed to achieve the top grade in his annual assessments, it was imagination, where he was scored more often than not as average. He was also highly gregarious, with a circle of friends and acquaintances which went far beyond the regiment and even the Army. Daphne was rather shy, almost anti-social, and already much preferred Cornwall to London. She favoured casual clothes, especially slacks and jerseys, over smart suits and pretty dresses. By the middle class standards of the day she was rather unconventional. On the other hand, if there was one characteristic she possessed in abundance, it was imagination.

What they shared immediately was a love of the sea. By the time they met, she was a highly competent sailor, who had graduated from a rowing boat to a motor boat, the *Cora Ann*, and then to a 32-foot yawl-rigged fishing lugger, the *Marie-Louise*, built for her by Jane Slade's grandsons. Boy also had a far wider range of interests than the average army officer, enjoyed literature and the theatre and was a natural conversationalist. Like her, he had a highly developed sense of humour. There was an immediate connection, with the result that they spent not only the day of their meeting, but also the following two in each others company.

There was also a considerable physical attraction. Daphne was not classically beautiful, but she was undeniably attractive, with light brown, almost blonde hair, clear blue eyes and a boyish figure, whilst he had a strong face and, even in his late thirties, an athletic build. He was naturally courteous and attentive to women but, perhaps more importantly, he had a strong personality and could be very masterful, in contrast to Carol Reed.

Notwithstanding that Boy had only just been posted to the 2nd Battalion, he was able to take yet more leave and was back at Fowey within a week, visiting again and again as spring moved into summer. 'We spend most of the time' wrote Daphne to Tod, 'cursing each other for spoiling the paint on the boat and yelling warnings if a lobster pot floats near the propeller'[5] and this easy familiarity was one of the factors which made him realize very quickly that this was the woman with whom he wished to share his life. He proposed marriage, but Daphne rejected him initially on the grounds that she did not believe in the institution of matrimony. It took a visit to Pirbright to meet some of his brother officers to persuade her otherwise. Boy arranged for her to stay with Eric and Estelle Dorman-Smith and it was Chink, much taken with Daphne, who persuaded her that to live together without getting married would spell the end of Boy's career. Daphne subsequently turned the tables by proposing to Boy herself, a typically unconventional act.

Once they had agreed to wed, Boy had to obtain the permission of his Commanding Officer, Paddy Beaumont-Nesbitt, but he was a friend and posed no problem. However, Peter Carrington, the son of a Grenadier and later an officer in the regiment himself, recalled his father being disgusted that there was opposition from a number of officers who felt that marrying the daughter of an actor was inappropriate.[6] The visit to Rousham to meet Nancy and Grace went very well, as did the one to Uncle Monty at his house near Winchester. Daphne was much more nervous about how to deal with Gerald.

Gerald had in fact burst into tears when he first heard of the impending engagement. However, by the time Daphne took Boy to meet him and Muriel on 6 July, he had become reconciled to the new development. Gerald's brother Guy had been killed in the Great War and Gerald, who had served briefly and without any distinction at the end of the war,[7] had developed a great regard for the Army and was impressed by Boy's DSO. He gave his blessing and the engagement was announced three days later.

Though Daphne had given in about getting married, she got her way on the wedding itself. There were to be no society church or Guards Chapel, no line of Grenadier officers forming an arch with their swords, no large reception and almost no guests at all. The ceremony took place at the beautiful old church of St Wyllow at Lanteglos, near Polruan. Gerald and Muriel were there, but the only other relative present on either side was Geoffrey Millar, Daphne's cousin. The Hunkins were also invited, with George acting as Boy's best man. Daphne's two sisters were away on holiday and, for some reason, neither Nancy nor Grace came nor any other members of the Browning or Alt families.

Early in the morning on 19 July Daphne, her parents and Geoffrey travelled by *Cora Ann* to the Pont bridge, walking up from there to the church, whilst Boy and the Hunkins followed in *Ygdrasil*. Immediately after the service, Boy and Daphne left in his boat for the Helford River, mooring in Frenchman's Creek and pottering about for a week, only interrupted by Boy's batman, Richards, rowing out provisions from time to time.

Chapter 9

Marriage (1932–1939)

After their somewhat unconventional honeymoon, it was down to earth for the newlyweds. Boy had his work to return to at the 2nd Battalion in Pirbright, plunging straight into the collective training programme for the year. At the beginning of 1933 he was transferred to the 1st Battalion on a temporary basis as second-in-command and stayed for just over a year, three months of which were spent at the Senior Officers School at Sheerness.

The purpose of the Senior Officers School was to prepare majors for battalion command and, at the same time, to inculcate the students with a common military doctrine. It was moderately successful in the first objective and largely unsuccessful in the second. Brigadier 'Tommy' Lindsell, one of the great logistics officers of his generation, was the Commandant. In his report on Boy he wrote: 'A really good type of officer who will make a first rate C.O. He has sound ideas and is prepared to back them with sound arguments. A keen student of his profession. He shows marked capacity as a leader and as an instructor. He has plenty of energy and drive.' It was clear that marriage would make no difference to Boy's professional life or diminish his personal ambition.

For Daphne, the adjustment to married life was much more difficult. Boy turned out to be not quite what she had expected; indeed his ability to show a different face to her from the one he showed to the rest of the world was and would continue to be very marked. To almost anyone else, he appeared to be strong, confident and decisive. To her, it seemed that at times he was looking for an emotional prop. This manifested itself initially in two ways. Boy was still suffering from the recurring nightmares he had experienced since the Great War, and would frequently wake up screaming, looking to her for comfort. He also suffered on occasion from 'me tum' and other minor ailments which she, initially at least, put down to some form of hypochondria. Instead of dominating her, as she had rather expected, she found that she was in some ways the stronger partner.

Realizing that his choice of career ran the risk of forcing her into the sort of life which she would find uncongenial, Boy bent over backwards to make her comfortable with her new situation. He took on the du Maurier nicknames and the codewords they used in everyday speech, whilst the two of them developed their own unusual form of English, to some extent based on Cornish dialect, not only for speech, but for letters to each other. Boy and Daphne also adopted a number of routines, called 'routes', such as meals at fixed times, although these were probably derived more from his habits than hers.

By inclination, Boy was at heart a social animal, whereas she was a lone wolf. Any wish on his part to go on weekend house parties or to formal dinners or dances, as he had done as a bachelor, was not reciprocated by her. She made a particularly poor Army wife, with no enthusiasm for participation in regimental events and little interest in the wives and families of the other ranks. 'Can't see myself giving away prizes to the Troops and asking after the sergeant-major's twins', she wrote to her confidante Tod.[1] Boy, for his part, was happy to indulge her likes and dislikes as much as he possibly could.

Luckily the 1st Battalion was at Wellington Barracks during 1933, so it was possible for them to live for the time being in one of the two cottages at the bottom of the garden at Cannon Hall, which Gerald had given Daphne as a wedding present.[2] The cottage was sufficiently detached for the couple not to live in the senior du Mauriers' pockets and they were able to develop some joint friendships, including the tennis player Bunny Austin and his wife Phyllis. However, Daphne found the role of housewife very difficult. She appealed for help to her father's friend the actress Gladys Cooper, who recommended that she take on Lily Bocock, one of her own former staff. Lily came as cook and fitted in well with the household, even going as far as to succumb to the amorous advances of Guardsman Richards,[3] whom before long she had married.

By the time of her own wedding Daphne had already had published a second book, *I'll Never Be Young Again* and had finished writing a third, *The Progress of Julius*, neither of which received the acclaim of her first novel, but now the novelty of marriage and the demands of creating a home called a temporary halt to her writing. Moreover, within months she was pregnant and her first child, Tessa, was born on 15 July 1933. Daphne was almost as reluctant a mother as she was a housewife, taking on a nanny immediately and leaving the care of the infant almost entirely in her hands. Rather like the heroine of *The Loving Spirit*, she had desperately wanted a son and could work up little interest in her daughter. Boy, on the other hand, was an attentive father as far as his duties allowed.

Shortly after his return from the Senior Officers School, Boy was posted back to the 2nd Battalion as second-in-command to Beaumont-Nesbitt. The battalion was located first at Windsor and then at Aldershot, so the couple rented the Old Rectory at Frimley. Daphne felt much happier outside the metropolis and turned to writing again, but she was set back in her tracks by the sudden death from cancer of Gerald in April 1934. Although the event brought her much closer to her mother than she had ever been, she was devastated, but she derived a great deal of comfort by writing a biography of her father, *Gerald: A Portrait*, which was published before the end of the year to excellent reviews and even better sales. Her creative powers restored and encouraged by Boy, she decided that she would spend as much time in Fowey as she could, writing her next novel, *Jamaica Inn*, which turned out to be one of her most popular.

Boy in the meantime was continuing to impress his superiors, all the more so when Beaumont-Nesbitt was sent on the one year course at the Imperial Defence

College, leaving his right hand man in effective command. It was Boy's good fortune that the battalion was now in 1 Guards Brigade, which was commanded from May 1935 by Thorne. The latter was still a strong supporter, but whilst he wrote in Boy's confidential report in 1935 that 'I would much rather have him as a C.O. in peacetime or on active service than many more senior officers', he was also perceptive enough to remark, 'he must learn to realize that there is a breaking point and that reserves of nervous energy are difficult to build up at times.' The GOC-in-C of Aldershot Command, General Sir Francis Gathorne-Hardy, whilst recommending him for advancement, made another point: 'Major Browning is himself capable of continuous exertion and therefore at times may be a hard taskmaster. In command he will, I have no doubt, learn the limits of others.' Boy was clearly continuing to stretch both himself and his subordinates.

Daphne, on the other hand, rather resented her new duties whenever she was at Frimley. She wrote to Tod that she was 'having to visit all the soldiers wives in the battalion as I am Mrs C.O. now. Can you picture me, going round the married quarters and chatting to *40* different women?'[4] She was shocked at their living conditions, which were clean enough, but very cramped and crowded. She was equally reluctant to participate in the social events demanded of officers' wives.

On 1 February 1936, Boy was promoted to lieutenant colonel and succeeded Beaumont-Nesbitt in command of the 2nd Battalion. By this time it had become apparent that a considerable upheaval was imminent for the Brownings, as the battalion was bound for Egypt.[5] Preparations were interrupted by the death of King George V[6] and it was the new Colonel-in Chief, King Edward VIII, himself a former Grenadier, who inspected the battalion, in service dress and greatcoats but already wearing sun helmets, in the stygian gloom of a raw March morning at Chelsea Barracks. A week later Boy, Daphne, Tessa and the nanny embarked with the battalion in the SS *Cameronia*, bound for Alexandria

Egypt had been occupied by the British since 1882 and had become a protectorate in 1914. In 1922 the country became notionally independent, but defence and the protection of foreign interests remained the responsibility of the British Government, much to the resentment of the majority of educated Egyptians. In 1936 a new Anglo-Egyptian Treaty was signed, handing over control of the Egyptian Army to local commanders, albeit with a large British Military Mission attached. However, there was still a sizeable body of British troops in Egypt, not least because relations with Italy, which had invaded Ethiopia in the previous October, were very poor and a potentially serious threat was perceived from the substantially larger Italian forces in neighbouring Libya.

Most of the British troops were to be found in three formations, the Cairo Brigade, the Canal Brigade and the Cavalry Brigade. Boy's battalion was based in Alexandria, at the Mustapha Barracks, for the duration of its tour of duty, although it was initially in the Cairo Brigade and then in the Canal Brigade. Boy's immediate superior in the latter was Brigadier W. T. Brooks, an old friend who had been a company commander at Sandhurst during Boy's time as Adjutant. The other battalions in the Canal Brigade were stationed along the Suez Canal itself.

For the most part the programme of training continued as if the battalion was in England, with platoon and company drills and musketry dominating the early part of each season, followed by collective training for the whole battalion, the last made much easier by the space and lack of population in the Western Desert. Whereas collective training in the UK was a summer event, followed by brigade exercises in the autumn, in Egypt these were delayed to October and February to take advantage of the cool weather. A new feature was a series of small expeditions into the desert, a number led by Boy himself. One important reconnaissance took place from 12 to 16 November 1937, its purpose being to investigate defensive positions against an attack from the west. The party of thirty-six was divided into two groups, each with four trucks and a water cart, the first group also including Boy's Hillman Hawk. Three further trucks carried supplies and spare parts to an intermediate point. The entire party travelled together from Alexandria to El Alamein, before turning south along a desert track to Naqb Abu Dweis, at the edge of the Qattara Depression, where they camped for the night. On the next day the groups divided, with one travelling south-west to Qara and the other following a track to the same destination along the top of the cliffs lining the Depression. On the third day the combined party travelled south-east to the furthest point at Qaret Agnes at the western end of the Depression, before going north and eventually retracing their steps back to Naqb Abu Dweis and Alexandria. The total distance covered was 560 miles. After this particular exercise, Boy wrote an appreciation of the country, giving his opinion that the Qattara Depression itself was effectively impassable to large bodies of troops, especially in vehicles. He concluded that the best defensive position lay on the shortest line between there and the sea at El Alamein, whilst the alternative, many miles further forward at Mersa Matruh, was likely to be untenable. Some five years later he would be proved correct.

Other activities for the battalion included sports, with which Boy remained personally involved wherever possible. Athletics, football, cricket and swimming were all encouraged, with frequent matches played against other units, not only from the Army but also the other two services, whilst in early 1937 a football match was arranged with the visiting German cruiser *Emden*, which the Germans won 3–1.

Daphne loathed Egypt. It was her misfortune that she arrived there after the end of the cool season, when the weather was beginning to become very unpleasant. She and Boy settled into a house at 13 Rue Jessop, where at least she had an establishment of domestic servants, but she was unable to go for the long walks she enjoyed in Cornwall, she disliked watching the races or polo and she found the local expatriate community boring and parochial. 'The English colony', she wrote to Tod, 'is comparatively small. We don't care a pin for any of them.'[7] *Jamaica Inn* had by then been published very successfully and she was on to a new project, a history of her family titled simply *The Du Mauriers*. Writing in the heat of the Egyptian summer was more than a chore, but she stuck to it and was able to send the manuscript back to her publisher, Victor Gollancz, in August.

Shortly afterwards she discovered that she was pregnant again. The climate was doing her no good at all, but she and Boy, with Tessa and the nanny, managed to take local leave in the mountains of Cyprus in September, which was a great success. Nevertheless, and although on her return to Alexandria she found the weather improving considerably, while her condition allowed her to excuse herself from the parties leading up to Christmas, she and Boy decided that she would have to go home for the birth and she sailed on the SS *Otranto* in mid-January.

Flavia was born on 2 April 1937 and this time Daphne was not so disappointed about the baby not being a boy. Boy came home on three months leave in May, which allowed Daphne to begin work on a new novel whilst she was still in England. Leaving the children with Nancy and Grace at Rousham, the two of them returned to Egypt together at the end of July, right into the middle of the Egyptian summer, where she worked tirelessly but often fruitlessly, on *Rebecca*. Deeply homesick and loathing the social life, her sense of inadequacy was reflected in the character of the unnamed heroine, the second Mrs de Winter. These feelings were given more weight by her jealousy of Jan Ricardo, which still lingered and was, in some ways, to remain with her for many more years. The novel also introduced to the world, had it realized it, another obsession of Daphne's, this time for a house. The Manderley of the novel was Menabilly, which Daphne had discovered during her walks around the Fowey countryside and which she was determined somehow to make her own.

The 2nd Battalion's posting to Egypt came to an end in December 1937. It arrived back in Southampton on the 14th of the month, moving directly to London and exercising its privilege of marching through the City with colours flying, drums beating and bayonets fixed, before being greeted at the Mansion House by the Lord Mayor and the Sheriffs. Boy returned with his reputation enhanced. Brooks had written an excellent report on him, endorsed by Lieutenant General Sir George Weir, GOC British Troops in Egypt, who thought that he would make a good brigade commander.

The battalion was much depleted after its return to England, with a large number of guardsmen coming to the end of their period of service and going into the Reserves. By May 1938 it was restored to full strength in time for its return to Wellington Barracks and to ceremonial duties for the first time since it left for Egypt. On the 25th of that month it received new colours from its third Colonel-in-Chief in two years, the Abdication having taken place whilst it was away. The old colours were laid up in St Paul's Cathedral.

The countdown to the next global conflict was now beginning and Boy, like some others, began to show signs of extreme frustration at the slow progress in modernizing the Army, frequently venting his opinions on both his superiors and their political masters to his family and friends. The only way in which he could directly make a contribution was by bringing his battalion to a very high level of efficiency. Peter Carrington, who joined the battalion from Sandhurst in January 1939, was astonished by the relaxed attitude of a number of officers in the Grenadiers, who he felt were completely unprepared for the war which by that time everyone thought was coming. The exception was Boy, whom he considered dynamic in his efforts to improve matters, albeit exasperated by the lack of equipment, notably transport and up to date weaponry. Boy was unable to do very much about poorly performing officers, other than through their annual reports, but he had a free hand with the NCOs and Carrington remembered him reducing eleven sergeants in rank after an exercise on Chobham Common. Carrington thought that he was a very good commanding officer, with a striking personality, albeit that his explosive temper made him a terrifying figure to a young subaltern.[8]

By this time it was known that all three regular Grenadier battalions would be included in any expeditionary force to be sent to the Continent in the event of war, but Boy was not destined to go with them, as on 1 August 1939 he was removed from the Regimental List, unemployed but on full pay. He took advantage of his temporary idleness by going cruising for a fortnight with Daphne in the sailing yacht they had recently acquired, *Restless of Plyn*. At the beginning of September he was promoted to colonel, with seniority backdated to 1 February, and appointed Assistant Commandant of the Small Arms School.

Chapter 10

Brigadier (1939–1941)

The Small Arms School had its origins in the School of Musketry, established in Hythe in 1853 on the orders of Lord Hardinge, the Duke of Wellington's successor as Commander-in-Chief, with the purpose of providing advanced instruction in personal weapons. The new name was adopted in 1919 and the school was expanded to include the Machine Gun School at Netheravon in 1926. There was a permanent staff, formed initially as the Corps of Instructors of Musketry and renamed the Small Arms School Corps in 1929.

The School ran a number of courses for officers and NCOs, lasting from a few days to ten weeks. These taught the use of a large variety of weapons, from pistols at one end to the 2-pounder anti-tank gun at the other. The school was also used to test new and modified weapons prior to their acceptance by the Army. In 1939, the size of the establishment was still modest, the full-time staff numbering about forty at each of the two wings at Hythe and Netheravon, with an additional number of attached officers.

Boy was Assistant Commandant for exactly a month before being promoted to brigadier and appointed Commandant. On their return from Egypt, he and Daphne had rented a house called Greyfriars at Church Crookham in Hampshire, which Daphne had liked, but they now moved into the Commandant's house in Hythe, with which she was less pleased. *Rebecca* had been published to great acclaim in 1938, since when there had been something of a pause in her writing, partly necessitated by the nanny going off sick for some time after the return from Egypt.

As usual, Boy threw himself into his work, as demand for more and better courses meant a rapid expansion in the number of instructors, achieved by calling back reservists and transferring some of the best of the infantry students. Having attended a course himself back in 1928 he was broadly familiar with the school, but it needed to be put on an entirely different wartime footing, which played well to his organizational skills. Among other new initiatives, it was decided to open up an establishment at Foulness to carry out experimental work. There were no battle schools at this time, let alone a School of Infantry, so the Small Arms School was one of the few places at which junior officers and NCOs could be taught minor infantry tactics involving fieldcraft and weapons handling, making it a most valuable resource for the Army.

Well aware of the importance of his task, Boy was nevertheless profoundly discontented. In a letter to his Aunt Helen in October 1939 he wrote: 'I feel rather an upstart sitting at home here and getting promotion while so many of my old brother officers are out in France.' At the end of August 1939 he had even written to the Military Secretary in an unsuccessful attempt to have the appointment cancelled, due to the imminence of a state of war, but his hopes of active service had been dashed and he was ordered to report for duty as instructed. He nevertheless remained determined to go over to France to see for himself what was happening, finding an excuse to do so in January 1940, when he paid a three-day visit to the BEF.

At the beginning of the second week of May 1940 he was back in France again, ostensibly to introduce a new pamphlet on the Bren Gun to the Director of Military Training at GHQ. He used the trip to visit his old 2nd Battalion and the 1st Battalion, now commanded by John Prescott. At GHQ he found two old school friends, Robert Bridgeman, a contemporary in 'Pop' at Eton, and now the GSO1 (Staff Duties) and Philip Gregson-Ellis, the GSO1 (Operations) and a fellow Grenadier. To make the Old Etonian party complete, Oliver Leese arrived on 10 May as Deputy Chief of Staff. On the very same day the Germans attacked in the West and it was immediately made clear that all extraneous personnel should leave[1]. Carrying a letter from Leese to his wife, Boy returned to England immediately.

Other than to effect a quick handover and to pick up his kit, he was not to return to Hythe. While he had been away a signal had arrived from the War Office, ordering him to take immediate command of 128 Infantry Brigade, where the incumbent had been taken ill. As he was on the move, it failed to reach him and further increasingly strident signals followed him round France and back to England. By the time Boy arrived at his new formation on 14 May, he was in a foul temper at being harassed in such a way and his Brigade Major had to take him for a very long walk to calm him down.

The Brigade Major was a man on whom Boy would rely a great deal for much of the rest of the War. Gordon Walch had been a cadet at Sandhurst during Boy's time there as Adjutant, following which he was commissioned into the Loyal (North Lancashire) Regiment in 1926. His career had consisted mostly of service with his regiment in India and England, broken only by a short posting to the Netheravon Wing of the Small Arms School. He was nearly as new to the brigade as Boy and this was his first staff appointment after completing the short wartime course at the Staff College.

128 Brigade comprised three Territorial Army units, 1/4th, 2/4th and 5th Battalions of the Hampshire Regiment and was thus inevitably known as the Hampshire Brigade. The parent formation was 43 (Wessex) Division, a first-line Territorial division which, at the time of Boy's arrival, was preparing to go to France. In the event, the collapse of the Allied forces on the Continent and the evacuation of the BEF meant that its planned move was cancelled and, as the best equipped division in the UK by the end of June 1940, it became a key component of the country's defence against invasion.

On the day after Boy assumed command, the three battalion commanders, two Territorials and a Regular officer, were instructed to report to him. The first two entered, saluted Boy, who was seated at his desk, and sat down in chairs opposite him. The Regular CO also saluted, but remained standing to await the Brigadier's pleasure. Walch was summoned immediately and ordered to take the Territorials outside and instruct them in the proper manners required in appearing before a superior officer, only after which could the meeting begin.

The full weight of his personality now imposed on his immediate subordinates, Boy could begin to lick the rest of the brigade into what he considered was the proper shape. His first action was to draw up Standing Orders, the first of which stated in large letters: 'Any officer or other rank who falls out on the line of march WILL be court-martialled.' Other orders followed in the same vein and the brigade very quickly got the message about the standards to which it was expected to conform.

Boy's arrival was generally well received. Tom Balding, who was sent to Brigade HQ as a liaison officer, wrote subsequently: 'It was our great good luck to have him....He looked us over and told us that we were of good quality but not yet alert... He gave us two months to get it right and we did. It was a great moment for the assembled officers of the brigade when later he said he would be proud to lead them in battle.'[2] Balding continued: 'It was a bit of luck for me to go to his headquarters. He was the only commander I met during the war that, if you carried out his orders as he gave them, you did right. With others I found that they complained, putting the blame elsewhere.' It was evidently a happy HQ, with Boy solicitous for the well-being of his staff. Balding recalled that, on the occasions when Boy provided wine for the senior table in the mess, he would also do so for the junior table, not wishing to see his subalterns spending all their meagre pay in the pub.

Brigade HQ was at Evercreech in Somerset, in the heart of the division's recruiting area, but, a week after Boy arrived, orders were received to move to Hertfordshire and on 25 May a new HQ was opened at Tatmore Place, near Hitchin. Activity increased significantly, the immediate priorities being to reconnoitre the surrounding area, to identify sites for road blocks and to establish liaison with the police and civil defence organizations. The Local Defence Volunteers, soon to become the Home Guard, came under operational command.

An early visitor was Field Marshal the Earl of Cavan, a former CIGS whom Boy had first encountered as the commander of the Guards Division in 1915 and had known as a senior Grenadier subsequently. Cavan proffered the use of a number of his retainers, whom he had formed into a motor cycle reconnaissance section. As they knew the area well, this was immediately accepted and the field marshal became a regular guest in the officers' mess.

43 Division, with 2 Armoured Division, formed IV Corps, which had been chosen to act as the Home Forces strategic reserve, its role being described in its first operational order as 'delivery of the decisive counter-attack which can only be effected by mobile and ruthless action.' Corps exercises began in the late summer. In the brigade itself, training was focused on battle drill and street-fighting practice, whilst night patrols were introduced and reconnaissance parties sent out into neighbouring Suffolk and Essex. Equipment was still woefully short and Boy

ordered Walch to buy up all the motor cycles available for sale locally to provide some additional mobility.

If Boy was totally at home in this new environment and, indeed, pleased to be carrying out at last what he considered was a role to match his talents, Daphne was at something of a loss, as well as being effectively homeless. Although the children were spending much of the time at Rousham with their grandmother, she was reluctant to live there herself. However, no separate accommodation was provided for the brigade commander, who was expected to live in the mess at Tatmore Place and, from mid-August, at a new HQ at Kingswaldenbury. She thought that she should at least be near at hand and Boy's batman Johnson[3] was instructed to look for a suitable billet for the family.

According to Brian Urquhart, Johnson was a man of few words, indeed he only ever heard him utter one word, 'Sir', used with 'infinite expressiveness' 'Sir' affirmative, 'Sir' questioning, 'Sir' enthusiastic, 'Sir' grateful, 'Sir' acknowledging, and so on.[4] On this occasion, Johnson must have plumbed hidden depths of volubility, as he succeeded in persuading the owners of Langley End, a large Lutyens house near Hitchin, to accept Daphne, Tessa, Flavia and the nanny as paying guests. Christopher and Paddy Puxley were both in their early 40s and were themselves childless. Christopher was notionally a gentleman-farmer, but in practice did very little other than read and play the piano, although he was a member of the Home Guard. They welcomed Daphne and the two girls with open arms, Paddy becoming an immediate favourite with the latter. Their stay initially was quite brief, as Daphne was pregnant again and decided that it would be only fair to the Puxleys if she moved out when the birth was imminent. She took the lease on another nearby house, Clouds Hill, in October and her longed-for son, Christian, was born on 3 November.

Relations between Daphne and Boy were starting to show signs of strain, largely because he was extremely busy and would come back to Langley End or Clouds Hill at the weekends tired and very often fraught. The war was not going well and he was highly critical of the War Office and some of the higher commanders. Moreover, in addition to the shortages of equipment still plaguing him, there were frequent frustrations involved in dealing with the civilian population, whom he often found obstructive.

In company he was often much more relaxed. The Harrison family, who owned the building in which brigade HQ was situated, boasted six beautiful daughters who were popular not only with the HQ staff, becoming known as the 'Brigade Butterflies', but also with their commander. Boy was quite capable of being an entertaining member of any social gathering and would give demonstrations of his own party piece, a Cossack dance executed with considerable *brio*. He was also rather better with his two daughters at this stage than was Daphne, readily entering their games. It was his wife who suffered the brunt of his frustration.

As always he was showing yet another face to his subordinates, for whom he continued to set a high example. John Collins, who was in charge of the brigade signals section, said that 'he inspired unusual loyalty – partly for his fierce rejection of any outside interference with his command ... chiefly for his self-confidence, complete calm and decisiveness ... we subalterns looked on him with awe: we realized his humour and humanity, but, frankly, we generally preferred his more magnificent qualities.'[5]

He also continued to find favour with his superiors. His divisional commander, Major General Val Pollok, wrote that the way in which the brigade responded to his command was inspiring, although his tactical judgement was sounder than his administrative and that he was apt to dash in where angels fear to tread. He recommended Boy for divisional command and Lieutenant Generals Nosworthy at IV Corps and Williams at Eastern Command broadly concurred, although they both felt that he needed more time.

In November 1940, 43 Division moved again. There had been a change in the leadership of Home Forces during the summer, with Alan Brooke replacing Edmund Ironside as Commander-in-Chief. The latter had kept his mobile reserve north of London, where in theory it could strike at landings in East Anglia as well as along the Channel coast. Brooke was convinced that any invasion would come on the shortest route from France and that his best equipped formations should be positioned to meet it. The division was thus moved to the eastern end of Kent, 128 Brigade being given responsibility for the coast of the Isle of Thanet between Whitstable and the North Foreland, with Brigade HQ located at Sarre, between Canterbury and Margate. The division now came under the command of XII Corps and it was of no small advantage to Boy that the corps commander was Andrew Thorne, a longstanding supporter.

Boy left Hertfordshire a week after his son was born and, although he was back for a week over Christmas, with invasion still a real possibility he had few subsequent opportunities to return to Clouds Hill. On the other hand, he was reluctant to bring the family into the part of the country most exposed to attack. It was with some relief to both him and Daphne, therefore, that she received an invitation from the Puxleys to return to Langley End when her lease expired in January 1941. From this time onwards she and Boy led an increasingly detached life which, had they but known it, would last for another eighteen years. In his absence she turned increasingly for comfort to Christopher Puxley, a handsome and engaging companion who was always there. She was also writing again, this time a historical romance which took its title from the place where she and Boy had honeymooned, *Frenchman's Creek*. She required time and solitude to do this, which she was only able to do thanks to the ministrations of the Puxleys, the nanny and nurse-maid.

On the other side of London, Boy was continuing to attract favourable attention. Pollok once again recommended him for a divisional command, strongly endorsed this time by both Thorne and Williams, giving as an alternative recommendation that he be considered for a training appointment as a major general. It was, in fact, in the latter role that he was initially considered for promotion and, indeed, selected to be Inspector of Infantry. It is possible to detect Brooke's hand in this appointment, which was being made to replace Major General Charles Loyd, who was becoming the C-in-C's Chief of Staff. In the event, it was almost certainly a good thing for Boy that it never took place, notwithstanding that his promotion to acting major general would have come nine months earlier than it eventually did. The duties of Inspector of Infantry, largely confined to advising on aspects of training, devoid of power and with no troops to command, would have driven him mad. As it was, another opportunity emerged and the appointment was rescinded.

The new posting was as Commander of 24 Guards Brigade Group. Brigade groups were divisions in miniature, operating independently, in most cases with much the same infantry component as a standard brigade, but with their own field regiment and anti-tank battery, engineering field company, field ambulance, ordnance field park and other supporting units. On 19 February Boy left Sarre, along a road lined by the cheering men of 128 Brigade, and travelled directly to his new HQ at Addington Golf Club in South London, where he took over from Brigadier the Hon. William Fraser, a fellow Grenadier and an old friend, with whom he had served in the 3rd Battalion ten years earlier.

Whilst 24 Guards Brigade Group was not a division, it was the next best thing and much to Boy's liking. There was no Grenadier unit, but there were the 1st Battalions of the Scots, Irish and Welsh Guards, with a relatively high proportion of regulars. The first two of these had gone with the brigade to Norway in March 1940 for the forlorn campaign in that country and as a result had experience of active service. There was also an additional infantry unit, the 2nd Battalion Royal Warwickshire Regiment. There were not one, but two field regiments and two anti-tank batteries, so it was a powerful little force. Its task was to defend London from an attack from the south, for which purpose it was concentrated in the Wimbledon–Purley–Norwood triangle.

Once again good fortune smiled on Boy, as his immediate superior, the GOC London District, was none other than his namesake and one-time commanding officer, 'Boy' Sergison-Brooke. Boy was also in luck with his Brigade Major, yet another Grenadier. George Gordon Lennox, known to all as Geordie, had been at Sandhurst during Boy's time as Adjutant and had won the King's Medal. He had also served with his new brigade commander in the 3rd Battalion. Notwithstanding the fact that his new chief staff officer had passed Staff College and was already well-known to him, Boy summoned Walch to instruct Gordon Lennox on how he liked to have his HQ run. Walch quickly established that Gordon Lennox knew exactly what to do and departed as soon as decently possible after a gin and a lunch.

During the spring, summer and autumn of 1941 there was a long series of exercises, starting with one in Ashdown Forest in early March for the whole brigade group, with the Irish Guards as the enemy, moving on through the rest of that month and April to four consecutive London District exercises, carried out not only in Kent and Sussex, but also in the Thames Valley. Also involved were 20 and 30 Guards Brigades, the latter commanded by Boy's old friend, Alan Adair. One feature of the exercises involved counter-measures against landings by parachute and glider-borne troops.

By May the focus had switched to working in conjunction with the neighbouring IV Corps to the south and XII Corps to the south-east. At the latter, Thorne had been relieved by an officer not at the time well-known to Boy, Lieutenant General Bernard Montgomery. Montgomery came up to Addington to visit the brigade group HQ and, when he left, requested Boy to find an officer to serve on his staff from his battalion of the Warwickshires, Monty's old regiment. Boy duly asked the CO to make a recommendation and the officer was promptly despatched to Monty's HQ at Sevenoaks. Three weeks later he was returned with a complaint that he did not know how to write staff letters properly. Boy was furious, making the comment that he believed in leading officers not sacking them. It was not the best start to what would become in due course a key relationship, but a better understanding was reached when the brigade group played the enemy in XII Corps' Exercise 'Morebinge' in August.

There was more to Boy's life than exercises. He kept his subordinate commanders on their toes by conducting surprise inspections. On one occasion he found that one of the battalion HQs was unguarded. Ordering Edward Ford, one of his staff officers, to collect all the papers he could lay his hands on and bring them back to Brigade HQ, he then summoned the luckless CO and showed him the evidence of his slackness. Typically for Boy, after he had vented his considerable wrath, he invited the man to stay on for a glass of sherry. He had to manage the local Home Guard with a lighter touch: in the predominantly middle-class area of South London, its members were often solicitors, insurance brokers and even judges, some of whom became friends in later life. By this time the Home Guard at least had rifles, but was woefully short of other equipment and was forced to resort to a strange collection of cheap but ineffective weapons. It had nevertheless to be fitted in to the overall defence plan.

There were other duties as well, one of them distinctly unusual. On 4 and 5 August, Boy was a member of a court martial convened by Sergison-Brooke to try Josef Jacobs, a German spy who had landed in Huntingdonshire by parachute on the night of 31 January/1 February, but had injured himself and attracted attention by firing his revolver. After being found guilty, Jacobs was put before a firing squad on 14 August at the Tower of London, the last ever person to be executed there.

There was little time for relaxation as the Blitz continued throughout the winter into spring 1942 and on 16 April the area was particularly heavily hit, with the whole HQ staff out all night fighting fires locally. The site of the HQ on a large golf course did, however, tempt a number of the staff to bring their clubs with them and play whenever work permitted. Boy never took up golf, but enjoyed going round with his bow and arrow, matching his flights against their shots. He had kept in practice at Tatton Place and Kingswaldenbury, where he used to impress his officers with his feats of archery.

The visits to Langley End became fewer, although he managed to take a week's leave in mid-August, spent with Daphne on a boat trip on the Ouse. She had been seriously ill with pneumonia during the early spring, following a severe bout of flu, and remained weak for some time afterwards, although she managed to resume writing *Frenchman's Creek* in May and had the novel finished by early July, helped by having the children packed off to their grandmother Nancy at Rousham. She had by now become infatuated with Christopher Puxley, whose calm sympathy stood in contrast to Boy, who always seemed to arrive tired and keen to vent the frustrations which he was unable to express at work. Daphne's relationship with Puxley up to this point was emotional rather than physical, but the very effort of concealing her feelings added to her stress when Boy was around.

As Boy's professional life prospered, his private life suffered and a change was about to take place which would exacerbate the divisions between the two. It was very clear by now that Alan Brooke wholly approved of Boy. In this he was almost certainly encouraged by his cousin, the GOC London District, who was one of only a handful of people in whom the C-in-C Home Forces was able to confide wholeheartedly. The two of them dined together frequently and it is very likely that Sergison-Brooke, as a long-time supporter of Boy's, strongly advanced his case for a divisional command.

The case may have been strengthened by Boy's performance in Exercise 'Bumper', the largest Home Forces exercise to that date, involving a quarter of a million troops in twelve divisions and three independent brigades, including Boy's. Brooke himself was in overall control, with his HQ in Oxford, whilst the exercise covered a vast area in the east and south-east of England and ran from 29 September to 3 October. 24 Guards Brigade Group formed part of Southern Command's forces, under Harold Alexander, and it was attached to 4 Division[6] for much of the exercise.

On the night of 30 October, the brigade group was ordered to cross the Thames in order to support a divisional attack on the flank of Eastern Command, the 'enemy' army. Boy commandeered a number of London buses to augment his transport and, using Chelsea Bridge, Blackfriars Bridge and the Blackwall Tunnel, managed to establish his troops in a secure position before Eastern Command had realized that they were there. His target was the HQ of II Corps and, on the next day, he ordered Charles Larking, one of his liaison officers, to pass through the enemy lines and, wearing an umpire's white armband, penetrate the HQ and establish the enemy positions on the map. When Larking expressed surprise at this deception, Boy simply said '*ruse de guerre*' and ordered him to get on with it.

Armed with this vital information, Boy attacked on 1 October and captured the II Corps HQ. With half of Eastern Command's forces now utterly directionless, the exercise would have been brought to a complete and premature halt, but the Chief Umpire decided, 'reluctantly' according to the brigade group's war diary, that it should be withdrawn. It was, nevertheless, a considerable feat.

Later that month Boy's immediate future was settled. Brooke's diary on 22 October 1941 reads: 'Picked up Bertie Brooke at his flat and took him down to 24 Guards Brigade Group to watch a demonstration by Browning of attacks on tanks. A first class show, very well staged and full of useful lessons. I am arranging to have it made into an instructional film which ought to be useful. Also informed Browning that he had been selected for command of the Airborne Division, and what I wanted him to do about it.'[7]

Less than a fortnight later, on 3 November, Boy reported to GHQ Home Forces. He did, however, leave behind him at 24th Guards Brigade Group one enduring reminder of his stay, the formation sign. As an independent entity, it was entitled to one of its own and he was asked to suggest a design. He proposed his own family crest, a pair of wings in red on a blue background, the colours of the Brigade of Guards. It was to survive for nearly sixty years.[8]

Chapter 11

Pegasus (1941–1942)

Boy has often been called 'The Father of the Airborne Forces'. It is certainly true that he took this important new branch of Britain's armed services from infancy to maturity in three short years, but he was not present at the conception. The real father was the Prime Minister, Winston Churchill, who had been greatly impressed by the German glider and parachute landings in Holland and Belgium on 10 May 1940, and particularly by the glider-borne *coup de main* at Fort Eben Emael. On 6 June, two days after the last British soldier was picked up from the beaches at Dunkirk, he sent a minute to his Chief Staff Officer, Major-General Hastings Ismay, outlining a number of measures for taking the offensive back to the Germans, including 'Deployment of parachute troops on a scale equal to five thousand'. This was followed by a further minute on 22 June, asking for a plan from the War Office.

Churchill was doomed to disappointment in the short term. Whilst activity began immediately with the opening of the Central Landing School (shortly afterwards renamed the Central Landing Establishment or CLE) at Ringway, Manchester and the allocation of No. 2 Commando to parachute duties, it became apparent very quickly that his target of 5,000 troops was unlikely to be achieved for at least another twelve months, the major constraints being the availability of aircraft for training and the complete lack of military gliders. The main opposition came from the RAF which, not unnaturally, considered that its priorities were first to defend the country from invasion through Fighter Command and secondly to take the war to the Germans through Bomber Command. The supply of both trained pilots and suitable aircraft were constrained by this policy, which was driven from the very top of the Air Staff. The only aircraft which the RAF was prepared to make available for parachuting and glider-towing were a few obsolete and unsuitable Whitley bombers, whilst not until September 1940 was an initial order placed for 400 Hotspur training gliders, with deliveries to commence in the following spring.

There was also some reluctance in the Army to let its best men transfer to an unproven organization, although the strong support of a number of senior officers, notably Brooke and his successor in late 1941 as C-in-C Home Forces, Bernard Paget, would over time prove invaluable in overcoming opposition from that quarter.

Notwithstanding these difficulties, the CLE began its work under the overall command of Group Captain L.G. Harvey. The army side was headed by Major John Rock and the RAF by Wing Commander Sir Nigel Norman, whilst the Parachute Training School (PTS) came under two commanders before the appointment in

July 1941 of Squadron Leader Maurice Newnham, who would be associated with it for the rest of the war. No. 2 Commando was renamed 11 Special Service Battalion and was organized into a headquarters, a parachute wing and a glider wing. In February 1941 the first ever British parachute operation took place, when a party of seven officers and thirty-one other ranks parachuted into Italy and mounted an attack on the Tragino Aqueduct, with the objective of disrupting water supplies to Taranto, Brindisi and Bari. The operation was successful, but the whole party with one exception was captured and the impact was negligible. Nonetheless, some useful lessons were learnt about the mounting of such operations.

Urged on by an impatient Prime Minister, the War Office and the Air Ministry began work in early 1941 on a joint paper on the development of the airborne forces. Little progress had been made by the time Churchill visited the CLE on 26 April and he came away profoundly depressed. Yet more pressure was applied and at the end of May the joint paper was submitted which, among other things, proposed the formation of two parachute brigades and two airlanding brigades, one of each in the UK and the Middle East respectively. This led to the formation in September of 1 Parachute Brigade under Brigadier Richard Gale, comprising 11 Special Air Service Battalion, now renamed 1st Parachute Battalion and under the command of Lieutenant Colonel Eric Down, and the newly raised 2nd and 3rd Parachute Battalions under Lieutenant Colonels Edward Flavell and Gerald Lathbury. In the following month 31 Independent Brigade Group was converted into 1 Airlanding Brigade Group, with the command given to Brigadier George 'Hoppy' Hopkinson. In the meantime a small number of glider pilots were trained on civilian gliders until the arrival of the Hotspurs, whilst the first prototype of a larger troop-carrying glider, the Horsa, was flown on 12 September 1941.

This was the situation in the autumn of 1941, when the War Office decided that a separate headquarters was necessary to coordinate the expanded airborne forces. Brooke, as C-in-C Home Forces, carried considerable weight in proposing that the new commander should carry not only administrative but operational responsibility and, indeed, that the new organization should be constituted from the outset as a divisional headquarters. Thus, when Boy arrived at GHQ Home Forces in Storey's Gate on 3 November 1941, it was as Commander Para-Troops and Airborne Division[1]. He had been asked whom he wanted as his GSO1 and chose Walch, who reported for duty on the same day. On the following day they were joined by Nigel Norman from the CLE as Air Adviser and the other members of the staff arrived over the ensuing weeks.

Some of the staff were handpicked by Boy. There were two Grenadiers, Lieutenant Colonel John Goschen, the AA&QMG, and Major Richard des Voeux, the GSO2 (Operations), both of whom had served under Boy in the 2nd Battalion. Major Dick Shorrock, the DADOS, had been on the staff of 128 Brigade and Captain Brian Urquhart, the GSO3 (Intelligence), had been recommended to Boy whilst serving in 43 Division. The remaining staff officers were Colonel Austin Eagger, the ADMS, Lieutenant Colonels Geoffrey Loring, the ADOS, and Mark Henniker, the

CRE, Majors John Cowan, the DAQMG, W. T. Williams, the DAAG, and 'Pigmy' Smallman-Tew, the SO Royal Signals. Together with Staff Sergeants Watson and Dexter, the Chief Clerk and his assistant, they comprised the 'Dungeon Party', so called because they were located in a basement in the depths of Storey's Gate.

Almost all these men were to remain associated with the airborne forces in some capacity for the next three years of Boy's career, indeed Walch, Cowan, Eagger, Loring, Shorrock and Urquhart moved with Boy to successive HQs and ultimately to I Airborne Corps, achieving promotion as they went. Boy always rewarded loyalty when it was given to him. On the one hand this was a great attribute and produced a tightly knit team, each of whom understood what the others were doing. On the other, an infusion of new blood from time to time might have instilled new ideas in the execution of staff duties, whilst the lack of experience on active operations of most of his staff was to prove a considerable handicap in the autumn of 1944.

Perhaps because he was not from the Army and thus the difference in seniority was less important, the man closest to Boy was Nigel Norman, a deep friendship developing between the two men. The others either knew Boy well already or quickly came under his spell. In Brian Urquhart's words, 'Once you got used to Browning's mannered arrogance – wearing his cap at meals in the mess[2] and always slightly aloof and challenging – you found a delightful and imaginative man and a loyal friend.'[3]

Boy did not come to his new role entirely cold. He had for some time been seriously interested in the possibilities of airborne warfare and, whilst commanding 128 Brigade, he and members of his staff would retire to his room after dinner in the mess to work out the men, weapons and equipment which would be needed for an airborne army. He had conveyed his views on a number of occasions to the War Office and to Brooke, whom he admired enormously, and it was said that he even copied his letters to his former comrade from the trenches, now the Prime Minister.

He also had some modest theoretical experience. Shortly after assuming command of 24 Guards Brigade Group, he had been asked to take part in a tri-service exercise without troops in South-West Area (Devon and Cornwall) as the commander of an 'invasion force' which would land at Start Bay and attempt to take Plymouth. His allotted force was one infantry division, one parachute regiment and twelve dive bombers. He asked Basil Liddell-Hart to help him with a plan, one part of which involved an airborne landing between Plymouth and Tavistock. The reviewing panel concluded that he would have succeeded in taking the former, although there was some criticism of the dispersed nature of the parachute landings and their distance from the seaborne invasion force. This problem would be played out on a much larger scale later in the war, but Boy was clearly already thinking about the issues.

From Brooke's perspective Boy was the ideal candidate. He was known to be determined and energetic but also personally ambitious, which meant he could be counted on to throw himself into the role and make a success of it. He was a natural leader, who would inspire those under his command. He was a good organizer, who would overcome any obstacles put in his way. Whilst no intellectual, he was entirely open to new ideas, unlike many of his contemporaries. Finally, he was very well connected, not only to Brooke himself, who was about to become the professional head of the British Army as CIGS, but to other senior officers and politicians, even to Churchill himself. He had even been known for many years to the Royal Family: there is no suggestion that this played a role in either his appointment or his later achievements, but the visible interest of the King and Queen in the airborne forces was helpful in building morale and establishing a reputation among the wider public.

The task before Boy was nothing less than monumental. There were no good recent precedents for raising an entirely new type of fighting organization. The nearest equivalent was the formation of the Tank Corps in the Great War, so Boy arranged a lunch with Major General J. F. C. Fuller, one of the first armoured warfare pioneers, to draw on his experience. Boy knew that, although a great deal of work had been done over the previous eighteen months, much more needed to be resolved, starting with the composition of the division. It had been accepted that there would be a parachute brigade and an airlanding brigade, but there was no guidance as to what would constitute the divisional troops. Henniker, as Boy's Chief Engineer, recalled that his first problem was to work out exactly what airborne engineers would do. This in turn depended on the role of the division itself. Would it land in small parties behind enemy lines, in which case the engineers' role would combine sabotage and demolition, or would it operate as a whole, when the role would be more conventional and include building bridges, preparing landing grounds, laying and lifting mines and organizing water supplies? If the latter, how would they get the equipment into action, given that they would have no heavy ground transport? Problems like these were multiplied across the various arms and services.

One thing was clear. The HQ would have to move out of London, preferably to an area where the main formations could be based and train. 1 Parachute Brigade was located at Hardwick Camp, near Chesterfield, which was relatively convenient for parachute training at Ringway, but otherwise remote. 1 Airlanding Brigade Group had recently moved to the Newbury-Basingstoke area. Boy thought that the best place to concentrate would be around the British Army's traditional training area on Salisbury Plain and Walch was despatched to find a suitable location. As it happened, it was a part of the world the GSO1 knew well as his parents-in-law lived in Brigmerston House, near Netheravon. He quickly identified Syrencote House, half a mile away, as ideal for the divisional HQ. Previously the residence of the Commandant of the School of Artillery at Larkhill, it was occupied by a number of girls from the ATS, who were summarily ejected. The HQ moved there on 22 December 1941, with Boy, Walch and Norman billeted at Brigmerston House, Walch's in-laws having moved to another house owned by them locally.

With good grass airfields nearby at Upavon and Netheravon and plenty of space to train on Salisbury Plain, this was an excellent location and Boy brought 1 Parachute Brigade south in April 1942. There had been some movement on the RAF side as well. Two exercise squadrons, 296 for glider training and 297 for parachute training, were formed in January 1942 and consolidated that month into 38 Wing, commanded by Nigel Norman, who was now promoted to group captain. He located his HQ initially alongside the Airborne Division at Syrencote House, before moving to Netheravon airfield. Norman was given the responsibility for all air training, but the number of aircraft received was far below the planned establishment and progress was agonizingly slow, causing great frustration to both him and Boy.

Boy's first priority was to mould his new command into the shape he wanted, much as he had done for every other sub–unit, unit or formation he had ever led. He was not entirely pleased with what he found. The original paratroops had been formed from an army commando and, whilst excellent fighting men, had adopted a somewhat relaxed attitude to discipline. The two newer parachute battalions were manned by volunteers from every regiment in the Army and, once again, they had stepped forward in order to see some excitement, not to drill or polish brass. The four airlanding battalions, although regular in origin, had been diluted by conscripts and officers with emergency commissions.

To Boy, discipline had always been the cornerstone of military success and he therefore took steps to improve every aspect of it, primarily by importing a number of NCOs from the Brigade of Guards, but also by ensuring that his subordinates understood the standards to which they should aspire. A second key plank of his philosophy was *esprit de corps*, driven by his experience in the Grenadiers, who epitomized this. He wanted everyone in the airborne forces, from generals to drivers, to identify with the whole organization, not just their own part of it, to wear the same uniform and badges and to take pride in themselves and in the achievements of all the others. Realizing this objective, he reasoned, would be assisted immeasurably by distinction of dress, the way by which parts of the British Army have traditionally differentiated themselves.

For entirely practical reasons, variations in dress were already being introduced by the time he arrived. It had been learnt very early on that the Mark I helmet, worn since the Great War and still in use for the bulk of the army, was entirely inappropriate, indeed positively dangerous for parachuting, and that a design would be necessary which did not jut out so far from the head. A new pattern was produced and adopted which was both practical and quite distinctive from the Mark I. A helmet was also designed for glider pilots to use whilst flying – on the ground they used the same type as other airborne troops – and another, known as the 'rubber bungee' was used for parachute training. Similarly, a number of different smocks or jump jackets were introduced, the prime purpose of which was to prevent items on the outside of the wearers battledress getting entangled in the parachute harness.

Whilst he approved of all of these, Boy wanted something which would single out a man as a member of the Airborne Forces when he was not in battle and the obvious item was the headgear. The Royal Tank Regiment had adopted the black beret in 1924 and its use had also been sanctioned for the newly raised Guards Armoured Division. The beret was an eminently sensible piece of clothing, easy to put on, take off and stow away when necessary, and potentially a great deal smarter than the ubiquitous field service cap. It was also easy to produce in different colours and Boy realized that this would make it the most recognizable part of the uniform. Ironically, he himself was mildly colour blind, but he put together a committee to produce some alternatives, which were paraded by Guards NCOs at Wellington Barracks before a representative audience. The choice of colour was whittled down to two, maroon and light blue, and the former was chosen as the latter was too close to that of the newly formed RAF Regiment.[4] The light blue was not forgotten, however. Boy also insisted on the same identifying badge being worn on the battledress of every single man in the Airborne Forces, regardless of his unit or formation. The theme was to be Bellerophon mounted on his winged horse, Pegasus, in light blue on a square maroon background,[5] the final design being created by the artist Edward Seago. Beneath the badge, in identical colours, was the word AIRBORNE.

None of this took place as quickly as Boy would have liked, as the dead hand of bureaucracy lay heavily upon such decisions. At the monthly meeting of all his commanders on 9 February 1942, attended by representatives from the War Office, the changes were reported to be in the hands of the Directorate of Staff Duties. Boy made it clear, referring to a meeting with the C-in-C Home Forces and the CIGS a month earlier, that the two most senior officers in the Army 'had already agreed that the new uniform was a necessity for the Airborne Division, and had ordered that it should be provided. He requested that GHQ Home Forces and the War Office should push the provision of this uniform with the greatest vigour'. Sensing delay, he arranged a meeting with the VCIGS, Archie Nye, to lobby for more vigorous action to be taken, but it was not until May that the beret and Pegasus badge were finally approved by the War Office.

Problems with suitable equipment also multiplied. Personal weapons needed no adaptation, but heavier guns were an issue when it came to loading them onto gliders. The axle of the 6-pounder anti-tank gun had to be narrowed to fit it into a Horsa, whilst the American 75mm pack howitzer proved to be more suitable than its British 3.7 inch counterpart. It was another piece of American equipment, however, which was to make the greatest impact on the airborne forces.

A problem which had been identified early on was the mobility of the division once it had landed. Heavy vehicles would not fit in the Horsas and there would be limited availability of a larger type of glider, the Hamilcar. Light cars were not powerful enough to pull trailers or artillery over rough ground and Universal Carriers, though used in small numbers in the airlanding brigade, lacked speed and agility. The solution emerged whilst HQ was still based in the Dungeon. A call came in to Walch from the US Military Attaché, Colonel Wells, asking if he and Boy would be interested in seeing a new type of vehicle, the Jeep, the first two prototypes of which had just arrived in the UK. Boy accepted enthusiastically and the two of them had a trial drive down Piccadilly at some speed. They agreed that it would be just what was required, only provided that it fitted in the Horsa. One of the vehicles was driven at once up to Ringway, where the first few Horsas were by then located, and it was discovered to be about half-an-inch too wide. Wells sent an immediate signal back to the USA and the design was altered just in time to go into production. The jeeps still required further modification when they arrived, with the help of a mock-up Horsa fuselage, as did the glider itself: the tail could be removed in later production models of the Horsa I, whilst the Horsa II also had a hinged nose.

Boy's style of leadership required him never to ask his men to do something he had not done himself. Like every man in the parachute brigades and many in the supporting services, this meant that he had to learn how to parachute. He was neither a good nor a keen jumper and, in a much later conversation with Roy Urquhart, revealed that he had done two jumps and hurt himself both times.[6]

Qualifying as a glider pilot was quite another matter. The Glider Pilot Regiment was formed with a single battalion on the last day of 1941 under the command of John Rock. Boy's relationship with Rock was never close, but it was much better with George Chatterton, initially Rock's second-in-command and then the CO of the 2nd Battalion when it was formed in August 1942. Chatterton's philosophy of warfare was close to Boy's and he both introduced a strong ethos of discipline in the regiment, assisted by two company sergeant majors from the Brigade of Guards, and developed the concept of the 'Total Soldier', whereby his men would be not just pilots, but also fully trained infantrymen. He also taught Boy to fly.[7] As he later wrote: 'teaching a General of over forty-six[8] to fly was no easy matter, particularly this one, for he was a very determined person, and highly inflammable! Nevertheless, he was amazingly good, and quickly learnt the technique of flying an aeroplane. He went solo in eight and a half hours, which is the average for a young man of twenty-one, and very creditable to General Browning.'[9] After qualifying, Boy always wore the Army Air Corps wings, designed by himself and still in use to this day.

Encouraged by Brooke, Boy decided quickly that the division should be prepared to fight as such, rather than in small parties or even as brigades or brigade groups, a policy promoted by one school of thought. Building a division with what was initially a very small HQ was a frustrating business. To create the divisional troops, a number of units, including a light artillery battery, a reconnaissance squadron and a field park company were detached from 1 Airlanding Brigade Group before the end of 1941, with the other units from the brigade following progressively during the course of 1942. Henniker was able to assemble a properly functioning HQ Royal Engineers in February, whilst both divisional signals and a field ambulance were formed that April.

The first opportunity for men from the division to see action, however, was in exactly the sort of small-scale operation which the alternative school of thought espoused. Operation 'Biting', better known as the Bruneval Raid, brought Boy into working contact for the first time with the raid's sponsor, Lord Louis Mountbatten, a man who would later play a major part in his life. Mountbatten had become Adviser Combined Operations in late 1941 and his mandate, among other things, was to develop opportunities for taking the war to the enemy. With the strong support of Churchill, he was given access to the resources of all three services.

There was great concern at the time in the RAF about serious bomber losses, which were attributed in part to the Germans' development of a new radar system.

One of the radar sites was believed to be at Bruneval, on the French coast near Le Havre, and a plan was hatched to parachute in a party to remove the equipment for evaluation, using the RAF to get it there and the Royal Navy to take it out again.

Boy's first conference with Mountbatten on the operation was on 8 January 1942 at Combined Operations HQ at Richmond Terrace. The two men had met before, but only incidentally. Now, working together for the first time, they found that they thought very much alike. Boy was immediately attracted by the plan, which would showcase the capabilities of his paratroopers, and set about delivering his part of it, reporting back to Mountbatten just over two weeks later. Not wanting to use his most experienced unit, 1st Parachute Battalion, in case it was required intact for a larger operation, he asked the 2nd Battalion to select the party, which was drawn from C Company. Under the command of Major John Frost, it began training on Salisbury Plain at the end of January.

The operation was a near perfect success. The landing party, which included a detachment from the Airborne Division's Royal Engineers, was dropped into France from Whitleys[10] on 27 February 1942. It landed some distance from the objective, the building where the radar was housed, but made its way there and took the Germans by complete surprise. The withdrawal involved some alarming moments, but the majority of the party, together with their valuable prize of a *Würzburg* radar set, was lifted safely off the beach and returned to England by sea. The casualties amounted to three killed, two missing and seven wounded, a very low number proportionately for airborne operations. Churchill was delighted and invited Frost to address a meeting of the War Cabinet on 3 March, which was also attended by the Chiefs of Staff and by Mountbatten, Boy and Walch.

Immediately after this meeting, Boy went on nine day's leave – the first time that he had been able to take more than a day or two off at once since early November. Daphne was still living at Langley End. *Frenchman's Creek* had been published in the previous autumn, Daphne subsequently acknowledging that the privateer hero was a combination of Boy and Christopher Puxley. She continued her infatuation with the latter, but not long after Boy's leave had ended, she was discovered in his arms by an astounded Paddy Puxley, who had no idea of what was going on under her nose. The parties behaved with some dignity, but it was clear that Daphne and the children would have to leave.

It had been Daphne's intention to go down to Fowey for the summer and the move was now accelerated. Ferryside had been partially commandeered by the Royal Navy and there was no room for the family there, so she rented 8 Readymoney Cove, a large cottage at the seaward end of the town. She could not get Christopher out of her mind and her next writing project was *Hungry Hill*, a novel based closely on the Puxley family, about whom she had become well informed over the previous eighteen months. Christopher continued to see her, coming down to stay at the Fowey Hotel and spending the days with her at the Watch House, a tiny building on the cliffs near Polruan, overlooking Lantic Bay. Boy remained entirely ignorant of the affair.

Chapter 12

Expansion (1942)

On 16 April 1942 Winston Churchill visited the Airborne Division with General George C. Marshall, the US Army Chief of Staff, who was on his first wartime visit to Britain. The two men and their entourage were treated to a display of parachuting and glider landing at Everleigh, a short distance from Netheravon. Every available aircraft from 38 Wing was used, twelve Whitleys for the parachute troops and nine ancient Hector tugs towing Hotspur gliders. The day was cold and blustery and there was a parachute fatality, but it was not this which upset the Prime Minister. Boy spelt out succinctly the issues facing him, notably the lack of aircraft and gliders, so Churchill, deeply concerned by the lack of cooperation from the RAF, convened a meeting for the following month to address the problem.

The meeting took place on 6 May and was chaired by the Prime Minister himself. In addition to Boy, the attendees were Brooke, Ismay, Air Chief Marshal Portal, the Chief of the Air Staff, Colonel Ian Jacob[1] of Churchill's staff, Colonel J. J. Llewellin, the Minister of Aircraft Production, with his Permanent Secretary, and representatives from both the Air Ministry and the War Office. Boy addressed the meeting and described how, in terms of personnel, the Airborne Division would be complete by the end of the month but, whilst trained for ground action, could not be trained for airborne operations without adequate aircraft. With such aircraft, he envisaged that training could be completed quickly, although he still expected both a three to four month delay before further special equipment was delivered and a bottleneck in the training of glider pilots due to shortages of gliders coming off the production lines.

Portal was clearly reluctant to release further bombers, proposing that pressure be applied to the Americans to provide suitable transport aircraft, in the absence of which sacrifices would have to be made elsewhere. By this time, however, the Prime Minister had the bit between his teeth. After further debate, he issued a memo to Portal: 'Please make me proposals for increasing the number of discarded Bombers which can be placed rapidly at the disposal of the Airborne Corps. At least 100 should be found (Boy had asked for 96) within the next three months. We cannot go on with 10,000 men and only 32 aircraft at their disposal.' Three days later Portal replied, grudgingly agreeing to allocate 83 Whitleys between May and September, with 10 heavy bombers (Halifaxes) to tow Hamilcar gliders. Strong opposition, however, continued from the RAF, and specifically Bomber Command, and this would dog the development of the airborne forces for some time yet as the debate continued at the highest level, with Brooke and Portal the leading protagonists.

Boy was also lobbying in other directions. Realizing that Mountbatten carried some influence, at least with the Prime Minister, he had met him a few days before Churchill's visit to the division, eliciting a memo from the Chief of Combined Operations to the Chiefs of Staff on 15 April. 'I wish to draw the attention of the Chiefs of Staff', wrote Mountbatten, 'to the desirability of employing airborne forces in larger numbers than hitherto for raids.' Boy then invited Mountbatten to deliver a lecture at the Divisional Tactical Week and ensured that he remained an ally on the Chiefs of Staff Committee, where the debate was about to intensify. In September, as Brooke confronted Portal again on the issue, the CIGS was briefed to advance Mountbatten's view that the airborne forces would be an essential part of any major operation against the Continent.

Boy was also able to demonstrate tacit support from the Royal Family, when the King and Queen paid a visit to the Airborne Division on 21 May, accompanied by Paget from Home Forces and Sir James Grigg, the Secretary of State for War. The day's activities started with an inspection of the 1st Parachute Battalion, the Glider Pilot Regiment and the RAF, and a static display of gliders and aircraft, followed by a film on parachute training. The royal couple then inspected the rest of the division before lunch at Syrencote House, followed by a demonstration of parachuting and glider landing. It was the first of a number of visits engineered by Boy, which did a great deal for the morale of the troops and, because it was widely reported in the press, for their standing with the public.

In the following month a significant development took place at the War Office. Since its formation, the responsible department had been the Directorate of Staff Duties, where the airborne forces' interests had been handicapped by the lack of relevant experience. It was now decided to appoint a Deputy Director for Air, reporting to the DSD. The officer selected was Gale, who reluctantly handed over 1 Parachute Brigade to Flavell. He was an excellent choice, a no-nonsense infantry officer, but one with a good sense of humour, who commanded a great deal of respect throughout the Airborne Division and was also well liked by the RAF. He and Boy had developed an excellent relationship, not least because Gale subscribed wholeheartedly to Boy's view that the division should be trained and employed as a whole and not piecemeal. Gale took as his GSO1 Gerald Lathbury, another outstanding airborne soldier. Relations between the War Office and Boy's HQ, never easy during the first six months of 1942, improved immeasurably.

By the summer of 1942, other than in respect of aircraft and gliders, the equipping of the Airborne Division was proceeding much more satisfactorily. At the beginning of May a committee was set up 'to co-ordinate arrangements for the development, production, supply, transport and storage of all equipment for airborne forces, and to secure rapid decisions'. Under the chairmanship of Sir Robert Renwick, an industrialist seconded to the Ministry of Aircraft Production, its members included technical experts from Renwick's ministry and senior officers and civil servants from both the Air Ministry and the War Office, together with Boy himself. It had the effect of reducing to a minimum the bureaucratic hold-ups which had dogged the airborne forces since their inception.

Boy's efforts to instil *esprit de corps* were also going well and morale was generally rising, although he was constantly seeking ways to improve it. The Glider Pilot Regiment had been constituted as part of the Army Air Corps, but the parachute battalions, which had accepted men from nearly every regiment in the British Army, were initially without any affiliation. In August 1942 it was decided that they should form a new regiment, the Parachute Regiment, which would also be part of the Army Air Corps, but would develop its own its own traditions and honours. The first Colonel Commandant was Field Marshal Sir John Dill, Brooke's predecessor as CIGS and now Head of the Joint Staff Mission in Washington and British representative to the Combined Chiefs of Staff. With Brooke himself appointed as Colonel Commandant of the Glider Pilot Regiment, there was no doubt about the level of support from the very top of the Army.

Another opportunity to improve morale emerged in 1942. Boy received an approach from Captain Jock Pearson of the Glider Pilot Regiment, who had been concerned with some of the financial difficulties being experienced by the men under his command and elsewhere in the regiment. Like the parachutists, the glider pilots came from every conceivable regiment, but it had proved difficult to tap into regimental funds once they had transferred elsewhere, so he had decided on his own initiative to set up the Glider Pilot Benevolent Association. He now asked Boy if he would consider a fund for the whole of the airborne forces.

Boy was enthusiastic, agreeing with Pearson that no soldier should have to worry about his financial affairs and that all of them would take comfort from knowing that their dependants would be looked after if they were killed. A trust deed for the new Airborne Forces Security Fund was drawn up by a firm of solicitors, offices were found and with the help of Mr Gordon Boggon, a philanthropist, the services of a full-time controller were secured. At a meeting on 19 May attended by Boy, Pearson, Walch and Chatterton, those present were appointed Trustees, together with Goschen and Eagger, with Boy becoming the first Chairman. A considerable amount of funds were attracted from the public and from commercial organizations associated with the airborne forces.

Whilst morale improved, the emphasis on discipline did not necessarily work to Boy's favour in terms of his personal profile in the division. There was a great deal of resentment to start with among men who were looking for a chance to see action and who failed to understand how drill and standards of turnout could be relevant. He was quietly but widely known as 'Bullshit' Browning among those who found themselves subjected to his regime, but who failed to comprehend his motives. Even amongst some longer serving regular officers, there was a feeling that he was more concerned with burnishing his own reputation than with fighting the Germans.

This was manifestly unfair. There is little doubt that Boy was personally ambitious and that he saw the fortunes of the airborne forces as intimately linked with his own. There is equally little question of his genuine belief that he had been given the responsibility for building a potentially war-winning organization and of his determination to do what was necessary to make it work. If that meant using all his connections in the corridors of power, so be it. In fact, there were probably few men of his seniority who could have marshalled such an array of supporters in the face of the active opposition of the RAF and the dead hand of bureaucracy.

On a more personal level, Boy was almost invariably highly regarded by those with whom he came into the closest contact. Among his seniors, his admirers included Brooke, Sergison-Brooke, Paget and later Montgomery and Mountbatten, although he was to experience difficulties with the Americans. Some of his peers undoubtedly found him pushy and begrudged his access to high places, which, to them at least, seemed to give him preference, but once again, those with the most immediate exposure to him generally appreciated his virtues. The members of his staff, both in the airborne forces and subsequently, were mostly devoted to him, as were those who worked for him personally, such as Johnson and Boy's longstanding driver, Alex Johannides. Part of the reason was that he was so evidently concerned for their well-being, as was demonstrated by his response to a serious parachute accident to Brian Urquhart. The latter incurred injuries which were life-threatening, with a potentially disastrous medical treatment only averted by Boy's intervention and insistence that the Army's Chief Orthopaedic Surgeon should take the case.

Notwithstanding his background, there was absolutely no trace of snobbishness in Boy's character and those who actually met him, of whatever rank, found that he would talk without looking down on them. Henniker told the tale of an animated conversation between Boy and a corporal in one of the RE field companies. Henniker asked afterwards what they had been talking about, to be told in detail with the conclusion 'He's really a very intelligent General, Sir!' He discovered subsequently that Boy thought that the corporal, too, was very intelligent and took this as epitomizing the bonds between the men in airborne forces. However, Boy could not meet everybody and his magic, unlike that of Montgomery or Slim, seems only to have worked at short range.

The airborne movement as a whole was by now gathering pace and by mid-1942 a number of Great Britain's allies had established parachute units and formations, the most advanced of whom were the Poles. Colonel Stanislaw Sosabowski, who after a number of adventures had escaped from both Poland and France, had formed an Officers' Cadre Brigade in the summer of 1940, based in Scotland. In February 1941 he was given permission to send a number of his men for parachute training at the PTS at Ringway and, on their return, decided to constitute his formation informally as a parachute brigade. In September of that year, at a ceremony attended by Gale and Newnham, General Sikorski, the Polish C-in-C, announced that it would in future be known as 1 Polish Parachute Brigade. Relationships between the Poles and their British counterparts were good. They were popular at Ringway, where they established a permanent group of instructors, whilst small groups from the Airborne Division visited their brigade in Scotland and vice-versa. Early in 1942 Sosabowski called on Boy and received a warm welcome, with Boy undertaking to help the Poles with equipment, and later in the year thirty Polish officers were attached to the Airborne Division for instruction

Other countries also established parachute units in the UK, notably the Free French in battalion strength and the Norwegians, Dutch and Belgians as independent companies, whilst a party of Canadian officers arrived for training at the PTS in August. It was clear, however, that it was Britain's newest allies across the Atlantic who would create the largest and most sophisticated force. Colonel Wells at the US Embassy had remained in close contact following his success with the jeeps and in early April, shortly before Marshall's visit with Churchill, Boy invited him down to spend four days with the division. At the end of May, Brigadier-General Bill Lee, who had commanded the first airborne soldiers in the USA and went on to raise 101 Airborne Division, visited Boy's HQ and inspected 1 Parachute Brigade. Some weeks later 2nd Battalion, 503 Parachute Infantry Regiment,[2] under Lieutenant Colonel Edson D. Raff, disembarked in the UK and came under the temporary command of the Airborne Division, based at Chilton Folliatt, near Hungerford. The Americans trained with their British comrades, establishing for the first time a close bond which would last through the war. Boy arranged for them all to receive airborne berets, although these could not be officially worn, and he was generally well received by the battalion's members.

On 11 July some more important visitors arrived for a demonstration of parachute and glider landing by the 2nd Parachute Battalion and the Advanced Divisional HQ near Larkhill. At their head was the Secretary of State for Air, Sir Archibald Sinclair, with Portal and the DCIGS, Ronald Weeks. Perhaps more significantly from Boy's perspective, there were two American Generals in the entourage, Dwight D. Eisenhower, who had arrived in the UK just over a fortnight earlier as the newly appointed Commanding General, European Theatre of Operation, US Army, and Mark W. Clark, who was in command of US II Corps and was leading the planning for the future invasion of French North Africa.

The demonstration went well at first, although the wind was really too strong for safe parachuting. The Advanced HQ party, however, was dropped far too close to the VIP line and Brian Urquhart, last out of his plane, landed just in front of Eisenhower and was blown straight through it. According to Urquhart, Ike was perfectly charming, although less than impressed when Urquhart released a carrier pigeon, which flew to a nearby bush and refused to go further. 'I see that we shall have to do something about your communications,' said the future Supreme Commander.[3]

It was time for a return trip. In April, Dill had written to Brooke from Washington: 'It would, I think, be mutually beneficial if you could spare Browning for a very short visit to parachutists here. I am very favourably impressed by what I have seen. Browning might get some ideas and would certainly give some.'

Boy arrived in the United States on 20 July and was given a friendly welcome by the American Army. He was immediately struck by the close resemblance which the US Airborne Divisions bore to the British, in spite of the fact that they had different origins, the British putting together existing brigades, the Americans converting an infantry division. He spent most of the time touring units with Lee, going as far afield as Texas and Florida, but was also invited to lunch alone with Marshall and to share ideas with him. He found the US Army Chief of Staff impressively well informed on airborne matters and a strong supporter generally of the new arm.

Boy focused much of his attention on the Americans' basic parachute training, coming away with the impression that their courses were too short, but also concluding that the British equivalents were, in the light of what he had seen, rather too long. He also felt that the Americans, still very new to the use of airborne troops, had some way to go to master other fundamentals such as the seizure of ground around the drop zones, the use of AA and anti-tank guns and the concealment of troops from the air. He expressed his opinions forcefully, as was his habit, and experienced for the first time something of an adverse reaction. 'I gathered the impression,' he wrote later in his report to Paget, 'which was confirmed by General Lee when I discussed quite frankly my reactions before leaving, that officers of his rank and below are fully aware of the necessity of these things, and for learning from us, but that the more senior officers take the following view – "the British Army has not done sufficiently well to lay down the law to the American Army and in consequence we have got little to teach them." I know our people out there are fully aware of this attitude and take the line that we are prepared to accept a certain measure of their remarks about the British Army, but emphasis should be laid on the fact that we have learnt from painful mistakes and experience what not to do, and that they should at least listen to that.'

It was these attitudes on both sides – the British over-inclined to lecture their new allies on how to wage war, the Americans resentful of what they perceived as unjustified arrogance – which were to impair relationships at a senior level in the two armies as soon as they began to work together and to make a significant and long-lasting contribution to the anglophobia of some top US generals. In his conclusion to Paget, Boy wrote: 'I personally would have no qualms, from what I have seen of the [US] Army, about the amount of co-operation which can be expected as long as we know their outlook and meet them more than half way, which is not always easy for an Englishman.' In his own case achieving a meeting of minds with the Americans would prove to be far from easy.

In most other respects, Boy was impressed by what he had seen on his tour. He believed that the American approach to discipline, 'a curious blend of the strict and the easy going', would serve them well in battle and that their inherent military qualities and determination to achieve their objectives would bring success. He was astonished by their engineering capabilities when it came to constructing facilities of any sort and envious of their lavish equipment and notably their transport aircraft, the C.47 Dakota. Returning from the United States on 4 August, Boy lost no opportunity to spread the message about cooperation. He followed up his letter to Paget with a meeting, lectured both the Airborne Division and the RAF on what he had learnt and on 13 August held a joint exercise involving night landings by 2/503

Parachute Infantry and 1 Airlanding Brigade, opposed by 1 Parachute Brigade and 2nd Armoured Battalion, Irish Guards.

This frenetic level of activity left little time for the family and, after his ten day leave in March, Boy was only able to spend the occasional night at Readymoney Cove. The children would always know that he had arrived by the tell-tale smell of eau-de-cologne and cigarettes. To them he was always fun. His main party piece, other than his celebrated Cossack dance, was to walk past their bedroom window, simulating going down a flight of steps. He would disappear entirely and then spring up again to howls of delight from inside.

For Daphne his visits were more stressful. The only colleague he ever brought with him was Nigel Norman, whom she took to immediately, but more often he came by himself and once on their own he felt he could share some of his burdens. He managed to take a week off in July, but it was very frustrating for both of them that wartime restrictions meant they were unable to sail. 'Yggy' had been laid up in Hunkin's yard for the duration, but *Restless* was still afloat and the two of them used to take a picnic out to her.

A return visit by Daphne to Netheravon in October was less successful. Boy worked all hours and she virtually never saw him, writing to Tod that she was grateful that she had brought her typewriter with her. She very much hoped that he would be able to take a longer period of leave over Christmas 1942, but it was not to be. Eight days beforehand he left for North Africa.

Chapter 13

Setbacks (1942–1943)

As the summer of 1942 drew to a close, the Airborne Division was at last beginning to look like a complete formation. In July 2 Parachute Brigade was formed under the command of Eric Down. 4th Parachute Battalion, which had been raised to join the three original battalions in 1 Parachute Brigade, was transferred to the new brigade, but it was no longer possible to rely on volunteers, so two Territorial units were converted to become 5th and 6th Parachute Battalions.[1] By this time 1 Airlanding Brigade Group had lost almost all its ancillary units, which became divisional troops. The latter were nearly up to establishment in their complement of engineers and signals, whilst 21 Independent Parachute Company was established to act as pathfinders and there was even a light tank squadron. The most deficient arm was the artillery, which was still only in battery strength in each of howitzers, anti-tank guns and anti-aircraft guns. A second battalion was formed in the Glider Pilot Regiment and Chatterton transferred to the 1st Battalion after the death of Rock in a glider accident in October.

Ground training had also moved forward. On 1 September a divisional battle school was opened, in response to Paget's decision to create such establishments throughout Home Forces. By the middle of that month, Boy felt that the division was ready to hold Exercise 'Merlin' over two days, the first time it had been possible to carry out any such event on a divisional level.

On the RAF side too, progress seemed initially to have been made, with the expansion of 38 Wing in August by two additional squadrons, 295 and 298. However, a major setback occurred in the following month, when it was rather belatedly discovered that the Whitley was unable to tow a fully loaded Horsa. Pending increased production of the new Albemarles and the release of larger bombers, Halifaxes and Stirlings, from Bomber Command, this was to have a significant impact on the conversion of glider pilots from Hotspurs to Horsas and the ability of the airlanding brigade to complete its training. Churchill was furious, but there was no obvious immediate solution.

Worse was to follow as the argument continued within the Chiefs of Staff Committee. In August Arthur Harris, the AOC-in-C of Bomber Command, wrote in a memo highly critical of the airborne forces' demands, 'is Bomber Command to continue its offensive action by bombing Germany or is it to be turned into a training and transport command for carrying a few thousand troops to some undetermined destination for some vague purpose?... I find it hard to resist the conclusion that the raising of the airborne division was undertaken without adequate appreciation of how it would be transported, or where and when it could be employed with any prospect of material contribution to victory.'

Brooke challenged Portal to say whether or not he agreed with Harris's comments on the airborne forces. The Chief of the Air Staff replied that the AOC-in-C had possibly overstated his case, but that he himself doubted if airborne forces could be used effectively against stiff opposition. On 29 September he submitted a memo arguing that the current airborne establishment should be reduced and used for raiding and minor operations. The CIGS countered on 10 October with a memo of his own, pointing to the use made of airborne forces by Germany[2] and concluding: 'The airborne division is an essential formation and our present airborne forces cannot be considered sufficient.' Two meetings later, it was clear that stalemate had been reached and Portal suggested referring the whole matter to Churchill for a decision. The memos setting out the positions of the two sides were sent to the War Cabinet on 7 November.

It was not a particularly good moment to approach the Prime Minister, who was much preoccupied with events in the Western Desert and the preparations for Operation 'Torch'. He was, moreover, known to be a strong supporter of the strategic bombing campaign against Germany, the one way in which he could mollify Stalin on the lack of progress in establishing a second front in Europe. The War Office sensed the arguments slipping away from them and Gale wrote to Ismay on 7 November to say that he was concerned that the Air Staff 'are progressively closing down on progress in connection with airborne forces on assumption paper will go in their favour.' Gale was right to be concerned, as Ismay himself was moving towards Portal's position, supporting the reduction of airborne forces to two parachute brigades and a small glider-borne force.

Brooke's backing, on the other hand, became all the stronger for a visit he had paid to the Airborne Division on the occasion of its first anniversary on 3 November. In his diary for the day he wrote: 'Made an early start and motored down to Andover to visit Airborne Division. Started with inspection of the Border Regiment, a first-class show and a real workmanlike organization for an airborne battalion. Then proceeded to lunch at Syrencot House, the HQ of the division. This brought back many memories of 3 of the happiest years of my life.[3] After lunch inspected Parachute Bn, grand lot of men, and then representative groups from all the units. Was also shown method of loading gliders, ambulance and RE organization, etc. After tea was shown glider using parachute to allow of steeper descent. Also had a trip in a Wellesley aircraft fitted with 'Rebecca', a new homing system for finding objectives. I was then taken in a Horsa glider pulled by an Albemarle from Netheravon to Shrewton. A delightful and most inspiring trip. Came away more convinced than ever that there is a great future for airborne forces.'[4]

Without the strong support of Brooke, there is little doubt that the British airborne forces would have been reduced to a minor role by the end of 1942. Their future, as perceived by Portal and Ismay, was as raiders or supporters of conventional operations in brigade strength at most. To counter this, Boy was assiduous in ensuring that not only Brooke, but the other members of the Army Council and those who were backers elsewhere, such as Mountbatten and Air Marshal Sir Arthur Barratt, AOC-in-C of Army Cooperation Command, were kept fully in the picture on both progress and difficulties.

However, for the time being the argument was going Portal's way, confirmed by the Prime Minister's adjudication on 19 November, endorsing the CAS's proposal. From the point of view of Brooke, Paget, Boy and Gale, this was a serious setback. Brooke persuaded Churchill not to break up the Airborne Division, but he was unable to prevent a slow-down in glider production. In the meantime the RAF had stopped any further issues of aircraft with effect from 19 October and 298 Squadron was disbanded, so further training and operations were forced to make do with what was already available until either the Air Ministry resumed the supply of aircraft or the Americans made alternatives available.

In spite of these problems, the airborne forces were about to see real action. On a very small scale another operation was conceived by Combined Operations HQ. This was the raid of 19 November on the German heavy water plant at Vermork in Norway, codenamed 'Freshman', carried out by a party of Royal Engineers. Because of the heavy equipment which was thought necessary, the party went in by gliders, two of which were towed across the North Sea by Halifax bombers. Radar direction failed and one aircraft and both gliders crash landed, their crews and passengers either dying as a result or being executed subsequently by the Germans. By any standards this was a complete disaster, quite different to the Bruneval Raid.[5]

Much more significant was the first deployment of airborne forces overseas in support of a conventional campaign. At the end of September Boy was informed that 2/503 Parachute Infantry Regiment was to be required for Operation 'Torch', the invasion of French North Africa. In addition to his existing duties, he had been appointed the British adviser on airborne forces to Commanders-in-Chiefs in all theatres of war and, in this capacity, he immediately made strong representations both to the War Office and to the 'Torch' planners that a larger airborne element should be employed, proposing 1 Parachute Brigade. The RAF was unable to supply the necessary aircraft, but the USAAF stepped enthusiastically into the breach and the brigade was hastily retrained on Dakotas.

Not for the last time, this resulted in Boy ceding operational control of part of his command, with Flavell being instructed to report directly to Lieutenant General Kenneth Anderson, the commander of First Army, who would dispose of the formation as he thought fit. The brigade left by sea on 1 November and landed at Algiers eleven days later, in the wake of the successful seaborne landings. On 12 November the 3rd Parachute Battalion made the first operational drop at Bone, followed by the other two battalions elsewhere later in the month and from then until the end of April 1943 the brigade was almost constantly in action in Tunisia, fighting from the end of November as conventional infantry.

Boy saw this as an opportunity both to show off the capabilities of his men in action and to use their deployment as an excuse to create another brigade. The latter was duly authorized in early November and three more infantry battalions[6] were converted to the 7th, 8th and 9th Battalions of the Parachute Regiment and formed into 3 Parachute Brigade, with Lathbury moving from the War Office to take command.

Boy also needed to see for himself what was happening on the ground, so on 17 December he and Norman flew to North Africa for a short visit, meeting not only Flavell, but also the relevant senior commanders, Eisenhower, Anderson and Lieutenant General Charles Allfrey of V Corps, under whom 1 Parachute Brigade was operating. In miserable weather, wet and cold, he also visited the three battalions over Christmas. The men of the 2nd Parachute Battalion, who had just come out of the line after heavy fighting around Medjez-el-Bab, during which they incurred severe losses, were less than impressed by the arrival of the immaculately uniformed general and a number of them showed their displeasure by melting away during his address.

The visit was useful, however, in that a number of lessons had been learnt. Neither Boy nor Flavell were happy with the dispersion of the brigade, indeed Flavell had been able to exercise only limited control. Boy himself had recommended that the whole brigade be used in a major *coup de main*, but he had been ignored. The USAAF, whilst keen, had proved to be poorly trained. Most importantly the knowledge of airborne operations within the various superior HQs was poor and Boy's proposal for liaison officers to be attached to them had been rejected. All these failings needed to be rectified.

Although he had missed Christmas in Cornwall, Boy was back in England before the end of the year and on New Year's Day 1943 he went up to London to meet both Brooke and the Prime Minister, using the opportunity to vent his frustration. As both were preoccupied by the forthcoming Casablanca Conference, he prepared a report on the operational state of the airborne forces, which he sent to GHQ Home Forces on 10 January, copied to Brooke. In this he pointed out that 1 Parachute Brigade had suffered 443 casualties in North Africa and was still 150 men under strength, even after reinforcements from 2 Parachute Brigade. The latter was accordingly considerably depleted, whilst 3 Parachute Brigade was still forming. 1 Airlanding Brigade was well trained for ground operations and fit for war, but was seriously lacking in equipment, as were the divisional troops. The number of aircraft was totally deficient and, although there were sufficient Horsas, there were not enough tugs to ferry them to Africa.

Boy went on to say that, since July 1942, he had been urging the formation of an Airborne Forces HQ in addition to the Airborne Division HQ, to take some of the administrative and advisory responsibilities off the shoulders of the GOC, failing which a much larger divisional HQ would be necessary. He had received no backing for this or for the appointment of an airborne commander at First Army. His conclusion was bleak: 'The Division is not ready for war even in a ground role and the air situation precludes even unit training in the air role.'

Brooke reacted immediately. On the day before he left for Morocco he issued another memo to the Chiefs of Staff pointing out that the proposals advocated by Portal and Ismay would result in the disintegration of the airlanding brigade, the destruction of the right balance between parachute and glider-borne troops in the Airborne Division, a serious reduction in the striking power of the Airborne Division and the restriction of the role of airborne forces to minor operations. He asked for a rescission of the order to curtail glider production, a request to the United States for the use of their Waco Hadrian gliders and the acceleration of the provision of transport aircraft from whatever source.

Boy had also sent a copy of his report to Ismay, writing in the covering letter: 'In order that the authorities may be fully aware of the state of readiness of the Airborne Division, I have put this paper through official channels. I am sending you a copy for your private information and for such action as you consider necessary.' Just off to Casablanca himself, Ismay could do nothing immediately but it is very likely that he showed it to Churchill, which was certainly Boy's expectation. In the event, January 1943 turned out to be the low point of the airborne forces' political fortunes, as the conference was about to produce some decisions which would propel it forward faster than could possibly have been imagined at the turn of the year.

Unaware of this, Boy lost no opportunity to spread the word, among other things arranging for a number of Members of Parliament to visit the division on 28 January. The MPs were given the full treatment, with an introduction by Boy and Nigel Norman on their arrival, followed by an inspection of the division's gliders. Those who wished were offered a short trip by glider, embarking in two Horsas from Netheravon and landing again at Dumbell Copse. Boy himself flew in one of them and it had the misfortune to make a very hard landing. One of the MPs, Ellen Wilkinson, suffered a broken ankle and was rushed off to Tidworth Hospital, whilst others suffered minor injuries, including Boy himself, who damaged his shoulder. He struggled through the rest of the day, but by the following morning it was clear that the injury was more serious than had been supposed and he was admitted to Shaftesbury Hospital.

Daphne was informed and rushed up from Cornwall, staying in a pub near the hospital. In addition to his shoulder problem Boy had also developed a blood clot on one knee, which required bed rest. Nevertheless, he insisted on returning to duty on 3 February. Daphne went up to London for a few days, but returned to find him back in bed on Eagger's orders because of the blood clot. After the clot had dispersed she remained in Netheravon to look after him.

On 26 February, still feeling the after effects of the accident, Boy went up to London to see Brooke for the first time since the latter's return from Casablanca. Plans had moved on remarkably fast at the conference, where it had been agreed that the next step for the Allies after the end of the Tunisian campaign would be the invasion of Sicily. Two days before their meeting, Brooke had issued another memo to the Chiefs of Staff outlining the plans, which among other things envisaged the use of three British and two US airborne brigades. As the complete Airborne Division would be required, Brooke continued, it would be necessary to raise another in the UK to replace it, and he called for the resumption of the glider production programme and some encroachment on the bomber effort. Brooke attached to his memo a telegram to Eisenhower, in response to a formal request from the latter, agreeing to send the rest of the Airborne Division to North Africa and continuing: 'Also propose sending General Browning in advance with small staff to assist in planning for British airborne forces.' The message about the lack of its own experience seemed at last to have got through at Allied Forces HQ.

After considering the implications of what was for both of them an enormously positive development, which even the RAF would be powerless to prevent, the CIGS ended the meeting on another note by delivering a rocket to Boy for writing letters to politicians, a major crime in Brooke's eyes.[7] However, Brooke went on to comment on how ill Boy looked after his accident and ordered him to take at least two weeks leave.

Handing over temporary command of the division to Hopkinson, Boy spent his leave down at Fowey, the longest period he was to have off at any one time during the war. Daphne relished the opportunity to have him to herself, which had never really been possible at Langley End and only briefly on the short breaks he had been able to take subsequently. They managed to resume their 'routes' and to restore some of their earlier intimacy, taking picnics out to *Restless* and enjoying each other's company, their mutual sense of humour breaking any ice which had existed.

It was all too short. Although Daphne thought that he was still far from fit, Boy returned to the division on 16 March and began a series of meetings preparatory to leaving for Algiers. On 28 March he was briefed by the VCIGS, Lieutenant General Nye, under whose orders he was to go. He lunched that day with Lieutenant General Ira Eaker of the US Eighth Air Force and with Eisenhower's successor in London, Lieutenant General Andrews, and on the following morning he flew from Hendon down to Portreath, where he met his small party for the journey ahead.

Chapter 14

Adviser (1943)

Boy travelled to North Africa wearing a new hat. As far back as June 1942 he had been making representations both to the War Office and to GHQ Home Forces that his responsibilities as the Airborne Division's GOC went far beyond those of a normal divisional commander. In particular, he was responsible for much of the general development activity of the airborne forces and acted as an adviser on airborne matters to superior HQs. In August he submitted a paper on the subject to the War Office, which was in turn passed to a committee headed by the VCIGS. With no progress by early October, Boy went to see Brooke and persuaded him that it would be necessary to set up a separate Airborne Forces HQ, which would take over the advisory work in all theatres of war and assume responsibility for the Airborne Forces Depot at Hardwick and any development and experimental work deemed necessary.

GHQ Home Forces was in partial agreement with the proposal. It recognized the need to separate certain responsibilities from those of the divisional commander, but considered that these would be best run by a small staff within Home Forces itself. Boy felt strongly that this was not the right solution, but there the matter rested at the end of the year. Once again, it was the Casablanca Conference which proved the catalyst for change. The mobilization of what was now called 1 Airborne Division for active service in the Mediterranean, the agreement in principle to raise a second division, the request from Allied Forces HQ for assistance in planning the invasion of Sicily and the formation of a new development centre all pointed to the desirability of a new Airborne Forces HQ.

It was thus as Major General Airborne Forces and Airborne Adviser to the Supreme Allied Commander, Allied Forces Headquarters (AFHQ) that Boy set out once again.[1] Hopkinson, who had been sent to Algiers to represent Boy during the latter's sick leave,[2] returned to assume command of 1 Airborne Division. Leaving Walch behind to set up the new HQ at Brigmerston House, Boy took with him Nigel Norman, now promoted to Air Commodore, and two staff officers.

After an overnight stay in Gibraltar, the party landed at Maison Blanche airfield outside Algiers on 31 March. For the next three weeks, Boy and Norman had a hectic schedule. On their first day they met Eisenhower and Major General Charles Gairdner, General Alexander's Chief of Staff at Force 141, the overall planning organization for Operation 'Husky', the invasion of Sicily. They then flew on consecutive days to meet Alexander himself at his HQ in Tunisia, Air Chief Marshal Tedder and General Spaatz of the USAAF in Constantine, Mark Clark in Oujda and finally Montgomery at Eighth Army's Tac HQ near Gabes.

Boy had two immediate priorities, to find out what tasks were being planned for the airborne forces in 'Husky' and to make arrangements for the arrival of 1 Airborne Division, which was expected early in May. On 9 April, he was formally appointed as Eisenhower's Adviser on Airborne Training & Operations, with orders to establish a small HQ for planning and liaison, in which role he would also have some oversight of the training and administration of the US airborne troops, who were expected to land in North Africa at much the same time as their British colleagues.

On the next day Boy and Norman left Algiers for Cairo, where they arrived two days later after an overnight stop at Tripoli. Montgomery had established Force 545 there, his own planning staff for the Eighth Army element of 'Husky', led by one of his two corps commanders for the operation, Boy's old friend 'Bimbo' Dempsey. After a day of meetings in Cairo, the two men flew on again, this time to Palestine to inspect 4 Parachute Brigade, which was due to join 1 Airborne Division on its arrival in the Mediterranean, and to agree its future role with the commander, Brigadier Shan Hackett.

The evolution of 4 Parachute Brigade had been quite different from its UK based equivalents. Nearly two years earlier, the joint paper from the War Office and the Air Ministry had proposed that both a parachute and an airlanding brigade should be formed in the Middle East, just as in the United Kingdom, but this had proved impossible to implement from the manpower available in the theatre, the only one in which the British Army was in constant contact with the enemy. The solution was to bring from India 151st Parachute Battalion, which had been formed there in late 1941 out of volunteers from infantry battalions in the country. Renumbered 156th Parachute Battalion, it had been well trained and was now based at Ramat David, near the Brigade HQ at Nazareth in Northern Palestine.[3] A decision had also been taken to raise 10th Parachute Battalion from volunteers in the Middle East, although this was substantially untrained. To bring the brigade up to full strength, 11th Parachute Battalion was in the course of being formed.

Boy had met Shan Hackett shortly before he left for Algiers, when the latter had visited 1 Airborne Division in the UK for a week. Hackett had had an eventful war, fighting with the Transjordan Frontier Force in Syria and with his own regiment, the 8th Hussars, in the Western Desert, where he had been wounded at Gazala. After a short period as GSO1 Raiding Forces, he was promoted and ordered to form the new brigade. He already had a reputation as a highly capable officer, but his relationship with Boy would always be more distant than those of some of the longer standing members of 1 Airborne Division.

After two days in Palestine, Boy and Norman returned to Cairo for some further, more detailed planning with Dempsey and his staff. They then flew to Malta, where they stayed with the Governor, Boy's fellow Grenadier, Lord Gort, now a field marshal. Boy was particularly keen to see Sicily for himself and arranged with the AOC-in-C, Air Marshal Sir Keith Park, to take a flight over the invasion area in a Beaufighter.[4] He spent two and a half hours on the mission, reconnoitring the proposed dropping and landing zones, and was encouraged by the ease with which features could be picked up from the air.

Boy and Norman arrived back in Algiers on 19 April and spent the remainder of their visit at AFHQ, working on detailed plans and administrative arrangements, during which time some differences between Forces 141 and 545 came to light, requiring the plans to be recast. Hopkinson and the advanced elements of 1 Airborne Division arrived on 26 April, to be fully briefed on all the decisions which had been taken and on 1 May Boy and Norman took off again for England, arriving there two days later, after being delayed by bad weather in Gibraltar.

Boy's priority on his return was to ensure that everything was in place for the formation of 6 Airborne Division. Gale had been appointed the GOC and arrived at Syrencote House a few days later. He had done an excellent job on behalf of the Airborne Forces at the War Office, where the Directorate of Air had been recently greatly strengthened by the upgrading of the Director to a major general's rank and the appointment to the post of Kenneth Crawford – invariably called by his forename initials KN – who was to make a significant impact there for much of the rest of the war. Crawford was well known to Boy, having served previously as BGS Home Forces.

6 Airborne Division experienced some of the same frustrations as its now departed forerunner, but its build-up was significantly quicker and many of the equipment problems had been solved. Moreover, by that time both planes and gliders were becoming more readily available. The core of the division was 3 Parachute Brigade, which had remained behind when 1 Airborne Division left for North Africa, although it had been severely depleted by providing replacements for 1 Parachute Brigade's casualties. It did at least have the benefit of an experienced commander, James Hill. 6 Airlanding Brigade and 5 Parachute Brigade, the latter not raised until July, were both new formations, comprising existing infantry battalions which required training from scratch: neither of their commanders, Hugh Kindersley and Nigel Poett, had previous airborne experience. Gale, however, was helped by having a leavening of officers on his staff who had served in 1 Airborne Division or the Directorate of Air.

One major decision, taken jointly by Boy and Gale very early on, was that the members of the new division would wear exactly the same Pegasus badge as those in 1 Airborne. Gale subscribed wholeheartedly to Boy's view that the airborne forces formed part of one family and that there should be no distinction between them.

With trusted men in the key airborne positions in the UK, Gale at 6 Airborne Division and Crawford at the War Office, Boy now considered himself free to devote time to his other function, as adviser to Eisenhower on the airborne role in Operation 'Husky'. After snatching a few days leave in Fowey, he took off again for North Africa on 19 May. His journey came in the aftermath of a personal and professional shock, the death of Nigel Norman, who was the only man killed when the Hudson in which he was flying crashed shortly after take-off. Waiting to fly himself, Boy scribbled a note to Daphne on the back of a bank statement. 'His death' he wrote 'is an absolute tragedy for our affairs and I honestly don't know how we'll replace him.'[5] Norman had been his confidant since the early days of the Dungeon Party and had become a close friend and companion: he was, to that extent, irreplaceable.

Boy had to break the news by telephone to Lady Norman, who said that she had feared and expected this moment for seventeen years, ever since they had married.

One of the perks of Boy's new job was the allocation to him by Eisenhower of his personal Dakota, which had also conveyed him on his earlier trip. It had an American crew, Joe Beck as pilot and George Denny as navigator, and in accordance with USAAF custom they had painted on its nose the plane's name, *Boy's Boys*. The party, including Walch and Brian Urquhart, stopped off at Gibraltar, Urquhart noting that 'As usual, the admiral, the Governor-General, and everyone else of consequence had been to school with, played polo with, sailed with or fought in World War I with Browning.'[6]

Boy's staff was established within Force 141 at La Marsa, outside Algiers. The allied airborne forces had been gathering since he had been away, with 1 Airborne Division concentrating in its training area near Mascara, south-east of Oran. 2 Parachute Brigade had arrived even before the end of his previous visit, 1 Parachute Brigade moved from Tunisia in early May and the convoy bringing 1 Airlanding Brigade docked just after Boy's return. 4 Parachute Brigade was due from Palestine in the first week of June. The American airborne contingent had also arrived in the shape of 82 Airborne Division, which was located further west near Oujda.

The wisdom of appointing an overall coordinator was now apparent, as there were numerous HQs involved in planning for 'Husky'. At the top there was Eisenhower's AFHQ in Algiers. Initially Alexander's 15th Army Group, which had absorbed the staff of Force 141, was close to AFHQ, but it subsequently moved to Tunis. Eighth Army still had its planners in Egypt, whilst George Patton's US Seventh Army's HQ was in Morocco. The air and naval HQs were likewise dispersed, so Boy had a lot of travelling to do and a formidable job of reconciling conflicting interests.

In this he was only partially successful, due to the constraints of available resources and notably planes and gliders. The latter posed a particular difficulty for the British. The lack of suitable tugs meant that very few Horsas had reached the theatre and it was necessary for the airlanding brigade to use American Waco Hadrians, on which it and the glider pilots had to be hastily retrained. The planes for use as glider tugs and to carry parachutists were to come substantially from XII US Troop Carrier Command, whose pilots had no experience of such operations and virtually none of night flying. Their allocation to the Americans and the British was in Boy's hands and he fell foul of both parties.

Boy got off to a particularly bad start with Matthew Ridgway, Commanding General of 82 Airborne Division, a down-to-earth soldier who brooked no interference with his command. Ridgway considered that Boy had a patronizing attitude towards the Americans. This was a miniature version of a scenario which was being played out across the allied forces in North Africa, in which the British were apt to point to the relative lack of experience of the Americans, whilst the Americans were quick to respond that the British had little to be proud of in their conduct of the war thus far. Whilst Eisenhower was able to rise above this rivalry, Alexander had offended the Americans some months before by his critical response to their performance at Kasserine, Montgomery was equally dismissive of their capabilities and, on the other side, Clark, Patton and Bradley, whilst not explicitly anglophobic, were deeply suspicious of their allies and wont to seek advantage for the American side at all times.

Boy, for his part, believed that he had the full authority of Eisenhower and Alexander and was inclined to use this when a more diplomatic approach might have paid dividends. The differences between him and Ridgway began over aircraft, where there were not enough Dakotas to satisfy both airborne divisions. In Ridgway's words: 'A running argument developed with General Browning as to how these planes were to be allocated between my division and the British 1st Airborne Division. I also began to feel that General Browning, from his post at Supreme Headquarters, was in a position to exert undue influence, both on the allocation of aircraft to American airborne troops and on their tactical employment.'[7]

Worse was to follow. One of Ridgway's battalion commanders was informed that Boy was to arrive on the following day on an inspection. On making enquiry of Ridgway, he found that the latter knew nothing about it and was incensed when he heard. It was indeed at best discourteous of Boy not to have gone through the divisional commander and his action did nothing to improve a steadily deteriorating relationship. The situation was further exacerbated by Boy then informing Ridgway that he was coming to see his plans for 'Husky'. Ridgway responded that no plans were available for scrutiny until they had been approved by Patton. The Seventh Army commander supported Ridgway and the matter was escalated to Eisenhower, whose Chief of Staff, Walter Bedell Smith, read Ridgway a stiff lecture on cooperation, causing him to back down. The damage, however, had been done and would affect relationships in the future, although Boy was in general a great admirer of the Americans.

Although Hopkinson was also unhappy about his allocation of aircraft, the main problem with him was of a different order. The newly appointed GOC of 1 Airborne Division was keen to demonstrate his independence from his former commander and, as they were now of the same rank, did not see that he should be dictated to. His tactic was to ignore Boy for as long as he could get away with it, even to the extent of disappearing from his HQ whenever the latter arrived. Without consulting Boy he went directly to Montgomery and sold him the concept of a glider-borne operation on the night before the beach landings on Sicily, its objective being the strategically important Ponte Grande, a bridge just inland from Syracuse. Montgomery, who had no concept of the limitations of such an operation or understanding of the difficulties of the airlanding brigade in its conversion to Hadrians or the total lack of experience of the American tug pilots, seized on the proposal with enthusiasm, as it solved a conundrum for him. Boy was horrified when he heard of it, as he could see major problems, particularly regarding the landing zones, which were composed of small fields divided by stone walls. He was also unhappy about the approach over the open sea. However, he was in no position to change Montgomery's mind and was effectively ignored. Chatterton, who was to lead the glider force, thought that the plan was mad and duly pointed out all the obstacles, only to be told by Hopkinson that if he did not accept it he would be replaced.

There remained a huge task for Boy's HQ to carry out, including the provision of all the necessary supplies for the forthcoming operations and liaison with the two air forces over reconnaissance and air to ground support. It was also responsible for coordinating the movement of both divisions to their final staging point at Kairouan in Tunisia, carried out in late June and early July. There was little time for relaxation, although Boy managed to visit 24 Guards Brigade, which had fought in the closing stages of the North African campaign and was now resting near Tunis. The composition of the brigade had changed since his departure in November 1941, with 5th Grenadiers replacing 2nd Warwicks. The former was now commanded by Geordie Gordon Lennox and the battalion's chaplain was Boy's cousin, Denys Browning[8], who had followed his father Bertie into the church.[9]

Boy moved to Malta shortly before the invasion of Sicily and remained there until after the first phase, his main concern being to ensure that the AA batteries in the vicinity of the landing zones were neutralized by RAF Beaufighters. The glider operation on the night of 9/10 July, as he had predicted, was disastrous. Many of the gliders were cast off far too early by the inexperienced tug pilots and went down in the sea, including, ironically, the one in which Hopkinson was flying. Those which landed in Sicily were dispersed over a wide area, only one reaching the correct landing zone, its occupants seizing the Ponte Grande, where they were joined in due course by others, including Walch, who had accompanied the 1 Airlanding Brigade and who took command of the party. The Italians counter-attacked in strength and overran the positions, but the bridge was later recaptured intact by the seaborne forces.[10] The total casualties of the brigade were 490, of whom 252 were drowned.

In the American sector, there was also initial chaos as the paratroops were dropped in widely separated parties far from their intended landing zones. In their case, however, they did manage to create considerable confusion among the German and Italian defenders by taking vigorous offensive action wherever they could and disrupting lines of communication. Although its execution was far from the original conception, this airborne operation nevertheless made a considerable contribution to the successful lodgement of Seventh Army. The 82 Airborne Division later formed part of the Provisional Corps, which carried out a wide flanking movement to Palermo.

1 Airborne Division mounted one further operation, the seizure of the Ponte di Primasole, another key bridge, this time over the Simeto River in the Plain of Catania. Carried out on the night of 13/14 July by Lathbury's 1 Parachute Brigade, it was similarly blighted by the inaccuracy of the drops, due to the inexperience of the Dakotas' pilots. A party from 1st Parachute Battalion did capture and hold the bridge, removing all the demolition charges, but was forced off on the following day. Nevertheless, by removing the charges and then dominating the bridge from the south, the paratroopers subsequently enabled it to be captured intact by ground forces.

The conclusion of the Sicily campaign in early August marked the effective end of Boy's appointment as Adviser to Eisenhower and Alexander. He attended the Board of Enquiry into 'Husky', set up by Eisenhower in late July, at which he was sharply critical of the performance of the USAAF and RAF pilots and navigators.

Alexander had written a report which was positive overall. 'The recent operations', it read 'have proved the value of airborne troops, and given us a peep into their great possibilities if they are properly organized, equipped and employed.' He pointed out that where the troops were accurately dropped the results had been excellent, was enthusiastic about the quality of the troops themselves, but was critical, just like Boy, of the pilots of the two air forces.

Alexander may have been supportive, but Boy was deeply frustrated. He had, in effect, been cut out of any real involvement in operations by the two army commanders, Patton and Montgomery. Following attempts by Boy to discuss aspects of the operations with Monty's two immediate subordinates, Leese and Dempsey, the Eighth Army commander had gone as far as to write to Lieutenant General McCreery, Alexander's Chief of Staff: 'Browning must discuss the employment of airborne troops with me and not with my Corps commanders. The conduct of operations in Sicily is nothing to do with him and suggest you inform him accordingly.' In the face of such an attitude and having in particular had his advice on the glider landings dismissed out of hand, it was little wonder that Boy questioned the value of his role.

In early August Boy returned to England, where he participated in some preliminary discussions being held on the employment of airborne forces in the invasion of North-West Europe. The RAF was by this time much more inclined to cooperate and a key meeting, attended by Boy, Gale and Crawford, was held on 10 August to consider the role of 6 Airborne Division in the invasion. It was chaired by Air Marshal Sir Trafford Leigh Mallory, then the AOC-in-C Fighter Command, but shortly to be designated the Air C-in-C of the Allied Expeditionary Force, and both its content and its tone demonstrated a significant improvement in inter-service relationships since the beginning of the year.

Boy's time back in England was all too brief, although he managed to take a whole week in Fowey at the end of August. He was about to leave on a long odyssey, the main objective of which was to advise on the development of airborne forces in India. With a small party consisting of Walch, Major Bill Bradish, Boy's DAQMG, and Lieutenant Colonel Anthony B. Harris, his American liaison officer, he departed again in early September, calling in on Allied Forces HQ in Algiers and 15th Army Group HQ in Bizerta, before flying on to visit 1 Airborne Division in Taranto just as the command had unexpectedly changed hands.

The division had landed in Italy on 9 September in an infantry role, transported to Taranto by Royal Navy cruisers. Though the Germans in the area were relatively few in number, they had put up a spirited defence. Hopkinson, eager to see what was happening in the front line, had been visiting 4 Parachute Brigade and, ignoring warnings from Hackett and others about snipers, had stuck his head over a protecting wall and been shot. Seriously wounded and unconscious, he had been taken back to the field hospital and in the meantime Eric Down had taken over command on 11 September with the approval of Montgomery. Hopkinson died of his wounds on the next day, just before Boy arrived.

The other two brigadiers, Hackett and Lathbury, were not entirely happy about the appointment of Down, who, whilst thoroughly competent, had a reputation as one of the most abrasive officers in the Army. Possibly because of this,[11] Boy signalled to Eighth Army and the War Office to enquire if he should assume command instead, but was ordered to proceed to India in accordance with his instructions. He flew on to GHQ Middle East in Cairo and then to New Delhi, where he arrived on 17 September.

On 22 September Boy had the first of several meetings with Major General Orde Wingate, who had recently returned from accompanying Churchill to the Quadrant Conference in Quebec. Wingate had impressed Roosevelt with his account of the first Chindit expedition and the President ordered that he was to be offered every facility, including the use of American planes and gliders for his next operation, which was being planned for the spring of 1944. Boy's task was to discuss with Wingate cooperation between the Chindits and 50 Indian Parachute Brigade and the use by the former of Hadrian gliders, but Walch remarked subsequently that Wingate was not a good listener and took little notice of what operational experience Boy's team had to offer, although, by way of mitigation, he was suffering from malaria at the time.

Boy's main priority was to visit the only airborne formation in the country, 50 Indian Parachute Brigade, under the command of Brigadier Michael Hope-Thompson, formerly CO of 4th Parachute Battalion in the early days of 1 Airborne Division. Already well trained and ready for action, it was based at Campbellpore in the Northern Punjab, and consisted of 152nd (Indian), 153rd (Gurkha) and 154th (Gurkha) Parachute Battalions, together with a parachute squadron of the Royal Bombay Sappers and Miners and its own signals section and machine gun and medical companies. The arrival of Boy's party coincided with the end of the Hindu festival of Dussehra and they were entertained to singing and dancing by the Gurkhas. Boy gave a spontaneous demonstration of his Cossack dance, which was greatly admired.

Boy's visit to the parachute brigade had been made in company with the C-in-C India, General Sir Claude Auchinleck and the AOC-in-C, Air Chief Marshal Sir Richard Peirse, and when he returned to New Delhi, he had a number of meetings with both men and with General Sir George Giffard, the GOC-in-C Eastern Army. The outcome was a series of decisions, including the expansion of 50 Indian Parachute Brigade, which was still short of men, the formation of an airborne forces depot, the appointment of a Director of Air at GHQ India, the creation of an Indian Army Air Corps and, most significantly, the raising of an airborne division. In connection with the last of these, a signal was sent to the War Office London on 13 October requesting the despatch of a divisional commander designate, together with a GSO1, GSO2 and DAQMG.

Whilst Boy was in New Delhi, Mountbatten arrived to take up his appointment as Supreme Allied Commander South-East Asia and on 14 October Boy met him for a briefing on all matters airborne. This appointment was especially pleasing as Boy could leave India knowing that, with Auchinleck firmly on side as well, he had two strong supporters at the top of the military hierarchy there. He returned directly to the UK and to a new and much more promising job.

Chapter 15

Corps (December 1943–June 1944)

On 20 August 1943, before leaving for India, Boy sent a long letter to the War Office which was to be the catalyst for major changes to the organization and control of the airborne forces. It was born out of his extreme frustration at the impotence of his position as Major General Airborne Forces and his assessment that, with the invasion of North-West Europe likely to take place in the following year, a more efficient structure and chain of command was vital.

In the letter he pointed out that many of the difficulties encountered in Sicily had been the result of the British and American airborne divisions coming under the command of higher formations whose commanders and staff had no experience of their use. His own rank of major general and role as adviser had not allowed him to exercise command himself and his lack of authority had meant that his advice had on occasions been ignored. He went on to say that he believed that it would be desirable to use airborne formations in at least divisional strength, and possibly in corps strength, in the forthcoming campaign and that it would be necessary to set up an organization which could command more than one division on operations and to train them accordingly. He also recommended that there should be a single higher authority with whom the RAF could deal when it came to the allocation of aircraft and the training of glider pilots.

His conclusion was that there should be a major upgrading of the existing Airborne Forces HQ. In addition to the existing roles of Major General Airborne Forces, as adviser to the War Office and to supreme commanders and commanders-in-chief at home and abroad, and as commander of all airborne training, depot and experimental establishments, the HQ should be given the administrative and operational command of all airborne forces.

The letter was duly considered by the War Office during his visit to India, but no decision had been made by the time of his return and he raised the issue with Brooke when he met the CIGS on 28 October. On 12 November James Steele, the Director of Staff Duties, sent a minute to Ronald Weeks, the DCIGS: 'When 1 Airborne Division returns to the UK, there will be in 21 Army Group two airborne divisions in addition to certain allied para units. C-in-C 21 Army Group asked for the appointment of a "Commander Airborne Troops" to command all formations and units in the Army Group as well as any SAS units, and to act as his airborne adviser. He considers that this commander should be entirely under his orders and have no dual responsibility. He has asked in addition that Major-General Browning should be appointed to this post.' Importantly at this juncture, Steele went on to write: 'There would…be no question of commanding all the airborne troops in operations.'

This was not quite what Boy had in mind. Indeed, he had specifically proposed that the organization should be constituted as an airborne corps to command both 1 and 6 Airborne Divisions and allied contingents other than the Poles. This had not been asked for by Paget, who had moved from Home Forces to be C-in-C 21st Army Group in the summer, and it was considered by Steele to be wrong in principle. Boy had made two further proposals, first that the Commander Airborne Corps should have direct access to the War Office through the Major General Airborne Forces and secondly that he should have the rank of lieutenant general. On the first, Steele thought that the position of MGAF was no longer justified and that access should be through the Director of Air. On the second he felt that there were arguments for and against, whilst Paget had an open mind.

Somehow, Boy managed to have his way on the major issues. On 4 December the new HQ Airborne Troops, formed on a nucleus of its predecessor, HQ Airborne Forces, opened at High House, Hammersmith, close to 21st Army Group, under whose command it was to come. It was to take under its own command 1 and 6 Airborne Divisions and the Special Air Service Brigade, which was about to be formed. The responsibility for the Airborne Forces Depot and Development Centre was passed to the War Office. Boy's Directive No 1 was explicit about nomenclature: 'The Title of the Force is officially Headquarters Airborne Troops (21 Army Group). All correspondence will bear the official title, but verbally it will be known as the Airborne Corps and I will be referred to as the Corps Commander.' On 9 December he was promoted to acting lieutenant general.

Boy retained a presence at Brigmerston House and the first corps commander's conference was held there on 8 December, chaired by Boy and attended by Down, Gale, Flavell, Walch and his chief administrative officer Bower. This was to be one of Down's last appearances as GOC of 1 Airborne Division, as on 7 January 1944[1] he handed over command to an officer who was new to the Airborne Forces, Roy Urquhart.

There have been allegations that Boy dismissed Down because he was too abrasive, but there is no evidence to support this. Indeed, according to Urquhart himself, Boy contested the decision to remove Down but was overruled. Although Down was apparently disgruntled at the prospect, he was leaving with good reason, because he had been nominated to lead a new airborne division to be raised in India. 1 Airborne Division had only just returned from the Mediterranean and was unlikely to see action for some time, with 6 Airborne Division certain to be committed to battle next. He was therefore both available and admirably suited to the job, although it was to prove to be even more frustrating than Boy's experience in 1942.[2] The position of GOC 1 Airborne Division was not, in any event, in Boy's gift, although he was consulted on the subject. On being asked if would accept someone from outside the airborne forces, he agreed as long as the individual was 'hot from battle'.[3]

The first choice, as it happened, was not Urquhart at all, but Brigadier 'Swifty' Howlett, who had been commanding 36 Brigade throughout the Tunisian campaign and on into Italy. The day after he was told of his appointment, he was killed by shellfire on the River Sangro. Urquhart had the advantage of already being in the UK, where he was the BGS at XII Corps. Moreover, he met Boy's criterion as he had seen plenty of action, as GSO1 of 51 (Highland) Division from El Alamein to the end of the North African campaign and then as commander of 231 (Malta) Brigade Group, earning a DSO and bar in the process. The latter formation had been involved in heavy fighting in Sicily and had gone on to land in Italy, where Urquhart had been slightly wounded. He was a favourite of Montgomery's, who possibly suggested and was certainly consulted on his promotion.

Urquhart duly reported to Boy on his first day in command, only to be given a mild rebuke for being improperly dressed for a general, in his Highland Light Infantry tartan trews. The two men never developed a close relationship, but by most accounts they got on well professionally. There was some feeling in the division that command should have gone to Lathbury, as the most senior brigadier and an experienced airborne soldier, but Urquhart came in due course to earn its respect. On the other hand, whilst some considered that his appointment helped to dispel some of the mumbo-jumbo about airborne operations, others were left with the impression that he considered parachuting and glider operations as just another way to get into battle, according insufficient prominence to some of the unique problems which would be faced as a result. However, he inherited an experienced staff and had many months to familiarize himself with the issues.

In any event, Boy's immediate concerns were less with 1 Airborne Division than with forming his HQ and establishing the role which the airborne forces would play in the invasion of North-West Europe. The first was relatively straightforward. Walch was promoted and appointed the BGS. The staff of HQ Airborne Forces moved over *in toto*, whilst others transferred from the newly returned 1 Airborne Division. At the end of December the HQ moved from High House to Ashley Gardens, where it was adjacent to HQ I Corps, under which it had been provisionally decided that 6 Airborne Division would operate in the forthcoming invasion.

There were two men who were on Boy's personal staff in addition to Johnson and his driver, Johannides.[4] Like all of his rank he had an aide-de-camp and for most of 1944 it was Major Harry Cator. In spite of his relatively junior rank Cator was actually only a month younger than Boy, had been at Sandhurst at the same time and had won a Military Cross serving with the Royal Scots Greys in the Great War. After that war he had left the Army and become a farmer, rejoining in 1939. He had had an exciting war, largely in North Africa with the commandos, becoming Commander HQ Raiding Forces. Far from a typical ADC, his age and background made him more of a friend and confidant than a subordinate. Boy's other key aide was his Personal Assistant, Eddie Newberry. Newberry was a delightful man, but an unlikely soldier. A civil servant in the London County Council prior to joining up, he was highly organized and carried out many of Boy's more tiresome errands with great devotion to duty.

The second priority, the plan for D-Day, took longer to agree and, when it was first revealed to Gale, he found it most unsatisfactory. Boy travelled down to Syrencote House on 17 February to discuss the proposal, which was for a single parachute brigade and an anti-tank battery to seize the two bridges over the Caen Canal and the River Orne at Benouville and Ranville, coming thereafter under the intermediate command of 3 Division. Gale was deeply disappointed that the whole division was not to be used and Boy sympathized with him. The problem, as ever, was with the RAF, which was initially only prepared to allocate the aircraft of 38 Group to the operation. Further representations were made – Gale wrote later of Boy that it was 'the effect I knew he would make on our behalf that really formed my only solace'[5] – and on 23 February a revised plan was announced, which envisaged the use of 46 Group RAF as well. This would permit the two parachute brigades and a small glider-borne *coup de main* party to go in on the first lift and take the two bridges already allocated, but also to destroy others over the River Dives to prevent German reinforcements coming forward and to eliminate the Merville Battery, which would dominate some of the landing beaches. Gale would still not get his whole division over in a single lift, but the airlanding brigade would be brought in later on D-Day.

The relatively small amount of time needed to change the plan showed how far relationships with the RAF had changed. There was a new commander of 38 Group, Air Vice-Marshal Leslie Hollinghurst, who would be a key member of the whole airborne team in the future. His group had expanded to ten squadrons, four each equipped with Albemarles and Stirlings, and two with Halifaxes. 46 Group of Transport Command, which had other duties but would be available for specific operations, numbered five squadrons of Dakotas. During the spring these two groups moved to airfields in Gloucestershire, Oxfordshire, Wiltshire and Dorset.

At the beginning of February, Boy submitted a paper on the Airborne Base, which would provide the necessary interface between the airborne forces themselves, the RAF and, where necessary, IX US Troop Carrier Command, organizing the reception of troops at the airfields, the army element of air supply, the despatch of the various lifts and any subsequent reinforcements. Members of his staff were attached to the RAF and USAAF formations, whilst others provided airborne control sections at the airfields, near to each of which transit camps were established. The number of staff at HQ Airborne Troops burgeoned and it became necessary in mid-April to relocate from Ashley Gardens to the imposing clubhouse of the Moor Park Golf Club, between Northwood and Rickmansworth. At the same time the name of the organization changed formally to HQ I Airborne Corps.

Amongst all this activity, there was little time for Boy to see his family. Just before he had set out for India, a major event had taken place, when Daphne achieved one of her heart's desires by taking a lease on Menabilly. She had coveted the house ever since she and her sister Angela had discovered it in 1926, shortly after Gerald had bought Ferryside. It had featured strongly as Manderley in *Rebecca* and would appear in later books. For years she had been badgering the owner, Dr Rashleigh, and he now agreed to grant a twenty year lease at a peppercorn rent, but with the proviso that it be fully maintained by the tenant. As it was in appalling decorative condition and, among other things, needed a new roof, the total cost was substantial. The house was effectively uninhabitable and Daphne hired workmen to patch it up during the autumn of 1943.

Knowing what he did of the house's condition, Boy was at first highly dubious. On receiving her letter with the news of the lease, he remarked to Eagger, his ADMS: 'I think you'd better hurry down to see my wife – she must have gone clean crazy!'[6] However, on his return from India, he was impressed by what Daphne had achieved. One whole wing had been shut off, but the rooms which were to be used had all been attractively decorated and the roof appeared to be watertight. The move from Readymoney Cove was achieved just before Christmas 1943 and Boy managed to take a whole week off. The main problem was the lack of heating in what turned out to be a particularly cold winter, as open fires and paraffin stoves were quite inadequate for the large, high-ceilinged rooms; but nothing could detract from Daphne's evident happiness.

If he could not visit more often, Boy could at least write, indeed he was an assiduous, almost daily, correspondent. For the most part his letters were scribbled in pencil on whatever paper he could find. The language was peculiarly their own, whilst the contents tended to focus on domestic issues and matters of common interest, such as boats. As far as the war was concerned, there were constant expressions of hope that 'this filthy business' would soon be over, so that they could settle back to their 'routes' and enjoy sailing again.

The topic which received more mention than any other reflected Boy's desire to own a much larger boat than either 'Yggy' or *Restless* once the war was over. By this time his main form of relaxation, carried out in his room at HQ once the business of the day was over, was the design of such a craft. His ideal was a motor fishing vessel, like those to be seen round the coasts of the UK, which would be called *Fanny Rosa*, after the feisty heroine of Daphne's most recent novel, *Hungry Hill*. He spent many hours sketching out the dimensions and the arrangement of the accommodation and specifying the rig and equipment, including the engines. Although he had pronounced views on what he wanted, Boy realized he needed professional help and enlisted the services of a Scottish naval architect called McBryde. The latter's role was to translate Boy's vision into reality, but the chances of achieving anything were scuppered by the lack of building materials, all of which had strategic wartime priority. Letters went to and fro, with Boy becoming increasingly frustrated at the lack of progress. There was also the issue of cost and Boy, impecunious himself, began to work on Daphne to bankroll the project.

Back in the real world Boy now had one new formation under command, the Special Air Service Brigade, which had a very different history to the airborne divisions and an even more different ethos. Formed in the Western Desert in late 1941, initially as 'L Detachment', under the command of the charismatic David Stirling, it had distinguished itself over the following eighteen months by a series of daring raids behind the Axis lines. Not all of these were successful, but some were spectacularly so. After Stirling's capture in February 1943, his own 1st SAS Regiment had been broken up into the Special Boat Squadron and the Special Raiding Squadron. In the meantime, Stirling's brother Bill had raised the 2nd SAS Regiment and both it and the SBS and SRS played a raiding role in Sicily and Italy. At the beginning of January 1944 SRS, now transformed back into 1st SAS Regiment, and 2nd SAS Regiment returned to the UK and were formed into the SAS Brigade with the two French parachute battalions and the Belgian parachute company which had been part of Airborne Forces for some time.

The new brigade was placed under the command of Rory McLeod, who had commanded the 1st Airlanding Light Regiment in 1 Airborne Division. He was an outsider, but he had a very good grasp of the capabilities of his men and the type of warfare to which they were best suited and fought tenaciously to ensure that they were properly employed. He was not so successful in integrating them with the rest of the airborne forces, indeed there was a mutual and lasting jealousy between the two. Whereas the paratroopers and airlanding regiments had been subjected to Boy's tight discipline and trained to fight with complete obedience as a team, the SAS was altogether more informal, accustomed to operate independently in very small groups with limited interference from above, and it resented any attempt at change. The matter came to a head with Boy's attempt to impose the maroon beret. The SAS men were intensely proud of their sand coloured berets and, other than on parade in front of senior officers, refused to wear the new issue.

With the French and Belgian parachute units absorbed into the SAS Brigade, the largest independent Allied airborne formation, other than the Americans, was the Polish Parachute Brigade. Relations at the senior end, very cordial back in 1942, were becoming strained. The root of the problem was an undertaking which Brooke had given to General Sikorski that the brigade would remain under Polish command and only be used in Poland. By the autumn of 1943, however, two things were apparent. First, there had been a breach in relations between the Soviet Union and the Polish Government-in-Exile and, with their strength growing after Stalingrad, it seemed unlikely that the Russians would accept any force offered by the London Poles. Secondly, it had become a matter of principle that Allied units from occupied countries would serve under whatever command was appropriate. This was already the case with Anders' Polish Corps in Italy, whilst it was understood that Maczek's Polish Armoured Division would come under British (later Canadian) command in North-West Europe. The position of the Polish Parachute Brigade was thus an anomaly, and an increasingly unattractive one to the British, who did not themselves have an abundance of human resources.

The death of Sikorski in a flying accident in July 1943 did not help, as his successors failed to command the same level of respect. The British began to apply pressure to the Poles to release their parachute brigade for use other than in Poland itself, primarily through Lieutenant General Edward Grasett, who had responsibility at the War Office for liaison with Allied Forces. Boy was also prominent in this initiative, creating probably justified suspicion in the mind of Sosabowski that he was angling for control of the Poles. According to Sosabowski, Boy at one point offered him the command of a joint British-Polish airborne division which, with the shortage of local volunteers at the time, would have made some sense, although Sosabowski felt that it was purely politically motivated. Boy made a direct appeal to Sikorski and his successors to release the brigade on more than one occasion, as did Brooke and in due course, Montgomery, but they were rebuffed each time.

Under further pressure, in March 1944 the Polish Government-in-Exile offered the brigade to 21st Army Group for a single operation, on the condition that it would be withdrawn after it had suffered 15 per cent casualties, but Montgomery was unsurprisingly not prepared to accept any formation with strings attached. Immediately after D-Day the Poles capitulated and agreed to let Montgomery have the brigade without restrictions, but by then some damage had been done to relationships, particularly in the British attitude to Sosabowski, who was thought to have been behind the stand on independence. In the meantime the Polish Parachute Brigade had been accorded a low priority in terms of equipment and training and was far from battle ready.

For Boy, relationships with allies were to get no easier. Having begun on the wrong foot with the Americans in the USA and again, much more significantly, in North Africa, he continued to offend them. In November 1943, Ridgway sent his Assistant Divisional Commander, Colonel Jim Gavin, to London to advise COSSAC, the organization set up to plan for D-Day ahead of the appointment of a Supreme Commander, on the American participation in airborne operations. Before he left, Ridgway warned Gavin about Boy's 'machinations and scheming'.[7] Gavin met Boy shortly after he arrived, only to be the recipient of a remark by the latter about Ridgway not having parachuted into Sicily, which Gavin considered unkind. Furthermore Major General Ray Barker, COSSAC's American Deputy Chief of Staff, described Boy to Gavin as 'an empire builder'.[8]

It would be easy to dismiss these episodes as merely reflective of a clash of style and culture which was only too evident at all levels between the two western allies or as an over-sensitive reaction by the Americans to what they widely perceived as British arrogance: there would be some truth in both of these, but they are not an excuse. It is likely that Boy intended no offence and was merely expressing his views frankly, as was his practice. Nevertheless, the hostility which his personal attitude quite clearly generated and the impression that he was out for his own advantage were to have uncomfortable consequences for him later in the year.

For the time being, however, Boy had no direct relationship with the Americans and there were none of the arguments about the allocation of aircraft which had dogged 'Husky', as it had been agreed that each airborne division on D-Day would use those of its own country's air force. He was thus able to focus his energy on ensuring that 6 Airborne Division was ready for battle. Although the division would come under the operational command of Lieutenant General John Crocker's I Corps in Normandy and Gale and his staff were accordingly liaising constantly with the latter's HQ, for administrative purposes and as far as both transportation and supply was concerned it remained the responsibility of HQ I Airborne Corps. Boy thus had frequent meetings with Gale and Hollinghurst on the one hand, and with 21st Army Group on the other.

His relationship with Montgomery had not been soured by being sidelined over Sicily – Boy was never one to hold grudges – and he became a trusted adviser to the latter. On 8 March Montgomery, wearing the maroon beret which Hopkinson had given him in North Africa, with the badge of the Parachute Regiment alongside his general's badge, went down to inspect 6 Airborne Division on Salisbury Plain, accompanied by Boy and Crawford. For Boy, this was the culmination of the immense progress made in raising the airborne forces and preparing them for war. Not only were there many men present who had served under him in 1942, including James Hill of 3 Parachute Brigade, 'Pigmy' Smallman-Tew of the Divisional Signals and two unit COs, Geoffrey Pine-Coffin of the 7th Parachute Battalion and Alastair Pearson of the 8th Parachute Battalion, but the division, in his words to Gale afterwards 'showed a standard which I have always hoped airborne forces would attain and maintain; whatever anyone else thought, I, at any rate, was fully satisfied...'[9] On 19 May came the icing on the cake, when Boy escorted the King and Queen and Princess Elizabeth on their visit to the division.

The principle role of HQ I Airborne Corps in the run-up to D-Day was to provide the critique for both planning and training which the inexperienced HQ I Corps would lack and, in order to familiarize himself thoroughly with the terrain on which the landings would take place, Boy insisted on flying a reconnaissance mission over Normandy, just as he had done over Sicily. The climax of the training programme came in late April with Exercise 'Mush', set and conducted by Boy himself as a full-scale rehearsal for what was in store. With 1 Airborne Division playing the enemy, it tested to the full 6 Airborne Division's readiness for battle. In Gale's words, the exercise 'helped me enormously to clarify my mind on many points, and left us all confident that the plan would work.'[10]

Boy was on much less firm ground with the SAS Brigade. He had lobbied successfully for the inclusion of this formation in his command, on the grounds that there was no other suitable headquarters, but neither he nor his senior staff had any real concept of what it should do. Although a dedicated section of his HQ was formed to look after it, Boy had little time to spend on the brigade due to his other commitments. When the initial plan for its commitment to operations in Normandy was issued on 29 March, it proposed a blatant misuse of the formation. It envisaged the whole brigade being dropped up to thirty-six hours prior to D-Day, inserting itself between the German infantry divisions near the coast and the armoured divisions, which intelligence had correctly identified as being held back in reserve. It would then establish a blocking line to prevent the German armour moving forward.

Bill Stirling was horrified, believing that this would be a suicide mission, likely to result in the needless destruction of a force which could be much more effectively employed, and threatening resignation if it were so used. McLeod agreed and work began to get the plan changed. To Boy's credit he saw the point and on 8 May he wrote to 21st Army Group, proposing that small groups from the SAS Brigade should be sent in after D-Day to establish contact with the French Resistance, disrupt communications and harass any German panzer divisions moving to the front. On 28 May a new plan was issued, which proposed four operations, focused on widely dispersed areas of France from which German reinforcements might be directed. These would be initiated by two-man reconnaissance parties working alongside three-man SOE/OSS/Free French 'Jedburgh Teams', which were being parachuted in to make contact with the Resistance. Once conditions were right, the main parties would follow, of anything between 50 and 150 officers and men, equipped with jeeps, explosives and anti-tank guns.

In due course the number of SAS operations in France was to burgeon, utilizing most of the manpower of the brigade and performing outstanding work in the rear areas. Bill Stirling, however, deeply disenchanted, carried out his threat to resign and was lost to the SAS. Boy himself had at best clearly not kept his eye on the ball during the planning period and was to give relatively scant attention to the SAS subsequently, as he was much preoccupied elsewhere. He did, however, take a great deal of pride in the brigade's achievements.

It was understood from early in the planning of Operation 'Overlord' that airborne operations would not necessarily conclude with the landings on D-Day. HQ I Airborne Corps had to be prepared to draw up other plans at short notice and to commit 1 Airborne Division or any other formation which Montgomery required to achieve his tactical objectives. Accordingly it was decided that Boy and a few of his staff would join the Tactical HQ of Second Army, now commanded by his old friend Dempsey, for the early days of the invasion. Having visited as many units of 6 Airborne Division as possible in their transit camps, he boarded Dempsey's HQ ship, which sailed for France on the evening of 5 June.

Chapter 16

Frustration (6 June–9 September 1944)

etween 6 June and 9 September 1944, no fewer than fifteen airborne
operations were planned in support of Allied ground operations in France,
Belgium and the Netherlands and all of them were cancelled, some at very
short notice.[1] Boy himself travelled to and from the Continent thirteen times during
these three months, initially for several days at a time, latterly more often than not
just for the day as the pace of activity increased.

The landings in the early hours of D-Day by 6 Airborne Division and 82 and
101 US Airborne Divisions did not go exactly to plan, but they achieved most of
their objectives. The glider borne *coup de main* operations to seize the bridges over
the River Orne and the Caen Canal were outstanding successes, a model of their
type. Boy and Gale had both had their doubts about this aspect of the plan, but a
demonstration of precision glider landing in a night-time exercise had convinced
them of its possibilities and their judgement was rewarded. The parachute landings
in the dark, on the other hand, were far too widely scattered in both the British
and American sectors, but small groups managed to concentrate as best they could
and to carry out their appointed tasks. By the time night fell on D-Day, 6 Airborne
Division, with Lord Lovat's 1 Special Service Brigade under command, was in a
relatively strong defensive position at the seaward end of the eastern flank of the
beachhead, whilst the Americans had joined up with the landings over Utah Beach
and were holding key points pending an advance into the Cotentin Peninsula.

Boy was able to visit Gale during the following days, remarking at one point on
the exposed situation of his HQ, but I Corps retained operational control. Between
10 and 13 June the division was engaged in very heavy fighting, culminating in the
capture of Bréville. Thereafter it was ordered to adopt a static defence, anchoring
the far left of the Allied line, where it met the sea. The division was to remain in
Normandy until the break-out and advance to the Seine in mid-August, fighting
as normal infantry, but with limited artillery support. It only returned to England
in early September, much depleted as there were few trained reinforcements other
than in 1 Airborne Division, which was being maintained intact pending future
operations. It had achieved everything which had been asked of it, a source of deep
satisfaction not only to Gale, but also to Boy.

Boy spent the first week of the invasion at Second Army's Tac HQ. The first three
operations proposed by 21st Army Group and considered by Boy and his planners
involved the reinforcement of the Allied forces by part or all of 1 Airborne Division,
in the event that it was no longer possible to land troops over the beaches, whilst the

fourth proposed landing the division to prevent German reinforcements reaching the front. These essentially defensive operations were all cancelled, the first three because the necessity never arose, the last because it was obviously bound to end in failure. From thenceforward, the operations proposed were offensive in nature, virtually all of them designed to unlock a door to ground troops.

The first was 'Beneficiary', timed to take place at the end of June or beginning of July. The plan called for 1 Airborne Division, augmented by 1 Polish Parachute Brigade, 504 US Parachute Regimental Combat Team, 878 US Airborne Aviation Engineer Battalion and a SAS squadron, to land near St Malo and Dinan, capture both towns and the nearby airfield and seize the port and the beaches. US XX Corps of two divisions would then land from the sea and fan out into Brittany. The operation was cancelled because the airborne commanders were unable to guarantee that there would be no opposition to the seaborne landings.

For the first time, HQ I Airborne Corps was to accompany the force and take command of the operations on the ground. This presented some problems. Against Boy's better judgement, HQ Airborne Troops had not been originally constituted as an operational headquarters, but as a planning and administration organization and, because no operational role was envisaged on D-Day or in its immediate aftermath, it remained that way after its change of name. Now, for the first time, it was being asked to perform such a role without having the full capacity to do so. To be fair to Boy, he had constantly lobbied the War Office to bring his HQ up to its full active service establishment, but had always been fobbed off, on the grounds that other HQs known to be going into action should have priority. As a result, by the end of June he was contemplating taking into the field a HQ which lacked a number of the basic necessities for controlling operations on the ground, notably a dedicated signals unit.

It was far from uncommon for a corps HQ to enter a major campaign without previous experience, indeed this was the case with three of the four British corps in Normandy. However, by this stage of the war, most of their staff officers, from their commanders downwards, would have themselves seen action of some sort, often at a divisional or brigade HQ or at least in a fighting unit, and would have a clear idea of the operational imperatives. This was not the case with I Airborne Corps, which was populated at a senior level largely by those who had gone up the tree with Boy himself in administrative HQs and had no experience of the control of operations. Perhaps most importantly this applied to Walch, who as BGS would have a key role in action as Boy's right hand man.

Thomas Firbank, who joined the HQ as GSO2 (Ops), and who had himself seen action with 1 Airborne Division's Reconnaissance Squadron in Italy, was scathing about the situation. 'Corps Headquarters had been so concerned with bigger issues,' he wrote subsequently, 'that it had perhaps overlooked the fact that many of its personnel, though bright at clerking, were rusty from disuse as soldiers.'[2] Brian Urquhart moved the men in his Intelligence section out of their comfortable billets around Moor Park and into tents on the golf course, but 'Even then we had a formidably unmilitary appearance.'[3] In order to provide some relevant training, three battle courses, each of a fortnight, were arranged in the Peak District for groups from the HQ: they improved physical fitness but failed to instil much tactical awareness.

Operation 'Beneficiary' would have included the Polish Parachute Brigade and this formation, now supposedly fully committed to 21st Army Group, was still causing Boy concern. Returning from the initial planning conference in France, he instructed his GSO1 (Ops), Charles Mackenzie, to go up to Scotland to inform Sosabowski that the brigade, which had just begun a two week programme of mobilization for active service, would be required for the operation and to outline its role. Mackenzie arrived on 22 June to be told that the brigade would not be ready for action until early August, on the grounds that it was still deficient in both equipment and training. Sosabowski phoned Boy, who asked him to come down to Moor Park on 25 June. The Polish commander then appealed to his C-in-C, General Sosnkowski, with a view to his intervention if the brigade was ordered into action before it was ready, but they agreed that nothing would be said until the results of the meeting were known.

On the day before the meeting with Sosabowski, Boy convened a preparatory conference, attended among others by Down, who had been back in England since April. It was agreed that, immediately after Boy had seen Sosabowski, Down would visit the Polish Parachute Brigade, taking with him representatives from each branch and service to sort out any issues which were preventing it from declaring full readiness. Moreover, the brigade would move as soon as possible from Scotland to the Stamford-Peterborough area, close to where 1 Airborne Division was concentrated.

The meeting on 25 June, attended also by Down and Walch, was a difficult one. In Sosabowski's word, Boy's greeting was 'stiff and rather curt; our relationship had changed in any case, as previously I had been independent and I was now under his command. I think that our opposing views at this conference affected our attitude to each other for the rest of the war.'[4] Cutting short any preliminaries, Boy asked Sosabowski if his brigade would be ready by 6 July and was told that it would not. Boy expressed a view that it was already better trained than 1 Parachute Brigade when it left for Tunisia, which surprised Sosabowski, as he felt that Boy was in no position to judge, having not visited the Polish units since early 1943.[5] Boy went on to ask whether, if he insisted on Polish participation in 'Beneficiary', Sosabowski would appeal to his C-in-C, to which the Polish commander confirmed that he would. Boy made it clear that he wanted the Poles to be battle-ready by 1 August, to be told that Sosabowski and the Polish Inspector General of Training believed that this would take two months. At this point Boy, who was as ever on a short fuse, snapped, making it clear that 1 August was the deadline and that Down would be available to ensure it was met.

As usual Boy's temper subsided quickly and the meeting ended on a more conciliatory note, but relations between the two men would never be as cordial as before. Boy, for his part, was confirmed in his view that Sosabowski was, at best, difficult to deal with. It is evident, moreover, from Sosabowski's own testimony, that the Poles still had another agenda – participation in the liberation of their own country. Towards the end of July, he received secret orders from Sosnkowski to have one parachute company ready to jump into Poland to assist the Home Army in the Warsaw Rising, which was about to start. Luckily for the paratroopers they were never to participate in this tragic episode, but that such an action was even considered reveals a less than full commitment to the campaign in North-West Europe, a stance always suspected by some on the Allied side.

On a more positive note, however, Down stayed on with the Poles and did an excellent job which was much appreciated. On 2 and 3 August Boy attended a full-scale exercise by the Polish Parachute Brigade at Netheravon and on 8 August he declared the brigade fully operational. Two days later he placed it under the command of 1 Airborne Division.

In the meantime, more operations had been considered and rejected, the largest of which was 'Hands Up', the capture of the Quiberon Bay area to enable a new Mulberry port to be established there, as Cherbourg was thought at the time to provide insufficient capacity for the American armies. The plan was first considered at a conference in the UK on 9 July and Boy travelled to and from Normandy three times that month to discuss it with General Bradley's newly formed 12th US Army Group, which would command I Airborne Corps and Patton's Third US Army. The proposition was for 1 Airborne Division to capture Vannes airfield, into which 52 (Lowland) Division would be flown, the combined force then forming a beachhead on Quiberon Bay itself. It was agreed that the operation would not be launched until Patton had reached a line St Malo-Rennes-Laval, but in the event, he moved so quickly that it was unnecessary.

This was the first time that 52 Division had appeared in the order of battle of the Airborne Corps. This all-Scottish formation had trained extensively for mountain warfare, with a view to being employed in Italy, but it was decided by the War Office that it should be retrained as an air-portable division. The method of approach to battle differed in material respects from the airlanding brigades in the two British airborne divisions. These used gliders to land in open country, whereas 52 Division was to be transported in Dakotas, which meant that it could only be brought in to reinforce the glider forces and paratroops once a suitable airfield had been secured. Its advantage was that it could deploy more and heavier artillery and equipment; indeed once on the ground it looked much the same as a normal infantry division. Boy visited the division on 1 August and two days later it was placed under his command.

In early August another significant event took place. It was thought to be increasingly likely that British and American airborne forces would be used on joint operations, indeed this would have been true of 'Beneficiary'. Moreover, whilst each nation had used its own air force for D-Day, it seemed that larger operations would require a pooling of resources. Even before the invasion, therefore, the staff at Supreme

Headquarters Allied Expeditionary Force (SHAEF) had been considering setting up a combined airborne headquarters and initially recommended, although he was probably unaware of it, that Boy should get the command. There were different reactions to the outline proposal from those consulted. 21st Army Group was in favour, but asked that implementation should wait until SHAEF had assumed direct operational control of ground forces. Bradley, on the other hand, rejected it outright. Boy thought that it would only make sense if it also took under command IX US Troop Carrier Command and 38 and 46 Groups RAF, whilst Leigh-Mallory would only support it if it did not. The US Chiefs of Staff were behind the proposal, but only if the commander was an American. Reconciling these views was impossible, but, with Marshall behind him, Eisenhower took the decision to go ahead with forming First Allied Airborne Army (FAAA) and to appoint Lieutenant General Lewis H. Brereton as Commanding General.[6]

Brereton was a senior airman with a chequered wartime history. He had had the worst possible start as Commanding General of the US Far East Air Force in the Philippines, when the majority of his bombers were destroyed on the ground by the Japanese on 8 December 1941. It was not entirely his fault as he had sought, and not been given, the authority to attack Formosa, which would have taken the bombers away at the time of the raid. General MacArthur attached no blame to him, sending him with the remaining bombers to safety in Australia, but Brereton was thought to have felt the disaster deeply. A short period in command of the American air contingent in the ill-fated ABDACOM (American, British, Dutch and Australian Command) was followed by his appointment to lead the USAAF in North Africa in the summer of 1942. There he built up what became Ninth Air Force, notable among other things for the bombing raid on the Romanian oilfields at Ploesti.

In September 1943 Ninth Air Force was transferred to the UK, where it became the tactical component of the USAAF in the European Theatre of Operations, being successfully employed before and during the invasion of Normandy and in support of the American troops on the ground during the campaign. Brereton, however, was not always easy to deal with,[7] being actively disliked by some of his compatriots, including Bradley, the most senior US ground forces commander, and it was possibly because of this that Eisenhower and Marshall decided to move him. Although he had absolutely no experience of airborne operations, he did know both the USAAF and the RAF very well at a senior level.

Boy was not at all happy with this decision. He was slightly senior to Brereton in his appointment as lieutenant general and he knew a great deal more about airborne operations. However, it is quite clear that he would have been totally unacceptable to the Americans, who at this point neither liked nor trusted him. Boy, for his part, did not care much for Brereton, whom he had met in North Africa and more recently in the UK. He nevertheless accepted the appointment as his deputy, whilst remaining GOC of I Airborne Corps, a situation which led to some confusion in the command structure. Although FAAA now took overall responsibility for training, supply and equipment and, through its direct command of IX US Troop Carrier Command and

38 and 46 Groups RAF, coordination with the air forces, the planning of operations fell between several stools. As far as Boy was concerned, his links to 21st Army Group and Second Army remained intact, as did his personal relationships with both Montgomery and Dempsey, and he continued to be the primary recipient of new proposals generated by them.

Another development took place at the same time, the formation of XVIII US Airborne Corps, which took under command 82 and 101 US Airborne Divisions, now returned from Normandy, and also 17 US Airborne Division, beginning to form in the UK under Major-General 'Bud' Miley. Ridgway, still highly suspicious of Boy, was appointed to command the new corps, with Gavin replacing him at 82 Airborne Division.

The first operation to be planned after the creation of FAAA was 'Transfigure', which envisaged 1 Airborne Division, 101 US Airborne Division and 1 Polish Parachute Brigade landing in two lifts to cut off the retreating Germans by closing the Paris-Orleans gap. They would be accompanied by 878 US Airborne Aviation Engineer Battalion and the newly formed Airborne Forward Delivery Airfield Group ('AFDAG'), which would respectively construct and operate an airfield for the arrival of 52 Division. All the troops would be under the command of I Airborne Corps, which had carried out the planning, as HQ FAAA was still in the course of formation.

The employment of an airborne corps HQ in such operations was by this time a matter of policy at the highest level. When Eisenhower wrote to Marshall on 28 July justifying the creation of FAAA, he had said: 'Assuming that an airborne attack by two or three divisions took place within a single area, a temporary corps commander would be designated to conduct the fighting on the ground. He would operate under directives issued by this headquarters until his forces could join up with the nearest army, whereupon he would be taken over by the army commander both operationally and logistically.'[8]

Boy flew to France to meet both Bradley and Montgomery on 9 August and, on his return, held a conference of all his subordinate commanders. Boy had decided to take with him an Advance HQ, consisting of 120 of the approximately 275 personnel at Moor Park, together with 78 British and 28 American signals personnel, who were allocated specifically for the operation. On 15 August Advance HQ relocated to the airfield at Harwell, where the gliders for the operation were all loaded, but by 17 August it was clear that Patton's Third Army was moving so quickly[9] that the operation would no longer be necessary and all the troops were stood down, Advance HQ returning to Moor Park on the following day.

More small abortive operations followed, including one to seize bridgeheads over the River Seine and another to capture Boulogne, but, like their predecessors, they were overtaken by events. Towards the end of August, an operation even larger than 'Transfigure' was planned, with a view to controlling the roads leading north through Tournai, Lille and Courtrai and thus cutting off the Germans retreating in front of Second Army. On 1 September Dempsey sent explicit instructions to

Boy to 'Facilitate in every way the move of 30 Corps to Brussels. This will include guarding all bridges in your area; policing all cross-roads in your area; and keeping all your own and civilian traffic off the roads which 30 Corps are using … Inform me by wireless of the location of your HQ directly it is established, together with the map reference of the nearest landing ground for light aircraft.' It was quite clear from this that Dempsey expected the Corps HQ to be on the ground controlling operations.

Operation 'Linnet' called for the 'Beneficiary' force to be further augmented by 82 US Airborne Division and the troops from all the formations concerned were moved to their airfields on 30 August, with Advance HQ of I Airborne Corps going once again to Harwell. On this occasion it was not so much events as weather which caused the cancellation. By 2 September, D-1, it had turned to heavy rain and that evening it was cancelled. In the event XXX Corps had an almost unimpeded advance to Brussels, Guards Armoured Division making a triumphal entry into the city on the next day.

This time the troops remained at their airfields as Brereton had an alternative plan in mind, 'Linnet II'. This involved landings by the same force in the Aachen-Maastricht area to block any retreat through the gap between the North Eiffel and the River Maas. It was conceived in haste and Boy protested to Brereton that maps of the area could not be distributed in time for an adequate briefing. On being told that the operation would only be cancelled on the orders of SHAEF or if the weather did not permit, he responded that he would submit a formal letter of protest on behalf of himself and his divisional commanders.

Once Boy had left the meeting Brereton summoned Ridgway and asked him if he thought the divisional commanders would join Boy's protest. Ridgway replied that he was sure that Gavin and Maxwell Taylor of 101 US Airborne Division would do as they were ordered without question, a characteristic of American commanders generally. He was asked to stand by to assume command if Boy persisted with his threat. The letter from Boy duly arrived, which not only registered a protest but said that the difference of opinion made it difficult for him to continue as Deputy Commanding General of FAAA and that he was therefore tendering his resignation.

Whether or not this was a bluff on Boy's part – and he was certainly right to raise questions about a totally inadequately planned operation – it was called by Brereton, who told him on the following day that the letter would be forwarded to Eisenhower and invited him to attach his comments.[10] Boy, realizing that 'Linnet II' would go ahead under Ridgway, who would then be in a very strong position to command any future operations, withdrew his resignation. Brereton had completely outflanked him, leaving the threat of being replaced by Ridgway on the table and putting him in an exceptionally weak position to question further plans. Notwithstanding the cancellation of 'Linnet II', like all its predecessors, this was a turning point in the relationship between the two men and entirely to Brereton's advantage.

Until the middle of July Boy had been pleased with the role in which he found himself. He was close to the centre of events and was in no doubt that the airborne forces were to see more action before long. He was unable to visit Daphne and the family, but she wrote to Tod: 'Tommy backwards and forwards to France all the time, but seems in good spirits and when he is back he rings up quite cheerfully.'[11] His later letters to her, however, began to expose his growing frustration. He was 'in the throes of ... plans and counter-plans. They change every 24 hours with the result that we don't know whether we'm standing on we head or we heels.'[12] The appointment of Brereton did not help and neither did the mood in his command.

Morale was becoming a serious issue among the British airborne forces, particularly at 52 Division, which had been part of Home Forces since 1940 and was highly trained for active service, and at 1 Airborne Division, which had been unemployed for nearly a year. Roy Urquhart wrote subsequently: 'By September 1944 my division was battle-hungry to a degree which only those who have commanded large forces of trained soldiers can fully comprehend. In fact there were already signs of that dangerous mixture of boredom and cynicism creeping into our daily lives.'[13] Some of Urquhart's commanders, including Hackett, believed that, if it were not committed to action shortly, the division would lose battle-worthiness and require retraining.

Following the cancellation of 'Transfigure' Boy issued a message to the whole of 1 Airborne Division, saying that he realized their irritation and disappointment and continuing: 'Hard though these periods of waiting are, we must appreciate that we may be used for the decisive plan only, and not frittered away on an approach which the Supreme Commander does not consider as vital and which can be achieved by other and less important means.' The morale issue was so serious that Boy even wrote to 21st Army Group demanding that Montgomery should land both divisions and his own HQ on the Continent immediately for active operations. The lack of action was also causing concern at SHAEF where Eisenhower, since Sicily somewhat equivocal in his support for airborne operations, chafed at the thought of six-and-a-half divisions of the best troops in the Allied armies sitting unused in the United Kingdom. The pressing need from above and below to get them into action was about to lead to rash decisions.

The first manifestation of this was Operation 'Comet', which was entirely Montgomery's creation. On 3 September, the day after the cancellation of 'Linnet', he sent a signal to Freddie de Guingand, his Chief of Staff: 'require airborne operation of one British Division and Poles on evening 6 Sep or morning 7 Sep to secure bridges over RHINE between WESEL and ARNHEM.' This operation would be the first embodiment of a strategy which Montgomery had been developing for some time, a concentrated thrust by the maximum available force across the Rhine, in order to envelop the Ruhr from the West and to turn from there into the heart of Germany. Everything he had seen in the last few weeks, since the destruction of much of the German Army at Falaise, had convinced him that that the remnants were on the run and that a determined effort would slice through them and end the war.

In some respects Montgomery was right. For a few short days after the fall of Brussels and Antwerp, the Germans were indeed streaming back towards the Reich in disorganized and demoralized groups and a well-conceived and thoroughly supported plan to keep up the pressure might well have done what he envisaged. Time, however, was not on his side, and neither were the by now creaking logistics of the Allied armies, whose supplies were still coming from Cherbourg and the 'Mulberry' harbour at Arromanches. Boy was summoned to Montgomery's Tac HQ for a meeting on 5 September and then sent on to Dempsey to plan the new operation.

For 'Comet', only 1 Airborne Division and 1 Polish Parachute Brigade were to be used for the initial landings, 1 Airborne Division at Arnhem, Divisional HQ, 1 Airlanding Brigade and the Poles at Nijmegen and 4 Parachute Brigade at Grave. There would be *coup de main* glider operations at the Arnhem, Nijmegen and Grave bridges. I Airborne Corps HQ would land with the second lift, although this would still take place on D-Day, and 52 Division would be flown in as soon as an airfield was secured. XXX Corps, with Guards Armoured Division in the van, would race up the road and cross the Rhine. On 7 September Boy flew over to Brussels to receive his final orders. 'At long last' he wrote to Daphne, 'will lead me drop into action. Alan Adair's party (Guards Armoured Division) will be behind us which is good as we shall be sure of good support.'[14]

His extreme frustration over the cancelled operations, his concern over falling morale in his command, his desire to lead his troops into battle before the war was over and his optimism about the collapse of the German Army had now got the better of Boy. Whilst there is no doubt that 'Comet' was Montgomery's idea, Boy had confirmed to him the ability of an augmented 1 Airborne Division to do the job alone, although in retrospect it would always have lacked the strength to hold the bridges, even against the broken German formations then retreating through Holland. Boy probably also influenced moving the axis of advance from Wesel, Montgomery's original objective on the Rhine, to Arnhem. Wesel had the advantage of only two major water obstacles on the way, the Maas and the Rhine, and much greater proximity to the Ruhr, but it brought the landings perilously close to the heavily concentrated anti-aircraft defences around the latter area, which were anathema to the RAF. Nijmegen and Arnhem were also much closer to the airfields in England, whilst success would have the added benefit of cutting off the V2 rocket sites, whose activities were causing great concern.

Boy's attitude towards the state of the German Army was by no means uncommon, indeed it was shared by many of those concerned. There were a number of doubters about 'Comet', however, and they included Hackett and Sosabowski. Hackett was privately appalled at the risk being taken. Both in North Africa and in Italy he had developed a healthy regard for the Germans' ability to recover from apparent defeat and to conduct a stubborn defence out of very little. Sosabowski was of like mind. During a briefing on the operation by Urquhart he was moved to interrupt with the words 'But the Germans, General ... the Germans'. It seemed to him and to others that this operation was assuming an almost complete lack of opposition, which was hardly likely to be the case.

Sosabowski also asked Urquhart to confirm his orders in writing, not a request likely to endear him to a superior officer, with its implications not just of release from responsibility, but of disagreement with the plan in the event that the outcome turned out badly. He persuaded Urquhart to accompany him to see Boy, where he told the latter that the operation needed at least one more division. He was certainly right, but his intervention was equally certainly unpopular.

Montgomery, however, was also having second thoughts. His concerns centred on the supply situation, with significant shortages of ammunition and fuel caused by the restricted capacity of the available ports.[15] Moreover the lack of transport was causing delays in bringing reinforcements up from Normandy, whilst resistance to Second Army was stiffening on the Albert Canal. This view was reinforced by Dempsey. In his diary on 9 September he wrote: 'It is clear that the enemy is bringing up all the reinforcements he can lay his hands on, and that he appreciates the importance of the area Arnhem-Nijmegen. It looks as though he is going to do all he can to hold it. This being the case, any question of a rapid advance to the North-East looks unlikely. Owing to our maintenance situation, we will not be in a position to fight a real battle for perhaps ten days or a fortnight. Are we right to direct Second Army to Arnhem or would it be better to hold a left flank along the Albert Canal, and strike due East towards Cologne in conjunction with First (US) Army?'

With these sentiments prevailing, Montgomery cancelled 'Comet' on the evening of 9 September, much to the relief of many concerned, but at the same time he ordered Dempsey and Boy to meet him in Brussels on the following day to discuss another and much larger operation.

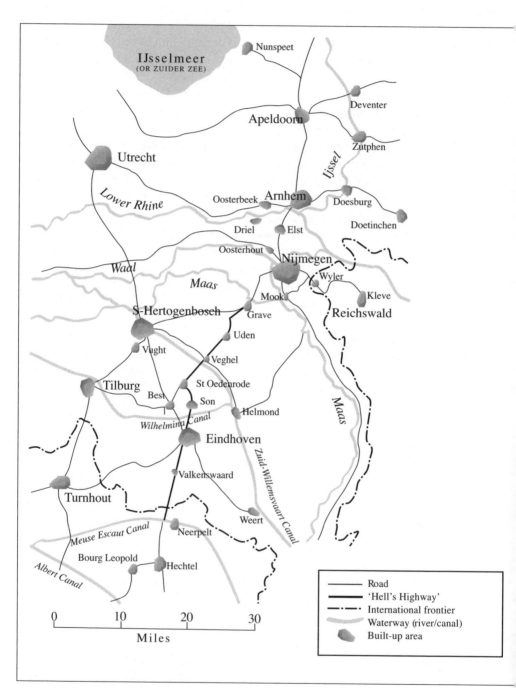

Map 1. The 'Market Garden' Battlefield

Chapter 17

Sixteen (10–16 September 1944)

Next to that of his first meeting with Daphne, 10 September 1944 was probably the most important day in Boy's life, the day on which the events were set in train which were to fix his place in history. There have been doubts expressed as to whether or not he actually saw Montgomery that day, but there is conclusive evidence that he did from the C-in-C himself, who recorded in his personal war diary: 'I had a conference with Dempsey and Browning and decided that we must use the whole Airborne Army on the air operations in the ARNHEM area; enemy resistance there is getting stronger.'[1] This is corroborated by an entry in the I Airborne Corps war diary: 'GOC to see C-in-C 21 Army Gp and Comd Second Army'.

The purpose of the meeting was for Montgomery to agree an outline plan for a scaled-up 'Comet', employing not only 1 Airborne Division, 52 Division and the Polish Parachute Brigade, but also both 82 and 101 US Airborne Divisions. The new operation was as audacious as its predecessor, the laying of an airborne carpet which crossed a series of water obstacles and passed through Eindhoven, Nijmegen and Arnhem. XXX Corps would advance rapidly up this corridor and on to the Ijsselmeer, cutting off all the enemy forces to the west and providing a platform to launch the Allied Armies into the North German Plain.

There is some question as to whose plan it was. Brigadier Charles Richardson, Montgomery's Brigadier (Plans), maintained subsequently that it was Boy's, which 'Monty enthusiastically adopted … as his own.'[2] Richardson had been heavily involved with the earlier operations on behalf of 21st Army Group and had spent almost as much time at Moor Park as Boy had done in France, so was close to the decision making, even if he was not himself at the key meeting. David Belchem, Brigadier (Operations), who was acting as Montgomery's Chief of Staff in place of Freddie de Guingand, then on sick leave in England, was clear that the plan was Montgomery's.

It was at this meeting that Boy supposedly introduced a new expression to the English language. The first mention of it came in Roy Urquhart's book *Arnhem*, published in 1958. According to Urquhart, Boy 'asked how long we would be required to hold the Arnhem Bridge. "Two days," said Monty briskly. "They'll be up with you then." "We can hold it for four," Browning replied. "But I think we might be going a bridge too far." '[3]

Considerable scepticism has been voiced as to whether Boy said any such thing. There were probably only three people present, Dempsey, Boy and Montgomery, the first two of whom never subsequently wrote or spoke publicly about the episode, whilst the last was not going to admit that any concerns had been expressed about the operation. Urquhart, whilst not present, was one of the first people to see Boy on his return from Belgium and thus a good witness, but an even better one was Walch, who wrote later:

> On being asked by General Montgomery for his general opinion of the proposed operation, General Boy said he thought it was possible, but that perhaps they might be going a bridge too far *with the air lift available* [author's italics]. His opinion was understood and appreciated; the operation was planned in detail by General Boy and he would be in command until the ground forces joined up.
>
> There have been differences of opinion as to whether or not General Boy did express the above comments to General Montgomery. I have no doubt about it. I was his chief staff officer. I had served under him for about three years and I saw him immediately after his return to Corps HQ to put the plan into operation. He told me exactly what I have recorded above, though for obvious reasons I was bound to complete secrecy. No doubt could be allowed which might affect the morale of the troops taking part in an operation which had been ordered and which though perhaps less certain of success than General Montgomery's former battles, was fully justified by the vital results which could reasonably be expected. Calculated risks have to be taken and the risks of this operation were fully calculated in the light of the information available. I have never previously broken my silence on this matter, but now, 45 years later, I think perhaps this statement may do more good than harm, if it gets any publicity.[4]

If Boy did say this, his reservations about stiffening resistance since the conception of 'Comet' were consistent with those of Dempsey, as expressed in the latter's diary on the previous day, although Boy would certainly have favoured an airborne operation over Dempsey's alternative of holding firm on the Albert Canal and driving eastwards towards Cologne with the Americans. Nevertheless, the operation only made strategic sense with the last bridge, an advance beyond which would cut off the enemy forces to the west and make available for the first time an excellent springboard into the Reich. Failure to get beyond Arnhem would leave the Allies in a dead end behind the Rivers Waal and Maas. However, it was no part of Boy's role to determine strategy, but rather to construct and execute a plan to deliver it. If Montgomery was set on it, which he clearly was, then his subordinate could offer an opinion. If this failed to change the C-in-C's mind, then he would have to make it work.

The operation has to be set in the context of the strategic debate which was now raging between Montgomery and Eisenhower and, if the Montgomery/Dempsey/Browning meeting was important, the one that followed between Monty and Ike at noon on the same day was even more so. Montgomery fervently believed that the way to end the war in 1944 was to concentrate the most powerful possible force in a single thrust across the Rhine downstream from the Ruhr, leaving the other Allied armies to hold their positions. The Supreme Commander was equally convinced that his forces should advance on a broad front, with identical prominence being accorded to each of the three army groups now in the field. In this he was motivated, at least in part, by political considerations: American public opinion would never have tolerated leaving Bradley and Patton without resources to the south-east, whilst a British-led northern thrust was afforded priority.

Eisenhower, who had flown up to Brussels from Normandy, had to remain on his plane as he had injured his knee and could only walk with difficulty. Montgomery had not met him since 26 August and now used this opportunity to pour out his grievances about the lack of supplies and his frustration at his superior's obduracy over the strategic issue. 'Steady Monty, you can't speak to me like that. I'm your boss,' said Eisenhower.[5] Montgomery, temporarily abashed, apologized but continued to advance his cause. Eisenhower refused to concede, but agreed to give limited priority to the northern thrust and, crucially, authorized the use of FAAA for the new operation. To Montgomery's disappointment he refused to scale down Patton's advance towards the Saar.

Two days later, Eisenhower appeared to change his mind.[6] Bedell Smith flew to Brussels on 12 September, to tell Montgomery that the Supreme Commander had agreed to halt the Saar thrust, divert the transport of three American divisions to 21st Army Group, give priority within Bradley's 12th Army Group to General Hodges' US First Army on Montgomery's immediate right and allow Montgomery to deal directly with Hodges. 'As a result of these changed conditions,' signalled Montgomery to Brooke, 'I have now fixed D (D) day for operation Market (rpt Market) previously known as Comet for Sunday next 17th Sep. So we have gained a great victory. I feel somewhat overcome by it all but hope we shall now win the war reasonably quickly.'[7] It was, unfortunately for all, an illusion. If Eisenhower did make such promises, he failed to keep them.

After a meeting later on 10 September with Dempsey, during which confirmation of the new operation was received from Montgomery, Boy flew back to England with the outline plan. He had previously signalled Brereton with the news that the operation had been authorized and the latter convened a meeting for the airborne divisional, brigade and regiment commanders, the air force chiefs and the key staff officers[8] at his HQ at Sunninghill Park, near Ascot, at 1800 that evening. Boy was the main speaker, outlining in clear terms the plan as it stood and the allocations of objectives to each of the formations. 101 US Airborne Division was to land along the main road from Eindhoven to Nijmegen and seize the bridges over the Wilhelmina Canal at Son, the Zuid Willemsvaart Canal at Veghel and the River Dommel at St Oedenrode. 82 US Airborne Division would land south of Nijmegen and take the bridge over the Maas at Grave, four bridges over the Maas-Waal Canal and the road bridge over the Waal at Nijmegen itself. 1 Airborne Division, with 1 Polish Parachute Brigade under command, was given the toughest assignment, the capture of the road, rail and pontoon bridges over the Lower Rhine at Arnhem. 52 Division would be flown in north of Arnhem once Deelen airfield had been captured.

The ground forces driving up the airborne corridor and out at the other end would be Brian Horrocks's XXX Corps, composed of the Guards Armoured Division, 43 (Wessex) Division and 8 Armoured Brigade, with 50 (Northumbrian) Division and the Royal Netherlands Brigade coming up behind. Simultaneous attacks would be launched by Richard O'Connor's VIII Corps and Neil Ritchie's XII Corps on either side of Horrocks, to expand the shoulders of the corridor.

There was some disappointment from the Americans that the British had been given the toughest assignment, but the justification was clear. Not only was 1 Airborne Division familiar with the target through its planning of 'Comet', but there would be political problems if Americans were left stranded north of the Rhine by a British relieving force. Ridgway was particularly unhappy. 'I well remember my bitter disappointment when General Brereton announced that he was giving command of this operation to General Browning. I had not anticipated this. We had two divisions committed to the operation. The British had one. We had won our spurs in three battles already – in Sicily, Italy and France. I felt in my heart that we could do a better job of commanding that operation than anyone else, and I imagine that I expressed these views, in private at least, with some fervor.'[9] Ridgway, with his extensive combat experience, was better qualified than Boy for command in the field. On the other hand he was wrong about the composition of the force, as the British were providing two-and-a-half divisions, including the Lowland Division and the Poles. He also ignored the facts that his own HQ was just one month old and that I Airborne Corps HQ had planned 'Comet' and was very familiar with the proposed battlefield. Finally he was naïve to ignore Boy's close personal relationships, both with Dempsey, the Army commander under which the corps would be placed, and with Horrocks of the relieving force.

The codename first allocated to the new operation was 'Sixteen', but by 11 September, when Boy received his formal orders from Brereton, it had been renamed 'Market' for the airborne element, whilst for those advancing from the south it became 'Garden'. The original target date was the night of 15/16 September, but this was in due course put back to the day of Sunday 17 September. The landings in Sicily and Normandy had been carried out in the hours of darkness and had been very largely inaccurate and scattered as a result. In this case there would be no moon from 17 September for a week, posing a high risk of a similar outcome. With growing allied air supremacy and a continuing lack of night flying experience in the USAAF, a daytime landing became not only possible but essential.

The first major issue to emerge affected all the formations. The available transports and glider tugs could carry no more than half the total force at one time and, with the likely losses of aircraft, three lifts would be required. Hollinghurst was prepared to carry out two lifts in one day, the first taking off before dawn, but Major General Paul L. Williams, the commander of IX US Troop Carrier Command, believed that crew fatigue and the need for maintenance during the turnaround prohibited this and insisted on the lifts taking place on consecutive days.[10] Brereton, himself an airman rather than a soldier, supported Williams and since a doctrine had been established that as far as air operations were concerned the air forces' view would have supremacy, the decision was forced upon the ground commanders. If there was one feature of the whole plan which doomed the operation to failure from the start, it was this.

There is evidence that Boy queried this decision, but he did not contest it vigorously and he has been much criticized for not doing so. He clearly understood the implications even before he went to Brussels and it appears from Walch's evidence that this was the very issue which had caused him to express doubts to Montgomery about the ability of the airborne forces to take and hold the last bridge. Although he might on 10 September still have hoped for two lifts on the first day, he was now in no position to argue the toss with Brereton. Even if he had made an issue of it, Williams was widely respected and Brereton stood behind him. Boy had already discovered what would happen if he made this a matter of principle: nothing would change except that Ridgway would assume command in his place. Montgomery, when he heard of the detailed plan two days later, did query spreading the lifts over three days and sent Belchem to Brereton to try to persuade him to change his mind, but Brereton refused to budge.

Within each of the formations other problems emerged. Major General Maxwell D. Taylor of 101 US Airborne Division complained that he was being asked to land on too many drop and landing zones on too long a corridor. He was concerned that his men would be so widely dispersed that they would not have sufficient force anywhere to take his objectives. He appealed to Brereton and in this case the air forces had no objection to a greater concentration. Because this aspect of the plan had come from Second Army, Brereton sent Taylor in person to see Dempsey, who approved a revised plan with fewer drop and landing zones. One feature of the new plan was that there would be no drop on the south side of the canal bridge at Son.

The main issue for 1 Airborne Division was the location of the drop zones and once again this was driven by airmen, in this case led by Hollinghurst. The area of open ground nearest to the Arnhem road bridge was immediately to the south, but the RAF asserted that it was unsuitable for gliders, being low-lying polder with ditches and high banks.[11] Furthermore, there were believed to be strong anti-aircraft defences around the bridge, whilst the airmen feared that turning away after the drops would bring their aircraft over Deelen airfield, which was also thought to be heavily defended by flak batteries. Their solution was the open farmland and heath north of Heelsum for the first lift and Ginkel Heath, even further away, for the second. This would land the division some six to eight miles from its objective, with a lot of built-up area in between. Lacking adequate transport, the paratroopers would have to march there. Moreover, only 1 Parachute Brigade would be available for the attack on the bridge, as 1 Airlanding Brigade would have to remain close to where it had landed in order to protect the drop zones for the second lift.

Boy held Hollingworth in high regard and there is no evidence that he made any great attempt to change his mind. Urquhart pressed Boy for more planes for the first drop, but was told that the priority had to be 'bottom to top', so that the divisions reached first by XXX Corps should have the best possible chance of achieving their objectives. Boy was nevertheless concerned enough to consult his most experienced airborne commander, Gale, who was insistent that there should be a *coup de main* landing close to the bridge and said that if he had been in command he would have resigned rather than accept the plan as it stood. He was asked by Boy not to reveal the substance of this conversation, almost certainly to avoid damaging morale.[12]

For Gavin and 82 US Airborne Division, the problem was one of priorities. With two large bridges to capture, at Grave and Nijmegen, and several smaller ones, he would have to split up his force into small units. He had another issue to consider. Almost the only high ground in the area of operation lay south-east of Nijmegen, lying between the Maas and the Maas-Waal Canal on one side and the low polder along the Waal on the other. On either side of the little town of Groesbeek the heights faced the Reichswald forest, just across the German border. There was a serious concern that the Germans could attack out of the Reichswald and seize the heights, which would then allow them to dominate the route to be taken by XXX Corps as it crossed the Maas-Waal Canal. The extent of the possible threat was made more urgent by a report referred to in the SHAEF G2 (Intelligence) Summary of 13 September: 'One thousand tanks reported in Forest of REICHSWALD (E85) in Holland on 8 September, presumably a pool for refitting Panzer Divisions.'[13]

Boy and Gavin were of like mind about the priorities. Without the Grave Bridge and one or more bridges fit for tanks over the Maas-Waal Canal, XXX Corps would be unable to pass through, so the capture intact of these was imperative. The significance of the Groesbeek Heights meant that it too had to be a priority objective, not least because the second lift was planned to arrive on landing and drop zones dominated by this feature. The Nijmegen Bridge would thus have to have a lower priority, although Gavin proposed to detach a battalion against it in the event that the Groesbeek Heights were secured quickly. Once again, the insistence of the airmen on not carrying two lifts on the first day gravely compromised the operation.

As in five previous aborted operations, the Advance HQ of I Airborne Corps was to take to the field. It would consist of most of the 'G' staff, both operations and intelligence, together with liaison officers from FAAA, each of the American divisions and the Polish Parachute Brigade, four members of the Dutch Liaison Mission, a number of Civil Affairs officers, including two more Dutchmen, and a detachment from Phantom, the GHQ Liaison Regiment. Together these totalled 105 officers and men, with 12 jeeps and 10 trailers, between them requiring 14 Horsas. An additional 18 Horsas would be required for the newly formed signals section and the RAF Light Warning Units, which would supply radar coverage and control Second Tactical Air Force's ground attack operations. These would carry another 115 officers and men, 15 jeeps and 16 trailers. Six Waco Hadrians carrying 15 men and 6 jeeps would also be employed to bring in an American Air Support Signals party. The use of the 38 gliders, or more pertinently their tugs, would deny them to 1 Airborne Division, resulting in two-and-a-half companies from 2nd Battalion The South Staffordshire Regiment (2 South Staffs) and six 6-pounder anti-tank guns having to wait for the second lift.

Main HQ, totalling 107 officers and men, largely from the 'A' and 'Q' branches and the services –RAOC, RASC, REME and RAMC – would come up by road with XXX Corps, whilst a Rear HQ of some 60 would remain at Moor Park, dealing with aspects of resupply, providing additional wireless contact with 21st Army Group and Second Army and passing messages through to FAAA and the Troop Carrier Command Post. Gale was instructed to act as Boy's deputy at Moor Park during the operation.

The decision to take the HQ into the field has been widely criticized but once Boy had been appointed to command, as he had been verbally by Montgomery and Dempsey on 10 September, and in writing by Brereton on the following day, it was unthinkable that he could have done anything else. Montgomery was adamant that his corps and divisional commanders should be located as close as possible to the front line and would never have tolerated the exercise of control from hundreds of miles away. It was so far from established practice that is unlikely that the parties even gave this any thought. In any event, it was not the corps commander's own decision, other than at a purely tactical and local level, where to site his HQ, as he was at the disposal of his army commander, in this case Dempsey. The latter had made it quite clear that he wanted Boy on the spot for 'Linnet' and would have expected no less for a plan which placed the airborne forces even further away from the ground forces' start point.

From a personal perspective, Boy was desperate to lead his troops into action. Whilst waiting for 'Comet' to get the go ahead, he had written to Daphne to say that he envied 'the people who are strongly ensconced in France in command of their divisions or corps with no worries except the battle in front of they faces.'[14] In such a mood he was unlikely to want to do anything to prevent this happening and, although carrying out Montgomery's plan and not upsetting morale any further were also uppermost in his mind, he was not going to do anything to jeopardize his chances. Moreover, he genuinely believed that the Germans were on the run and his attitude was not uncommon. Brian Urquhart was one of relatively few 'worried by the state of mind of General Browning and my brother officers. There seemed to be a general assumption that the war was virtually over and that one last dashing stroke would finish it.'[15] This mindset was by no means confined to I Airborne Corps, but was prevalent at SHAEF, where in early September Eisenhower believed that he was on the brink of victory, at 21st Army Group and at FAAA, as Brereton had proved by his willingness to take a serious risk in 'Linnet II' without any real planning at all. Urquhart ascribed the attitude primarily to those who, like Boy, had participated in September 1918 in the breach of the Hindenburg Line and the capitulation of the German Army two months later. As he correctly surmised, it was about to contribute to a gross underestimation of the capabilities of the enemy. He expressed his concerns to Walch among others, but the BGS would hear no criticism of the plan.

Urquhart, as Boy's senior intelligence officer, was also becoming seriously worried about both the number and the quality of the opposing forces in the operational areas and specifically in the neighbourhood of Arnhem. Intelligence was largely derived from Second Army, where Dempsey, unlike Boy, was privy to the product of Ultra decryptions of German radio communications. The situation was a fast moving one, however, and Ultra was, if anything, becoming less valuable the closer the Germans got to their own country and the more they were able to use fixed lines rather than wireless. Nevertheless, in the fortnight leading up to the launch of 'Market Garden', Ultra produced some valuable information. Potentially the most alarming report came on 5 September when II SS Panzer Corps was said to be in the Venlo-Arnhem-'s-Hertogenbosch area, but thereafter it disappeared from view. On 13 September, Ultra described Army Group B as chiefly concerned with establishing whether the Allies were preparing to advance on Aachen or to Arnhem. On 15 September there were two relevant decrypts, the first identifying Army Group B's HQ as located in Oosterbeek, directly between 1 Airborne Division's landing sites and Arnhem, whilst the second indicated correctly that the probable intention of XXX Corps was to thrust forward on either side of Eindhoven to Arnhem to cut off German forces in the western Netherlands.

This information was not available to Boy or to Brian Urquhart, but the latter was growing concerned about suggestions in 21st Army Group's intelligence summaries and reports from the Dutch Resistance[16] that two panzer divisions, 9 SS (Hohenstaufen) and 10 SS (Frundsberg), might be in the Arnhem area. This was not entirely unknown to 1 Airborne Division, whose own intelligence summary on 7 September had stated: 'It is reported that one of the broken panzer divisions has been sent back to the area north of ARNHEM to rest and refit; this might produce 50 tanks ... .'

With neither Boy nor Walch sharing his concerns, Urquhart commissioned a low-level RAF photo-reconnaissance mission in the Arnhem area which showed tanks and other armoured vehicles within striking distance of the drop and landing zones. He rushed to Boy with these but was fobbed off with a comment that the vehicles were probably not serviceable. Not long afterwards Brigadier Eagger, the DDMS, sent him off on sick leave on the grounds that he was suffering from nervous exhaustion. Before Urquhart left, however, he had conveyed the information to others. On 12 September, in the course of a conference at Moor Park, Urquhart had an opportunity to show the photos to the division's brigade majors during their intelligence briefing, telling them that there was evidence from Dutch Resistance that the two SS divisions were located between Arnhem and Zutphen but that Boy had dismissed it. A flavour of this emerged in 1 Parachute Brigade's intelligence briefing on 13 September, which read: 'A reported concentration of 10,000 troops SW of ZWOLLE on 1 Sep may represent a battle scarred Pz Div or two reforming, or alternatively the result of emptying in ARNHEM and EDE barracks to make room for fighting troops.' Zwolle, whilst much further away than Zutphen, was still too close to Arnhem for comfort.

Urquhart was not the only one to be worried. The intelligence about the panzer divisions had been picked up at SHAEF by Major General Kenneth Strong's G2 (Intelligence) Division, appearing in its weekly summary on 16 September: '9 SS Panzer Division, and with it presumably 10, has been reported as withdrawing altogether to the ARNHEM area of HOLLAND: there they will probably collect some new tanks from the depot reported in the area of CLEVES.' Approaching Eisenhower, Strong was instructed to fly immediately to 21st Army Group's HQ with Bedell Smith. Smith saw Montgomery alone and suggested that the airborne drop should be strengthened, but at this late stage the C-in-C was not prepared to change the plan. Wing Commander Asher Lee, a senior air intelligence officer at FAAA, also became aware of the presence of German armour through other channels. With Brereton's knowledge he went to Brussels, but was unable to get any sufficiently senior officer at 21st Army Group to give him time and returned disappointed. There was, nonetheless, concern among Montgomery's staff, where Belchem pointed out the dangers and de Guingand even rang his chief from England to ask him to reconsider. Montgomery, however, was by now completely set on the operation and would allow no dissent. As far as outsiders were concerned, the staff followed his line.

The die was now cast. The plan, risky though it appeared to many, was set in concrete. Even some of the critics, like Shan Hackett, were keen to be in action as soon as possible rather than have another cancellation, as morale among the troops had risen again at the prospect. Boy himself, even if he harboured doubts about the plan, was totally committed. He genuinely felt that he would be participating in an operation which could end the war and that the chances of success were good. His last engagements before setting out for the airfield were a briefing for Prince Bernhard of the Netherlands and a cheerful lunch with Brereton.[17]

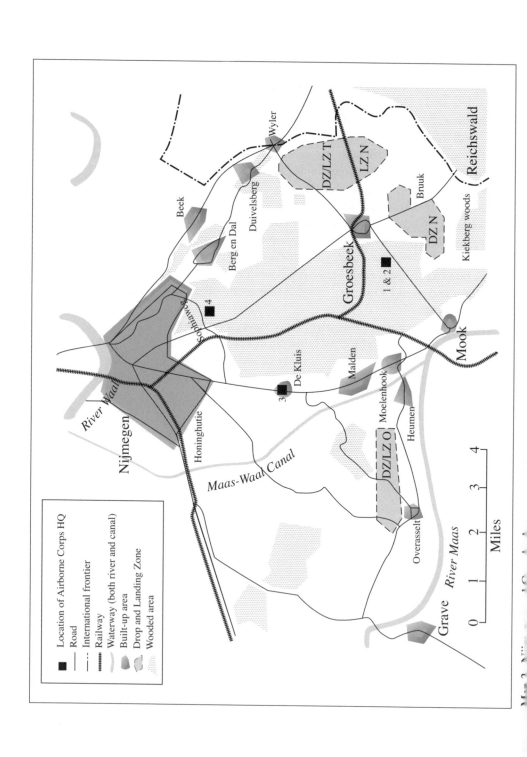

Legend:

- ■ Location of Airborne Corps HQ
- Road
- International frontier
- Railway
- Waterway (both river and canal)
- Built-up area
- Drop and Landing Zone
- Wooded area

Nijmegen

River Waal

Honinghutie

Maas-Waal Canal

Beek

Berg en Dal

Duivelsberg

Wyler

DZ/LZ T

LZ N

Groesbeek

Bruuk

DZ N

Kiekberg woods

Reichswald

Sophiaweg

■ 4

De Kluis

■ 3

Malden

Moelenhook

Heumen

1 & 2 ■

Mook

DZ/LZ O

Overasselt

Grave

River Maas

Miles

0   1   2   3   4

Chapter 18

Market (17–20 September 1944)

On 14 September the Advance HQ of I Airborne Corps moved to Harwell, where the gliders were loaded. Boy himself arrived there early on the morning of 17 September, a few hours before take-off. He was carrying kid gloves and a swagger stick and wearing his airborne beret with general's badge and a double-breasted uniform tunic of his own design, made up for him specially by a firm of tailors in London and based on that of a German Uhlan of the Great War.[1] He was in very high spirits, in spite of the fact that he was nursing a heavy cold, which he thought he had picked up from the flying helmet he had worn on his way to Brussels on 10 September.

There to see off the HQ were SHAEF's Deputy Supreme Commander, Air Chief Marshal Tedder, and Brereton's Chief of Staff, Brigadier General Floyd L. Parks. The latter was intrigued by the contents of Boy's glider.[2] 'I have never seen so much junk,' he told Brereton later, 'it looked like a gypsy caravan. There were bicycles, bazookas, bedding rolls, radios, and all sorts of stuff he planned to use for his Command Post.'[3] He would have been even more surprised had he investigated the contents of Boy's pack, which contained four items that went with him everywhere on his travels. Three were teddy bears and the fourth was a framed print of Albrecht Dürer's famous drawing *The Praying Hands*, which he had carried with him from the Great War onwards.

At 1120 Boy's glider was the first of the HQ to leave, pulled by a Stirling of 295 Squadron, piloted by Wing Commander Angel. His fellow passengers were Cator, Major Spencer Thomas, the GSO2 (Ops), Captain Louis, the HQ Medical Officer, and four other ranks, including Johnson and Boy's driver, Johannides. The pilots were Chatterton himself and Major Andy Andrews, with Boy positioned just behind them, perched on an old Worthington beer crate. In a letter to Daphne on the previous day, he described himself as the third pilot, 'in the event of them being shot in the backside.'[4] Across a wide swathe of Southern and Eastern England, 1,534 aircraft and 491 gliders were taking off from 24 airfields at much the same time, a colossal feat of planning and logistics. They had been preceded by thousands of other aircraft, bombers from Bomber Command and US Eighth Air Force and both fighters and bombers from Second Tactical Air Force and US Ninth Air Force, which had hit German airfields, flak batteries and barracks along the route and at the destinations.

The weather over England was dry and partly cloudy, the cloud melting away as the armada crossed the North Sea before bubbling up again after the Dutch coast had been crossed. Some light flak was encountered, but caused no damage. Advance HQ was to use Landing Zone N near Bruuk, south of Groesbeek. The tugs approached from west-south-west and cast off the gliders as they crossed the Maas. The gliders then flew on briefly over the edge of the Reichswald before turning north for the landing. Boy's glider touched down just before 1400 in an allotment full of cabbages behind some cottages, losing its front wheel in the process, but leaving the passengers and crew intact. It was followed immediately by the glider carrying among others Walch and Newberry and piloted by Major Billy Griffith[5] and then by the rest of the HQ. The BGS was surprised to see Boy leap out and run over to the nearby wood. On being asked on his return what he was doing he replied: 'I wanted to be the first Allied soldier to pee in Germany!'[6]

Mindful of a possible German reaction, the staff unloaded the gliders and moved off as quickly as possible to the agreed site for the HQ, which was just north of the road from Mook to Groesbeek and not far from Gavin's Command Post. There were only three casualties, Lieutenant Gee of the Royal Signals and his driver, who were blown up by a mine leaving the landing zone, and Wing Commander Brown of the RAF, the officer in command of the RAF Light Warning Units, who was killed on the landing zone later by a strafing Messerschmidt 109.

Three gliders failed to arrive, one after experiencing difficulties over the UK and one landing in the sea off Walcheren. The third, carrying members of the Corps HQ Phantom detachment and an American liaison officer, came down near Dongen, between Breda and 's-Hertogenbosch. The occupants were attacked by German soldiers and one of them was killed before they surrendered. The American officer, Lieutenant Prentiss, tried to burn the papers he was carrying, but some were not destroyed. It is probably these which were delivered to General Student at his HQ at Vught that afternoon and which he claimed contained details of the plan for the whole operation, although what survived was actually only the operational order for 101 Airborne Division. Student had some experience of losing plans himself when two of his officers had made a forced landing in a light aircraft in Belgium with plans for the airborne landings in 1940[7] and he may have welcomed the chance to prove that this could happen to anyone. Even if they were not the full plans those for 101 Airborne, which had landed in Student's operational area, would have been still very valuable, giving as they did details of the second and third lifts. Why an officer as junior as Lieutenant Prentiss was carrying such sensitive documents has never been explained.

Radio communication was established by I Airborne Corps with both 82 Airborne Division and Rear HQ in England, with Second Army on the Phantom net and, after some delay, with XXX Corps, but no contact could be made with either 1 or 101 Airborne Divisions. By early evening the news from 82 Airborne was good. It had achieved most of its immediate objectives, first and foremost of which was the bridge over the Maas at Grave, the longest in Europe, where a landing on the south side had taken the Germans by surprise. By late afternoon the lock bridge across the Maas-Waal Canal at Heumen had also been seized. Two of the other canal bridges were blown up in the faces of the attackers, whilst the Honinghutie rail and road bridges were badly damaged before their capture early on the following morning. On the most direct route for XXX Corps to Nijmegen, the Honinghutie bridges remained open to foot traffic and light vehicles, but could not carry tanks, which would now have to cross the canal at Heumen. This would bring them much closer to the high ground and increase the importance of continuing to hold it.

Gavin had also positioned troops at key points along the Groesbeek Heights and was sufficiently confident as night fell to be able to send 1/508 Parachute Infantry towards the Nijmegen Bridge. As the troopers approached they came under heavy fire, were forced to pull back and then cut off. A platoon from the 3/508 Parachute Infantry was also repulsed. Reinforcements were sent, but this only had the effect of thinning out the units facing the Reichswald, from which German infantry was now beginning to deploy.

Boy met Gavin on the evening of D-Day, driving over to the latter's Command Post. He arrived back at his own HQ to find that it was about to be relocated, as a German ammunition dump had been discovered nearby. With Gavin clearly on top of the situation, Boy's main concern was communications with the other airborne forces. It had been agreed in advance that 101 Airborne would come under the command of XXX Corps as soon as it had landed and would remain so until Dempsey, Boy and Horrocks agreed otherwise. Communications with Taylor were desirable, but not essential in the immediate future. Of far greater importance was 1 Airborne, which was under Boy's direct command and with which there was no contact at all.

As 18 September dawned, the news from the south was less satisfactory, as a report was received that Guards Armoured Division had been held up south of Eindhoven. In fact it had encountered serious resistance at Valkenswaard and had been forced to harbour for the night. Boy was also shortly to find out that 101 Airborne, which had taken the majority of its objectives on the first day, had failed in the case of the bridge over the Wilhelmina Canal at Son, possibly as a result of Taylor's decision not to land a party on the south side. Taylor had managed to get a small force across and now held both ends of a makeshift footbridge, but any vehicles would require a Bailey bridge, which could only come up behind Guards Armoured. The original timetable was now beginning to slip badly.

During the morning of 18 September the Germans continued to build up their forces facing Gavin from the Reichswald and along the road between Wyler and Nijmegen. The plan was for 450 gliders to arrive in the early afternoon, carrying much of his artillery and a battalion of engineers, followed by a major supply drop by parachute, but the Germans had infiltrated the landing and drop zones. Gavin immediately brought up what reserves he possessed and ordered them to clear the ground, but fighting was still continuing as the gliders arrived at 1400. Notwithstanding, the operation was highly successful with most of the guns and jeeps being recovered, together with 80 per cent of the supplies.

Boy spent the day visiting all parts of his extensive front. He knew by this time that the second lift of 1 Airborne had left England as planned, but he had news neither of its arrival nor of any other events at Arnhem. The first intimation of what was going on was not received until 0800 on 19 September, when a short signal reported that elements of 1 Parachute Brigade had penetrated into Arnhem, but were no longer in possession of the north end of the bridge. This, as it subsequently turned out, was inaccurate as John Frost's 2nd Parachute Battalion was still holding on tenaciously.

The fog of war now descended on Boy, as such news as he was able to garner from or about 1 Airborne, some of which came from the Dutch Resistance through the still functioning telephone system, was infrequent and often contradictory.[8] He did not know it, but by dawn on 19 December the situation was already dire. Frost still held the north end of the bridge and had successfully repulsed the 9 SS Panzer Division Reconnaissance Battalion, which had crossed the bridge on its way to Nijmegen before the arrival of the British paratroopers and then returned to try to retake it. The advance of 1st and 3rd Parachute Battalions, on the other hand, had been held up by blocking forces defending the roads into Arnhem. Urquhart, handicapped by non-existent communications, had gone forward into Arnhem with Lathbury of 1 Parachute Brigade to find out what was happening and been cut off, Lathbury being subsequently wounded. Philip Hicks, the commander of 1 Airlanding Brigade, had taken temporary command of the division, a situation not at all to the liking of Hackett, whose 4 Parachute Brigade had landed in the middle of a battle. With no forward progress possible, the divisional HQ had already been relocated to the Hartenstein Hotel in Oosterbeek, where it was to remain for the duration of the battle.

Other than his deep concern about events at Arnhem, 19 September started well for Boy when he was informed that Guards Armoured Division would be arriving at the Grave Bridge early in the morning. With Chatterton acting as his driver, he and Gavin rendezvoused at Overasselt to greet the Guards.[9] Boy now found himself among very old friends. The first tanks to arrive were those of the 2nd Battalion Grenadier Guards, in which he had served for most of the Great War and commanded immediately prior to leaving the regiment. Its Commanding Officer was Lieutenant Colonel Rodney Moore, who had been a subaltern in the 3rd Battalion in the early 1930s, whilst Moore's opposite number in the 1st Battalion, which provided the infantry element of the Grenadier Guards Group, was Lieutenant Colonel Eddie Goulburn, who had served under Boy in Egypt. The Grenadiers were followed by the 3rd Battalion Irish Guards whose Commanding Officer, Joe Vandeleur, had commanded another battalion of the same regiment in 24 Guards Brigade Group in 1941. At a more senior level Brigadier Norman Gwatkin of 5 Guards Armoured Brigade was, like Boy, a former Adjutant at Sandhurst, whilst the divisional commander, Allan Adair, was a longstanding friend of Boy's own generation.

Many of the Grenadiers were to remember seeing Boy standing by the side of the road, immaculately dressed as ever. They included Boy's cousin, Brian Johnston, and Peter Carrington, who recalled that Boy took one look at the dusty guardsmen and said 'I told you that it was better to come by air!'[10] The mood of festivity, however, was shortly to give way to more serious matters, particularly once Horrocks had appeared on the scene. As he wrote later: 'Boy Browning and I were old friends, and from now onwards we took all the major decisions together without any semblance of friction.'[11] In the light of future events, this might be seen as generous, but for the time being it was certainly true.

A meeting was held at noon between Boy, Horrocks, Adair and Gwatkin at Boy's new HQ, which had just moved to a house on the road to Nijmegen at De Kluis, north of Malden, so as to be on Guards Armoured's axis of advance. Adair recalled that 'General Browning was in his usual fine form – clear, definite, coping well with the involved situation and pressing the urgency to relieve the 1st Airborne Division.'[12] Gavin arrived later and he and Adair agreed that the Grenadier Guards Group should cooperate with 2/505 Parachute Infantry in an attack on the south end of the Nijmegen Bridge, but this was unable to kick off before 1700 hrs. As the Americans formed Gavin's divisional reserve, Boy arranged for him to receive the Coldstream Guards Group as replacements. However, in spite of outstanding cooperation between the British and the Americans, the paratroopers and Grenadiers were unable to break through the defences and the attack was called off after dark. It was now clear to all that the defenders were both more numerous and of better quality than they had been led to expect.

Apart from the surprisingly stubborn defence of the Nijmegen Bridge, the tentative attacks on the Groesbeek Heights and the difficulty experienced by Guards Armoured in breaking through south of Eindhoven, neither Boy nor his fellow commanders yet had a complete picture of the scale of the German response to Market Garden, which had been both swift and vigorous. It was coordinated by Field Marshal Model, C-in-C of Army Group B, who had been rudely surprised in his HQ at Oosterbeek by the arrival of 1 Airborne. Known as 'the Führer's Fireman', Model was a skilful, energetic and ruthless commander who had on numerous occasions pulled the Wehrmacht's chestnuts out of the fire on the Eastern Front. Decamping with some speed, he had arrived at General Bittrich's HQ II SS Panzer Corps at Doetinchen less than two hours later and immediately began to make his dispositions.

Bittrich himself was charged with defending Arnhem and the Nijmegen bridgehead with 9 and 10 SS Panzer Divisions, which had both arrived from Normandy significantly reduced in numbers and equipment. The full 1944 establishment of a panzer division was 14,700 men and 100 tanks; on 17 September 9 SS Panzer had approximately 2,500 men and no tanks, whilst 10 SS Panzer had approximately 3,000 men and a few tanks. However, both were composed of seasoned veterans of Russia and Normandy, who had been specifically trained in combating airborne operations, and possessed a variety of other armoured vehicles, including self-propelled guns. 9 SS Panzer, less its Reconnaissance Regiment, which had gone south to Nijmegen and been nearly destroyed on its return, was ordered to recapture the Arnhem Bridge and to hold off any further advance towards it by 1 Airborne. A motley collection of other units was put together under Lieutenant General von Tettau[13] to attack the airborne positions around Oosterbeek from the west. 10 SS Panzer was directed on Nijmegen, with orders to hold the bridge there and, in the event that there was any crossing of the Waal, the southern approaches to Arnhem. As the Arnhem Bridge was closed, the division would have to cross the Lower Rhine by the Pannerden ferry, whose limited capacity would slow its build-up.

South of the Maas, facing Second Army's front on the Meuse-Escaut Canal and on either side of the airborne corridor between Eindhoven and Grave, the command was placed in the hands of General Student at First Parachute Army. In order to attack the corridor, Model arranged for it to receive such reinforcements as could be spared, including 59 Infantry Division and 107 Panzer Brigade. The attacks on 82 Airborne from the Reichswald were to be the responsibility of Corps Feldt, composed of whatever units could be found, including a NCO school and some Luftwaffe and 'stomach and ear' battalions.[14] Model, however, promised to send immediately two parachute divisions, which were refitting near Cologne. These were in practice reduced to not much more than battalion strength, but they were composed of tough and experienced troops.

Particularly when they were on the defensive, the Germans had an extraordinary ability to form ad hoc *Kampfgruppen* (battle groups) of almost any size, led by the most senior officer, or even NCO, available. Each *Kampfgruppe* could be created out of a larger formation or from a variety of smaller units or parts of units and it could take any shape and absorb soldiers from all arms. A large number of these were formed during the course of Market Garden and many proved to be highly effective.

With stalemate at the Nijmegen Bridge, a further meeting was convened for the senior commanders at 2000 on 19 September. Boy had already impressed on Gavin the urgent need to take the Nijmegen Bridge and he now required a plan to achieve this. Moore, Goulburn and Vandeleur were all present, wearing the informal dress adopted by many Guards officers of corduroy trousers, suede boots and battledress top, behind which was an old school scarf, or a bright green one in the case of Vandeleur. 'They wore a most amazing air of nonchalance', wrote Chatterton, who was present, 'and gave the impression that this was not a battle but an exercise near Caterham barracks. In contrast to them Colonel Tuck,[15] the American commander, had a tin hat on which covered his whole face, a jumping jacket on which there were several decorations (including our own DSO), a pistol strapped under each arm, a knife on the right-hand side, long trousers and lace-up boots. He chewed a fat cigar and every now and then spat. Each time he did so a faint look of surprise flickered over the faces of the Guards officers.'[16] Even allowing for some hyperbole, this vignette encapsulates the differences between the officers of the two armies.

Boy had asked for a plan and Gavin arrived with one, but it required boats.[17] He proposed to put a battalion of Tucker's regiment across the Waal west of the town and attack both the rail and road bridges at their north ends. He asked Horrocks about the availability of the boats and, although these were well back in the XXX

Corps column, the staff thought that they could be brought up by daylight. Boy and Horrocks, the former evidently filled with admiration at its boldness, both gave their agreement to the plan.

On the morning of the following day, the Grenadiers and Lieutenant Colonel Ben Vandervoort's 2/505 Parachute Infantry moved against both bridges, but made very slow progress, whilst Tucker's men, supported by the tanks of the Irish Guards, cleared the river bank at the site of the proposed crossing. The boats, however, were seriously delayed by the traffic jam on the single carriageway road leading up from Eindhoven, which was already subject to attack from Germans. 107 Panzer Brigade had put in two vigorous attacks on the new bridge at Son and, although both were repulsed by 101 Division and British tanks, free movement had been halted. Time and again the crossing operation was postponed until it was eventually scheduled to begin at 1500, the boats arriving half an hour before that.

Shortly before the boats' arrival, Gavin was called away urgently by serious developments on his southern front, where the Germans had taken Mook, which was perilously close to the Heumen Bridge, and had also overrun the defenders at Beek, below the ridge looking north-east towards the Waal over the flat polder. These attacks were part of a coordinated operation involving three separate attacks, the third against Groesbeek itself, by *Kampfgruppen* which now included the German paratroopers from Cologne, who were to prove a much tougher proposition than the second-rate soldiers encountered earlier. Gavin rushed away initially to Mook, where the situation was on a knife-edge but was eventually restored with the help of the Coldstream Guards' tanks, and then to Beek and the nearby village of Berg-en-Dal, where the Americans had created a strongpoint around the hotel. The Germans focused on this, but Gavin was later to say that if they had slipped between the defenders, they would have had a clear run into Nijmegen. Fighting at all three sites was to continue through the night, but peter out on the following day, with the Americans retaining the key defensive positions.

Back on the Waal, Boy, Horrocks and Adair stood on the roof of the power station near where the Maas-Waal Canal entered the river, whilst the operation unfolded at their feet. Boy was now seriously worried. During the morning he had received the first direct signal from 1 Airborne and the news was not good. The division had no contact with Frost at the bridge, whilst Arnhem itself was by now entirely in enemy hands. Intense fighting was being experienced and immediate relief was urgent. The only solution seemed to lie with the forthcoming assault crossing by 3/504 Parachute Infantry, led by Major Julian Cook. The boats, when they arrived, proved to be made of collapsible canvas, heavy, paddle-driven and difficult to manoeuvre. The river itself was 400 yards wide, with a current running at eight to ten knots, and on the far side there was 500 yards of polder to cross in front of an embankment.

Preceded by a barrage from rocket firing Typhoons of the RAF and supported by their own artillery and the guns of the Irish Guards' tanks, which put down a smoke screen, the Americans picked up the twenty-eight boats and carried them down to the river. The crossing was subject to heavy fire from the far bank, many boats were sunk and casualties were high. The survivors leapt out and rushed across the polder towards the embankment, many falling in the process, whilst the remaining boats turned round for further crossings.[18] Boy turned to Horrocks and said 'I have never seen a more gallant action.'

Overwhelming the defenders on the far embankment, Cook's paratroopers turned right and made for the bridges, taking the old Dutch Fort Hof van Holland on the way. In the meantime, heavy fighting was continuing in Nijmegen, where the Grenadiers and Vandervoort's paratroopers were inching towards the road bridge, having by now pushed the Germans back into a small perimeter around the old medieval fortifications of the Valkhof and the nearby Hunner Park, with its prominent belvedere. The defenders had received reinforcements from 10 SS Panzer Division and were resisting tenaciously, but gradually they were winkled out of their strongholds. On the other side, Cook's men reached the north end of the railway bridge, which they took and held, whilst a group had penetrated to about 1,000 yards north of the road bridge. A signal was received by the Grenadiers in Nijmegen saying that the far end of the bridge had been captured and, in the mistaken belief that this referred to the road bridge, a troop of Sherman tanks was made ready to storm across.

As the last defenders were pushed away from the southern end of the road bridge, Moore ordered Sergeant Robinson to lead the way. Initially the tanks were driven back by anti-tank fire, but with the light fading, another attempt was made. This time Robinson and Sergeant Pacey drove their tanks onto the bridge itself and raced forward. A brief duel ensued with a German 88mm gun positioned at the far end, but this was destroyed by accurate shooting and the two Shermans sped across, followed by another two on their heels and then by Peter Carrington, the second-in-command of the squadron, with two more. In a bunker close to the north end SS Brigadier General Harmel, the commander of 10 SS Panzer Division, who had been given strict instructions by Model not to destroy the bridge but to preserve it for a counter-attack, gave the order to blow it, but the detonators failed and the tanks passed across intact, whilst engineers cut the wires to the remaining charges.[19]

The last water obstacle before the Lower Rhine had been crossed. Although the Poles, 325 Glider Infantry Regiment of 82 Airborne and part of 327 Glider Infantry Regiment of 101 Airborne had yet to arrive on the field of battle, all the initial airborne objectives apart from the bridge at Arnhem had been secured and 'Market' was effectively at an end. 'Garden', however, was far from complete.

Chapter 19

Garden (21–24 September 1944)

The capture intact of the Nijmegen bridges on the evening of 20 September had been a cause for jubilation on the Allied side, as it seemed for a brief moment that nothing stood between them and Arnhem. This very quickly proved to be an illusion. The Americans in particular have always criticized Guards Armoured Division for not pressing on immediately after crossing the bridge, but in practice this would not have been a sensible military decision. It was 1900 before the small troop of tanks had collected and the light was fading fast. Although there were American paratroopers around, none of them were trained in working with armour and the Grenadiers' infantry was still mopping up in Nijmegen. Ahead ran a single carriageway road across totally flat polder, slightly raised, with no chance of lateral deployment and no fire support available from artillery or the RAF.

On the next day tanks of the Irish Guards did advance, but before they reached Elst and about six miles short of Arnhem they ran into anti-tank guns and four were immediately destroyed, blocking the road. Only infantry would be able to proceed further on the direct route and this would require 43 Division, which was only just arriving in Nijmegen. One positive development took place, however, when 64 Medium Regiment RA, with its guns at Hees just to the west of Nijmegen, established contact with 1 Airborne's Forward Observation Unit. This enabled the gunners to put down accurate fire from a distance of about twelve miles to break up attacks on the Oosterbeek perimeter.

Boy was deeply frustrated by the slow progress, although he did not necessarily show it. Gwatkin said later that he spent a lot of time at the 5 Guards Armoured Brigade HQ, but that he 'never fussed, never complained, never urged on great efforts: he knew that all that could be done was being done – but it does take more than just iron control to behave as he did. I thought then that I was too old to hang another picture in my Hero's gallery, but I put him up.'[1] One of Boy's other concerns was the performance of his own HQ and here he unburdened himself in a scribbled letter to Daphne late on 19 September: 'My staff is almost more inefficient than I could possibly imagine now we are in the field – I suppose its due to people being pushed up the tree too quickly without sufficient experience, but its really too frustrating for words. Gordon Walch has completely failed as chief of staff in the field – not entirely his fault I suppose but he seems unable to combine the two jobs.'[2] It is difficult to conclude that the failure was other than of Boy's own making, although the War Office's reluctance to provide him with a signals unit until the last minute, and then a totally inexperienced one, made a major contribution.

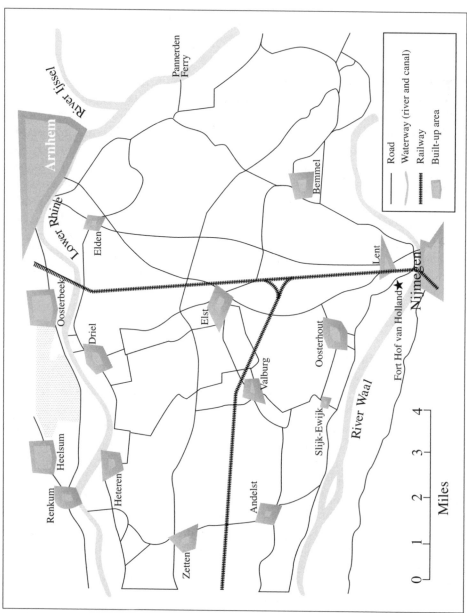

Map 3. The Island

On 20 September the HQ moved to the location which it would occupy until it returned to the UK. This was necessitated partly by geography, but more by the piecemeal arrival of the Main HQ by road. Eagger had turned up on the previous day and immediately made himself useful by organizing hospitals in the area with the assistance of the Dutch. Bower, the chief administrative officer, arrived twenty-four hours later and the balance of the HQ on 21 September. The choice fell on three empty villas found by Firbank, the GSO2 (Operations), on Sophiaweg, a pleasant wooded suburban thoroughfare which linked the main roads to Nijmegen from Mook and Malden at one end, from Berg-en-Dal at the other and from Groesbeek in the middle. The position was ideal, providing good communications to all parts of the Airborne Corps sector.

There was also an empty barracks close at hand (from which Firbank liberated a large quantity of wines and spirits) which was used as an alternative to tents by some of the staff and by the seventy glider pilots, who were supposedly providing the defence of the corps HQ, but were for the most part underemployed. They did, however, have to clear the surrounding woods of snipers left behind by the departing Germans and still proving a nuisance. An airstrip for light aircraft was constructed nearby and used for communication with Second Army. Boy's mobile caravan arrived with the Main HQ, which provided him with a ready-made office.

One of Boy's deep frustrations concerned the delays to the third drop, which had been due on 19 September. Increasingly irate signals were sent from his HQ over the non-arrival of the Polish Parachute Brigade and Gavin's 325 Glider Infantry Regiment, both of which were urgently needed. On 20 September the weather was still fine in Holland and Boy could not understand why they were still not being despatched. The weather in England, on the other hand, had closed in. FAAA was responsible for the decisions, but Brereton had decided to visit the front and was in Eindhoven on 19 September and then with Taylor at 101 Airborne on the following day. Ridgway, whose XVIII Airborne Corps was responsible for supplying the two American divisions, had travelled with Brereton initially,[3] later arriving at Nijmegen, where he turned up at Gavin's HQ just as the latter was tackling the crises at Mook and Beek. Gavin could spare him no time, but noted later that Ridgway was still unhappy not to be controlling the two divisions. With the two most senior commanders away, the decisions regarding further lifts were left to Parks, Brereton's Chief of Staff, who gave priority to resupply rather than fresh troops.

During the afternoon of 20 September a message was received at Rear HQ from Edmund Hakewill-Smith, the GOC of 52 Division. Passed on to the Advance HQ, it offered to fly in by glider one brigade and a mixed artillery regiment of 6-pounder anti-tank guns, 25-pounder field guns and 3.7 inch howitzers to reinforce 1 Airborne. Given that 52 Division had no training on gliders, this was a brave suggestion. On the previous day a message had been received that the division was now at the disposal of Second Army, so Boy needed Dempsey's approval to use it. He and Horrocks met Dempsey on the morning of 21 September and it is inconceivable that this was not discussed. In any event, Boy's clear priority was still to bring in the Poles and Gavin's glider infantry. There were already considerable difficulties being experienced in sustaining XXX Corps and to transport and supply another formation at this juncture, in addition to those already in the field or planned to arrive, would have put a huge additional strain on resources.

Boy's reply to Hakewill-Smith, not delivered until 22 September but almost certainly drafted on the previous day after the meeting with Dempsey, was nevertheless extraordinary: 'Thanks for your message but offer not repeat not required as situation better than you think. We want lifts as planned including Poles. Second Army definitely require your party and intend to fly you in to Deelen airfield as soon as situation allows.' If anything was to demonstrate his lack of understanding of the situation at Arnhem, it was this. On the previous day Frost's party at the bridge had been forced to surrender, after a most gallant resistance against overwhelming odds. The perimeter at Oosterbeek had contracted and was under constant attack from all sides. The one other potential river crossing point into the perimeter, the Heveadorp ferry, had been lost to the Germans and, although the Poles had landed on the south side of the Lower Rhine by the time the response was received by Hakewill-Smith, they were unable to get across without boats. There was absolutely no hope at all of taking Deelen in the near future. Brereton's subsequent comment on the message – 'As it turned out, General Browning was overoptimistic'[4] – was a major understatement, but Brereton had earlier described the message as 'encouraging', demonstrating clearly his own lack of comprehension of the position.

If Boy had been frustrated, Sosabowski had been even more so. Due under the plan to parachute in on D+2, his brigade's departure was put back time after time by the weather in England. Although the glider-borne element arrived with the second and third lifts, the latter was much depleted by losses on the way: those who survived the third lift had to fight their way into the Oosterbeek perimeter, but with only two of their ten anti-tank guns. Sosabowski was as short of information on the fate of 1 Airborne as everyone else and was becoming increasingly concerned about aspects of his own drop. On D+3 the drop zone was changed from just south of the road bridge to an area close to Driel five miles to the west, from where he would be able to use the Heveadorp ferry to cross to Urquhart's relief. The retention of the ferry was thus uppermost in his mind and he decided that he would refuse to go unless it was still held.

At 0700 on the morning of 21 September – D+4 – his British liaison officer, Lieutenant Colonel Stevens, told him that the ferry remained in British hands and shortly afterwards he received confirmation from Parks that he could fly. By early afternoon the weather had cleared and at 1415 Sosabowski's plane left the ground. The drop itself was successful, but one of his battalions had to turn back because the weather had again deteriorated, leaving Sosabowski with two weak battalions, comprising just 750 men. Sending out reconnaissance parties, he discovered to his horror that the Heveadorp ferry had actually been destroyed and that the far bank at that point was now held by the Germans. Shortly afterwards his Polish liaison and Riethorst along the Maas, where he lost the Kiekberg Woods. He was therefore greatly relieved when 325 Glider Infantry Regiment arrived at last on 23 September, four days late, to be put initially into reserve before being moved to Mook.

On the same day, the sector responsibilities were changed in order to free up Horrocks for the battle now developing on the Island as the low-lying land between the Maas and the lower Rhine was known.[5] Boy was allocated the Royal Netherlands Brigade, which was ordered to protect the Grave Bridge and to patrol westwards between the Maas and the Waal. On 24 September, a further reinforcement arrived in the shape of 157 Brigade Group, the seaborne echelon of 52 Division.[6] This formation had a single battalion of infantry, but it included the division's reconnaissance regiment, a regiment of field artillery, its own engineers, an anti-tank battery and an anti-aircraft battery, so it was a welcome addition to the corps. Over the course of the following week the reconnaissance regiment was tasked to patrol south-west of Grave, the field regiment was placed under Gavin and the remainder were ordered to protect a newly found airfield.

Boy had earlier sent out parties to locate possible landing grounds for Dakotas and on 21 September his Chief Engineer had discovered a grass airfield, previously unknown to the Intelligence staff, at Oude Keent, about three miles west of Grave. There was also an open space nearby which could be used for glider landings or as a fighter airstrip. Permission was immediately requested from Second Army to fly in 878 Airborne Engineer Battalion, AFDAG and 2 LAA Battery, with the intention of using the main airfield for supplies and, in due course, for the possible arrival of 52 Division. Second Army replied two days later, giving permission for it to be used, but it would be another three days before AFDAG and 2 LAA Battery were flown in, so the discovery was to make little contribution to the immediate battle.

Although there were a number of peripheral issues such as the airfield to be dealt with, Boy's priorities were twofold. First, he had to ensure that the Airborne Corps continued to hold its sector of the airborne corridor. With O'Connor now running all operations on the road between Eindhoven and Grave, his own remit incorporated Nijmegen and all the surrounding land between the Maas and the Waal, together with Grave itself, the south end of the Maas Bridge and the country immediately along the south bank of the river towards 's-Hertogenbosch. The most vulnerable sector remained that facing the German border along the edge of the Reichswald and extending from there to the Waal, but he had realized from the outset that Gavin was a highly competent commander, who should be given support when he asked for it, but could be allowed to operate with a minimum of supervision. Their relationship had improved immeasurably since the start of the operation, Walch writing subsequently 'The mutual trust and respect shown by General Boy and General Jim Gavin, working closely together in the Nijmegen area, was particularly good to see.'[7]

More pressing by far was the second priority, the relief of 1 Airborne. This could only be effected by XXX Corps and the battle north of the Waal was now unequivocally under Horrocks's control, in spite of his subsequent insistence that he and Boy took the main decisions together. Boy was still notionally responsible for 1 Airborne, but the continuing lack of good communication and his inability to be on the ground prevented him from exercising any command role. In Urquhart's absence, he was also Sosabowski's immediate superior, and here the sensible course of action, implicitly understood by Boy and Horrocks and later explicitly ordered, was to combine the Poles with elements of XXX Corps.

The halting of Guards Armoured Division on 21 September had been a setback, as 43 Division was still concentrating in Nijmegen and the small bridgehead to the north and was not ready to launch an attack. During that night, however, two troops of the Household Cavalry side-slipped through a gap in the German defences along the Waal to the west and looped round to link up with the Poles early the next morning. There they found two senior officers from 1 Airborne, Charles Mackenzie, the GSO1, and Eddie Myers, the Chief Royal Engineer, who had crossed the river in a rubber boat. For the first time, using the armoured cars' wireless sets, an accurate picture of the situation at Oosterbeek could be passed through to XXX Corps and thence to Boy. Plans were put in hand to get as many of the Poles as possible across the river on the night of 22 September, but in the event only fifty or so made it to join the defenders of the perimeter.

On the morning of that day, 43 Division began its advance on a two-brigade front, 214 Brigade moving north-west toward the Polish Parachute Brigade with the intention of effecting a crossing, whilst 129 Brigade advanced directly on Elst. The latter found the German defences too strong, but 7th Somerset Light Infantry from the former broke the strong resistance at Oosterhout, just north of the Waal, enabling 5th Duke of Cornwall's Light Infantry to pass through and join up with the Poles by the evening.

The difficulty of getting through in either direction meant that Mackenzie and Myers had remained with Sosabowski all day, but on 23 September they were taken back to Boy's HQ in Nijmegen in two Household Cavalry armoured cars. Mackenzie, who arrived the worse for wear following a narrow escape from the Germans after his armoured car had overturned, tried to impress on Boy and Horrocks the full scale of 1 Airborne's plight. However, although Boy told him that every effort would be made to get reinforcements and supplies over the river to Urquhart, he was less than convincing about the ability to put across a strong force and Mackenzie left with the impression that neither of the two corps commanders had really grasped the urgency of the situation. That night he crossed back over the river at the same time as another two hundred Poles, whose journey had been made under vicious fire from the Germans.

Early on 23 September, with the weather having deteriorated into heavy driving rain, Major General Ivor Thomas, the GOC of 43 Division, managed to slip the whole of 130 Brigade round the back of 214 Brigade. This enabled 214 Brigade to attack Elst from the west, but the town was proving a seriously difficult nut to crack. Having been forced back from the Nijmegen bridges, the Germans were now able to focus all their efforts on the Island into preventing the British from advancing any further north or east and continued to pour reinforcements across the now cleared Arnhem Bridge and the Pannerden ferry. Thomas, with two-thirds of his division committed to pushing back the Germans on the Island, only had one brigade available for any river crossing.

During the course of the day an outline plan was evolved between Thomas and Brigadier 'Pete' Pyman, the XXX Corps Chief of Staff, which involved a river crossing near the site of the Heveadorp ferry. Pyman took the plan down to Dempsey at St Oedenrode and that evening the Second Army Commander sent a message to Boy and Horrocks jointly, spelling out what he saw as the priorities. These were firstly to keep open the main axis from VIII Corps' sector so that supplies could get through and secondly to hold the Nijmegen bridgehead. Only then were they to establish a bridgehead in the Arnhem area. 'You know situation in North', wrote Dempsey, 'better than I do but if you consider task No 3 too difficult at present both to gain and to hold you may withdraw 1 AB without reference to me.' This was the first time that withdrawal had been seriously mentioned and the idea probably stemmed from a meeting that day between Dempsey and Montgomery at the former's Tac HQ. Writing about 1 Airborne in his personal diary on 23 September, Montgomery recorded: 'I am very doubtful myself now if they will be able to hold out, and we may have to withdraw them'[8] but in his message, Dempsey made it clear that he still relied on the judgement of Boy and Horrocks as to whether such a course of action would become necessary. For the moment, however, both were committed to a crossing and a meeting was convened to take place at 43 Division's HQ in Valburg, a few miles from Driel, on the following day.

The Valburg Conference on the morning of Sunday 24 September was a key moment in the whole operation and a source of much subsequent controversy. It was attended among others by Horrocks, who was in the chair, Boy, Thomas and Sosabowski, accompanied by Stevens, his Liaison Officer, and by one of his best English speakers, Lieutenant Dyrda. Sosabowski had earlier climbed the tower of Driel church with Horrocks to show the XXX Corps commander the lie of the land over which the forthcoming relief operation would take place. On the previous afternoon, a message sent by Stevens to Boy said that Sosabowski believed that 'it now requires a divisional operation to carry out a normal river crossing with full arty support & smoke. The high ground on the far side commanding the river is held by the enemy and must be neutralised by all the arty available.' Sosabowski was not to know it at that time, but the resources for a full divisional crossing were just not available.

It was unfortunate that Sosabowski and Thomas were both strong characters who clashed immediately. Thomas had the reputation of being one of the most difficult general officers in the British Army, although he was appreciated by his superiors as a man who would carry out the toughest orders without demur. Humourless and often regarded by his subordinates as something of a martinet, he did not brook dissent from his instructions.[9] When Sosabowski met him for the first time just before the meeting, he described him as giving out an air of well-being and satisfaction.

It possibly did not help that neither Horrocks nor Boy was on top physical form. Horrocks was still suffering from the after-effects of the very serious injuries he had received in North Africa in June 1943. These had put him out of the war for over a year and, when he was called back by Montgomery to take command of XXX Corps in Normandy in August 1944 he was still not fully fit. He experienced a number of relapses and was certainly under the weather at this time, as well as being desperately worried about progress and somewhat short-tempered as a result. Boy had failed to shrug off the heavy cold which he had developed just before leaving England and which had left him feeling very tired.

The plan produced by Thomas and Pyman involved not a division or even a brigade, but a single battalion, the 4th Battalion Dorsetshire Regiment (4 Dorset), together with the recently arrived 1st Polish Parachute Battalion. Sosabowski protested that it was he who should choose which of his troops should go on the operation, at which Thomas became very angry. According to the historian of 43 Division, Sosabowski then said, 'I am General Sosabowski, I command the Polish Para Brigade. I do as I like.' Horrocks replied, 'You are under my command. You will do as I bloody well tell you', to which Sosabowski's retort was: 'All right. I command the Polish Para Brigade and I do as you bloody well say.'[10] It was a most unhappy incident and was to prove in due course inimical to Sosabowski's career. Boy, Sosabowski's immediate superior, did not speak up in his defence, though it is possible that he deprecated and was embarrassed by such behaviour from one of his senior officers.

In further discussion, Sosabowski strongly recommended that the force should not cross at the selected point, where the German defences were strong. He favoured another point some way to the west, where he believed that the crossing would be unopposed, and argued that it should be in divisional strength. The matter of opposition is one of speculation, but the whole of the north bank was now crawling with Germans and it is likely that a crossing anywhere would have been seen and resisted. Moreover, there was no hope of conducting it on the scale which Sosabowski believed necessary. In any event, Horrocks and Thomas had made their decision and it was to stand. Thomas rubbed in his displeasure by conveying his detailed orders to Stevens, ignoring Sosabowski.

After the meeting Sosabowski drove back to Airborne Corps HQ where he had a further meeting with Boy. The latter admitted that the crossing might not succeed as the equipment available, by way of boats and bridging, was inadequate. Sosabowski expressed considerable surprise that such an eventuality had not been planned for and that the equipment had not been given priority but Boy pointed out the delays caused by the Germans cutting the road. Sosabowski, true to his character, spoke his mind very forcefully, which did not go down well with Boy who saw it as unmerited criticism of the British Army.

Horrocks, in the meantime, had travelled down to St Oedenrode to report to Dempsey on the proposed operation and to discuss possible outcomes.[11] Dempsey wrote that day in his war diary: 'Met Commander 30 Corps at St Oedenrode. Contact gained with 1 AB and 43 Div will pass a battalion over the river tonight to join them. Depending on the development of operations in the next 24 hours, 30 Corps during the night of 25/26 September will either: (a) pass a complete brigade of 43 Div across the river West of Arnhem, build a bridge and so establish a bridgehead; or (b) withdraw 1 AB south of the river and give up the existing slender bridgehead. I will give Comd 30 Corps a decision at 1200hrs tomorrow.' In fact, Montgomery had already told Dempsey that, unless strong contact was made with 1 Airborne, it would have to be withdrawn on the next day.

The die was now cast for the final episode of 'Market Garden'.

Chapter 20

Tragedy (24 September–9 October 1944)

harles Mackenzie had left his meeting with the two corps commanders at Airborne Corps HQ feeling that they did not understand the gravity of the situation and the urgency of relief. It is much more likely that by then, albeit very belatedly, they understood it only too well, but knew that the resources necessary to engineer a significant reinforcement of 1 Airborne's bridgehead just did not exist. Sufficient boats were not even available for a crossing in brigade strength, as Boy admitted to Sosabowski, so the single battalion from 43 Division, together with the 1st Polish Parachute Battalion, was the best they could provide.

Sosabowski subsequently criticized Boy for not making one final effort to get across the Lower Rhine in strength, but it was Boy, not he, who was in full possession of the facts; these did not allow for such an operation to be mounted in time to save what was left of 1 Airborne, which was becoming Boy's overriding priority. Although he went along with the agreement reached at the Valburg Conference, he already favoured withdrawal, as Sosabowski suspected, and it might reasonably be supposed that this carried weight with Dempsey. Urquhart could only be thankful that he did: 'Horrocks remained optimistic to the very last about the possibility of effecting a crossing to the west of the perimeter. In this I think he was being unrealistic; it is as well that Browning and Dempsey insisted that we came out when we did.'[1]

Boy's anguish was conveyed in a letter to Daphne written on the day of the Valburg Conference. 'We have had a very tragic time the last few days', he wrote, 'as we've been unable to reach the 1st Division in time to prevent their annihilation – its been a combination of weather, stiffening resistance and appalling country. I've got a major battle on me hands to keep the corridor open and hold the Boche on me southern flank,' going on to say later that he was 'worried as hell about the 1st Division although the latter is not now my battle but a matter for 30 Corps who are trying to reach them. Apart from the latter the thing has been a great success, but the whole thing is overshadowed by the tragedy in the north.'[2]

Boy's priority was given greater momentum by a message received on the Phantom net from Urquhart on the evening of 24 September. 'Must warn you', wrote the beleaguered GOC, 'unless physical contact is made with us early 25 Sep. consider it unlikely we can hold out long enough. All ranks now exhausted. Lack of rations, water, ammunition, and weapons with a high officer casualty rate … . Even slight enemy offensive action may cause complete disintegration. If this happens all will be ordered to break towards bridgehead if anything rather than surrender. Any

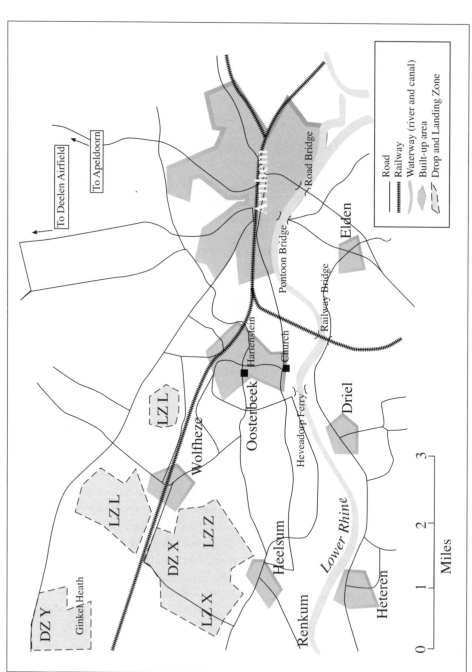

Map 4. Arnhem and Oosterbeek.

movement at present in face of enemy NOT possible. Have attempted our best and will do so as long as possible.' If this communication was not enough, the news that 'Hell's Highway' had been cut yet again meant that any last vestige of hope of bringing up reinforcements in time to swing the battle in the Allies' favour had vanished.

Horrocks had been caught at St Oedenrode, on the wrong side of the cut, and was only able to return by a cross-country route with a carrier platoon from 50 Division, not arriving back until the following morning. During his absence the operation to put 4 Dorset across the Lower Rhine had been a costly failure. The assault boats for the battalion had failed to arrive, two lorry-loads having gone off the road, whilst the other two had taken a wrong turning and ended up in the German lines. It was decided to transfer the boats allocated to the Poles to 4 Dorset, but after the delay it was past 0100 hrs on 25 September before the operation was able to commence. Many boats were destroyed on the bank or on the way across, and those men who landed on the far side found themselves under withering fire and showers of hand grenades from the Westerbouwing Heights, which dominated the landing site. Most of those who survived, including the CO, Lieutenant Colonel Tilly, were taken prisoner and a mere handful made it into the 1 Airborne perimeter.

One of the few to survive the crossing and arrive in the perimeter was the division's CRE, Eddie Myers. He carried with him a letter which Boy had given to him for Urquhart after the meeting at the Airborne Corps HQ on 23 September. It read:

Dear Roy

Sosabowski will be bringing you this, I hope tonight.

I will not labour your present position, and it may be little consolation to you and the 1st Division when I tell you that the opinion held this side of the river is that the action of the 1st Division has, apart from the killing of the many Boche it has undoubtedly achieved, enabled XXX Corps and the Airborne Corps between them to capture the Nijmegen bridges and to break clean through the main German defence line on the Waal.

From the information at our disposal, the German undoubtedly moved back the bulk of his forces from Nijmegen to Arnhem just before our airborne attack took place, and instead of the Nijmegen crossings being an acutely difficult problem, the Arnhem crossings have become most acute in consequence.

You can rest assured that XXX Corps are doing their maximum under the most appalling difficulties to relieve you. As you know, I am responsible for from inclusive Nijmegen down the narrow corridor for about 40 miles, and the road has been cut for 24 hours, which does not help matters much. It is now through again, and the Army is pouring through to your assistance but, as you will appreciate better than I do, very late in the day.

I naturally feel, not so tired and frustrated as you do, but probably almost worse about the whole thing than you do.

I enclose a letter from Field Marshal Monty,[3] and I hope to see you in a day or two.

officer with Urquhart arrived, having swum the Rhine, to report on 1 Airborne's precarious situation. He was sent back with a message that Sosabowski would try to cross as soon as he had the wherewithal to do so.

On 22 September, the weather in England closed in again and there was no resupply, let alone further reinforcements. 101 Airborne now came under Boy's command for the first time since the initial landings, in order to free XXX Corps for the impending battle north of Nijmegen. Since the action at Son two days earlier, the corridor had been relatively quiet, but Student was gathering his forces for a series of attacks from both sides. From the east, *Kampfgruppe* Walther, incorporating 107 Panzer Brigade, struck between Veghel and Uden and cut the highway, whilst *Kampfgruppe* Huber attacked from the other side close to the Zuid-Willemsvaart Canal bridge. Taylor had already brought up some of his troops who had been relieved further south by VIII Corps and these, together with those already in the area, drove back the attackers causing heavy losses, but the road remained under artillery fire and was effectively impassable. The German attacks became increasingly uncoordinated, improving weather created opportunities for the Allied air forces to strike back and the arrival of 32 Guards Brigade from the north, sent down urgently by Horrocks, tipped the balance. By the early afternoon of 23 September, the Germans were forced to pull back, but they had cut what was now called 'Hell's Highway' for 36 hours and delayed 69 Brigade, which was moving up to Nijmegen in the van of 50 Division, as well as other urgently needed supplies and equipment.

Further south the operations by VIII and XII Corps were going much more slowly than anticipated. The resistance to XII Corps to the south-west of Eindhoven had been particularly stubborn and it was only inching its way forward. VIII Corps had done better after a late start on 19 September, capturing Helmond and Deurne and seeing off 107 Panzer Brigade, and it was now in close contact with 101 Airborne. Dempsey met O'Connor on 22 September and told him that he was to take responsibility for clearing the road from Veghel to Grave. A further conference was held with Taylor on the following day and command passed from the Airborne Corps to VIII Corps that afternoon. For the short period during which it had been under his command, Boy had had no impact at all on 101 Airborne's battle, apart from concurring with Horrocks's decision to detach 32 Guards Brigade.

In 82 Airborne's sector the southwards attack by 32 Guards Brigade had deprived Gavin of his reserve, the Coldstream Guards Group, but he now received some armour of his own in the form of the Sherwood Rangers Yeomanry from 8 Armoured Brigade. This enabled him to extend his front across the low-lying polder to the south bank of the Waal east of Nijmegen. He was able to pull 504 Parachute Infantry back into his line after their heroic efforts on either side of the Nijmegen bridges and to hand over responsibility for the bridges at Grave and over the Maas-Waal canal, but he still urgently needed reinforcements. He found himself under a series of attacks from a number of *Kampfgruppen*, particularly on the Duivelsberg, a high point on the ridge between the two roads from Wyler to Nijmegen, and around Mook

It may amuse you to know that my front faces in all directions, but I am only in close contact with the enemy for about 8000 yards to the south-east, which is quite enough in present circumstances.

Yours ever

F.A.M. Browning

Delivered twenty-four hours later than anticipated, the contents of the letter were already out of date. Boy had handed over responsibility for the corridor later on the day on which it was written and the road had been cut again. Boy's assessment of the German movements around Nijmegen and Arnhem was quite inaccurate, largely because intelligence on the ground remained far from perfect. It is doubtful if the letter brought much comfort to Urquhart and the extent of his amusement or otherwise over the last paragraph has never been disclosed.

Myers also brought with him a more useful letter from Thomas regarding a withdrawal, codenamed Operation 'Berlin'. At 0800 hrs on 25 September Urquhart raised Thomas on the radio and told him that it had to happen that night. Together with Mackenzie, Myers and his remaining staff he then planned the withdrawal, based on the concept of the 'collapsing bag' derived from his knowledge of the Gallipoli campaign. This was to be covered by the artillery of 43 Division and XXX Corps and to be carried out by 16 assault boats manned by 43 Division's engineers and 21 motorized storm boats crewed by Canadian engineers, all under the control of the division's newly arrived CRE, Mark Henniker, formerly of Boy's staff.

In the meantime Boy and Horrocks had met on the latter's return from the south. It took them fifteen seconds to agree on evacuation and authority was given by Dempsey at 1215. Montgomery had been at Dempsey's Tac HQ again that morning and the two had discussed the situation fully. For the two most senior commanders, the Phantom message received by Boy from Urquhart on the preceding evening, and forwarded to Second Army and 21st Army Group, had been conclusive and Montgomery agreed that it was time to throw in the towel.

In the event the evacuation, across the river from the vicinity of Oosterbeek church, was a success thanks to good planning, bad weather, the discipline of the airborne troops and the devotion to duty of the sappers manning the boats. A total of 1,741 men from 1 Airborne (out of 8,969 who had flown in), 422 glider pilots, 160 Poles and 75 Dorsets were brought across, and a number of others were to escape individually or in small groups over the coming weeks and months, including Hackett and Lathbury. The wounded were left behind under the care of the division's doctors. After the crossing, the men were assembled at a reception area some way from the river and then most were transported by lorry to Nijmegen, although some had to march. Boy had sent Cator in his jeep to drive Urquhart back to Airborne Corps HQ. It surprised many at the time and has been the subject of criticism subsequently that he was not there himself to meet the survivors. The best that can be said is that it was atypical of him.

When Urquhart arrived at the HQ at 0300 he was offered a change of clothing and a bed but he insisted first on seeing Boy, who entered after some delay, immaculately dressed as always. In Urquhart's words: 'He looked as if he had just come off parade instead of from his bed in the middle of a battle. I tried to display some briskness as I reported: 'The division is nearly out now. I'm sorry we haven't been able to do what we set out to do.' Browning offered me a drink and assured me that everything was being done for the division. 'You did all you could', he said. 'Now you had better get some rest.' It was a totally inadequate meeting.'[4]

Quite what Boy was doing on the evening and through the night of 25/26 September has never been explained. He still had significant responsibilities elsewhere, but although there was constant shelling of 82 Airborne's positions and a number of small actions, this was a relatively quiet period on Gavin's front. It seems most likely that he was following the example of Montgomery, who invariably insisted on a proper night's sleep, regardless of the state of any battle in which he might be engaged. Whilst his attitude rankled with Urquhart, it was clearly not the time for a full debrief, but he could and probably should have shown more sympathy. As it was his Guardsman's reserve and stiff upper lip came to the fore, although to judge by one of his letters to Daphne he was far from critical. 'Roy Urquhart's party has done magnificently,' he wrote later, 'but have been very badly knocked about. They have covered themselves in glory and without them we couldn't have done what we have done.'[5]

He did better on the afternoon of the next day when he addressed the survivors, going to each of the three buildings in which they were housed. One of those from 1 Airborne described the scene: 'The Commander of the Airborne Corps entered with his retinue, and climbed a table in the centre of the hall. He had made many speeches in his time, but never one to an audience such as this. Their mood was dumb weariness, and a tremendous dignity. He realized that they were beyond authority, having no more to give; truth would be clear to them, insincerity would be scabrous. They were most expectant. It was difficult to hear, on all four sides of the General, and as they all wanted to hear, there was a little grumbling. It was a very courageous moment for him.'[6]

Boy had confided to Cator earlier that he was dreading this task. He decided that only the unvarnished truth would do and so he told them exactly what had happened, why they had dropped in three lifts and so far away from their objective, how the rest of the Airborne Corps had fared and what had happened to XXX Corps on its way north. He told them clearly that they should not regard their efforts as a failure, as these had enabled a springboard into Germany to be established at Nijmegen. Finally he assured them that they would be going back to England as quickly as transport could be arranged. The speech was well received, one glider pilot describing it as 'impressive and very sensible'.

Both this episode and the earlier meeting with Urquhart were examples of how Boy could keep his emotions under control, one of the most notable features of his character. He was, even at times of great stress, able to present a front to the world at large which was at odds with what he was really feeling. In replying to Cornelius Ryan's research assistant for the book of *A Bridge Too Far*, Daphne wrote: 'One thing I do know, although he did not talk about it, was that his grief at the loss of life at

Arnhem was very deep indeed, and although the casualties of battle is a hazard that all military commanders have to face, this particular loss was something to which he could never become reconciled. He truly loved the men under his command, and the various regiments that combined to make up the Airborne Forces, his pride and his faith in them was tremendous, I would say – next to his family – the dearest thing in his life.'[7]

Daphne herself had no idea at the time of what was happening. Although she knew that he was off on an operation on 17 September, there was silence after that, as any letters he wrote were subject to considerable delay. Not long after the evacuation, however, she was woken by a telephone call from a newspaper reporter at three in the morning to ask if it was true that Boy had been taken prisoner. A rumour had indeed been put about by the Germans that he had been captured. The War Office was roused into action and eventually Rear HQ managed to contact Chatterton and Loring, Boy's DDOS, who both confirmed that he was alive and well. Chatterton, returning to England ahead of Corps HQ, rang Daphne to reassure her.

The survivors of 1 Airborne Division moved to Louvain on 28 September and began to return to England on the following day. Urquhart's mood had not improved on the day after the evacuation, when he attended a dinner to celebrate the division's return, which he found an ordeal. When Sosabowski visited him, he found him 'in a low state, both physically and mentally ... his whole attitude was one of deep and bitter disappointment.'[8] Things began to look up when he lunched with Dempsey before going on to stay with Montgomery at his Tac HQ. Urquhart found Montgomery, unlike Boy, totally understanding, and he was asked to give a full account of the battle. When he left the following morning, Montgomery gave him a letter which was written in terms guaranteed to raise morale, also sending a copy to the Director of Public Relations at the War Office, with instructions that it should be published in all the newspapers on 30 September. The letter concluded: 'In years to come it will be a great thing for a man to be able to say: I fought at Arnhem.' It was a modest but nonetheless valuable consolation. Boy had also written to Urquhart, but in much more formal terms (see Appendix 1), whilst Montgomery's letter to Boy on 24 September was brief and to the point:

My dear Browning

I have been following with intense admiration the operations of your Airborne Corps. The whole Corps, British and American, has done magnificently. I send to you, and to all officers and men, my very best congratulations. Please let them all know how well I consider they have done.

Yrs sincerely

B. L. Montgomery

HQ Airborne Corps was to remain in Nijmegen for nearly a fortnight longer. On the face of it, there was still much to do. Horrocks was fighting what was rapidly developing into a slogging match for control of the Island. Progress on either side

Boy's father, Freddie Browning, at the time of his marriage to Nancy

Boy, or Tommy, as a baby with his mother, Nancy

Boy's uncle, Admiral Sir Montague Browning, in 1926

Tommy during the
prep school years

Tommy keeping wicket
at West Downs

Tommy at Eton

Boy in late 1917, just after
receiving the Croix de Guerre

Boy wearing his England
international athletics shirt

Boy as Adjutant of the 1st Battalion, Grenadier Guards, with his HQ officers and NCOs

The Adjutant – a caricature from
the *RMC Magazine & Record*.
(*Copyright Royal Military
Academy, Sandhurst*)

THE ADJUTANT

Boy with the Senior Under Officers at Sandhurst

Daphne in 1930, shortly before
her first meeting with Boy

Boy and Daphne relaxing on 'Yggy'

The officers of HQ 128 Brigade, with Gordon Walch second from the left in the front row

Boy on his visit to the United States in July/August 1942

Churchill's visit to the Airborne
Division in April 1942

Boy accompanies King George VI on
an inspection of 1 Airborne Division
in March 1944

Boy and Sosabowski

Boy in late 1944, shortly before leaving
for South-East Asia Command

Boy and Daphne, with Kits, Tessa and Flavia, at
Menabilly during one of his rare wartime leaves

The Top Team at SEAC – Slim, Wheeler, Mountbatten, Power, Park and Boy

'Supremo' confers with his Chief of Staff

Boy takes the VE-Day parade in Kandy, due to Mountbatten's indisposition

The signatures of Numata and Boy on the Japanese surrender document

The CIGS visits Singapore – Brooke, Dempsey, Park and Boy stand to the right of Mountbatten, with Christison to the immediate left, two away from Leclerc

SOUTH EAST ASIA COMMAND HEADQUARTERS

- 3 -

Supreme Commander, Japanese Expeditionary Forces, Southern
Regions, to make such translation into Japanese as he may
require.

for SUPREME COMMANDER,
JAPANESE EXPEDITIONARY FORCES,
SOUTHERN REGIONS.

for SUPREME ALLIED COMMANDER
SOUTH EAST ASIA.

1825 HRS TIME (GMT) 27 AUGUST 1945.
GOVERNMENT HOUSE, RANGOON

A portrait by Dorothy Wilding
of Daphne in the late 1940s

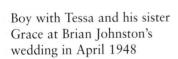

Boy with Tessa and his sister
Grace at Brian Johnston's
wedding in April 1948

Boy's Boats

Restless of Plyn

Jeanne d'Arc

Ygdrasil II

FANNY ROSA
FOWEY

Princess Elizabeth and the Duke of
Edinburgh aboard Fanny Rosa at
Cowes, Boy with his back to the camera

The Colonel of the Grenadier
Guards, wearing Boy's full dress sash

Kits, Tessa and Flavia –
Christmas 1950

Boy with Margot Fonteyn

Boy in attendance on Princess Elizabeth and the Duke of Edinburgh in Malta

The Queen and Duke of Edinburgh drive with Boy and Mike Parker from Clarence House to Buckingham Palace after the accession

Boy and Daphne sailing on *Jeanne d'Arc* after his retirement

Boy in the 1960s

of 'Hell's Highway' remained slow and for a time there was only the most slender of contacts with VIII Corps north of Uden. The front facing the Reichswald remained vulnerable with activity continuing around the Kiekberg Woods, from which a number of German attacks were mounted and which Gavin was anxious to retake, and the Den Heuvel Woods between Groesbeek and Wyler. The weather continued unsettled and Boy's cold, which had seemed to improve, started up again after he managed to get himself completely soaked.

Unlike 1 Airborne the Poles had not been withdrawn to the UK. Instead, after marching back to Nijmegen they had been sent to guard the airfield at Oude Keent, for which they were placed under the command of 157 Brigade. As a major general, Sosabowski was incensed at having to take orders from a much younger brigadier, believing that it was a deliberate slight by Boy. He sent a message asking to be released from 157 Brigade's control. Boy replied explaining that that move had been necessitated by the disorganization of the Polish Parachute Brigade after the fighting on the Island and the need for reinforcement of 157 Brigade, but also agreeing to bring the Poles back under the direct command of the Airborne Corps. They were ordered to guard the two bridges over the Maas-Waal Canal and hold a defensive position west of Grave. The episode did little to improve the relationship between the two men and made Sosabowski even more determined to maintain his brigade's independence.

Montgomery arrived in Nijmegen for the first time on 29 September and was received at I Airborne Corps HQ by a guard of honour from the Glider Pilot Regiment. He met Gavin, Taylor, Adair and Thomas and then held a conference with Dempsey, Horrocks and Boy, at which the immediate plans were discussed. Montgomery had already mentally cut his losses over the failure to get across the Lower Rhine and, as ever, remained outwardly optimistic about future operations. His priority was to retain the ground already captured on the Island, made more difficult the previous night by German divers destroying the Nijmegen railway bridge and severely damaging the road bridge. I Airborne Corps, with 82 Airborne Division, 157 Brigade, the Royal Netherlands Brigade and the Polish Parachute Brigade under command, continued to have responsibility for the whole area in Allied hands between the Waal and the Maas, and for the defence of Grave. On 1 October it also took responsibility for the immediate bridgehead north of the Waal and for the defence against future German raids of the Nijmegen road bridge and a newly constructed pontoon bridge.

Notwithstanding its responsibilities and continuing probing attacks against the 82 Airborne sector, Brian Urquhart, who had arrived from the UK following his 'sick leave' recalled that the HQ 'had virtually nothing to do in Nijmegen. We lived on the outskirts of the town in a villa which was periodically shelled by German 88mm guns and tried to keep ourselves busy, but nobody's heart was in it.'[9] After ten days, he found his position something of an embarrassment to himself and others and asked for a posting elsewhere, which Boy undertook to arrange. 'As usual' wrote Urquhart later, 'he was as good as his word.'[10] Boy wrote to Urquhart on

They rise gradually from the outskirts of Nijmegen to two ridges, one well-defined and facing north-east towards the Waal, the other much more broken and facing south-east towards the Reichswald. These form a bulwark against any advance from Germany itself between the Maas and the Waal, and in particular control the key roads to Nijmegen through Mook and Wyler. The ground rises to the north-east of Mook and its possession by the enemy would have threatened the bridge at Heumen, which was to prove the only one capable of carrying tanks. Furthermore, the Heights dominate the drop and landing zones around Groesbeek itself.

The tactical decision to seize and hold the Groesbeek Heights was bolstered by an intelligence report of German forces, including no fewer than 1,000 tanks, gathering in the Reichswald. Even if this report from SHAEF was not available to Boy and Gavin, it certainly was known to both Second Army and FAAA. Although it proved to be incorrect, Gavin was still to suffer attacks out of the Reichswald from the moment he landed and experienced some very tense moments, particularly on 20 September. Any breakthrough at Mook would have denied the Heumen bridge to the Allies, whilst around Beek and Berg-en-Dal, failure to hold the positions would have allowed the Germans direct access to Nijmegen.

The strategic priority was thus correct. Without the Groesbeek Heights, the road to Nijmegen via the Heumen bridge would have been barred and XXX Corps might never even have got past Grave. To have placed the Nijmegen bridge first and thus jeopardized the capture or retention of the other objectives, could well have led to complete disaster at Nijmegen as well as Arnhem. As Sosabowski was to say of his visit to Airborne Corps HQ on 24 September: 'It crossed my mind that if Operation 'Comet' had been carried out, the position which my brigade was supposed to have occupied near Nijmegen, without the friendly forces on that high ground, would not have been very pleasant.'[3]

The problem lay, as did so much else, with the timing of the lifts. Had Gavin been able to take in substantially his whole division on D-Day, he could have allocated sufficient troops to deal with the Nijmegen bridge. He particularly lacked 325 Glider Infantry Regiment, which could only fit into the original plan for arrival on D+2 and eventually arrived on D+6.

Verdict. Not guilty. The priorities were correct, in the light of the intelligence and the available resources, but they were the product of a thoroughly bad plan.

6. That he should not have turned down the offer by the GOC 52 Division to fly in a brigade group

The reply to the message received late on 20 September by Boy's HQ from Hakewill-Smith of 52 Division, offering to send in a brigade group by glider, was sent on 22 September, although it was apparently drafted on the previous day. Boy rejected the offer because to him, on the morning of 21 September, the outlook seemed encouraging. The Nijmegen bridges had been taken on the previous evening, 43 Division was arriving in Nijmegen and the corridor was open. There was some hope that Arnhem would be reached within 24 hours.

In fact Boy was deluded. The situation on the Island was static, with the Irish Guards held up and strong resistance being encountered at Oosterhout. Moreover, he had little idea of what was happening to 1 Airborne, where by this time Frost had been forced to surrender, the Heveadorp ferry had been lost and the remnants of the division had been forced back into the Oosterbeek perimeter. In the light of these events his reply was ridiculously optimistic.

His rejection of Hakewill-Smith's offer was not, however, necessarily wrong. Boy's priorities were the correct ones, which were to bring in the Poles, two-thirds of whom arrived on the afternoon of 21 September, and 325 Glider Infantry Regiment, which was yet again delayed. There was also an enormous demand on transport aircraft to bring in supplies to the rest of the Allied armies, which had been interrupted by the demands of Market Garden. 52 Division had received no training on gliders, which were completely different in a number of respects to the Dakotas designated to bring it into battle. Neither its jeeps nor its field or anti-tank guns, for instance, had been modified to fit into Horsas. There was no safe landing zone near Arnhem, whilst Landing Zones N and T near Groesbeek were in the middle of a battlefield. The only alternative was Landing Zone O near Overasselt, but this was required for 325 Glider Infantry Regiment and the remainder of the Poles. Later on 21 September the airfield at Oude Keent was discovered, but this was probably unknown to Boy when he wrote his reply.

Furthermore, it is highly unlikely that Boy would have received permission to use 52 Division. On 19 September a message had been received at Rear HQ to the effect that the division was now at the disposal of the Commander Second Army. Boy met Dempsey at Malden on the morning of 21 September, after he had received the offer from Hakewill-Smith, and it is unthinkable that the proposal was not discussed and that Boy's reply did not have Dempsey's endorsement. On the evening of 23 September, after Boy's reply had been sent, a signal arrived from Second Army confirming that the division should not be flown in without Dempsey's specific approval. It was by that time the only reserve available to Montgomery and Dempsey in the UK and, with one infantry division already disbanded to create reinforcements for others, it was not going to be squandered unnecessarily. Dempsey was perfectly prepared to use it to exploit success, but not to build on failure.

Verdict. Not guilty. It was the right answer for the wrong reason.

7. That he should have supported Sosabowski in his alternative plan to cross the Lower Rhine

The Valburg Conference on 24 September pitted Horrocks and Thomas against Sosabowski, with Boy playing little or no part in the proceedings. After the embarrassing confrontation in which Sosabowski had to back down on the use of his 1st Battalion in the crossing that evening with 4 Dorset, the Polish general had argued forcefully for a crossing by 43 Division and his own brigade further west than proposed, on the grounds that resistance would be much lighter there.

It was known by that time to Horrocks, Boy and Thomas that it would be impossible to effect a crossing in divisional strength. Two of the three brigades of 43 Division were heavily engaged in fighting the Germans around Elst and no further reinforcements were expected imminently. It was also known, as Boy confessed to Sosabowski later that day, and as was confirmed when the actual crossing was attempted, that there were not enough boats to carry it out. Although Horrocks wondered subsequently if he should have crossed further west, this might have been sensible two days earlier but was no longer a serious option. Even if a successful crossing had been effected, the troops would have had to have fought through the Germans to reach 1 Airborne.

Boy's priority at this time in any event, as suspected by Sosabowski, was to save the remnants of 1 Airborne and he almost certainly already thought that this would be more readily achieved by evacuation than by relief.

Verdict. Not guilty. Boy was better informed on the situation than Sosabowski and almost certainly felt that such an operation would prejudice any chance of bringing out Urquhart's men.

Conclusion

Loading the blame on Boy above all others for the failure of 'Market Garden', as some historians have done, is both facile and unfair. Nevertheless, as the co-architect at the very least of the outline plan and a willing accessory to the final plan, he must bear a significant share of the responsibility. Particularly after its modification by Brereton and Williams, the plan broke the fundamental tenets of airborne operations, namely that landings should take place in the maximum possible strength and as close as possible to the objectives, and that lightly armed troops should be assured of relief by conventional ground forces within a very short time. Montgomery expected that 1 Airborne would be relieved in forty-eight hours and Boy considered that they could hold out for four days, but the final plan, by denying to Gavin and Urquhart the resources necessary to capture the Nijmegen and Arnhem bridges on the first day, made this next to impossible.

There can be no question but that Boy was desperate to lead his troops into battle, but he would not have gone if he had expected other than success. His judgement was clouded by four factors, of which the achievement of personal ambition was only one. The others were his determination to use the weapon he had forged before it was too late and morale had collapsed completely, his understanding that Montgomery was completely set on the operation as the only way to achieve victory in 1944 and would not be swayed against it, and his grossly overoptimistic assessment of the German Army's capabilities, shared by most of his fellow senior officers and caused by recent experience and the memories of 1918.

As far as the execution of 'Market Garden' was concerned, HQ I Airborne Corps was not fit to go into action. In fact this made very little difference to events, as the operation stalled just north of the Waal and XXX Corps remained in control of the battle, although Horrocks did consult Boy on all the key decisions. With a highly capable and self-sufficient commander at 82 Airborne Division and little to do in the remainder of the Airborne Corps sector, Boy actually became irrelevant, except in one key respect. He was desperately anxious to save what was left of 1 Airborne Division and influenced the decision to evacuate it on the night of 25/26 September rather than encourage another, almost certainly vain, attempt to establish a new bridgehead further west. Roy Urquhart at least was later to give him credit for this.

Chapter 22

Aftermath (October–December 1944)

Montgomery described 'Market Garden' as 90 per cent successful. Although it was true that a valuable bridgehead had been gained, which would facilitate an attack through the Reichswald to clear the south bank of the Rhine in February 1945, on every other measure he was wrong. It was the end to his hopes of a 'Northern Thrust' to end the war in 1944. It left him with a vulnerable salient on either side of 'Hell's Highway' which attracted further reinforcements by the Germans and led to some extremely difficult battles before 21st Army Group could close up to the Maas along its entire length. Most importantly, it diverted him from what was most pressing, the clearance of the Scheldt estuary and the opening of the port of Antwerp, which did not happen until 28 November.

Boy was broadly in agreement with his mentor, although his assessment was based more on the purely tactical achievements of I Airborne Corps. In a letter to Daphne on 30 September he wrote: 'People don't seem to have been told that it [Arnhem and 1 Airborne Division] was only rather less than a third of the Airborne effort and that the whole thing was 80% successful. The two US Divisions which I have the honour to command have done marvellously and if it hadn't been for the atrocious weather and sheer bad luck the whole thing would have been 100% successful which in war would have been phenomenal.' Boy was constantly exasperated by the failure of the British press at the time and of historians later to give full credit to 82 and 101 Airborne Divisions. Both of them, in his view, had done all that had been asked of them and he had developed a high regard for both Gavin and Taylor. As he wrote to Hollinghurst: 'I only wish that the exploits of the two American divisions and everyone else during those hectic days when we were holding the corridor open, fighting the battle against the Germans in the Reichswald and struggling to force a corridor to the 1st Division, might be more fully appreciated.' Overall, just like Montgomery, Boy remained an 'unrepentant advocate' of 'Market Garden', but the anguish he felt over the losses incurred by 1 Airborne Division was to stay with him for the rest of his life.

Contrary to a commonly held belief, Boy received no British recognition for his role in the operation other than a mention in despatches, along with every other British corps and divisional commander in North-West Europe,[1] when these were announced in the following March. He had become a CB in the New Year's Honours of 1943, almost certainly in recognition of his work in raising 1 Airborne Division. He was not included among the knighthoods gazetted in July 1945 to all those corps commanders in North-West Europe and Italy who had not already received one, including Horrocks and Ritchie. He had to wait until 1 January 1946 before being awarded the KBE on the recommendation of Mountbatten. The Americans were more generous, putting him in for the Legion of Merit, whilst he also received the Order of Polonia Restituta from the Polish Government-in-Exile.

When Sosabowski wrote with congratulations on the award from his government, Boy replied to thank him and to acknowledge the honour, but also to say: 'I am going to be absolutely candid, and I say to you that the award of a Polish decoration, at the present time, to me is unfortunate. As you must be most fully aware, my relationship with you and your Brigade has not been of the happiest during the last few weeks.'[2] He was, in fact, deeply embarrassed, as he was shortly to put in motion the process which, two months later, would see Sosabowski relieved of his command.

The Sosabowski affair was an unhappy one which reflected poorly on the main British participants, but there can be no doubt that there was genuine displeasure about aspects of his conduct during the final days before the evacuation from Oosterbeek. This is reflected in the history of 43 Division, whose author was Brigadier Hubert Essame,[3] the commander of 214 Brigade during the battle. Essame had had no direct involvement with the Poles, as he was preoccupied with attacking Elst, but he was nevertheless close to the action, would have heard the views of Thomas and Essame's fellow brigadier, Ben Walton of 130 Brigade, shortly after the events described and would have conveyed them from their perspective in the history. Essame wrote of the attempt to put the Poles across on the night of 23 September, 'It must be recorded that General Sosabowski's attitude was the reverse of co-operative' and of the Valburg Conference, 'General Sosabowski's attitude at the conference cannot honestly be described as cordial.'[4] He made a further allegation of lack of cooperation by the Poles during the crossing on the night of 24 September. Whilst there may be sympathy for Sosabowski's stance on the crossings and some distaste at the way in which he was treated at the conference, it does appear that he caused considerable irritation at the time.

The reports which filtered back to the British military hierarchy were therefore certain to be unfavourable. As Sosabowski was serving under Boy's command, it is not too far fetched to imagine that the latter was taken to task by his fellow generals for his subordinate's behaviour. Whatever the case, he put in a report to Dempsey which was critical of Sosabowski and, by extension, the Polish Parachute Brigade. On his return to England Boy also mentioned this to the Director of Military Operations, Frank Simpson, who wrote to Montgomery asking for the C-in-C's views on the brigade's future.

Montgomery's reply, written on 17 October not to Simpson but directly to Brooke, was astonishing: 'Polish Para Brigade fought very badly and the men showed no keenness to fight if it meant risking their own lives. I do not want this brigade here and possibly you might like to send them to join other Poles in Italy.' It is possible that Sosabowski's lack of enthusiasm for the crossing at Heveadorp was misinterpreted as a lack of willingness to fight, whereas it was in fact a sensible appreciation of the dangers. It appears that there might have also been some criticisms of the

Poles' lack of discipline. Nevertheless, this was an unwarranted slur on a brigade many of whose members had, in an appallingly difficult situation, demonstrated great bravery. Montgomery was thought to be less than enamoured with the Poles generally and was rather grudging in his praise for the larger Polish formation in his army group, 1 Polish Armoured Division. He had also been personally exasperated by the earlier reluctance of the Poles to place the Polish Parachute Brigade at his disposal. However, the accusation levelled by him against the brigade cannot be supported in any way.

It was Boy, however, who was to wield the knife, in a letter (see Appendix 2) written on 24 November to Ronald Weeks, who as DCIGS was responsible at the War Office for relations with Allied formations. As Sosabowski's immediate superior, Boy was entirely within his rights to report on him. It cannot be determined whether what he said reflected just his own views and those of Horrocks and Thomas,[5] who are referred to in his letter, or whether it was also influenced in part by Montgomery's earlier judgement, but he must have known of the C-in-C's letter. Boy had met Brooke on 25 October and it is very likely that Montgomery's letter was discussed.

The most difficult statement to justify in Boy's letter is 'This officer proved himself to be quite incapable of appreciating the urgent nature of the operation', although by 'operation' Boy may have been referring specifically to the evacuation of 1 Airborne Division, which he felt would be put at risk by any further attempt to cross the Lower Rhine in force, as advocated by Sosabowski. The other criticisms, explicit or implied, cannot be so easily dismissed. Sosabowski was unquestionably difficult to deal with. He did not fall into line with decisions with which he disagreed, and whilst he may be admired for this in retrospect when he proved to be correct, his attitude at the time could be regarded as close to insubordination. He certainly had another agenda, the liberation of Poland, of which the British were highly suspicious, and he was keen to preserve his brigade as much as possible for this purpose. He had proved overall to be an awkward ally, and it did not matter, from this perspective, whether his views were right or wrong. Boy was perfectly entitled to deliver an adverse report on him in the knowledge that he would continue to be an impediment to Allied harmony. What Boy did not do was actually sack Sosabowski, as it was not in his power to do so. This could only be done by the Polish Government-in-Exile. Heavily leant on by the British they failed to stand up for him and their decision, delivered on 9 November, caused a near mutiny in the brigade, which was defused by Sosabowski himself.

There is no doubt that Sosabowski was shabbily treated by the British, Boy foremost among them, and that Montgomery's view, at least, was grotesquely inaccurate. It has been claimed subsequently by the Poles, by a number of the British veterans of Arnhem and by certain historians, that Montgomery and Boy used Sosabowski as a scapegoat for their own failure – indeed the rehabilitation of his reputation has depended on this allegation to a significant extent. There is not a shred of evidence for it. The two letters constitute the only written opinions of either man on the subject and it was only many years after the event that they came to light. Montgomery, who was not backward in delivering judgements on the operation as a whole, never referred to it again and neither did Boy, publicly or privately. They have nevertheless ironically become scapegoats themselves, in a campaign which led to Sosabowski being honoured posthumously by the Dutch Government in 2006.

After the climax and tragedy of 'Market Garden' it was difficult for Boy to return to whatever passed for normality. He continued in his joint appointments at I Airborne Corps and FAAA, but no further airborne operation was being considered for the foreseeable future. Boy's relationship with Brereton continued to improve and he accompanied him on a number of joint inspections, including of 38 Group RAF and 6 Airborne Division. The two men flew over together to France to inspect the 4th French Battalion SAS, to a number of whose soldiers Boy presented British decorations. He was also in demand to talk publicly about the recent operation, lecturing at both the Royal United Services Institute and at the Staff College.

Boy had not taken any leave since May. Daphne, in the meantime, had been busy with the continuing works at Menabilly and had little time for writing, although she had completed a play, *The Years Between*, which was in rehearsal at the time of Boy's return and was to open in London not long afterwards. Rather than have him come down to Cornwall, the two of them decided to treat themselves to a fortnight of relative luxury at Claridges.[6] He took only part of the time as leave, but she stayed there and he returned to the hotel each evening. On 14 November the two of them entertained Brereton, the other American generals and some of their staff to a cocktail party. The time in London was a success, but Daphne was already harbouring some doubts about how their relationship would fare once the war was over, whilst Boy remained determined to return to their 'routes' as quickly as possible. It was some time before this could be put to the test.

Boy's reputation in the higher reaches of the Army had not been diminished by the failure of 'Market Garden' and he continued to be held in high regard by both Brooke and Montgomery. In a letter to the CIGS of 28 September on the future employment of Urquhart and 1 Airborne Division, Montgomery wrote, 'If by any chance you took O'Connor for Egypt then I would ask you to let me have Browning for 8 Corps.'[7] In the event, O'Connor was to leave for India rather than Egypt,[8] but by that time Boy's future had been decided elsewhere. There is some evidence in any event, from the tenor of later letters to Daphne, that he was disillusioned with command in the field and was looking for something different. What he was to get was not, however, an appointment which he had either sought or was initially pleased with, the job of Chief of Staff to Mountbatten at South-East Asia Command (SEAC).

The genesis of this appointment lay in the ill health of Lieutenant General Sir Henry Pownall, who had gone out to South-East Asia with Mountbatten as his Chief of Staff in late 1943. A much older man than the Supreme Commander, Pownall had nevertheless got on well with and served as a steadying influence on his hyperactive superior. He had undergone an operation for a kidney stone in August 1944 and was away for two months following some complications. It seemed that Pownall might have difficulty with continuing to hold down his demanding job and with some reluctance Mountbatten began to seek a successor. He raised the issue with Brooke at the Cairo Conference, asking initially for either Archie Nye, the VCIGS, or John Swayne, Chief of Staff to Auchinleck at India Command. Brooke was never likely to give up Nye, his most invaluable deputy and the man who effectively ran the War Office whilst Brooke himself concentrated on grand strategy. Swayne, an outstanding staff officer with all the right qualifications, had only been in his job for six months and the move would certainly have been contested by Auchinleck. Brooke thus turned down both proposals, suggesting instead that the position be given to Bill Slim, the commander of the newly victorious Fourteenth Army. This was rejected by Mountbatten, who believed quite correctly that it was vital to keep Slim where he was.

A somewhat testy correspondence ensued between Mountbatten and Brooke, the former accusing the Army of failing to support him and threatening to promote Major General Wildman-Lushington, his Assistant Chief of Staff, the latter denying any failure to help and insisting that Lushington would be wholly inappropriate. It was then that Brooke came up with Boy's name, eagerly seized on by Mountbatten. Pownall reaction to the choice came in his diary: 'He is excellently qualified for it, my only reservation is that I believe he is rather nervy and highly strung, and if there's too much of that he's not a good half section for Mountbatten. Although the latter is now more restrained than he was he still wants a lot of looking after – the brake has to still to be put on pretty frequently and he doesn't want a Chief of Staff who eggs him on – very much the reverse.'[9] Pownall had certainly identified one key requirement of any COS for Mountbatten, the ability to keep him under control. He did not know Boy very well, however. 'Nervy and highly strung' was not an accurate description of him at this time, although he was a great deal less measured than Pownall himself.

Pownall's diary entry was made on 8 November, but it was not until 20 November that Boy was summoned to meet Brooke to be told of his appointment formally and it was some days later before it was made public. 'He took it well,' wrote the CIGS in his diary, 'but I doubt whether in his heart of hearts he was thrilled!'[10] In fact Boy had had wind of a new direction to his career some weeks earlier, writing to Daphne that he believed 'me won't be wearing the Red Beret very much longer but nothing definite yet and by the time 'ee comes up to London we will probably know more.'[11] He met Oliver Leese, who had just been appointed as the C-in-C Allied Land Forces South-East Asia (ALFSEA), to talk about the Far East on 30 October, and he may have had some inkling by then of what was in store for him.

As Brooke had suspected Boy was less than thrilled by the news of his new appointment. 'I've got a pretty awful job,'[12] he wrote to Daphne, but he was determined from the start to make the most of it. He was under orders to report to Mountbatten by the evening of 14 December, so there was little time to hand over his job as Brereton's deputy to Gale. On hearing the news Brereton himself noted in his diary, 'General Browning is a fine soldier and, despite differences of opinion between military men, I like and admire him very much. I wish him luck.'[13] There was one last occasion for Boy to share with the Airborne Forces before he left. On 6 December he and Urquhart led 320 survivors of Arnhem to Buckingham Palace. Major Robert Cain received the Victoria Cross from the King, the only one of four earned during the ground battle which was not posthumous, and seven DSOs and nineteen MCs were presented out of more than sixty decorations in all.[14] Three days later Boy flew out from Northolt.

Chapter 23

Kandy (December 1944–May 1945)

Boy's flight took him via Naples, Cairo and Karachi. Although the RAF failed to meet his deadline and eventually deposited him at Imphal on the morning of 15 December, Mountbatten was delighted to see him. Boy arrived just in time to witness a unique investiture, in which Field Marshal Wavell, the Viceroy of India, knighted Slim and his three corps commanders, Philip Christison of XV Indian Corps, Geoffrey Scoones of IV Corps and Monty Stopford of XXXIII Indian Corps, on the field of battle in recognition of their victories over the Japanese in the Arakan, at Imphal and at Kohima.

His appointments during 1943 and 1944 had left Boy very familiar with the theatres of war in the Mediterranean and North-West Europe and he was well acquainted with the leading personalities in both. Apart from his trip to India in September and October 1943, during which he had had no exposure to operations other than his unsatisfactory discussions with Wingate, SEAC was entirely new territory and he knew little about the 'Forgotten Army'. Most of the senior officers including Slim and Scoones were from the Indian Army, an organization which was almost entirely foreign to him. There were two divisional commanders, Pete Rees of 19 Indian Division and Douglas Gracey of 20 Indian Division, with whom he had served at Sandhurst in the 1920s, but the rest were strangers. Apart from Mountbatten, the man he knew best was Leese, a very old friend but one who had himself only arrived in the theatre just over five weeks earlier.

The deficiency was quickly remedied, as Boy was now to accompany Mountbatten on a comprehensive tour of the ALFSEA formations. They flew first to Kalemyo to see 11 East African Division, which had just completed an exhausting campaign to clear the Kabaw Valley of Japanese, and 2 Division, which comprised the advance guard of Operation 'Capital', Slim's pursuit of the Japanese into Central Burma with the objective of retaking Mandalay. The two men crossed the longest Bailey bridge in the world over the River Chindwin at Kalewa, which had been completed only three days earlier, before flying back to meet Stopford at his HQ. They then travelled up to Kohima, where they inspected 5 and 7 Indian Divisions and visited all the memorials to the battle. Boy particularly wanted to see the grave of a fellow Grenadier and friend, Willie Goschen, with whom he had served in the 1920s and who had been killed in action in command of 4 Brigade during the fierce fighting in May 1944.

On the next day, 18 December, Mountbatten and Boy had a half-hour lesson in close quarter combat from Lieutenant Colonel Grant Taylor, an expert in the subject who had learnt his trade with the FBI in Chicago. This nearly came in useful two days later, by which time the two were in the Arakan, first meeting Christison and inspecting 3 Special Service Brigade and 25 Indian Division, before moving on to the HQ of 82 West African Division. The GOC Major General George Bruce was a fiery character who sported ivory-handled pistols in the manner of Patton and insisted on driving the VIPs round his positions himself. Dispensing with the normal bodyguard, and with Boy and a staff officer suitably armed in the back seat of the jeep, Bruce took them not only up to but beyond his own forward posts, warning them to keep an eye out for Japanese snipers who had not been cleared from the area. After a hair-raising ride, during which it became clear that Bruce had little idea where the front line was situated, they managed to return intact but Mountbatten was not impressed. Following a similar incident some weeks later, in which Christison himself and Boy's American deputy Major-General Horace Fuller were pinned down under Japanese fire, Bruce was replaced.

The tour continued with a conference at Leese's HQ in Barrackpore, near Calcutta, which gave Boy the chance to meet some of the other senior officers of SEAC, including Admiral Sir Arthur Power, C-in-C of the East Indies Fleet, and Lieutenant General George E. Stratemeyer, the commander of Eastern Air Command, as well as Lieutenant General Sir Adrian Carton de Wiart, Churchill's representative to Chiang Kai-shek. Finally Boy and Mountbatten went on to New Delhi, where they held meetings with Wavell and Auchinleck and where Boy saw George Chatterton, who was on a visit to discuss the allocation and training of glider pilots with Eric Down. After more than a week on the move, they reached Mountbatten's HQ at Kandy on the evening of 23 December. 'Browning got here safely…' wrote Pownall, 'to my great content.'[1]

HQ Supreme Allied Commander South-East Asia (SACSEA) had been in Kandy, the former capital of Ceylon, since the previous April. It had been located before that in Delhi, but Mountbatten was keen to move away from the influence of India. Ceylon, as a separate Crown Colony, fitted the bill, even though it was five hundred miles further away from the front. Kandy was a pleasant town which, at 1,700 feet, lying round an artificial lake and surrounded by hills, had a much better climate than Colombo. Its various hotels were now occupied by senior members of the SEAC staff, as were a number of the houses around the lake, whilst the offices were in specially constructed buildings at the Botanical Gardens about three miles away. Mountbatten was occupying the Governor's residence, known as the King's Pavilion, and Boy was invited to stay there until he had secured appropriate accommodation for himself.

It was three days before Boy took over formally from Pownall, partly because Christmas intervened with a round of parties. Mountbatten's nephew, Lieutenant Philip Mountbatten RN, was staying at the King's Pavilion on leave from his ship, HMS *Whelp*, and Boy was invited to dinner there on Christmas Eve. It turned out to be a chaotic occasion, as the cook got drunk and served the meal back to front, but nobody appeared to mind. When sobriety returned there was much to do, not least to get to know all the main personalities. The most senior of these was the Deputy Supreme Commander, the American Lieutenant General Raymond A. Wheeler, universally known as 'Speck', a thoroughly competent administrator who was both liked and admired by his British colleagues.

Others who were important to Boy were his immediate subordinates, the Deputy COS, Fuller, and the Assistant COS, Wildman-Lushington, the latter succeeded by Major General Brian Kimmins in April 1945. The man to whom Boy really warmed was Wheeler's successor as Principal Administrative Officer, Major General Reginald 'Jack' Denning, who became the closest friend he had made since the death of Nigel Norman. The one service chief whom he had not met on his travels was the Air C-in-C. At the time of his arrival the position was held temporarily by Air Marshal Sir Guy Garrod, but he would be replaced by Air Chief Marshal Sir Keith Park in February 1945. There were also numerous Chinese, French and Dutch generals, 'but what they all do', Boy wrote to Daphne, 'I really don't know.'[2]

Boy had brought four members of his personal staff with him, his Military Assistant Eddie Newberry, now promoted to major, his American ADC Captain Jim Collins, and his longstanding batman and driver, Johnson and Johannides. He found that he desperately needed a competent senior staff officer and requested as his GSO1 Geordie Gordon Lennox, who had been commanding 5th Battalion Grenadiers Guards with great distinction in Tunisia and Italy for two years and who needed a rest from action. Gordon Lennox arrived in February 1945 and made an immediate impact. Boy's GSO2 was Major, later Lieutenant Colonel, Geoffrey Sherman, a Royal Marine who subsequently took over from Gordon Lennox in late 1945. Last but by no means least was Maureen Luschwitz, an officer in the Women's Auxiliary Army Corps (India), who joined him as his Personal Assistant after holding the same position with Garrod and in due course took over Newberry's job. She worked for him in various incarnations for nearly ten years and in due course became a close friend of the family.

In one way, the choice of Boy as Mountbatten's Chief of Staff was an extraordinary one. He was, without question, the most senior staff officer in the British Army during the war who had never attended Staff College. What Brooke had appreciated, from Boy's work at 1 Airborne Division in 1942, was that he was nevertheless very well organized, yet would not let himself be dominated, and this is exactly what Mountbatten needed. Mountbatten, apart from being a forceful character, had a propensity to get involved in minutiae. In one of his first letters from Kandy, Boy told Daphne that he was having difficulty 'persuading Dickie to hand over all the details to me instead of going into every detail himself which causes despondency and alarm and overworks him hopelessly.'[3]

Boy described HQ SACSEA as 'a very curious setup'. By the end of 1944 it had become a large and complex structure and dealt with a multiplicity of issues, inter-service, inter-allied and inter-theatre. It was the ultimate planning authority for military campaigns and was deeply concerned with political questions, particularly in liberated territories. Boy proposed 'to take charge of all staff detail so that he

[Mountbatten] can have plenty of time to get around and see the troops and make big decisions.'[4] His solution to taking control was to hold his own Chief of Staff's meeting every morning. Some of those who visited Kandy and attended this meeting regarded it as an extraordinary circus, but it was necessary to satisfy Mountbatten that progress was being made on all fronts and to keep him fully briefed, although at arms length on everything except matters of strategy and principle.

Boy had been asked by Brooke, who had been sceptical about Mountbatten's appointment and remained dubious about both his judgement and his military ability, to make regular reports to him and some of these were mildly critical of Mountbatten's need to be involved with everything, however small. On the whole Boy admired, liked and worked well with the Supreme Commander, although he found him tiring to deal with and on occasion difficult to keep under control. Though there were times, particularly initially, when both of them were away from Kandy together, Mountbatten preferred that Boy should be there whenever he himself was on his travels. This suited Boy, as it allowed him to get on with his business without interference.

Boy's first report to Brooke, written on Christmas Day 1944, was unequivocally upbeat about what he had seen. 'There is very little wrong with the discipline and morale of the troops in South-East Asia Command. In fact I was much impressed. There is no doubt that all ranks feel that they have got the measure of the Jap, and that the only problems are terrain, maintenance and resources of the right type. ... Oliver Leese appears to be settling down well and the Army and Corps Commanders are good. The same applies to Divisional Commanders ... I am convinced they are adequate for the task.'[5] His only complaint was that 44 Indian Airborne Division was not yet ready for operations. He asked subsequently for Walch, whom he continued to rate highly as a staff officer, to be sent out as Head of Airborne Operations at HQ SACSEA, to help speed things up and provide an airborne input into future plans.

In early January Boy flew up to meet Leese in Barrackpore – a journey which took the whole day from Kandy, starting with a three hour drive to Colombo – in an attempt to improve the poor relationship between the two HQs. Leese had been critical of the organization at Kandy, writing of Boy's arrival 'I am glad to get him out here, but I doubt if he can straighten out all the tangle at his end.'[6] There was friction, too, between ALFSEA and Fourteenth Army, the latter resenting the fact that Leese's staff officers, imported by him from Eighth Army, should tell it constantly how things had been done so much better in the Western Desert and Italy. These tensions were to come to a head some months later.

Leese paid a return visit to Kandy on 9 January. There was one serious operational issue on the agenda, the scarcity of aircraft available to support Slim in his drive on Mandalay and Rangoon. Slim was almost entirely reliant on air supply, as his overland lines of communication were very long and difficult. Now, just as the advance into Central Burma gathered momentum, three squadrons of US transport aircraft were withdrawn on the request of General Wedemeyer, Chiang Kai-shek's Chief of Staff, to support the Chinese in China itself. This could have had potentially disastrous consequences for any attempt to take Rangoon before the monsoon arrived in May. The situation was so serious that Mountbatten promised Leese that he would send Boy to London to make representations to the Chiefs of Staff. On 12 January Boy set off by plane.

Just after he left there was an exchange of signals with Whitehall, where the Chiefs of Staff considered that Boy's visit was unnecessary. Mountbatten persisted on the grounds that Boy was by then well on his way, asking that at least he should meet Brooke. In the event Boy arrived back in England on 16 January and was invited to attend the Chiefs of Staff meeting on 17 January, where he made urgent representations for the replacement of the aircraft. He was entirely successful. The Americans were persuaded to instruct Wedemeyer to return temporarily two of the three squadrons, which he did on 1 February, whilst one RAF squadron was sent to India from Italy and another from the UK. In due course two more squadrons were formed in India itself to replace the American aircraft.

Boy had been allowed some leave, as it was thought unlikely that he would be back for some time. He took five days at Menabilly with the family, but bemoaned the fact that it was too short for him to do all he wanted and to get back into 'routes'. Daphne reported to Tod: 'He likes Kandy and is thoroughly interested in his new job, and says that our 14th Army in Burma are wonderful and a higher class altogether than anything we have got in Europe ... I think he looks upon the war in Europe as a side-show now.'[7] On 25 January he left again, arriving back in Kandy three days later. He was not to see Daphne and the children for nearly eighteen months.

After such a disruptive start, Boy welcomed a few weeks on the spot to bring some order to his new job. Although he found Mountbatten personally good to work for, the demands placed on him were great and the transition from commander to senior staff officer difficult at first. 'Sometimes feel like applying for a new job ... unending meetings...' he wrote to Daphne.[8] He was also exasperated at having to entertain all the visitors who arrived in Kandy with great frequency but, true to form, he never showed his frustrations in public. He was certainly being appreciated and not just by Mountbatten. Slim wrote later: 'His advent was like a breath of fresh air to us and he made the Headquarters a much more likeable place.'[9] Boy continued to demand very high standards of his own staff and as usual could seem formidable, abrupt and even cold to those who did not know him well. His staff were devoted to him and those who managed to penetrate the seemingly arrogant exterior tended to like what they saw. Major J. H. Money, who arrived in Kandy early in 1945 to draft Mountbatten's Report on SEAC from its formation onwards, wrote much later: 'I was much impressed by Browning – a handsome man always impeccably dressed in uniforms which were said to have been designed by Daphne du Maurier,[10] a person of few words, a good judge of men, rather stern,[11] and a stickler for discipline. He was ready to help with information and advice whenever I approached him.'[12]

Outside work Boy's main priority was to find permanent accommodation and he soon located a suitable bungalow called Malabar House, which was up on a hill with a view over the lake. It required a great deal of work before it met his requirements, but this was handled by Jim Collins 'with the help apparently of most of the Wren officers here!'[13] Possibly the fact that Wrens were all fans of Daphne's contributed to their enthusiasm. Boy moved eventually in early March, sharing the bungalow very harmoniously with Denning and Desmond Harrison, the Engineer-in Chief. The only disadvantage was the building's proximity to the Buddhist Temple of the Tooth, whose priests were apt to start banging drums early in the morning!

Boy continued to travel within the theatre. On 20 February he flew up to New Delhi for meetings at GHQ India. India was outside SEAC, except for those areas in which ALFSEA formations were operational, but it remained both the main base and the recruiting and training ground, so relationships with India Command were of vital importance. It helped that the C-in-C, General Auchinleck, was on good terms with Mountbatten, whilst Swayne, the Chief of the General Staff, had been known to Boy for many years, initially as a fellow battalion CO in the Cairo Brigade in 1936, then as a divisional commander in 1941 and CGS Home Forces in 1942. After leaving New Delhi, Boy went on to Barrackpore for a Commanders-in-Chief's conference before returning to Kandy.

He was only back for just over a week before leaving again, this time to accompany Mountbatten to China. They flew initially to Monywa on the Chindwin to see Slim and then to Myitkyina to meet the American Lieutenant General Dan Sultan, the Commander of Northern Combat Area Command (NCAC), a largely Chinese formation driving down into Burma from the north. They then left for Kunming, where they saw Claire Chennault, the commander of the US Fourteenth Air Force. On the afternoon of 7 March they landed at Chungking, where Chiang Kai-shek was waiting to meet them at their house, an unusual honour. After two days of meetings, Mountbatten and Boy flew back over the 'Hump' to Jorhat and then went their separate ways, Boy returning to Myitkyina to inspect the Chinese divisions there, before flying on to Lashio to see the newly reopened Burma Road and then south to visit 36 Division, the only British formation serving in NCAC. On 13 March he was off again, first to see the situation around Mandalay, which fell shortly afterwards, and then to meet Christison in the Arakan. After stop-offs in Calcutta and New Delhi, it was an exhausted Boy who arrived back in Kandy on 18 March.

It was apparent by now that Mountbatten had become highly reliant on his new Chief of Staff, the more so when the 'Hapgift',[14] one of Mountbatten's two Dakotas in which Boy was flying, was reported missing on its first leg from Jorhat. It proved to be a false alarm but Mountbatten wrote subsequently: 'It wasn't until I was faced with the prospect of your having been extinguished that I realized how very much you had come to mean to me in these last few weeks and what a tremendous difference you have made to the whole command. I could not even begin to think of the name of anybody who could in any way replace you.'[15] Boy certainly seemed to have the measure of how to handle the Supreme Commander by now. He explained to Daphne how Mountbatten 'never for one moment stops talking. Me maintains a masterly silence during the torrent of words and every now and then puts in a dampening remark which silences him for sufficient time to get in a few well chosen remarks which are essential and to the point!'[16]

As usual, Boy was giving everything to his job and this and the climate were starting to take something of a toll on his health, even leading to a mild recurrence of 'me tum'. He realized that he was smoking and drinking too much and although he managed to reduce both he felt increasingly tired, yet often unable to sleep. He was off on his travels again only ten days after his long trip, back to New Delhi before going on to see Eric Down at 44 Indian Airborne Division, and then, in mid-April, to the Arakan, Calcutta and yet again to Delhi, where among others he met Hollinghurst, now AOC Base Air Forces South-East Asia. Every so often he was able to get up for a day or two in the hills, where at least the temperature and humidity were much lower, but the tempo at SACSEA was rising as the campaign in Burma approached its climax.

Chapter 24

Victory (May–November 1945)

'Well we've got Rangoon and beaten the monsoon by about an acid drop,' wrote Boy to Daphne on 4 May 1945. Mountbatten was in bed with an extended bout of dysentery at the time, albeit 'distressingly hearty', and so Boy had to take the salute on his behalf at the Victory Parade in Kandy on 8 May for the joint celebration of the fall of Rangoon and VE-Day. There were considerable festivities that night, during which Gordon Lennox played the piano and Boy performed his Cossack dance, leaving him very stiff on the following day.

Rangoon had been entered following a seaborne landing, with a parachute drop at Elephant Point by 50 Indian Parachute Brigade, which particularly delighted Boy. The landing had been proposed by Slim, just in case Fourteenth Army became bogged down by the weather in its advance from the north, and was strongly supported by Mountbatten, against some resistance from Leese. The relationship between the Supreme Commander and the C-in-C ALFSEA had in fact been showing signs of deterioration and matters were about to come to a head.

The problem had manifested itself initially two months earlier with a mild case of lese-majesty, in which Leese had referred to HQ SACSEA as the 'other HQ', which was not considered by Mountbatten as adequately reflecting ALFSEA's subordinate position. Boy had warned Brooke about the situation in a letter at the end of March, also pointing out that Leese was not getting on with his fellow C-in-Cs and ascribing his attitude to fancying himself as a second Montgomery, but lacking the necessary talent. HQ ALFSEA became increasingly inclined to take decisions which did not fall within its remit and to try to keep Kandy at arm's length, which infuriated Boy. 'The worst trial in we lives here', he wrote to Daphne on 19 April, 'am Oliver Leese and his HQ. There am no doubt about it that he is tricky and dishonest with overwhelming ambition – the combination makes it almost impossible to deal with him … . All very surprising and disappointing.' He enjoined Daphne to keep it to herself 'as no whisper must get about to destroy the outward harmony of the proceedings.'

Shortly before the fall of Rangoon, a sharp exchange of signals took place between Mountbatten and Leese over the activities of the Civil Affairs Service (Burma). Leese was responsible for the administration of Burma through CAS(B), but Mountbatten had overall accountability for policy. The latter therefore felt that he had every right to ask questions regarding the organization's activities, but Leese interpreted this as dissatisfaction with his exercise of command and asked that the valuable time of his staff should not be wasted by such enquiries. Mountbatten then made it clear that he could ask for information from a subordinate whenever he wished and expected loyalty from Leese in return. He subsequently reported the reprimand to Brooke. Swayne, who was back in England from New Delhi in mid-March, also told Brooke that he thought that trouble was brewing between the Supreme Commander and his land forces C-in-C.

What brought matters to a climax was Leese's inept handling of Slim. Boy had himself met the commander of Fourteenth Army during his long trip to China and Burma in March and had noticed that he was showing signs of tiredness. This was unsurprising, as Slim had been in almost continuous action for over a year, but Boy reported his concerns to Leese on his way back to Kandy. Leese flew immediately to see Slim, who confirmed that he would like four month's leave after the capture of Rangoon. Leese was surprised at the request, which suggested to him that Slim was exhausted and almost certainly needed replacing. On 3 May, the day after Rangoon was entered by Allied troops, he visited Kandy for a meeting with Mountbatten, described by the latter as 'a very important and not too easy interview.'[1] Leese proposed that Fourteenth Army should be withdrawn to India to plan Operation 'Zipper', the invasion of Malaya, and placed under Christison, who had experience in amphibious operations, whilst Slim would be left to mop up in Burma in command of a new Twelfth Army. Mountbatten was far from convinced, but authorized Leese to sound out Slim.

Leese flew on to the Arakan, where he outlined his proposal to a delighted Christison. He then met Slim at the latter's HQ at Meiktila, where he explained to him what he had in mind. Slim's immediate reaction was that he was effectively being relieved of his command, in which case he would decline the offer of Twelfth Army and retire. Leese said that he should reflect on the proposals and later rang Boy to report on the meeting and to say that he believed that Slim would in due course accept them. Slim understood quite differently, continuing to believe that he had been sacked. He confided only in his immediate staff and then went on a few days' leave with his wife to Shillong, arriving back on 13 May when he informed his other corps commanders, Stopford and Frank Messervy.

The cat was now out of the bag, the news spreading like wildfire around Fourteenth Army and in India and being almost universally received with dismay. In the meantime a storm was also brewing in London, where Brooke had received a letter from Leese describing his proposals, but replied to say that he would not countenance the relief of Slim from Fourteenth Army without the strongest reasons being given by both Mountbatten and Leese. Brooke also wrote to Mountbatten demanding to know why he should agree to a change in an army commander without prior consultation. Auchinleck happened to be in London, where he too expressed his concerns to Brooke. In his diary for 17 May the CIGS wrote: 'Leese is going wild and doing mad things, prepared a fair rap on the knuckles for him!'[2] Four days later Leese arrived back in Kandy, where Mountbatten made it quite clear that Slim should be reinstated, on which Leese backed down and the status quo ante was duly confirmed. Boy wrote to Brooke on 24 May confirming that matters were settled, but expressing an opinion that Leese's handling of the matter had adversely affected both those involved and the morale of Fourteenth Army. He queried whether Slim could in future serve comfortably under Leese.

There the matter rested for a month, helped by the fact that Slim went on leave to the UK. Mountbatten travelled to Rangoon for the Victory Parade there on 15 June, with Boy holding the fort in Kandy, but Boy was asked to represent the Supreme Commander 'to see fair play' at subsequent talks held on HMS *Cumberland*, moored on Rangoon River, between the soon-to-be reinstated Governor of Burma, Sir Reginald Dorman-Smith[3] and the Burmese politicians headed by Aung San.[4] Mountbatten was convinced of the need to bring Aung San and his colleagues, who had sided with the Japanese during the occupation, into some form of partnership with the British, against the inclinations of Dorman-Smith who considered initially that they should be treated as traitors. Boy had fully adopted Mountbatten's position, but even the latter was surprised by the way in which he handled the matter. 'I was staggered to find that Boy Browning, who was my representative at this meeting, had himself pressed and got the Governor to agree that Aung San's forces should have their title changed to 'Patriotic Burmese Forces' and that Aung San should be made Deputy Inspector-General of the regular Burma Army, with the rank of Brigadier; a very far cry indeed from arresting him and declaring his Army illegal!'[5]

Boy flew from Rangoon by Sunderland flying boat through monsoons storms to New Delhi, where he attended a Supreme Commander's conference. This turned out to be Leese's last appearance at such a forum. Brooke, who held the same opinion as Boy of the likely relationship between Leese and Slim, and had in any event always doubted the former's ability, wrote to Mountbatten on 19 June advising him to replace Leese with Slim and offering Dempsey as the latter's successor. On 2 July a letter from Mountbatten was delivered by hand to Leese informing him that his appointment had been terminated. Boy's role in the affair had not been central, but his advice to Mountbatten and his reflections to Brooke had almost certainly been influential. In spite of his long friendship with Leese[6] all Boy's sympathies lay with Slim, whom he greatly admired.

Boy now had other problems to contend with, the most difficult of which was the 'Python' scheme. Immediately after the end of the war in Europe, the British Government announced that all those who had served for more than three years and eight months overseas would be repatriated immediately. This had an immediate effect on SEAC, many of whose British units, and particularly those in Indian Divisions, had been serving in the theatre for much of war. Matters were made considerably worse when the Secretary of State for War, Sir James Grigg, unexpectedly announced in the House of Commons on 8 June that the qualifying time would be further reduced to three years and four months. This meant that the numerous formations and units which had arrived in India as reinforcements during the first half of 1942, including 2 Division, would no longer be available for 'Zipper', now being planned for August or September.

Boy was incandescent with rage. 'The idiot [Grigg]', he wrote to Daphne, 'did it without asking us about the repercussions and without any warning, a pure electioneering stunt which will probably have the effect of prolonging our part in the Jap war by six months. It really is too infuriating. There's an <u>enormous</u> 'block' of chaps who are now caught within the four shorter months and their going has <u>completely</u> bitched our next operation – there will be one hell of a row with the chiefs of staff when they realize what it means ... we've been so rude to Grigg over this business that we shall all come back soon I suspect with small bowler hats plonked firmly on our heads.'[7] It might have been this which persuaded Boy to vote Liberal in the General Election that saw Churchill defeated, and he predicted correctly to Daphne that the troops would vote for Labour if they voted for anyone.

Daphne, at the time, was hard at work on another book, based on an episode in the history of Menabilly. *The King's General* had as its hero Sir Richard Grenvile, a leading Cavalier during the English Civil War. Boy liked the title, although Daphne herself expressed some concern that the readers might think that Grenvile's character reflected his own. Initially Boy was unworried: 'About people thinking it was me – well – we can take it!'[8] He suggested that it might be dedicated to Mountbatten, but she insisted that it should be him. The dedication duly appeared as 'To my husband, also a general, but, I trust, a more discreet one'. However, when Boy read the book many months later, he was dismayed. A suggestion from him that it should have a happy ending had been ignored and although he thought it beautifully written he had two observations: 'to wit (a) the chap is so unpleasant that it makes the book a bit unpleasant and (b) the word 'discreet' in the dedication is nothing like enough to deal with the matter!!'[9]

Any chance that Boy might have hoped for in the way of leave in the UK was dashed by an increase in his workload, juggling the resources required for 'Zipper', dealing with political issues in Burma, where nationalism was gathering pace, and beginning to consider the possible implications of an end to the war not only on Malaya, but also on the wider SEAC area. Mountbatten was away from 11 July to 14 August, first on a visit to his fellow Supreme Commander, General MacArthur, in the Philippines, and subsequently to attend the Potsdam Conference. Daphne was hopeful that Boy would accompany him, 'but', as she wrote to Tod, 'the lights and the music of Kandy must have been too much for him.'[10] This was symptomatic of her mood at the time, believing that he did not want to come home and beginning to question her own feelings for him. She was still seeing Christopher Puxley, who came to stay at Menabilly during July, but the affair was nearing its end.

Mountbatten's return to Kandy was preceded by momentous news. At Potsdam he had been let into the secret of the atomic bomb and had been authorized by Churchill to send a signal to Boy that the Japanese were expected to capitulate on or about 15 August, although he was unable to provide the reason. This changed every assumption that SEAC had been making about the prosecution of the war and its aftermath, but Boy was able to put in hand the preliminary planning for the new circumstances by the time of Mountbatten's return. This would involve the occupation not only of Malaya, but also of Hong Kong, Thailand, French Indo-China and the Netherlands East Indies.

The atomic bombs were dropped on Hiroshima and Nagasaki on 6 and 9 August respectively and the Japanese duly capitulated on 15 August, just as Churchill had forecast. It did not help the planning that Boy had been ill with a septic throat which required him to be hospitalized and given 'frightful pills' every four hours. He was well enough to meet Mountbatten on his return, but the Supreme Commander noted that he was still looking very ill. He was far from fully recovered a week later, but this did not stop him being sent as Mountbatten's representative to conduct the preliminary surrender negotiations in Rangoon. MacArthur had decreed that no formal surrenders should take place until he had signed the overall instrument in Tokyo Bay on 2 September, but there was a mass of detail to agree in respect of local arrangements before then.

Lieutenant General Numata, the Chief of Staff to Field Marshal Count Terauchi, Commander-in-Chief of Japan's Southern Army and thus Mountbatten's opposite number, arrived by plane at Mingaladon airfield outside Rangoon on the morning of 26 August. He and his delegation were received by Stopford, in his new capacity as Commander of Twelfth Army, and then escorted to Government House in Rangoon. Numata and two of his colleagues sat facing a row of Allied officers in the Throne Room and, when Boy entered at 1215, the meeting began. The Japanese were presented with a document which made Terauchi fully responsible for enforcing the cease fire, for removing all minefields, for making all signals in clear and not in code and for maintaining law and order until the Allies arrived. Other matters addressed included arrangements to drop doctors and medical supplies into POW camps and twenty-four hour reconnaissance flights over occupied territories.

The Japanese had come in the belief that they would be able to negotiate the terms of any agreement, but Boy made it quite clear that he would only permit clarification. When Rear-Admiral Chudo asked for separate arrangements for the Japanese Navy, this was denied, as the Tenth Area Fleet was under Terauchi's operational control. The meeting came to a standstill when the Japanese realized that some of their objectives were not going to be met and they had to withdraw to confer amongst themselves, but understanding that they were not going to make any progress, they reluctantly agreed to continue. Further meetings on matters of detail took place on that day and the next and the preliminary surrender agreement was signed by Boy and Numata at 1825 on 27 August.[11]

With the capitulation, the SEAC area had increased enormously and now included Malaya, Singapore, Borneo, the southern half of French Indo-China, the Netherlands East Indies and Thailand. Both politically and militarily, the last of these proved to be the easiest to handle. Although nominally neutral, it had been occupied by and cooperated with the Japanese, but with no colonial history and a government only too anxious to please the Allies, it could be largely left to its own devices, although the HQ and a brigade of 7 Indian Division was sent in during the first week of September to oversee the Japanese surrender and to release the many

POWs in the country. In Borneo, Australian troops had already landed and were speedily augmented, whilst Operation 'Zipper' took place as a tactical exercise to facilitate the re-occupation of Malaya. 5 Indian Division arrived in Singapore by sea on 5 September.

The French and the Dutch were as anxious as the British to resume their former colonial roles and sent large delegations to HQ SACSEA to establish their positions. Neither country, however, had any military units in the Far East and, as nationalist sentiment was known to be vigorously opposed to re-colonization and unrest was almost certain, ALFSEA was compelled to provide the necessary troops to keep order. Advance elements of 20 Indian Division arrived at Saigon on 13 September, where Gracey took control of Terauchi's HQ and established a SACSEA Control Commission, whilst 23 Indian Division began to land in Java at the end of the month.

On 12 September, Mountbatten took the formal unconditional surrender of all the Japanese forces in the SEAC area in the Council Chamber of the Municipal Buildings in Singapore, accompanied by Wheeler, the Land, Sea and Air C-in-Cs and representatives from China, India, Australia, France and the Netherlands. Boy was not present, as once again he was holding the fort at Kandy, but he deputed Kimmins and Sherman to organize a suitably impressive ceremony. He flew to Singapore with Gordon Lennox later in the month, where he met Mountbatten and Dempsey who had recently arrived to assume command of Fourteenth Army. On 27 September the three of them drove round the island, visiting the released POWs and inspecting the various military and naval installations. They then went to meet the new Secretary of State for War, Mr J. J. Lawson, in Boy's words to Daphne 'a very decent old chap and quite shrewd [and] certainly honest – but he would have been more suitable if he was ten years younger.'[12] Boy returned to Kandy the next day, accompanied by Lawson, but leaving Gordon Lennox behind to represent him in Singapore.

It had already been decided that the HQs of SACSEA, ALFSEA and Air Command South-East Asia would be relocated to Singapore as soon as practicable, but to Mountbatten's displeasure the Admiralty decided that the East Indies Fleet, which had come under SEAC, should remain in Colombo, whilst the Pacific Fleet would have its base in Hong Kong, which was outside the SEAC area. Boy needed to plan the SACSEA move at the very time its staff was rapidly diminishing, due to both demobilization and an insistence from the British Government that cuts should be made for budgetary reasons. In a situation where the demands on the HQ in particular were heavier than ever, this placed a great deal of strain on him.

Boy's first concern was with RAPWI, the Repatriation of Prisoners of War and Internees. There were about 125,000 Allied prisoners and civilian internees in Japanese hands at the time of the surrender, most in extremely poor physical condition, and all of them needed to be released, provided with food and medicine and, as soon as they were fit to go, returned to Europe, Australasia or America. The problem of looking after them was largely taken over by Lady Louis Mountbatten who, as Superintendent-in-Chief of the St John Ambulance Brigade and Chairman of its Joint War Organization with the Red Cross, had already had similar experience in Europe.

The task for Boy and his staff was first to distribute supplies, then to transfer the prisoners to safety and finally to juggle the required shipping with the simultaneous demand for the repatriation of the tens of thousands of servicemen who had been promised demobilization by the British Government. The first RAPWI vessel sailed from Singapore for the UK on 10 September, only five days after the colony had been liberated, and by the end of the month over 53,000 former prisoners had been evacuated from the SEAC area. The number rose to 71,000 by the end of October, but slowed thereafter as many of those released had required hospitalization and were not fit to travel. Some were in any event domiciled in the area, including many of the Dutch civilians interned in Java and Sumatra.

For the time being SEAC was responsible for all aspects of the government of the liberated territories and the next most significant concern was to ensure the provision of essential foodstuffs, notably rice and flour, in circumstances where the annual crops had been much reduced. Once again, the adequacy of shipping was the major problem. Furthermore, seaways had to be cleared of mines and the ports converted back to non-military use. Entirely new skills were demanded of the SEAC staff to ensure a return to peacetime normality.

It quickly became apparent that the colonial possessions of Britain's European allies were going to prove troublesome. The problem surfaced quickly in Indo-China, where the Viet Minh under Ho Chi Minh declared a republic in Vietnam on 17 September. The British, who had gone in primarily to disarm and in due course repatriate the Japanese, found themselves involved in internal politics. As temperatures rose to boiling point between the local French and the nationalists, Gracey concluded that it was essential to proclaim martial law, although this was contrary to Mountbatten's orders. It was popular with the French, however, and gave General Leclerc, who had arrived from Europe, time to assert control over the key Saigon area. French troops began to arrive during the autumn, allowing 20 Indian Division to withdraw early in 1946.

The situation in the Netherlands East Indies (NEI) was much more complex, although the intelligence on the ground was so poor that it took the Allies longer to realize it. The advance party from 23 Indian Division landed in Java only on 25 September, followed by Royal Marines from HMS *Cumberland* and then an infantry battalion. The division's GOC, Major General Hawthorne, arrived on 30 September in the company of Christison, now Commander Allied Land Forces, Netherlands East Indies who had been briefed prior to his departure by Boy. The main centres of Western Java were speedily occupied, followed by other major cities. In the meantime 26 Indian Division landed in Sumatra.

Boy was already frustrated by the 'bone-headed' attitude of the Dutch, who clearly wanted to restore the position they had held prior to the Japanese occupation and were reluctant to enter into any substantive discussion with the nationalists.

Mountbatten, by instinct a liberal who sympathized with the nationalist view, was not always helpful. 'Supremo is showing signs of cold feet', wrote Boy to Daphne, 'over such things as the press (who are a perfect nuisance) and the setting up of British courts in Dutch territory owing to the fact that there are no Dutch courts and someone has to deal summarily with those Indonesians who commit crimes against our troops and against normal law and order.'[13] The military situation rapidly deteriorated, with the Japanese temporarily rearmed in order to be able to assist their former enemies to retain control of the key centres.

With most of the other issues under control and civilian rule gradually being introduced in the British possessions, the NEI problem completely dominated the coming months and the strain began to take a toll on Boy's health, with another attack of 'me tum' in mid-October. He was also dismayed to find that he now needed glasses for reading. The impending move to Singapore filled him with gloom, although it had the advantage of being much closer to the action.

Chapter 25

Singapore (November 1945–July 1946)

On November 23, HQ SACSEA formally relocated to Singapore, where it took over the Cathay Building, a ten-storey office block built as recently as 1939. Boy's enormous office, containing a conference table as well as his own large desk at the far end, was close to Mountbatten's on the top floor and commanded a fine view over the harbour.[1] He had located a good-sized bungalow in the grounds of Government House, Mountbatten's residence, and he, Denning and Harrison moved in there, although Harrison was to leave for the UK early in 1946.

Mountbatten himself arrived on 1 December, in time to greet Brooke, who was on a world tour. The CIGS had never visited the theatre during the war and had shown little interest in it relative to the Mediterranean and North-West Europe. Now on the spot for the first time, he found his opinion of Mountbatten improving, whilst he also agreed to support him in taking a firm line with the Dutch on the question of their relationship with the Indonesian nationalists. Boy used the opportunity to send Christmas presents back to the family in Brooke's plane.

1946 began well for Boy when his knighthood was announced in the New Year's honours list, bringing a flood of congratulations. Boy had been able to warn Daphne in advance: 'As 'ee knows me doesn't want a K and we failed to prevent Supremo for putting a man in for it,'[2] but he was nevertheless gratified. Another honour to come his way was the Colonelcy of the Indian Parachute Regiment, emphasizing his stature at the time as the pre-eminent airborne soldier. The regiment had been formed in March 1945 and was composed of four battalions, one Hindu, one Moslem and two Gurkha, and four independent companies. Two of its battalions had seen action at Sangshak, during the Battle of Imphal/Kohima, but the regiment had thereafter had been unemployed, much to Boy's chagrin, until the successful drop by a composite Gurkha battalion at Elephant Point as part of the operation to retake Rangoon. The distinctions of its British counterpart – the maroon beret, the parachute cap badge and the Pegasus shoulder badge, the last two with the addition of the word INDIA – were all adopted by the new regiment.[3]

For the first five months of the year, Mountbatten spent more than half his time travelling, not only in the SEAC area, but to India, Nepal, Australia and New Zealand. Boy, on the other hand, was more firmly rooted to the HQ than he had been in Kandy, indeed his sole overseas visit during this time was to Batavia and Surabaya for a week at the end of February, to see what was happening on the ground and participate in discussions with the Dutch.[4] The absence of the Supreme Commander was a mixed blessing, as he told Daphne: 'Being away so much we lose our grip on him and his short visits back to his own HQ merely stirs up a lot of unnecessary turmoil about things that don't matter.'[5]

For the HQ as a whole, the demands began to diminish as 1946 progressed. Control of French Indo-China passed to the French at the end of January, although the last British battalions did not leave for another two months, whilst first Burma and then Malaya and Singapore moved from military to civil government. Before Malaya and Singapore did so, Boy had one of the very few outright disagreements with Mountbatten of his whole tenure as Chief of Staff. The issue arose when left-wing Chinese trade unionists called a series of strikes in February. Mountbatten allowed protest marches to take place, but agreed initially that up to fifty of the leaders who were Chinese nationals should be deported. Ten were arrested and recommended for deportation, but to the consternation of his staff, his civilian advisers and the officers of Malaya Command, the Supreme Commander changed his mind on the grounds that those detained had been unaware of the possible consequences of their action.

Dempsey and Boy both disagreed profoundly with the decision and Boy put his views in writing. 'You have always encouraged me to express my considered opinion on any subject for your own private information. I feel it my duty to say that I fundamentally disagree with the policy outlined in your paragraph 5 (the decision not to expel the Chinese). I am convinced that all steps which are legal, and which can in any way improve conditions in the country, should be taken as soon as possible, and that SACSEA should hand over to the Civil Government the best regulated country which it is possible for the former to achieve.'[6] Mountbatten appeared not to hold it against him, replying, 'I do appreciate your writing so frankly to me and am glad to have a Chief of Staff who gives me his views so frankly and fully even when he knows that I am not likely to agree with him.'[7] Much to Boy's irritation, however, when Mountbatten's confidential report on him appeared three weeks later, it gave him top marks for everything, but concluded 'As a staff officer, in spite of no previous experience, he has shown outstanding ability and *though his political judgement still requires development* [author's italics] his loyalty in carrying through a policy is unquestionable.' Boy wrote indignantly to Daphne that political judgement should not have even been touched on, as soldiers were not supposed to have political views, and that, in any event, the Colonial Office had agreed with him!

As responsibility passed to other nations or to civil authorities, the numbers at HQ SACSEA diminished rapidly. From a peak of 600 officers and 3,000 other ranks during the war, by 1 June 1946 the numbers were down to 20 officers and 60 other ranks. The Americans, with no further interest in the area, had been the first to leave but they were followed by all those British regular servicemen who were subject to Python and the very large numbers of emergency commissioned officers and conscripted other ranks who were due for demobilization. Gordon Lennox and Newberry both returned to the UK, the former to pursue a highly successful career in the army, the latter to re-enter civilian life with a well-earned MBE for which he had been recommended by Boy in recognition of nearly four years of faithful service. Johnson had already gone, to be replaced by Guardsman Poulter, a more than adequate substitute, although apparently not quite as good as his predecessor at polishing leather. Johannides remained to drive Boy's large Cadillac.

Boy was working as hard as ever, indeed the prolonged absences of Mountbatten meant that the full burden of decision-making was falling on his shoulders, although he continued to have the support of Jack Denning. His health was not of the best, with more frequent occurrences of 'me tum', together with other, mostly minor ailments. In general he felt tired and had lost a lot of weight, whilst his hair was showing signs of turning grey. He was concerned that he was also mentally jaded and unable to come up with any new ideas, although coping satisfactorily with the issues which crossed his desk. At the insistence of Mountbatten, he was having his portrait painted by the official war artist,[8] which he thought a good likeness, although it made him look 'pretty grim'.

The social life in Singapore played an even more significant part of Boy's job than it had in Kandy and he was expected to entertain or be entertained on most nights. There were an enormous number of visitors, many of whom were extremely tiresome, although he welcomed friends such as David Burghley and Adrian Carton de Wiart, the latter still the Prime Minister's Representative to Chiang Kai-shek. Whilst he liked most of those with whom he came in regular contact – he was on good terms with Lord Killearn, who had been brought in as Special Commissioner to handle food distribution and also to deal with many aspects of the negotiations between the Dutch and the Indonesians, and with Malcolm MacDonald, who arrived to be Governor-General of Malaya and Singapore and Commissioner-General for South-East Asia – the constant social round after work left Boy little time for relaxation. His only regular exercise was walking in the Botanical Gardens. In April he managed to take his first leave since a week off in the previous August in the aftermath of his septic throat. This time he went to Fraser's Hill, a small hill station in Malaya which was at least much cooler than Singapore, but even there he had a bout of his stomach trouble.

Part of the problem was that he was smoking and drinking too much. He was rarely seen without a cigarette and he put his daily consumption of alcohol as four strong gins between 7pm and dinner, a couple of glasses of white wine with dinner and two whiskies and water before bed. He had convinced himself that he sweated it out, so that it was the equivalent of less than half what it would have been in England. However, it seems more likely that it was a major contributory factor to his poor health. In mid-June he reported to Daphne that his left leg hurt so badly after a walk that he had been hardly able to get home. This was possibly a harbinger of the circulation problems which were to blight his last years.

Although the demands of both work and his social life occupied most of Boy's time, his attention began to turn to aspects of his return to the UK, which he could be certain would take place within the year. The one topic which occupied his thoughts more than anything else was sailing, indeed this clearly provided great relief from the stresses of his job. Increasingly his letters to Daphne contained instructions regarding their existing boats, *Ygdrasil* and *Restless*. 'Yggy', for which he had enormous affection and which would continue to serve for 'routes doings', had survived the war in relatively good shape, although he was keen to install new engines and there was an extensive correspondence on her repainting. Given his appointment at the Royal Fowey Yacht Club, he insisted that she should be a 'smart and snappy looking Commodore's barge'. *Restless*, on the other hand, had deteriorated badly and there was some doubt about whether or not she could be rescued, given the lack of materials, particularly wood.

There was one new addition to the fleet, its purchase also inspired by Boy's position as Commodore of the RFYC, which he felt required him to have a boat in which to compete in regattas. In the late 1920s a local Fowey boatbuilder had designed an 18-foot all-wood, open deck boat with a lead keel, which had performed exceptionally well. A number of leading members of the RFYC ordered identical boats and the new class was named after the fictional town of Troy, a thinly-disguised Fowey, in the novels of Sir Arthur Quiller-Couch,[9] then the Commodore of the club. Most of the boats were named after precious stones, but the one which now came up for sale and was duly purchased was *Shimmer*. It was raced by Dick Bunt, a retired seaman who had become friendly with the family and acted as their unofficial boatman, and then by Tessa, the only one of the Browning children who inherited any interest in sailing.

The majority of Boy's attention, however, was devoted to something on a much larger scale. Such leisure time as he had enjoyed during the war had been taken up with designing his proposed motor fishing vessel (MFV), the *Fanny Rosa*. He believed that such a craft would allow him and Daphne much more room and greater freedom to cruise than they had enjoyed with either 'Yggy' or *Restless*. He also felt strongly that they deserved it 'after all these weary years'. Boy's ambition to build it in the UK had been thwarted by the lack of building materials and he determined to see if he could do better in the Far East. To hedge his bets, however, Boy had been in touch with others, notably the naval architect Jack Laurent Giles, to whom he had submitted an outline design for a sailing cruiser to be called *La Mouette*, after the hero's ship in *Frenchman's Creek*, and the celebrated American boatbuilder Frank 'Huck' Huckins, whom he had met during his trip to the United States, and to whom he wrote about the possible purchase of one of his Fairform Flyer motor yachts. Pending the possible building of *La Mouette*, he even asked Daphne to consider buying *Flica II*, a famous 12-metre boat designed by Laurent Giles which had come up for sale, but she was non-committal.

Soon after arriving in Singapore he approached the naval authorities to see if it might be possible to build *Fanny Rosa* to his own design in the dockyard. 'Terrific doings!' he wrote to Daphne at the end of January. 'The Port Commissioner who runs the whole of Singapore harbour has offered to build in seasoned teak the hull, decks, bulkhead – in fact everything except the fittings and engines ... at cost price!!'[10] He thought that this would be half the price of an equivalent boat in the UK. Discussions took place with a local naval architect, decisions were made on the building materials and then, six weeks later … 'Terrible disappointment – the Port Commissioner has worked it all out and wants £8,000 just for the hull. I've told him to put it where the monkey puts the nuts – wherever that may be.'[11] The order cancelled, he started to look for a Chinese junk builder.

Shortly afterwards there was a promising new development. The Royal Navy had itself employed a large number of MFVs for all sorts of miscellaneous work and a number of these had found their way to Singapore, where they were now declared surplus to requirements. They were of much the same dimensions as the planned *Fanny Rosa*, 61-foot long, with similar accommodation space and engine position. Within days Boy had taken one to sea and, apart from the vibration of the engines, thought it would be highly suitable for conversion. He managed to have it allocated to him for his personal use, so that he could take it out at least once a week to get the feel of it, and arranged to have it surveyed in a dry dock by Thornycrofts, which had recently re-established its yard in Singapore. He also looked at an alternative MFV, built in South Africa, which lacked engines but seemed to be a better proposition.

One problem, as always with Boy, was money. Although he had been relatively well paid as Chief of Staff and had managed to save part of his salary, he did not have nearly enough both to pay for the boat and to undertake a complete refit. He began to work on Daphne as soon as there was some prospect of moving forward with the project and expressed the hope that she might come up with 'a little pressie'. Daphne, never confident about money herself, was actually very comfortably off, especially after the film rights to *The King's General* were acquired by Alexander Korda for the then enormous sum of £65,000. She baulked at some of his propositions, such as buying the Fairform Flyer, but eventually agreed to come up with what was needed for *Fanny Rosa*, despite somewhat resenting what she saw as a raid on her own savings. With her support assured, Boy acquired MFV 224, the vessel with no engines, for the sum of £1,050 which he paid himself. He arranged with Thornycrofts not only for the company to carry out some basic work in Singapore, but for the boat to be delivered to its yard in Southampton for more extensive fitting-out as soon as it arrived in the UK. Boy also persuaded the Royal Navy to carry the vessel in the next available homeward bound landing craft.

By early April the only area for which SEAC retained political as well as military responsibility was the NEI, where violence continued between the Indonesian nationalists and what they saw as the occupying force of British, although Dutch troops were at last arriving in the country. The low point had been reached at the end of October 1945 with the murder of Brigadier Mallaby in Surabaya, but there had been little improvement in the situation before the end of that year and Christison had been forced to request reinforcements in the shape of 5 Indian Division. The Dutch Lieutenant Governor-General and chief negotiator, Dr van Mook, having initially shown considerable reluctance, was leant on by Mountbatten to begin substantive negotiations with Soekarno and the nationalists, but on agreeing to do so was disowned by his government.

The Dutch stance was so obdurate that Mountbatten had delivered an ultimatum. Either they would negotiate with the Indonesians, in which case the British would continue to maintain order in all the key centres, or, if they continued to reject negotiations, the British would confine themselves to disarming and repatriating the Japanese. Not entirely surprisingly the Dutch agreed to negotiate and at the end of January Sir Archibald Clark Kerr was sent by the British Government to act as an intermediary.[12] This had an immediate beneficial impact, as did Soekarno's agreement to step back in favour of his more tractable colleague, Dr Sjahrir. Although in many ways the British remained unpopular with both sides and sporadic violence against them continued, a dialogue was begun and the piecemeal arrival of Dutch troops meant that the British formations could gradually begin to withdraw, although not without the occasional crisis intervening.

By the end of April the rationale for the continued existence of a combined HQ, with its origins in the Grand Alliance of the Second World War, was beginning to be questioned in London, although Mountbatten campaigned vigorously for its retention. From a personal perspective, however, the Supreme Commander felt that he had completed his task and was keen to resume his career in the Royal Navy. Supported by his three C-in-Cs, Boy and Denning, he made strong representations to this effect to the Chiefs of Staff, who agreed that he should leave the theatre at the end of May. The question of his successor was not resolved, but it was decided that Stopford, who had succeeded Dempsey as C-in-C ALFSEA, would serve simultaneously as Acting Supreme Commander, but that the practical aspects of the job would be assumed by Boy.

Having dined quietly with just Boy and Denning on 27 May, Mountbatten wrote to the former on the day of his departure from Singapore three days later to say that he was sad to be leaving 'the happiest and most efficient team I have ever worked with.' The letter continued: 'This, as I am certain you must know, is almost entirely due to yourself. Ever since you arrived you have halved my work and helped me stay on my right level, but what I find most remarkable is that on the very rare occasions when I have had to overrule you, you have not only accepted it loyally (as one would expect), but I know have gone out of your way to support my decision at every level, both officially and unofficially.'[13] He went on to say that Boy would really be SACSEA himself from then on. The letter accompanied the gift of a cigarette box.

Boy replied in like terms on 1 June, writing: 'Its been a great adventure and I've loved working with you – its been so good for me to work with someone who has more energy and drive than I have.'[14] He went on to say that Mountbatten's opinion of him was exaggerated, for instance that he was not in the same class as Dempsey, or for that matter as McCreery, Horrocks, Leese – 'if he regains his balance!' – O'Connor, Swayne or de Guingand. He ended with a PS: 'One sting in the tail. Please remember to be considerate to your staff – not people like Jack and me 'cos that you always were to us – but to the "stooges". One small fault in a big man!'

In spite of this mild reproach, Mountbatten could be counted on to reciprocate Boy's loyalty. He met the Military Secretary, General Sir Colville Wemyss, two days after his return to the UK and informed him that most of the success of SACSEA was due to Boy, who in his opinion was one of the three or four soldiers who really counted in the Army. Lecturing shortly afterwards at the Imperial Defence College on the invitation of Slim, now its Commandant, he told the assembled students, all senior officers of considerable promise: 'When General Pownall left, I lost the most experienced staff officer in the British Army ... He was relieved by an officer who had never attended this college, or any other form of staff college or held any other form of staff job. He took on the most difficult staff job in the whole war, and I have no hesitation in saying that he was the best Chief of Staff anybody had. I do not say that there is any connection between his training and his performance. I merely state these two unrelated facts to show the overriding importance of character and ability.'[15]

Mountbatten had agreed to lobby for the urgent relief of both Boy and Denning, and his meeting with Wemyss was to that end. Boy himself had been having second thoughts about even remaining in the Army. By the time he wrote his letter to Mountbatten on 1 June, his thoughts had clarified: 'You know I have no desire for recognition or advancement and curiously enough I have taken an absolute dislike of soldiering during this war and I have enjoyed this job with you much more than any command I've held, and the thought of having to command troops again fills me with horror. That is the truth and I want you to know it. I may get over it, but I doubt it.' The personal legacy of Market Garden was clearly apparent, even if it had taken Boy eighteen months to appreciate it fully. However, he had no ideas about what else he might do and had no financial resources to fall back on other than an army pension.

In fact Boy's future had already been decided by the time Mountbatten met Wemyss. Boy was to relieve none other than Wemyss himself, who had been in his job for four years and was looking forward to retirement. It was at least a staff job and not a command appointment and it promised employment for some time, albeit in London and thus separated once again from the family in Cornwall. He wrote to Daphne with the news – 'Duck you know God is being good to me ... we have a great deal to be thankful for'[16] – also suggesting that they might moor *Fanny Rosa* on the Thames and live there in the summer months.

The date fixed for his relief took some time in coming and in the meantime things were going badly again in the Netherlands East Indies, so he was completely preoccupied right up to the end with the situation there, the handover to his successor, Major General 'Dixie' Redman, and the arrangements for transporting MFV 224. He had persuaded Air Chief Marshal Pirie, Park's successor, to allocate him an Avro York for his personal use, which enabled him to bring back not only his kit, but also presents for the family and a generous supply of alcohol. He also took with him his Personal Assistant, Maureen Luschwitz, who he had discovered had never visited England, having been brought up in Australia prior to working in India.

Boy flew out from Kellang airfield near Changi on 12 July, reflecting that he could look back on the previous eighteen months with a certain amount of satisfaction. A few days later Pirie wrote to Mountbatten: 'I am afraid that SACSEA is now beginning to disintegrate with the departure of Boy Browning from Changi the other evening when the scene reminded me of the departure of famous film stars from Los Angeles airfield, the glamorous Maureen standing at the doorway of the York with an enormous bunch of flowers.'[17]

Chapter 26

Return (July 1946–December 1947)

To many of the servicemen returning from the war, and to their wives, fiancées or girlfriends, the reunion was a disappointment, and so it proved to be for Boy and Daphne. Boy's arrival at Northolt on 19 July – he had broken his journey in New Delhi to take farewell of Auchinleck and the many friends and colleagues he had made there, and in Cairo, where he stayed with Dempsey, now C-in-C Middle East – was a much more formal affair than Daphne would have wished. She looked somewhat askance at Maureen Luschwitz. Boy had mentioned his Personal Assistant in a few of his letters, but she could not help wondering if this attractive girl was in some way romantically involved with her husband (although this had never been the case). Even when they reached the London flat where they would stay for the first night, there was a distinct lack of passion and this was to continue throughout Boy's leave, which was spent largely at Menabilly.

The reasons for their failure to connect, mentally or physically, are difficult to pin down precisely but there seem to be two possible candidates. Firstly, Boy had been working in top gear – as he knew no other – for so long that he could hardly remember how to relax. Secondly, both of them had changed over the six years since they had last lived together. Boy was less open and more reflective, and had moreover been deeply affected by his experiences of the war, not all of which had been good. Daphne was even more independent than she had been, successful in her chosen career and reluctant to prejudice in any way what she had achieved. Whatever the reasons, the upshot was that both of them waited in vain for the other to demonstrate their love. Daphne in particular felt rejected, but was unable to discuss it openly. The only common ground they shared was sailing but, although they spent time on 'Yggy', the erstwhile emotions failed to emerge.

Daphne may have felt rejected, but it was actually she who had suggested in a letter over two months before Boy's return that he should have a separate room at Menabilly. He had conceded that he was so used to being in his own small shell that it was impossible to say how he would react on his return and agreed that she should prepare a room for him, although he had expressed a preference to share with her. In the event he moved straight into the separate room, whose connecting door remained firmly closed from both sides.

Whilst Boy and Daphne had changed, the same was also true of the children, simply because they were all eighteen months older. Tessa, still a child in 1944, was now a pretty teenager. Flavia had been old enough to remember her father before he left for the Far East, but to Kits he was virtually a stranger. Having had no real experience of children other than the occasional brief wartime visit, Boy experienced great difficulty in dealing with them. With Tessa, who was now eating with the adults whilst her siblings were still confined to the nursery, he made the mistake initially of trying to treat her as grown up and was consequently disappointed when she was unable to respond appropriately. The two younger children frequently proved to be an irritation and the old flashes of temper returned, although as usual they never lasted for long. He tried hard, for instance by inventing a game called the Monkey Olympics, which among other events involved the two younger ones participating in a race over obstacles set up in the house, with Boy's teddy bears playing the role of spectators on the sofa, but still Flavia and Kits were upset by the disturbance in what they had come to believe was the natural order and were frightened by his outbursts. Having been allowed a lot of freedom, the imposition of greater discipline was not to their liking.

Daphne did little to help manage his attitude. Her letters had kept him abreast of most of the family developments and she had on one occasion asked him to write to Tessa about looking after her personal appearance, but other than ensuring that Kits was put down for the right house at Eton he had not been asked to make any decisions and she was prepared for this to continue. She was highly protective of Kits, always her favourite, partly as a result of which Boy found it difficult to establish a strong rapport with his son.

Another issue was the presence of Tod in the house. With the children growing up and needing some education, which she had little inclination to provide herself, Daphne had asked her old governess to fulfil the same role with the next generation. With Boy's agreement, Tod had been installed in the autumn of 1945 and had been a great success with her three charges. Unfortunately she and Boy reacted like oil and water. She had a tendency to pontificate on matters on which she was not an expert, but about which he knew a lot, which infuriated him. The atmosphere could become poisonous, especially after one episode in which Tod had complained of a sore throat and asked if anyone knew a good remedy. 'Cut it, my dear Tod', had been the reply, occasioning barely suppressed hilarity in the family, but sending Tod off in high dudgeon to her room, from which she was only persuaded to emerge after Boy had been forced by Daphne to make an abject apology. The feud continued, although he readily acknowledged that she was necessary not only to the education of the children, but also to the running of the household, in which Daphne showed scant interest. He delighted in making snide comments to Tod, particularly when she rose to the bait.

On the positive side, any issues which may have arisen in Daphne's mind over Maureen Luschwitz were quickly dispelled. She was invited down to stay at Menabilly and found favour not only with Daphne, but also with the children. Of a much younger generation than their parents[1] and naturally vivacious, she was able to join in their games and become a friend to them all. She was to make her home in England and to continue working for Boy until her marriage in 1955. Boy, for his part, continued to get on well with Daphne's mother Muriel, and was very fond of her two sisters, Angela, who was living with Muriel in Ferryside, and Jeanne, who was painting in St Ives.

In other ways some semblance of peacetime normality began to emerge. Boy loved cars and owned a number of different types after the War, but those he had left behind in 1944 remained his favourites. One of them, a Ford V8 originally purchased in 1932 and always known as 'Fordie', had been rescued from its mothballed state and painted Eton blue, but the other, an MG sports car garaged in London, needed attention before it could be made roadworthy. Daphne had now bought Hunkin's boatyard, which was starting to find new work under the auspices of John Prescott, who had retired from the Army and lived close by, whilst Boy assumed his position as the Commodore of the Royal Fowey Yacht Club and was able to hoist his pennant on 'Yggy', now fully functional again. However, in spite of these small improvements to life, the two months of Boy's leave were not quite the soothing balm for which he and Daphne had hoped and it was with some relief to them both that he reported for duty as Military Secretary on 16 September.

The title of Military Secretary is an old one, dating back to 1795. Until 1904 the appointee had been the right-hand man of the Commander-in-Chief of the British Army, and as such was in a position of considerable power and influence, but with the abolition of the role of the C-in-C in 1904, the allegiance of the Military Secretary was transferred to the Secretary of State for War and his authority significantly diminished. His department remained, nonetheless, a very important one, dealing as it did with the appointment, promotion and retirement of officers, with selections for staff and extra-regimental appointments and with honours and awards. The Military Secretary himself was expected to have at his fingertips the backgrounds and current appointments of all general officers and those colonels and brigadiers[2] who were deemed suitable for promotion. When there was a demand for a particular position to be filled, he was required to produce appropriate suggestions. He was the Secretary of the No 1 Appointments Board,[3] which dealt with all appointments of general officer rank and which was chaired by the CIGS, with the Adjutant-General, the Quartermaster-General, the VCIGS and the GOCs-in-C of Eastern Command and Anti-Aircraft Command as members. He also vetted all proposals for orders and decorations, which he passed on with his recommendations to the Secretary of State prior to their being placed before the King. His part in these processes meant that he was liable to become the subject of discreet lobbying by his brother officers, at least to ensure that their names were uppermost in his mind when it came to appointments or honours. He therefore had to be himself an officer of impeccable probity.

The Military Secretary necessarily had a close relationship with the Secretary of State for War, to whom he acted as adviser on all these issues and thus straddled the divide between the military and the political. When Boy took up the role the Secretary of State was still J. J. Lawson, whom Boy had met in Singapore and for whom he entertained some regard. He was succeeded almost immediately by F. J. Bellenger, for whom Boy had much less time, and then in late 1947 by Emmanuel

Shinwell, whom Boy admired greatly in spite of the gulf between their respective backgrounds.[4]

The holders of the office of Military Secretary had for the most part been distinguished soldiers, but they had veered between those on their way up and those on their way out. Boy's predecessor, Colville Wemyss, might be regarded as one of the latter, whilst Lord Gort in 1937 was certainly one of the former, holding the office immediately before becoming CIGS. Notwithstanding the constitutional attachment to the Secretary of State, the appointment was usually in the hands of the CIGS[5] of the time and it is certain that Boy himself was recommended by Brooke, who retired in June 1946, and approved by his successor, Montgomery. (Brooke had in fact, back in 1945, considered Boy suitable for appointment as VCIGS, but Montgomery was committed to bringing into this role one of his close protégés, Frank Simpson, in the event a highly capable officer.) Once again, Boy's lack of a Staff College qualification did not stand in his way.

From his office in Hobart House, Boy approached the new job with his usual vigour. This was a difficult time for the British Army, during which there was intense political pressure to reduce its size in the pursuit of lower government expenditure, whilst at the same time maintaining the old imperial commitments, some left-over business from the war, such as the involvement in the Dutch East Indies and the demands of an army of occupation in Europe. The manpower was shrunk over two years from nearly three million to just over one million. As far as generals were concerned, the strategy was to retire officers in their mid-to-late 50s and concentrate on the substantial pool of talent and experience available among the younger ones. This required great tact, especially as Montgomery had pronounced views about most of the general officers in the Army and was ready to express them forcefully. He favoured those who had seen active service over those who had served largely in the War Office or on other static staffs, notwithstanding the fact that many of the latter possessed skills which would be much in demand. Unlike Brooke, who had tended to convey bad news himself, Montgomery delegated this to Boy.

Montgomery, however, was away on his travels for much of the time, and the work of the War Office was led by his Vice-Chief, Simpson, with whom Boy had a good relationship. Of the other members of the Army Council, the one with whom he had most day-to-day contact was the Adjutant-General, his old friend O'Connor. The Adjutant-General's Department dealt with all personnel matters in the Army and there was thus something of an overlap with the Military Secretary's Department. During the Second World War, as had also happened in the Great War, there had been some movement in responsibility from the former to the latter, the most significant one being the management of the careers of all regular officers. Towards the end of Boy's time as Military Secretary a committee was established to look at the issue again, with the result that career management reverted to the Adjutant-General, although the Military Secretary retained the role of court of appeal for officers[5] who were dissatisfied on matters relating to their promotion.

Boy was anxious to meet as many as possible of the senior officers on whom he was expected to hold an opinion. Accordingly he travelled around all the commands in the UK and, in the second week of February 1947, he set off on a longer journey. His knowledge of both ALFSEA and India Command was good, but he was very much out of date with what was happening in Europe. His first call was to the largest contingent, the British Army of the Rhine. He flew initially to Cologne where he met Dick McCreery, the GOC-in-C, and then embarked on a special train which took him in great comfort to all the key subordinate HQs on the way to Hamburg. The winter of 1946/7 was a particularly harsh one – at Menabilly all the pipes froze and there were power cuts, leaving the house freezing cold – but a thaw had set in briefly and his progress was unimpeded by the weather. From Hamburg he flew on to Berlin, where he stayed with Brian Robertson, the Deputy Military Governor of the British Zone in Germany and one of the few very senior generals previously unknown to him.

Germany was at the time in a desperate state and Robertson and his staff were struggling to provide sufficient fuel and food for the devastated country to get through the bitter winter and simultaneously to create the conditions for reconstruction. Boy was particularly horrified by the condition of Berlin, which was still in ruins after being nearly destroyed by the Russians. However, although he found the country 'pretty grim', the mood among the officers he met was more cheerful than he had experienced at home. He flew from Berlin to Vienna, where he stayed in the house of the absent British High Commissioner, before travelling on to Klagenfurt in the British Sector, once again by train and this time in the Royal Coach, which was attached specially for him. Boy had one final destination, Egypt, where he stayed once more with Dempsey and where he was pleased to see some sunshine before experiencing again the rigours of the winter.

Boy was now living during the week in Whitelands House, a solid block of flats overlooking the Duke of York's Headquarters, near the Sloane Square end of the King's Road. The flat, on the sixth floor, had three small bedrooms, a bathroom, a sitting room and a small kitchen and was rather gloomy. It was within walking distance of his job, but he usually drove, as he was able to keep his car in the garage underneath the building. There was a small restaurant on the ground floor from which it was possible to order a meal to be sent up and whilst he was out the flat was looked after by his daily help, Mrs Lester, who adored him and used to do whatever mending he required. His sister Grace and her close friend Helen McSwinney had lived there during the war[6] and the lease was owned by Helen's mother. Grace was now living most of the time with her mother Nancy[7] at Rousham, where she took up farming. Helen bought a house in Dorset, where Grace joined her after Nancy's death, following which Boy took over the Whitelands lease.

Without the matter ever being openly discussed, Daphne made it quite clear that she was not going to live in London, indeed that she would be there as seldom as possible. Boy therefore embarked on a pattern of life which he would continue until he retired, working in London all week and catching the night sleeper from Paddington on a Friday evening. On Saturday mornings he would be picked up by Mr Bunny's taxi from Par station, have breakfast at Menabilly and then, depending on the time of year, go out on one of his boats, usually accompanied by Daphne.

On Sunday evenings the process would be reversed and he would return on the sleeper, going from there straight into his office. More frequently than he would have wished, he was otherwise occupied at the weekend and unable to go down to Cornwall. On the other hand Daphne was occasionally inveigled into a visit to London, but only for some important function. This arrangement perpetuated the semi-detached nature of their marriage, which had begun in 1940 and which Boy found unsatisfactory but could do nothing about. There were no prospects of work for him in Cornwall and having only just turned fifty he was too young to retire. He was acutely conscious of money, of which he never had enough, and was forced on more than one occasion to ask Daphne to bail him out. Continuing to generate his own income was thus a high priority.

Boy did not sit around at the flat alone, however. He remained a highly sociable person and, as well as enjoying the company of a large circle of friends and acquaintants, began to develop some extramural interests. Inevitably some of these had a service connection. He had continued as Chairman of the Airborne Forces Security Fund whilst he was away in the Far East, but the pressure of work as Military Secretary caused him to step down in January 1947 in favour of Harvey Bowring, one of the original trustees who had taken the chair during his absence. He did remain a trustee himself and attended meetings whenever he could. He was also invited to become a vice-president of the Officers Association, a service charity whose prime function was to help former officers to find employment and in some cases offer financial support.

Boy's sporting background brought him appointments as President of both the Combined Services Rugby Football Club and the Army Rifle Association. Perhaps more prestigious than either of these was the Deputy Chairmanship of the British Olympic Association (BOA). The Chairman was his old friend, David Burghley, and the Treasurer was E. J. Holt, who had proposed him in 1921 to be a member of the South London Harriers. Boy also took on a simultaneous appointment as 'Commandant' of the British team for the 1948 Olympic Games, which were to be held in London. From his message to the team in their Handbook, it is apparent that not even he quite knew what being the Commandant meant, and it seems that he was in some ways purely a figurehead. The chief administrator, known as the *Chef de Mission*, was Evan Hunter, the long time Honorary Secretary and then General Secretary of the BOA,[8] who carried out the role for five consecutive Games from 1928 to 1952. The trials began in the summer of 1947 and Boy attended whenevert he could.

The one leisure activity which eluded Boy was sailing in *Fanny Rosa*. The MFV had been brought back from Singapore by the Royal Navy in the autumn of 1946 and had been taken to Thornycroft's yard in Southampton for the engines, lighting and plumbing to be installed and for the deckhouse and aft accommodation to be fitted out. There she stayed, with no progress possible until certain permits had been obtained. By early 1947 Boy was getting so frustrated that he was threatening to sell her and to look at buying a second-hand boat in her place. The problem was solved, but it was late spring before any work was started and September before he and Dick Bunt were able to go down to Thornycrofts and get her ready to go to sea. She was then sailed round to Hunkin's yard for the final fit-out of the forward accommodation, but they had missed the summer sailing season.

Boy would have far preferred to take his annual leave cruising in *Fanny Rosa*, but with this no longer an option he agreed to accompany Daphne on a two-week holiday to Switzerland. If either had hoped that the holiday would change things significantly between them, they were to be disappointed. They went for long walks together and became more relaxed in each other's company, but the old magic did not return. Love was still there certainly, and friendship too, but no romance and certainly no passion. One important quality which they shared, however, was a great sense of humour and they retained their ability to laugh together at the absurd.

In the autumn of 1947, Daphne had to travel to the United States to contest in court an allegation of plagiarism against her in the writing of *Rebecca*. The action involved not only her but the producers of the film of the book and her American publishers, Doubleday, and it was Nelson Doubleday who invited her to stay with him and his wife, Ellen, in their Long Island house. She determined to take Flavia and Kits with her and also Tod, who would look after them while she was engaged in court or in the various publicity events which Doubleday was setting up. Tessa was now of an age to go to boarding school, something to which she herself was looking forward, and her start at St Mary's, Wantage was hurriedly arranged by Grace for September, with Tessa passing through London in the care of Maureen, who was already proving herself an invaluable adjunct to the family. In early November Daphne embarked in the *Queen Mary* and was away for a month, attracting favourable notices in American society and seeing off the case against her and her co-defendants by her strong performance in the witness box.

Boy was now among the thirty most senior serving officers on the Army List. His promotion to substantive lieutenant general had come through shortly before he left SEAC, with his seniority backdated to 25 August 1944, putting him ahead of Horrocks, amongst others. During his peregrination around Europe by train in January he had given serious thought to his future and confirmed to himself and to Daphne his desire to leave the Army, first expressed in the Far East, although at the time he still felt that he might have more to do. He had nevertheless let it be known that he was not seeking an active command, which meant that, unless he could secure one of the positions on the Army Council, he was unlikely to have any further hopes of advancement.

Boy's dissatisfaction was compounded by the circumstances of Montgomery's treatment of O'Connor. The latter, whilst not a great Adjutant-General was much admired in the Army, not only for his wartime record but also for standing up for what he believed to be right. In August he objected strongly to the Government reneging on an agreement to bring home a certain number of men on demobilization from the Far East and, with some reluctance, he submitted his resignation to the Secretary of State. Montgomery, who O'Connor had believed would support him, failed to do so, even giving the impression that O'Connor had been dismissed and – contrary to what was the case – telling him that the other Military Members of the Army Council had lost confidence in him. Boy was charged with producing the announcement, and made clear to O'Connor his own opinion on the situation, but a leak from one of Bellenger's aides disclosing the name of the new Adjutant-General meant that it had to be rushed out without O'Connor's express approval. It was a sad end to a most distinguished career and Boy clearly found the whole episode distasteful.

He was therefore keen to leave but seemingly had no job to go to. However, other minds were at work, notably Mountbatten's, who had been left in no doubt as to Boy's feelings back in the summer of 1946. A significant event was about to take place which would provide just the opportunity for Boy's future employment, and Mountbatten was to act as the catalyst. On 10 July the engagement had been announced between Princess Elizabeth and Mountbatten's nephew, Philip, whom Boy had first met in Ceylon in December 1944. The wedding was fixed for 20 November and it had been decided that the newly married couple would move out of Buckingham Palace and into the nearby Clarence House. The Princess had always been looked after by the King's Household, but it was agreed that she should now establish a household of her own, in addition to the existing Ladies in Waiting, who remained with her. Jock Colville, who had been one of Churchill's private secretaries during the War, was speedily identified as the Private Secretary, whilst the newly created Duke of Edinburgh[9] brought in Lieutenant Michael Parker, a great friend from the Navy, to be his Equerry. All that was needed to complete the team was a Comptroller and Treasurer and Mountbatten proposed Boy.

'Boy' wrote Mountbatten to his nephew, 'has drive, energy, enthusiasm, efficiency and invokes the highest sense of loyalty and affection in his subordinates. His judgement in all matters that he understands[10] is absolutely sound, and he would sooner die than let his boss down ... he is not a "yes man" or even a courtier and never will be. He will fearlessly say what he thinks is right ... Frankly, Philip, I do not think you can do better.'[11] Following the receipt of a handwritten letter offering the position from the King's Private Secretary, Sir Alan Lascelles, Boy was received by the King on 21 October in an audience which was effectively a job interview. They had known each other for many years and Boy had recently had contact with the sovereign as part of his duties as Military Secretary, so there were never likely to be obstacles from that direction.

On 22 December 1947, Boy's appointment was announced and, although he would not formally retire from the Army until 5 April 1948, his notice and accrued overseas leave allowed him to begin his new job on the first working day of the New Year.

Chapter 27

Princess (1948–1952)

Boy's appointment as Comptroller and Treasurer to the Household of Princess Elizabeth suited the parties directly concerned and seemed to fall into line with the wishes of a number of others. From Boy's perspective, it played well to his talent for organization and his wide network of contacts. It also kept him in London, and although this was far from ideal in terms of his marriage, in the circumstances there seemed to be no alternative. The King and Queen had known him since before the war, whilst to Princess Elizabeth he was familiar both as a distinguished Grenadier – she had become Colonel of the regiment on her sixteenth birthday, 21 April 1942, on which day Boy had attended her first inspection at Windsor Castle – and as a senior general during the occasions on which she had visited various airborne formations with her parents. The Duke of Edinburgh knew him less well, but had the recommendation of Mountbatten on which to rely. The Duke was not totally at ease with the Royal Household, whose members were inclined to dictate what he and the Princess should and should not do. It was heavily populated by former Guards officers, who included the King's two Assistant Private Secretaries,[1] the Comptroller and Assistant Comptroller[2] of the Lord Chamberlain's Department and the Master of the Household, whilst the ranks of the Lords in Waiting, Gentlemen Ushers and Equerries were full of them. Now the Duke would have one of his own, who was prepared to stand up to the senior courtiers.

Many of those courtiers regarded the Duke as a potential threat to the status quo, so from their perspective the appointment of an establishment figure might have promised a welcome degree of control over the young couple. Outside the Palace others, including Montgomery, were concerned about Mountbatten's influence and thus also welcomed Boy's appointment. In fact the Duke was no puppet of Mountbatten but unequivocally his own man, concerned only for the welfare of the Princess. Boy, for his part, was totally unambiguous from the outset as to where his loyalties lay: he was certainly not prepared to act as a spy on behalf of any other individual or group. Had there been any conflict between the Duke and the King, he might have been placed in a difficult position, but there was never any hint of this. Boy's feelings for Princess Elizabeth already amounted to little short of adoration, whilst he was to develop very quickly a considerable regard for her husband.[3]

Much older than the Princess and the Duke and any of the members of their Household, Boy, whilst deferring to his employers, naturally assumed a position somewhere between general manager and elder statesman. His reputation had gone before him and Jock Colville was to write later that at first they were all, 'from

Princess Elizabeth downwards, rather dreading the arrival of an awe-inspiring figure. But in no time at all awe turned into affection …'[4] Boy had, in fact, mellowed considerably during his time in the Far East and at Whitehall and his reputation as a strict disciplinarian with an explosive temper, at least as far as his working life was concerned, belonged in the past, although these character traits remained visible to his family. Neville Wigram,[5] who had served in the Grenadiers before the war and encountered Boy again when he became the Regimental Adjutant in 1950, thought that he had lost some of his fire, but found him very easy to deal with on all matters concerning the activities of the regiment's Colonel.

Boy's primary responsibility was the management of the Household, from hiring and firing the staff to looking after property, or paying the bills. It had been decided that the royal couple would occupy Clarence House, but the building was in a terrible state requiring extensive refurbishment and would thus not be available for many months, so they were allocated a suite at Buckingham Palace where Boy's office was also situated. The intention had been for them to have the use of a country house as well and the initial choice fell on Sunninghill Park, formerly Brereton's FAAA HQ, but it was burnt down shortly afterwards in mysterious circumstances. Boy located an alternative, Windlesham Moor near Sunningdale, which was set in spacious grounds and was comfortable but not particularly large, with only five bedrooms and four reception rooms.

In addition to his general management duties and his role as the main point of contact with the senior Palace officials, Boy was also frequently required to attend either or both the Princess or the Duke on formal visits or at functions, especially if there was either an armed services or a sporting connection. The Duke's first solo outing in his new capacity was as the guest of honour at the Army v Navy rugger match at Twickenham and Boy, as President of the Combined Services Rugby Football Club, was there to receive him. The Duke took a considerable interest in sport, first evidenced by his becoming President of the National Playing Fields Association (NPFA) in 1948 and his subsequently spending some time working in its offices.[6] Boy himself was Vice-Chairman of the NPFA and active in promoting its interests.

For the first eight months of 1948 and particularly during July and August, Boy was involved with the Olympic Games as Commandant of the British team and deputy Chairman of the BOA. That the Games were held at all in a post-war Britain which was effectively bankrupt and still, among other difficulties, subject to food rationing, was something of a triumph. They were financed on a shoestring and used existing facilities, the most important of which was the Empire Stadium at Wembley which housed the opening and closing ceremonies and the athletics. There were 59 participating nations, but neither Germany nor Japan was invited and the USSR declined to attend. There was no Olympic Village, the contestants staying in redundant army camps or even tents. Great Britain came 12th in the medals table with 23 medals of which only 3 were gold, a poor return for the host nation, but the Games were judged overall to be a great success and were a welcome boost to morale in what was still a very difficult time.

One sport in which Boy and the Duke shared a keen interest was sailing and both would regularly attend Cowes Week, where the Duke competed in his yacht *Bluebottle*, a wedding present from the Island Sailing Club. By the summer of 1948 *Fanny Rosa* was fully ready for sea and Boy and Daphne took her to Cowes for the regatta, where they entertained the Princess, the Duke and a number of other friends. In the following year, with the Duke aboard, Boy managed to steer *Fanny Rosa* aground on Ryde Sands, much to his embarrassment. The vessel was left high and dry for ten hours, listing at 50 degrees, and became an object of interest to large numbers of holidaymakers who were able to walk out and inspect her before she was floated off again at the next high tide. The Duke was forced to remain on board instead of transferring to *Bluebottle*, which was taking part in the Dragon class championships.

In October 1948 Boy paid his first visit to Balmoral, one of many over the coming years, although when Daphne was invited she usually found a reason not to accept. On this occasion he was the only guest. He thought that the Queen was 'too perfect and in terrific form' and the King 'very nice but has a touch of sciatica after too much stalking'.[7] The King's condition was unsurprising, given that much of the time was given over to field sports. Boy himself was a fine shot with a rifle and killed a stag after eight hours of stalking, wearing his old airborne smock, which was much admired by the gillies. On the other hand he was rusty with a shotgun and failed to register any hits on the first drive of the grouse shoot, much to the King's delight. The two of them had much more success later, with Boy shooting fourteen grouse and a snipe to the King's eighteen grouse.

During visits to Balmoral, Holyrood House and other royal residences, Boy had to forego his weekends at Menabilly, but otherwise he took them as often as he could. His awkwardness with the children after his return from the Far East became a thing of the past and Boy enjoyed playing with them while they were still young and later taking them on outings to the theatre and the circus when they came up to London. For their part they were no longer frightened of him, but found him fun to be with. Tessa shared his love of boats and he would support her when she was racing in *Shimmer*, hovering around the edge of the course in 'Yggy' and trying not to appear concerned. On the other hand, neither Flavia nor Kits liked sailing and he got very upset when they both became seasick on a trip in *Fanny Rosa* to Poole Harbour and had to return home by train. Flavia much preferred horse-riding, which Boy strongly encouraged. Kits followed his father to West Downs in September 1948, where he began to enjoy sport, giving them for the first time a common interest. Boy told him that he would never be bored keeping wicket at cricket and was duly delighted when Kits emulated him in the first XI for two years, also playing for the first XI football team. In early 1950 Flavia followed Tessa, now in her last year, to St Mary's, Wantage.

One guest, in April 1950, was the Duke himself. He and the Princess had expressed great enthusiasm for the idea during Boy's first stay at Balmoral, but no earlier opportunity had emerged and it would be many years before the Princess would come. Boy got into a terrible state over the correct way to lay the table, this never having been a priority in the house, and he and Tod nearly came to blows. Daphne confined herself to decorating the house with flowers, but was the most relaxed of them all once the Duke arrived. The Duke subsequently remembered the occasion as having been rather chaotic but great fun.

Notwithstanding the regular routine of his weekends Boy found the whole experience unsettling, the pleasure of being at Menabilly and on his beloved boats being offset by the thought of having to return to his dismal little flat. The du Maurier family had a great penchant for nicknames – Daphne was variously known as 'Bing', Track' and 'Tray', whilst she and Boy usually called each other 'Duck' – but Boy's moods on a Sunday afternoon now spawned another, 'Moper', by which he became commonly known in the family and to very close family friends. He could still derive considerable enjoyment from his time at Menabilly and he and Daphne were more than capable of both bursting into spontaneous laughter whenever anything remotely ridiculous caught their attention. However, the contrast between his private and public persona became even more marked than it had been, the former characterized by informal clothes and by genuine pleasure interspersed with bouts of introspection sometimes amounting to depression, the latter by authority, charm and impeccable dress.

In June 1948 Daphne persuaded Boy to accompany her to the United States to stay with the Doubledays. From the time of their first meeting in late 1946 she had been obsessed with her hostess, Ellen, fantasizing about their being together and even using her as the inspiration for Stella, the heroine of her new play, *September Tide*. Ellen, whilst flattered by the attention, was unable to reciprocate in kind and there was never anything physical between the two women. This might have led to some awkwardness on the trip, but in fact Boy and Ellen hit it off immediately and he was particularly delighted when she invited Eisenhower to dinner, as the two men had always got along well.[8] For Daphne the visit was less successful, as Ellen made it clear that, whilst they could continue as good friends, a closer relationship was out of the question. They kept in regular contact and even went on holiday to Italy together, but to Daphne's disappointment Ellen allowed no real intimacy.

September Tide introduced a new object of attraction to Daphne in the form of the actress who played Stella, Gertrude Lawrence. 'Gertie', some nine years Daphne's senior, had been one of her father Gerald's lovers twenty or more years earlier. Unlike Ellen, she was receptive to Daphne's advances and the two women began to see much of each other. There can be little doubt that Daphne was emotionally 'in love' with Gertie, as she had been with Ellen, but the extent of their physical relationship, the subject of constant conjecture, has never been conclusively proved one way or the other. One thing is certain: when Gertie died in 1951, Daphne's grief was so intense that she went into something approaching a catatonic state. Boy remained as blissfully unaware of his wife's inclinations towards the two women as he had been over her affair with Christopher Puxley.

Possibly because these relationships stimulated her creative gifts, Daphne became more prolific in her writing. She had come to something of a halt after the publication of *The King's General* but 1949 saw not only *September Tide*, but also a new novel, *The Parasites*, the first book to be written in the shed which she had had erected in the Menabilly garden and to which she would retire in almost all weathers, for long periods and in complete solitude. It was a critical failure but was followed in 1951 by one of her very best and most enduringly popular works, *My Cousin Rachel*, whose eponymous heroine was once again inspired by Ellen.

Boy's gloom about returning to London every Sunday night was understandable. Although he spoke to Daphne every morning on the phone, he was bereft of family life and his boats for the next five days and had to return every night to a lonely and featureless flat which had little attraction for him. On the other hand he was hardly short of activities outside his job. He remained highly sociable and rarely had to spend an evening on his own. When not in attendance on the Princess and the Duke, he would often be invited to events in his own capacity and on the evenings when he was not otherwise engaged, he had a number of friends whose company he enjoyed. These included old wartime companions like Dempsey, Hollinghurst and Freddie Gough, who had served with distinction in 1 Airborne Division,[9] and family members such as George Browning and two cousins on his mother's side, Brian Johnston, already establishing a reputation as a cricket commentator and broadcaster, and Victor Noel-Paton, who was to become one of the first life peers in 1958 as Lord Ferrier. Another friend of whom he saw a great deal was Augustus Agar, a retired Royal Navy captain who had won the VC in the Baltic in 1919 and whom he had first met in Alexandria in 1936.

Entertaining, impossible at Whitelands House, was made much easier for Boy by following his father into a directorship of The Savoy Hotel Limited, whose board he joined in 1949. The D'Oyly Carte family had remained friends and, although Rupert had died in the previous year, his daughter Bridget, who headed the D'Oyly Carte Opera Company and had helped her father in the hotel, was now herself a director. This was to be Boy's only paid appointment outside his full-time job, but he commented that his directors fees were more than consumed by his expenditure in the bars and restaurants of the Savoy itself and its sister establishment, the Berkeley, which was located at that time in Piccadilly and was thus conveniently close to Clarence House and Buckingham Palace.

Boy and Bridget D'Oyly Carte found common ground in musical theatre, for all types of which he had a considerable enthusiasm. This was the golden age of the Broadway musical, with productions of *Carousel*, *South Pacific*, *Annie Get Your Gun* and *Kiss Me Kate* all coming to London in the late 1940s. Boy would see every one of these and many others, taking the children with him, and then bring the music on records down to Menabilly. However, his abiding passion was for ballet. He attended whenever possible every production at Covent Garden and Sadler's Wells and became very friendly with both the dancers and with other members of the classical music establishment, so much so that he was invited to become a Member of the Executive Committee of the Royal Academy of Dancing[10] at the end of 1950. Margot Fonteyn became a close friend and spent a day at Menabilly, Boy justifying the visit to Daphne on the grounds that he needed to demonstrate to the prima ballerina the proper use of a bow and arrow for a ballet which she was rehearsing.

In his enthusiasm for this particular art form, Boy even wrote a script for a new ballet, called *Jeanne d'Arc* and based on the story of France's great heroine. He suggested that it should be set to music by one of Benjamin Britten, Ernest Block, Ralph Vaughan Williams, Malcolm Arnold, Gordon Jacob or Leonard Bernstein, who between them certainly covered the waterfront in terms of musical styles. The composer Sir Arnold Bax, to whom he also sent the manuscript, was dubious about the concept, replying that 'dancing is incapable of suggesting very much beyond its own beauty and the simplest of dramatic ideas'.[11] Sir Arthur Bliss, a fellow member of the Royal Household as Master of the Queen's Music, was deputed to talk to Vita Sackville-West, who had written a biography of Joan, but she also doubted that it would make a good ballet scenario, whilst Dame Ninette de Valois pointed out that the real difficulty was that by half way through Joan would be attired as a soldier, presumably in armour and could no longer be used as a dancer. Princess Margaret, on the other hand, told Boy that she could not wait to see Fonteyn in the role. Undeterred by the lack of interest from the musical establishment, Boy persevered in his search for support for about five years before eventually accepting that the project was never going to get off the ground.

Boy had one other intellectual pursuit, his membership of the Kipling Society. He had long been an avid reader of Rudyard Kipling's works and on the death of the president of the society, Field Marshal Earl Wavell, Boy assumed the position 'with engaging modesty'[12] at the annual luncheon in October 1950. He was to continue in the role for over a decade and to take the chair at the luncheons almost every year. Not all his reading interests were so literary. One of his great enthusiasms was for the 'Biggles' novels of Captain W. E. Johns, and he was also fond of Peter Cheney's 'Lemmy Caution' novels and anything by Damon Runyon.

Boy retained numerous connections with the military and particularly the airborne forces. His continuing involvement with the Airborne Forces Security Fund brought him into regular contact with the leading personalities from the wartime years, including Gale, Frost and Lathbury, and when Harvey Bowring resigned as Chairman in September 1951, the trustees unanimously voted to ask him to accept the appointment once again. This he did and was present thereafter at the vast majority of their meetings. He would also always attend, if he could, the Airborne Forces Memorial Service each November and sometimes read the lesson.

In 1948 Boy was in the chair at the annual dinner of airborne officers, at which the guest of honour was Brereton. Any differences which he may have had with the Americans during the war were now, if not always forgotten by them, at least forgiven, and he also became the first president of the British chapter of the United States-British Comrades Association. Never one to bear any grudges himself, Boy was appalled when he discovered that his old rival Ridgway had not received any British decoration after the war, unlike many of the most senior American officers. 'I personally feel very put out over this,' he wrote to the then Military Secretary, 'as Matt Ridgeway [sic] was one of the few American Generals who personally commanded British troops in action. In my opinion he was quite the outstanding American General, certainly on any Corps or Army level, that I came across in the war. If anything can be done in the matter, perhaps you would let me know in time, so that I can make sure that The King is fully briefed on the subject if it should come up to him.'[13] At the time nothing could be done, as the opportunity had passed for the award of decorations to foreign officers in respect of their services in the War. To Boy's pleasure the injustice was rectified some years later, following Ridgway's tenure as Supreme Allied Commander both in Korea and in Europe, when he was made an honorary KCB.[14]

In May 1949 the Princess and the Duke were at last able to move into Clarence House, a most welcome development as Prince Charles had been born the previous November and the family needed more space. It was very much larger than Windlesham Moor but still of a manageable size. Boy had been working on the refurbishment project from the commencement of his appointment and had initially struggled to instil some order into chaos. The building had been lit throughout by gas and needed to be completely rewired. It was not only in a poor decorative state, but had been damaged by German bombs and was in some respects structurally unsound, so considerable remedial work was required, all the while under the constraints of a limited budget agreed with the Government. Both the Princess and the Duke were closely involved with choosing the décor, whilst the Duke, always interested in technology, was responsible for innovations such as an intercom system. The result of everyone's efforts was a bright, airy and highly functional house which the royal couple could make into a family home.

In October 1949 the Duke, who had held a desk job at the Admiralty immediately after his marriage, before going on a course at the Royal Naval Staff College at Greenwich and then working at the NPFA, was appointed First Lieutenant of HMS *Chequers*, the Leader of the 1st Destroyer Flotilla based in Malta. This pleased him enormously, but created some difficulties as the Princess was initially committed to a number of engagements in the United Kingdom. Nevertheless, she was able to join him after Prince Charles's first birthday in November and stayed in Malta until shortly after Christmas. She was back there for six weeks from the end of March 1950, returning to London in plenty of time for the birth of Princess Anne that August. Shortly beforehand, the Duke had been promoted to lieutenant commander and given his first command, the frigate HMS *Magpie*.

Boy accompanied Princess Elizabeth on her first visit to Malta in late 1949, returning to London when she did at the end of that year, the demands on him now including the recruitment of nannies for the royal children. At the beginning of 1950 Jock Colville returned to the Foreign Office, from which he had been seconded, and was replaced as Private Secretary by Martin Charteris. The Princess went out to Malta once more at the end of November and was joined by her sister Princess Margaret in mid-December. Boy escorted the latter, their plane arriving in the middle of a gale, and subsequently accompanied the two princesses on to Tripoli in Libya to visit the 1st Battalion of the Grenadiers which was stationed there.

As the spring of 1951 turned into summer, it became apparent that the King was far from well. A very bad attack of bronchitis in May was followed by a series of tests which in due course revealed that he had lung cancer, and in September he underwent an operation to remove his left lung. Two months before that it had been decided that both the Princess and the Duke would have to increase their royal engagements and much to the regret of both of them, because he was thoroughly enjoying his career and because their time in Malta had brought them closer to a 'normal' married life than they were to experience at any time, the Duke stood down from active service. One result of the King's illness was that he was unable to go on a planned tour of Canada and the United States. The Princess and the Duke were deputed to stand in for him and though their departure was initially delayed by the King's operation they eventually left on 8 October, accompanied by Charteris and Parker, Boy remaining at home. They were away for over a month and missed the annual Remembrance Day service and parade at the Cenotaph, during which Boy placed a wreath on their behalf.

Another marathon royal tour had been planned to Australia and New Zealand for early in the following year but it was clear that the King, whilst apparently making a recovery, would not be well enough for such an exhausting journey. The Princess and the Duke stood in for him again, beginning their trip with a brief holiday in Kenya, for which they departed on 31 January, accompanied once more by Charteris and Parker. In the early hours of 6 February the King suffered a coronary thrombosis and died in his sleep. The new Queen arrived back at Heathrow on the following day in the gloom of late afternoon, to be met by her Prime Minister Winston Churchill and members of the Cabinet. Boy stood with the reception committee on the tarmac.

Boy went to pay his respects to the late sovereign as he lay in state in Westminster Hall, possibly recalling the time, almost exactly sixteen years earlier, when he had stood guard over the coffin of his father with the officers of the 2nd Battalion. On 15 February he walked between Charteris and Parker in the funeral procession from Westminster to Paddington, whence the coffin and the mourners were taken by train to Windsor for the funeral in St George's Chapel. Daphne had been invited to the funeral as well, sitting next to Parker's wife, Eileen.

Chapter 28

Duke (1952–1956)

The accession of the Queen brought about profound changes for her husband and her staff, the most immediate of which for the latter was that she was now served instead by the enormous Household of the reigning monarch. Another consequence was a move out of Clarence House and into Buckingham Palace. The Duke, in particular, had hoped that they might stay in what had become a well-loved family home, whilst working in and holding formal functions at the Palace, but Sir Alan Lascelles, who had automatically become the Queen's Private Secretary, insisted that they should live there as well and he was strongly supported in this by Churchill. Clarence House was to become the residence of the Queen Mother, who would inherit its domestic staff.

Martin Charteris remained with the Queen to provide some continuity as an additional Assistant Private Secretary, whilst Mike Parker stepped into the role of Private Secretary to the Duke. With no physical establishment to run, Boy's job as Comptroller became redundant. Instead he was appointed Treasurer to the Duke alone, as part of a very much reduced Household in which his role was to reflect the future activities of his employer. He moved into a spacious office in Buckingham Palace, from which he ran a team which now comprised just himself, Parker, the Duke's new Equerry[1] Squadron Leader Beresford Horsley, five secretaries including Maureen Luschwitz as Boy's Personal Assistant,[2] the Chief Clerk, the Sergeant Orderly and a police officer. He was also responsible for The Duke's personal staff of two Pages, two valets and chauffeur. Parker dealt with requests for engagements and handled the general correspondence, while Horsley saw to the details of the engagements once they had been accepted, agreed the programmes and made the travel arrangements. Boy, as the Treasurer, looked after financial matters, including the allocation from the Civil List, and acted as the main point of contact for the Duke's numerous honorary appointments in the armed forces and his growing number of patronages.

Whereas the duties of monarchy were well defined, there was no constitutional role for the Duke. He supported the Queen in every way possible, but the position of consort was never likely to satisfy him on its own and he now had to forge alongside it a unique new career for himself, which would take some time to shape. Between his marriage and the Queen's accession he had accumulated a small portfolio of external interests, to which he felt that he could make a worthwhile contribution. The number now grew substantially and covered a wide range of activities, although there were some common themes, notably those of a sporting, maritime, educational and scientific nature. There was also a strong emphasis on youth.

As a man who had inherited all the energy and enthusiasm of his uncle, the Duke was not content with the role of figurehead in any organization to which he lent his support, but although his commitment to each of them was undoubted, he had limited hours available in the day and thus many of the more mundane matters landed on Boy's desk. In addition Boy found himself more significantly involved in several of these organizations, sometimes in his own right, examples being the NPFA and the Central Council of Physical Recreation, and in a few cases in order to provide a stimulus on behalf of the royal patron. There were two significant examples of the latter, the first being the Cutty Sark Preservation Society.[3]

The last of the tea clippers, the *Cutty Sark* had been privately owned until 1938, when it was presented to the Thames Nautical Training College for use as a training ship. Surplus to requirements after the War, its future was in doubt until the Duke and Frank Carr, the Director of the National Maritime Museum, formed the Society in 1951 to secure its preservation. Boy became a founding member of the Steering Committee which was formed that year, going on to join the Board of Governors and become Chairman of the Appeals and Publicity Committee, in which capacity he used his considerable contacts to help raise the necessary finance for the project. As a knowledgeable sailor himself, he was also involved with some of the technical aspects of the restoration, including the rigging. The campaign was highly successful and the ship was moved to its permanent berth at Greenwich in 1954 and opened by the Queen on 25 June 1957.

The second example of a deeper involvement by Boy concerned an initiative even closer to the Duke's heart and one which continues to bear his title. The Duke of Edinburgh's Award Scheme has been an enormously successful undertaking, dedicated to the personal development of young people from all backgrounds, who undertake varied and challenging programmes on their way to the achievement of Awards. It was conceived by the Duke himself in 1954, inspired by the vision and philosophy of Kurt Hahn. An Originating Committee was set up in November of that year, composed of representatives from a number of other organizations including the Amateur Athletics Association, the Central Council of Physical Recreation, the Royal Geographical Society and the Arts Council. Boy joined the committee, becoming the main link between the Duke and its members, and also sought on behalf of the Duke some reactions from industry and the regions, which were broadly favourable.

Boy was simultaneously a member of the Council of the Outward Bound Trust, and in this capacity he became directly involved with setting up the Pilot Scheme for the Award in September 1955, pending the formation of the latter's own administration. One of the other members of the Pilot Scheme's Working Party was Brigadier Sir John Hunt, the former leader of the successful Everest Expedition and now Assistant Commandant at the Staff College, who had been approached by Hahn himself to see if he would be interested in becoming involved. Boy sounded out a number of other parties and was able to advise the Duke that Hunt would be prepared to leave the Army and devote his life to the Scheme as its first Director.

Boy stepped back once the Scheme had been firmly established, but his contribution to its formation had been considerable.

There were a number of existing commitments to be satisfied by the Duke during 1952, one of which was his attendance at the Olympic Games in Helsinki that summer. The Duke had become the President of the British Amateur Athletics Board, his first action being to write a letter to each of the athletes, inviting them to represent their country. He travelled to Helsinki for the opening ceremony on 19 July and Boy flew there with the sixteen-year-old Duke of Kent to join the royal party six days later. They stayed to watch the Games, which produced an even more disappointing result for the British team than 1948, with a single gold medal in show-jumping out of a total of 8 medals, putting the country in 18th place. The Duke, Boy and Parker returned via Oslo,[4] where they attended the 80th birthday celebrations of King Haakon V, before travelling directly to Cowes for two days of the regatta.

Following the poor showing at Helsinki, an Appeal Committee was set up by the British Olympic Association, with the Duke of Beaufort as President and Lord Burghley and Boy as Joint Chairmen, its objective being to raise £75,000 to send the strongest team possible to the next Games in Melbourne in 1956. In the words of the BOA: 'It is essential that a team worthy of Great Britain should be there and that our competitors of many sports who are already in training should not be deprived of Olympic competition – the highest honour in sport – through apathy or lack of funds.' The much improved results were a fitting reward for a successful campaign by the committee, with 6 gold medals out of a total haul of 24, lifting the country into 8th place. The Games were opened by the Duke in November 1956, but Boy was once again holding the fort at home.

Back in 1952 the Duke's most immediate priority was his Chairmanship of the Coronation Commission. The event itself, on 2 June 1953, was a triumph of organization and as a national celebration was boosted by the news of the conquest of Everest, received that morning. Boy wore the full dress uniform of a general officer and, for the first time, the insignia of a Knight Commander of the Royal Victorian Order, an honour in the direct gift of the Queen to which he had been admitted on the previous day. He walked up the aisle of Westminster Abbey immediately behind the Duke and his page and between Horsley and Parker[5] and rode in the procession in the group following the State Coach. Daphne and Eileen Parker had seats above the peeresses in the gallery of the abbey.

Later that year Daphne found herself unable to refuse yet again an invitation to spend a week at Balmoral. She was dreading it long before she went, but found the experience better than the anticipation. She had met the Duke on several occasions and thought him good company and she felt very comfortable with the Queen Mother. Nevertheless, she found the relative formality of the house party intimidating and she was unable to participate in the field sports which formed an essential part of the programme, although she loved being out on the hills. By the time she left she was exhausted by the amount of nervous energy she had expended on doing the right thing all the time. On the other hand, when the Duke came to stay at Menabilly again at the end of a visit to the West Country, she was much more relaxed than Boy, who once more worked himself into a state about the arrangements and the condition of the house.

On the face of it, the relationship between Boy and Daphne went through a quiet stage in the early to mid-1950s. For her part, she had got over the loss of Gertrude Lawrence, whilst her friendship with Ellen Doubleday remained just that and there were no similar emotional distractions. For his, the weekend routine was well established, although he continued to be depressed at the thought of returning to London. At least whilst he was in Cornwall he had some new boats to enjoy. One of these was a replacement for 'Yggy' which, although not abandoned completely was now honourably retired, having been hauled ashore and positioned on the lawn at Menabilly some way from the house, for grandchildren to enjoy. *Ygdrasil II* was also a motor boat, but significantly larger and faster than its predecessor. Even more exciting was the culmination of a project which had occupied much of his spare time over recent years, just as *Fanny Rosa* had once done, the design and build of a new sailing yacht.

Jeanne d'Arc was a descendant in design terms of *La Mouette*, the alternative to *Fanny Rosa* which Boy had worked on during the War, but which had been shelved when the MFV became a realistic proposition. For the new project Boy enlisted the help of Maurice Griffiths, the longstanding editor of *Yachting Monthly* and designer of the Eventide and Waterwitch yacht classes, and the result was a beautiful wishbone ketch, much more elegant than anything previously owned by Boy and Daphne and capable of being raced with some success. Construction took place at their own yard and the boat was named by Mrs Hunkin. Inevitably the cost of the new boats fell on Daphne, who was as ever generous in this respect, although still with some mild resentment that Boy was digging into her capital.

In the meantime the three children were moving on. Kits followed his father to Eton in the autumn of 1953. On his last day at West Downs, Boy had taken him to meet his new housemaster and he continued to be interested in his son's progress through the school, among other things sharing with him a mutual detestation of Geometry. He would usually come down for the Fourth of June celebrations but Daphne always managed to develop a virus of some sort shortly beforehand to provide her with an excuse not to attend. It was the sort of social occasion she loathed, but at which Boy, who knew many of the parents, excelled. Kits remembered him being particularly charming to the ladies. Father and son became closer through their common interest in sport – via his connections with the Football Association, whose Secretary Sir Stanley Rous was a great friend, Boy arranged for Kits to train with Tottenham Hotspur in the late 1950s and on one occasion to meet the great Stanley Matthews – but Kits always felt that Boy was more like a grandfather than a father and regretted that he never came to know him better.

Tessa had been living in London for some time and had seen more of her father than the others. He greatly enjoyed taking her to the ballet and going on afterwards to dine at the Savoy and dance to the music of Carroll Gibbons. By this time she had already had one serious boyfriend in the person of Ken Spence, the son of a Grenadier and one of Boy's godsons. The relationship developed and met with the approval of both Boy and Daphne, especially the latter, but in spite of Spence being keen to marry Tessa broke it off. Instead she began to see more of another suitor, Peter de Zulueta, an officer in the Welsh Guards. Because of their fondness for Spence this was an unpopular move with the family at first, but both Daphne and Boy grew to like de Zulueta, who bent over backwards to help around the house and make himself otherwise agreeable. Tessa married him in 1954 and Boy's and Daphne's first grandchild, Marie-Thérèse, was born in the following year, followed by Paul in 1956.

Flavia left school in 1954 and went to Paris to learn French, staying with Daphne's friend, the young writer Oriel Malet. Her original intention on her return was to follow her grandfather Gerald into the theatre, but although she enrolled at RADA her interest later waned. In 1956 she married Alistair Tower, yet another Guards officer, this time in the Coldstream.

Daphne was still writing, but the first serious work after *My Cousin Rachel* was not one of her best. *Mary Anne* is the story of her great, great grandmother Mary Anne Clarke, the mistress of the Duke of York,[6] and it hints at some of the unhappiness in Daphne's own life, the loss of Gertrude Lawrence and the concerns she was now beginning to develop about Boy. While visitors to Menabilly would see a charming couple, calling each other 'Duck' and laughing together, under the surface there was some tension. Daphne was becoming exasperated by Boy's moods and depressions, sometimes manifested by criticisms about the state of Menabilly. The moods were exacerbated by drink. He would arrive back cheerful after a day's sailing, but would progress from being pleasantly chatty after the first gin to increasingly argumentative as the evening wore on and the alcohol took effect.

His physical health was even more worrying. He had frequent periods off sick from his duties at Buckingham Palace and in 1954 he was unable to accompany the Duke to the Empire Games in Vancouver because he was in hospital with amoebic dysentery, possibly a legacy of his service in the Far East. There were also bouts of 'me tum', alleviated to some extent by copious doses of Eno's Fruit Salts, and of lumbago, for which his remedy was to take to bed with bread and milk. He also became increasingly prone to bronchitis, which he had endured as a child and which was probably caused or exacerbated by his heavy smoking. In 1955 he went into a nursing home for a check-up, but the enforced rest had no permanent effect on his ailments and the tiredness of which he complained to the family.

Once again his public and private faces were quite different. To those with whom he worked, there were no signs of fatigue at all. Apart from his occasional absences through sickness, he remained the decisive and commanding figure which the Duke's Household had come to expect and he continued to carry out all his duties, including the numerous occasions on which he was required to be in attendance on his royal master, with no diminution of energy. He was highly regarded by those with whom he worked. Anne Griffiths, then one of the secretaries in the Household,[7] recalled that he had the perfect manners of an English gentleman and was regarded with great respect and much affection, but that he still retained a touch of vanity, telling her once that his Sam Browne belt was the same one he had first had at the age of eighteen. Mike Parker's daughter Julie, one of his numerous godchildren, remembered that he was always welcoming when she visited the Palace, invariably with a big twinkle in his eye.

Boy accompanied the Duke on several short visits abroad and, in April and May 1954, he escorted Prince Charles and Princess Anne on the maiden voyage of the Royal Yacht *Britannia* to Tobruk to meet their parents, who were on the last leg of the five-and-a-half-month Royal Tour to the West Indies, the Pacific, New Zealand, Australia, Ceylon and Uganda. Boy stayed briefly in Libya, accompanying the Queen and the Duke to the British War Cemetery outside Tobruk before flying home.

His weekday social life in London also continued unabated, as did his interest in the ballet. One memorable occasion was a dinner hosted by the Prime Minister and Mrs Churchill at 10 Downing Street in October 1953, at which the other guests were the Duke, Montgomery, the Foreign Secretary Anthony Eden and General Al Gruenther, the NATO C-in-C, the last two with their respective wives. Boy also found time to take on further outside appointments, including membership of the Executive Committee of the Gordon Boys School and the chairmanship of the United Appeal for the Blind which, with other very similar charities, was consolidated into the Greater London Fund for the Blind in 1956, with Boy becoming Joint Chairman.

Boy's humour was probably not improved by the spectre of 'Market Garden' arising once again. In the years immediately after the War a number of personal accounts had been published, including those of Brereton and Gavin, the former in his diaries, the latter in a book devoted to the history and future of airborne warfare. Boy himself had been extensively interviewed by those preparing the British Official History and had given a lot of his time to Terence Otway, who was writing a detailed and largely factual account of the British and Commonwealth airborne forces for the War Office.

By the early 1950s few objective historians had yet considered the battle in any detail, but an early and distinguished entrant to the field in 1952 was Chester Wilmot, who wrote at some length about the operation in his book on the wider North-West Europe campaign, *The Struggle for Europe*. Wilmot had been a war correspondent, in which capacity he had landed in Normandy by glider with 6 Airborne Division, so he understood something of airborne warfare. Moreover, he had interviewed many of the key participants of 'Market Garden', including Dempsey, Gavin, Horrocks, O'Connor, Thomas, Lathbury and Hackett.[8] The result was an outstanding account of the operation and an incisive analysis of its failure, which still stands favourable comparison with anything produced subsequently. In Wilmot's account there is no explicit or implied criticism of Boy himself, indeed he endorses Boy's decision to order Gavin to give priority to the Groesbeek Heights and excuses his rebuff of the offer of a brigade from 52 Division.

Boy, nevertheless, took exception to the relevant chapters, as he made clear in a letter of March 1952 to Horrocks, who was serving as Black Rod at the Houses of Parliament:

> He [Wilmot] appears to have got his thoughts considerably muddled, such as:
>
> 1. His criticisms of the landing area at Arnhem. As you know, it is only by dint of considerable argument that we even persuaded the Air Force to fly over that part of Europe in daylight, and their flack [sic] maps showed the Arnhem Bridge area being an extremely dangerous centre.
> 2. He entirely overlooks the fact the Bridges which Monty ordered to be captured were in fact captured.
> 3. He fails to see that the Operation up to and including Nijmegen, even if Arnhem could not be held, pushed the Second Army through about 40 miles of unpleasant country and produced a firm base on the higher ground in Holland for Monty to turn east through the Reichswald if he required.
> 4. His failure to appreciate that as an Airborne Operation the Airborne Corps was successful in carrying out what it was told to do.[9]

Boy's criticism was unfounded. In his book, Wilmot refers explicitly to the advice on flak at the Arnhem road bridge, although he makes no reference to any debate over the daylight drop. He concedes that the salient created was 'of immense tactical value for the purpose of driving the Germans from the area south of the Maas', but goes on to say, correctly, that it was a strategic blind alley. [10] He also admits that in terms of the number of bridges captured, the operation was the success that Montgomery claimed, but points out that the failure to secure the last bridge meant the frustration of his real objective. His analysis is difficult to argue with.

Boy asked Horrocks 'to write something straightening out people's ideas', but the reply was not the one he wanted. 'I am sorry that you have found Chester Wilmott's [sic] description of operation Market Garden inaccurate. I must re-read this part of the book, which I must say I found on the whole extremely accurate.'[11] Boy, it seems in retrospect, continued to hold the opinions he had developed in the immediate aftermath of the operation, emphasizing tactical success, but reluctant to concede strategic failure.

When his actions attracted criticism, which at this time was more implied than explicit, he reacted sharply. Nearly three years after Wilmot's book had been published, he received a letter from Major General Erroll Prior-Palmer, at the time the Head of Army Staff at the British Joint Services Mission in Washington. Prior-Palmer had commanded 8 Armoured Brigade[12] during 'Market Garden', and so was entirely familiar with the battle. He had been approached by Jim Gavin, now Chief of Military Operations at the Pentagon, for some support on the decision to give priority to the Groesbeek Heights in preference to the Nijmegen bridges, in the light of some adverse views which were beginning to emerge from those writing the

US Official History. As a man with further military ambitions, Gavin was keen to dispel any criticism and possibly to deflect some of the blame.

Boy replied robustly. He was adamant that he would have given the same order if he had his time again and was good enough not to say that Gavin had entirely agreed with him, placing any blame on himself, Montgomery and Dempsey. Not surprisingly Prior-Palmer reported; 'This has filled Jim Gavin with great delight and he has born down heavily on the civilian historians as a result.'[13] Boy finished the letter with the words 'Give Jim my love and I hope he likes working at an office desk!',[14] making it abundantly clear that the somewhat difficult relationship of the early part of the War was now a distant memory.

The historians' views were an irritant, but they were no more than that. Other aspects of Boy's life, however, were before long to cause much more serious distress.

Chapter 29

Breakdown (1956–1959)

In the autumn of 1956 the Duke set out in *Britannia* on a long tour of the Commonwealth, which included his visit to the Melbourne Olympic Games. He took Parker with him, leaving Boy behind at the Palace to handle his affairs. In February 1957, as *Britannia* was approaching Gibraltar on one of the last legs of the journey, the news broke that Parker's wife, Eileen, was suing him for divorce. At the time, the attitude towards divorce in the higher echelons of British society was almost invariably censorious, and divorce suits among those in public positions aroused considerable and occasionally sensational interest in the Press. Parker returned immediately to England, where he was told in no uncertain terms that the Palace establishment would not be standing behind him. He felt that he had no alternative but to resign, a considerable blow to the Duke, who had relied on him not only to perform his various duties, but also to act as a congenial companion and loyal confidant. He had been instrumental in bringing into the Palace what the Duke had described as 'the fresh air of the Naval Service' and he and Boy had together made a powerful team.

Parker's successor was Jim Orr, who had been Guardian (Head Boy) at Gordonstoun in the early part of the Duke's career at the school. They had renewed their acquaintance when *Britannia* docked at Mombasa, where Orr was serving in the Kenya Police. He had confided in the Duke that he was unhappy in his job and was thus delighted to receive a letter some months later inviting him to become the new Private Secretary. There was never the same familiarity between Orr and the Duke that the latter had enjoyed with Parker, but he was an effective and popular member of the team and he and Boy developed a warm relationship during the relatively short time that they worked together.

Orr had barely had a chance to get settled in before there was another upset to the Duke's Household and this time it involved Boy. Early in July 1957, shortly before he and Daphne were to have celebrated their Silver Wedding, he collapsed and was admitted to a clinic just off Harley Street. Daphne, summoned to London, was horrified by the state in which she found him, careworn, terribly thin and distressed to the point of tears. It was abundantly clear that he was suffering from a severe nervous breakdown.

The seeds of Boy's condition had been sown many years before, possibly as far back as the Great War. He had suffered from nightmares ever since, which were possibly compounded by his experiences in Holland in 1944. There were other causes, however, both physical and mental. He was as inclined as ever to work far too hard. This had been part of his nature ever since he had joined the Army and had led to the spell of nervous exhaustion in the late 1920s which had ruined his chances of attending Staff College. Although he had complained of fatigue at various points in his later career, notably at SEAC, he remained temperamentally incapable of slowing down, even if it meant burning himself out. This had finally happened.

Secondly there was his drinking habit. Whilst he was not an alcoholic, for many years he had consumed more than was good for him, just as his father had done, and this almost certainly contributed to his occasional bouts of depression and to his tiredness over the recent years. There was also growing evidence of damage to his liver. He had recognized his alcohol intake as a potential problem when he was in Singapore, but had shrugged it off at the time. After the War he had if anything stepped up his consumption, his preferred tipple being gin either with lime juice or as a very dry Martini, although he also enjoyed whisky.

However it was something more emotional than physical which had tipped him over the edge. It emerged that Boy had been leading a double life – not the public one in London of which Daphne was well aware, but another which was a complete secret. Boy had always been attractive to and enjoyed the company of women, but he had been faithful to Daphne during the War and for some years thereafter. More recently, possibly because the physical relationship had disappeared from their marriage, he had been diverted elsewhere. One manifestation of this was his attachment to a young girl who worked in a shop in Fowey, whom he used to take sailing with him. She was known in the family as 'Sixpence', derived from one of the du Maurier codewords, 'Shilling', which meant anything worthless or disappointing. There is no evidence that the liaison with 'Sixpence' was much more than a long drawn out flirtation, but he was clearly flattered by the attention. Daphne, for her part, mocked the relationship to his face but was deeply hurt about it, believing herself to be in some way responsible. Whilst she had written herself into *Rebecca* twenty years earlier as the second Mrs de Winter, with Jan Ricardo as the eponymous first wife, she now wondered if it was she who was really Rebecca, whilst Sixpence was the nameless heroine of the book.

Until Boy's breakdown however, Daphne was totally unaware of another affair, a real one this time which was taking place simultaneously in London, involving a woman whom Boy had met as a result of his connections with the ballet. Just after Daphne returned from the clinic to Whitelands House, this woman, subsequently codenamed 'Covent Garden', called on the telephone to reveal all. As if this was not bad enough, there was actually a second woman, of whose existence and identity Daphne never became aware. The relationship in this case had come about through Boy's Palace connections, was totally concealed from view and only ever became known to a very small number of people.

It was little wonder then that Boy, in addition to his purely physical problems, was suffering from deep feelings of guilt at the deception he was practising on his wife, whom he still continued to love. The accumulation of all these tribulations led almost inevitably to the breakdown.

Boy was placed under the care of Lord Evans, the Queen's Physician.[1] The symptoms diagnosed by Evans were both physical and emotional, the former evidenced by some problems with Boy's circulation and by a hardening of the liver. Drugs were prescribed to thin his blood and he was strongly advised to stop drinking. The psychological aspects of the case were much more difficult to address and the immediate treatment was brutal by modern standards, involving the administering of electric shocks. Boy described it later as torture and it is highly questionable whether it had any benefit to the patient, indeed it may have retarded his recovery.

Daphne immediately enrolled the assistance of Maureen and her husband since 1955, Monty Baker-Munton, whom Daphne had liked at first sight and had already grown to trust implicitly. They were asked to keep Boy company as much as possible, while Daphne returned to Cornwall to cancel the Silver Wedding celebrations and to prepare for his convalescence. Maureen sat by his bed every day, although at the beginning he was in such a bad state that he did not recognize her. The immediate family was told the full circumstances of the breakdown, but the story otherwise put out was that Boy was suffering from mild nervous exhaustion. The timing from the perspective of the Palace could have been worse, as the Royal Family was about to decamp for its long annual holiday in Balmoral, during which engagements would be fewer than normal.

Daphne's response to the shock of her husband's infidelity and his desperate physical and mental condition was two-fold. On the one hand, she decided immediately that there would be no divorce and that she would do her utmost to restore Boy to health and their marriage to some semblance of equilibrium. On the other, she was consumed with guilt about her own wartime affair with Christopher Puxley, which she confessed by letter to Boy, and by the impact which her obsessions with Ellen Doubleday and Gertrude Lawrence might have had on their relationship. Her mind was in turmoil, with fantasies about 'Sixpence', Jan Ricardo and Rebecca alternating with comparisons of Boy to the character Kay in Hans Christian Andersen's fairy tale *The Snow Queen*.[2] For a while she even became convinced that there was a plot against her, Boy, and even the monarchy, and that his life was in danger: it was Kits who coaxed her out of it by persuading her to see the ridiculous side of her fears and she emerged much stronger.

After three weeks in the clinic, Boy was driven down to Cornwall by Daphne's cousin, Peter Llewelyn Davies.[3] Boy spent the whole of August at Menabilly recuperating from his breakdown before being judged fit enough to return to work in September, after which Daphne spent much more time herself in London. When she was not there, Ken Spence was deputed to keep an eye on Boy and to monitor the situation with 'Covent Garden', whom Boy continued to meet on occasion, although the affair was effectively at an end. On the face of it he was fine. He resumed all his duties at the Palace and was even able to accompany the Queen and the Duke on their tour of Canada and the United States in October, which included a visit to his old friend Eisenhower, now the US President. In reality he was far from completely recovered. He still complained of severe fatigue and had slowed down in his work, although this was not immediately evident to the Duke's staff. More worryingly his bouts of depression continued and on more than one occasion Ken Spence went to the flat to find Boy with his old service revolver in his hand, threatening to commit suicide, although this seems to have been more a plea for help than a serious expression of intent.

Daphne was quick to recognize that he was far from cured, writing to Oriel Malet that November: 'Moper's physical health is better, but I don't think his mind is all right. All he seems to want to do is sit glued to his desk at the office, doing rather routine things, and when at home, he doesn't know what to do with his time. I think his brain is going on like a kind of machine, but the power has gone, and he's terrified of relaxing, in case it goes blank.'[4] Daphne's mother had died shortly beforehand and she herself was not in the best mental condition, feeling humiliated by what had happened and loathing her stays in London. She expressed her frustration in a letter to another friend, Evie Williams,[5] whilst waiting for Boy to return from Canada: 'I shall have to be up in this blasted city more than I used to be, because the doctors say Tommy must not exhaust himself by coming down for snatched weekends after a tiring week in London, so I've faced up to duty and told myself I must be more of a domestic wife now we've turned our Silver Wedding Anniversary.'

By early 1958, life had returned to some sort of pattern. Boy was able to hold down his job without attracting attention to what he himself thought were his deficiencies, but the effort of doing so left him exhausted at the end of each day. Daphne came more frequently to London than she had done before the breakdown, but was also able to resume writing, this time a collection of short stories, eventually published in the following year under the title of *The Breaking Point*, most of which reflected the emotional turbulence from which she was still suffering. She remained deeply concerned about Boy and eventually summoned up the courage to write to the Duke without Boy's knowledge, suggesting that it was time for her husband to retire. The Duke replied to say that he did not wish to lose Boy, but he suggested that a sabbatical might be the best thing for him, following which the situation could be reviewed. In mid-July Boy left the Palace on leave and did not return until the New Year.

His departure came as something of a surprise to the Duke's Household and to nobody more than David Alexander, one of the extra equerries, who was summoned at short notice to London to take on the duties of Acting Treasurer. A young Royal Marines captain, Alexander had been appointed an extra equerry nine months earlier on the strength of a recommendation from the Commandant-General and because he was already known to the Duke and the Queen.[6] He was ordered to join the Household in a full-time capacity on 17 July and immediately accompanied the Duke on a tour of Wales and the West Country. The only time he had met Boy was when he had attended his interview as an extra equerry, although they had talked subsequently on the phone. Alexander was given the full authority of the position and was able to go anywhere and do anything on the Treasurer's business as if he held the permanent appointment himself. He was the first to recognize, however, that it was Boy's influence, standards and style which still permeated the Household.

A month after beginning what they still believed would be a temporary break, Boy and Daphne went on holiday, their first together for several years. It took the form of a driving tour of France, the main objective being to watch the filming of Daphne's novel *The Scapegoat* which had been published early in 1957. The trip was not a success. Daphne was disappointed with the screenplay, which was substantially different from the book, and Boy remained depressed. On their return to Menabilly, she had the local doctor look at him and was pleased when he recommended a sensible approach involving a building back of Boy's physical reserves and a complete absence of stress.

The next few months passed uneventfully with Boy untroubled by the Palace and taking every opportunity to go sailing. On the family front, Kits had left Eton that summer and was looking for a job. Unlike his own father, Boy did not approve of National Service and was pleased that Kits was just young enough not to be called up. To his credit, he was wholly encouraging about his son's choice of career, which was to go into films. Daphne had bought Kits a cine camera and projector and he made a short film at Menabilly called *The Saboteur* in which Boy starred as the 'baddy', wearing a trilby hat and a white trench coat and acting particularly enthusiastically in the scene in which he was directed to shoot Tod! Daphne then secured Kits some work experience on the filming of *Our Man in Havana*, which was being directed by her old friend and one-time lover, Carol Reed.[7] Boy was thrilled to find that the actor Burl Ives was one of the stars as he adored westerns and one of his favourites was *The Big Country*, released only that year, in which Ives had played a major part.[8]

By the end of 1958 Boy believed that he had recovered sufficiently to be able to hold his own again, even if he was not restored to full health. He duly returned to work in the New Year, but it was not a great success. Although as usual he managed to keep up appearances, he realized that he had slowed down considerably and now found it difficult to make decisions. The Duke, as intensely loyal to his staff as they were to him, was reluctant to let him go, but accepted the inevitable. The news of Boy's retirement and the name of his successor, Rear-Admiral Christopher Bonham-Carter, were announced on 10 April.

Boy's last public duty was to take part in a procession during the state visit of the Shah of Iran on 5 May. Five days later his grade in the Royal Victorian Order was advanced to Knight Grand Cross,[9] a sign of particular esteem by the Sovereign, and on 14 May he was received privately by the Queen, both to be invested and to take his formal leave of her. Waiting in Whitelands House, Daphne wrote to Evie Williams: 'I am standing by while Tommy does his "hand-over" – today is his last day at the Palace, and it's rather emotional and trying for him, after so long. But it was no good his struggling on, he really could not keep it up. Actual organic health OK but his nervous system is worn out and he needs months of no responsibility, and relaxation. So we head for home and sailing, hoping this will do the trick.'[10]

Chapter 30

Finale (1959–1965)

Boy was aged only sixty-two when he left the Palace and he and Daphne should have had every expectation of a long retirement. For the first time since 1940 they were living together and this proved initially to be a strain. Boy was still deeply depressed, believing himself to be useless to anyone: on one occasion Daphne found him with a gun, much as Ken Spence had done, threatening to blow his brains out. Even if the threat was not serious, Daphne knew that her own independence would be profoundly affected by the need to look after him, especially as he tended to take a downward turn whenever she was absent. There were a number of reasons for her to be away, such as the birth of Flavia's son Rupert in August 1959 and her research for a new book, a biography of Branwell Brontë, but every time she left she had to make arrangements for someone else to stand in. Happily for the peace of the household Tod was no longer there, having gone to London to look after Kits, who was now living in Whitelands House. The gap was eventually filled on a permanent basis by a new housekeeper, Esther Rowe. She was only twenty-eight, pretty and vivacious, and her presence helped to lift some of the dark clouds hovering over Boy.

Boy had one project to carry out over the next year, which provided a welcome distraction. He was writing an account of the Queen's life between her marriage and her accession, with the full cooperation of the Palace. A letter to his sister Grace indicated that his old sense of humour had not completely vanished. 'It is curious', he wrote, 'how directly I started writing all the early days with her came back to me and I am really enjoying it. Thank goodness I have got my old secretary Molly Miller (now married and retired) to do the typing as (a) she is completely trustworthy and (b) is able to jog my memory if I'm stuck e.g. the names of the blasted Korgis [sic] we had at Clarence House and were always attacking the luckless sentry in the garden!'[1] The account was not meant for publication, but was lodged in due course in the Palace archives.

Boy also remained in touch with the Palace following his retirement by virtue of his appointment as an extra equerry to both the Queen and the Duke. The only occasion on which he was asked to fulfil the function was during the Duke's visit to the Award Scheme centres and various other organizations in Devon and Cornwall in June 1961. In July 1962, however, the Queen came at last to Menabilly, accompanied by the Duke. They were on their way to join *Britannia*, which was moored in the Fowey River for a brief voyage along the south-west coast. On this occasion it was Boy who was the calmer of the two, making the arrangements with military precision whilst Daphne was the one in a state of nerves, confining herself to arranging the flowers. The visit went off without a hitch, though Daphne was mildly upset that the royal couple had not eaten more of her sandwiches and cakes.

Boy gave up a number of the appointments which would have required regular visits to London, although he did remain a member of the Board of Governors of the Cutty Sark Society. At the end of 1960 he resigned as a Director of The Savoy Hotel Limited, but stayed on the boards of its sister hotels, Claridges and the Berkeley. As he was unable to attend meetings regularly, he also stood down from the chairmanship of the Airborne Forces Security Fund in 1961, to be succeeded by Gale, although he continued as a Trustee.

He did, however, take on some more local appointments. As a distinguished local soldier, he was a natural choice to be Chairman of the Cornwall Territorial and Auxiliary Forces Association, to which he gave strong support over the coming years. He was also made a Deputy Lieutenant of Cornwall in February 1960, but at that time this was more of an honour than an obligation to perform any services. He was friendly with both Sir Edward Bolitho, who retired as Lord Lieutenant in 1962, and his successor Sir John Carew Pole,[2] and it was Lady Carew Pole who was instrumental in bringing him a much more substantial appointment in October 1959. She was the Chairman of the Cornwall County Council Civil Defence and Emergency Committee, which was responsible for selecting Boy as County Group Controller of Civil Defence, a job he took very seriously.

The Cold War reached its height in the early 1960s and the measures to be taken in the event of either nuclear or conventional attack loomed large on the agendas of both central and local government, various contingency plans being drawn up for a range of emergencies. Boy's organization consisted of the Civil Defence Corps (CDC) of trained volunteers, together with a small number of full-time officials to recruit and train it, and a small Auxiliary Fire Service (AFS) to supplement the County Brigade. In an emergency the County Controller was expected to assume 'strategic control' of the both the CDC and the AFS which, together with the full-time police and fire services were then deployed to protect the civilian population. He was responsible to the Regional Commissioner, who would direct the overall response to any emergency from his HQ.

Cornwall was unlikely to be immune from nuclear attack. RAF St Mawgan and RNAS Culdrose were both dispersal airfields for RAF Bomber Command, while the nearby Plymouth Dockyard and naval anchorage would also have been targets. Regular CDC exercises were held to address the response to any attack, the overriding objectives being to ensure the continuation of government, to keep essential services going, to safeguard communications and to protect as much of the population as possible from fall-out. However, other civil emergencies such as floods and oil spillages also fell into the remit of the Civil Defence and Emergency Committee and needed to be trained for. This was thus a real, if part-time job for Boy and he was ideally suited for it, as his reputation carried some influence with local military commanders as well as with the civilian services. He went frequently to Truro on Civil Defence business and toured the county visiting local establishments and attending exercises.

Whilst these new interests provided a vital distraction, he still had a great deal of unaccustomed time on his hands. During the summers he was able to indulge his passion for sailing, but he was finding it more difficult to handle *Jeanne D'Arc* and in the winter of 1960/61 he decided to sell her. She was replaced by a much smaller sailing boat, the 18-foot *Echo*, but she too proved to be something of a handful, not least because she was very fast. His last boat was *Ygdrasil III*, another motor launch built at Hunkin's yard, which gave him a lot of pleasure during the summer of 1964. Boy refused to take the advice given by almost everyone that he should install diesel propulsion and instead put in two large Chrysler petrol engines. Not only were they expensive to run, but they made the boat very difficult to sell in due course. In 1962 Boy retired after eighteen years as Commodore of the Royal Fowey Yacht Club, and was made the Honorary Admiral.

His other interest was photography and he enjoyed travelling around Cornwall taking pictures with the box camera he had brought back from the Far East, always shooting his film on transparent slides and refusing to upgrade to a 35mm camera when these became commonplace. In winter, when there was no sailing, he used to like taking the family's West Highland terriers on long walks to the beach at Pridmouth or along the coast. As far as more sedentary pursuits were concerned, he had loved television ever since it was installed at Menabilly in 1956. Apart from westerns his main interest was anything to do with sport, whilst he was an avid viewer of 'The Brains Trust'. He and Daphne had both invested in one of the new independent television franchises, Westward Television, which covered the South-West and Daphne even joined the board. In a rather more off-beat direction, Boy was also fascinated by Unidentified Flying Objects and was convinced that they existed, making a study of the reported sightings.

Another welcome distraction for Boy was his grandchildren. Marie-Thérèse and Paul were growing up fast and used to spend a lot of their holidays at Menabilly, whilst the whole family gathered there for Christmas. Boy was also greatly taken with Flavia's son Rupert, who was much younger than the others, but had impeccable manners. Paul remembered his grandfather fondly but said that he often kept himself to himself, Daphne becoming the much more dominant figure in their lives. When he wanted peace Boy retreated into his study, off the end of the Long Room at Menabilly, where he continued to pursue his longstanding hobby of boat design, his drawings strewn over the table in the middle.

By 1962, the relationship between Daphne and Boy was back on an even keel. There can be little doubt that they loved each other deeply and visitors would see a cosy couple, who enjoyed mutual banter and continued to share a lively sense of humour. The dominant personality however, except when they were aboard one of the boats, when Boy inclined to be dictatorial, was Daphne. His reliance on her was inhibiting, whilst his health caused her both concern and frustration and she could not understand his inability to give up drinking, as his doctors insisted he should do. Nevertheless, and although she often felt the need to escape to the hut in the garden or on occasions further afield, she had become much more the dutiful wife than she had ever been.

The Brontë biography had attracted some favourable criticism and she completed an unfinished novel by Sir Arthur Quiller-Couch, *Castle Dor*, but otherwise Daphne was going through a relatively fallow period as a novelist in the early 1960s. The problem was not only her concerns about Boy, but also her fear about the tenure of Menabilly, which made it difficult for her to develop the required level of creative concentration. The house's owner, Dr John Rashleigh, died in 1960 just as she was about to sign a new twenty-three-year lease and it was clear that Philip Rashleigh, his heir, would want to take it back at some point. It was not until 1961 that he granted a seven-year lease and, greatly relieved, Daphne felt confident enough to start writing fiction again. *The Glass-Blowers*, based on the activities of her French ancestors, appeared in 1963 and *The Flight of the Falcon* in early 1965, following a visit by Daphne and Kits to Urbino in Italy, where the novel is set.

There were some mixed developments on the family front. Tessa's marriage to Peter de Zulueta was giving cause for concern, as he was turning out to be both a drinker and something of a philanderer. On the other hand, Kits produced a new girlfriend who was instantly approved of by both Boy and Daphne. Olive White was a strikingly attractive former beauty queen, with a personality to match. Boy reported subsequently to Grace: 'This weekend Kits brought down his lady friend (Miss Ireland 1961) to whom he is apparently unofficially engaged! Daughter of a Dublin plumber but none the worse for that because, like Daddy I go for the man rather than his birth … . We have found no faults in the girl up to date and one's only reservation is the extreme youth of Kits and her i.e. 18 and 22 respectively.'[3]

Boy and Olive (later to be known by her nickname 'Hacker') got on well from her first morning at Menabilly, when she was woken by him with a cup of tea and a cigarette. As he told Kits afterwards, 'one should always see what they look like first thing in the morning.' On Sundays thereafter they both used to worship, with Boy driving her in to Fowey and dropping her off at the Roman Catholic church before going on himself to the Anglican equivalent. He would then pick her up and whisk her away to the yacht club, where he was delighted to be able to show her off to admiring friends and acquaintances. Daphne and Boy both harboured doubts about either their son or his fiancée being ready for marriage, but did not stand in their way when the event was set for January 1964. Boy was not looking forward to the occasion, indeed he remarked that he would have preferred to have gone back into the trenches on the Somme. However, the family went to Dublin in force and Boy and Daphne, neither in any way a snob, got on very well with their son's new parents-in-law. Boy was no longer drinking and found the reception something of a trial, but Daphne thoroughly enjoyed herself and they both returned to Cornwall in good spirits.

Boy's abstemiousness at the wedding was the result of a major shock only the previous month. Since his breakdown in 1957 he had been advised to cut out alcohol, but he had been singularly unsuccessful in doing so. In early December 1963 he was driving in his Alfa Romeo to attend a Civil Defence meeting, having fortified himself with a few whiskies in advance, when he caused an accident that left two other people injured. He had been taking various types of medication and it is likely that these did not combine well with the alcohol. Two days before Christmas, accompanied by Tessa to provide moral support, he appeared before the magistrates in Truro and was found guilty of driving under the influence of drink or drugs, fined £50 – a considerable amount at the time – and ordered to pay costs, including a doctor's fee. Although the injured parties made a full recovery, Boy was mortified, not least because the incident and its consequences had been reported in both the local and national press. In his shame he completely overreacted, refusing to appear in public and resigning from his clubs. It was only through family loyalty that he was induced to go to Dublin for Kits' wedding.

This was only a temporary upset, but in September 1964 Boy's physical condition began to give more serious cause for concern. Although there had been periods during his retirement when he had seemed relatively fit, overall he had not enjoyed robust health, with frequent bouts of lumbago and bronchitis and a tendency to catch any virus that was about. He had been admitted to the hospital in Fowey during 1961 for observation but there was no major ailment diagnosed, apart from those of which everyone was already aware. Now, however, his left leg began to cause him serious pain and it was clear that action had to be taken.

Problems with his legs had occurred before. He had damaged one or both of them in the bobsleigh accident in 1924 and had been admitted to hospital in early 1943 with a clot on his knee after the glider crash. His first real complaint specifically about pain in his left leg, however, had come during his time in Singapore in 1946, when walking any distance had crippled him. Although continuing to trouble him on occasion the problem had been kept under control, but it now blew up. A clot was diagnosed in his left foot, which was treated by blood-thinning drugs but quickly followed by an infection. The pain was agonizing and it became clear that he was now suffering severely from ischaemia, a condition in which his arteries were no longer able to supply the required amount of blood to his foot. He was admitted to Greenwich Hospital, Plymouth, to undergo a lumbar sympathectomy, an accepted treatment for restoring circulation that requires a needle to be inserted in the side, to administer a drug to a group of nerves in the lower back which control the blood supply to the legs. Usually the procedure has a good success rate, but in Boy's case it had no effect at all and he remained in considerable pain.

Daphne was reluctant at first to resort to the alternative, which was to amputate the foot, and Boy returned to Menabilly where efforts were made to control the pain with drugs. He was provided with an electric wheelchair which allowed him limited freedom to move about, but there was no improvement. However, whereas Daphne had long suspected him of being something of a hypochondriac, he was now totally stoical in his acceptance of his condition. His grandson Paul went into his study on one occasion to find him rubbing his leg and almost crying out with pain, but refusing to let it get him down. At least night storage heaters had been installed at Menabilly earlier that year, which provided unaccustomed warmth through the winter, much to the occupants' pleasure. The family came down for Christmas and it was clear to all of them that more radical action would need to be taken. Boy and Daphne were persuaded to seek a second opinion and he was admitted to the

Lindo Wing of St Mary's Hospital, Paddington shortly after the New Year. There the medical advice was forthright: his left foot needed to be amputated, otherwise gangrene would set in.

A blood clot had to be removed first, but the operation took place ten days later on 14 January 1965. It was in itself a success, the blood flowing freely again to the rest of the leg, but Boy developed a high temperature possibly from a hospital infection, and had to be pumped full of antibiotics. Three weeks later, still very weak, he returned to Cornwall by train with Daphne. He put a brave face on his condition, writing a cheerful letter to Geordie Gordon Lennox expressing confidence in the future and leaving the visiting secretary of the Territorial Association with the impression that he had turned the corner. However, not surprisingly for one who derived a great deal of pleasure from driving and sailing, the thought of having to have an artificial limb, for which he went to Plymouth to have his first fitting at the end of February, made him once again intensely depressed.

The next two weeks turned into a nightmare. Prior to his trip to Plymouth, Daphne had contracted jaundice and was confined to bed for days, feeling desperately ill herself and losing a stone in weight, whilst Boy, still far from fully recovered from his operation, developed a serious attack of bronchitis. Writing to Oriel Malet, Daphne expressed her fear: 'He looks ghastly. I can't believe that he can get right after this, and his leg was going on quite all right. Why is it that a sudden Doom descends on people in a flash?'[4] Two nurses had been brought in to look after Boy, and they and Esther Rowe now found that they had another patient on their hands, although Daphne began slowly to recover. On 10 March Boy found the strength to scribble a letter to his sister:

My dearest Grace
Thank you so much for your letter and as usual I forgot your birthday which is nothing new!! Getting a beastly go of bronchitis on top of all the other nonsense was really the end and put me back weeks in my general recovery – one sometimes wonders whether it is all worth it at my age and it would really be more dignified to fade gradually out. Thank goodness Daphne is much better but is being very cautious this time and not risking the cold weather outdoors. Please give my love to Helen and Anthony and trust all goes well with the livestock.
From your loving
Tommy
P.S It is quite amazing how tired one gets just writing!!

As the letter suggests by this time he felt exhausted, yet was finding it difficult to sleep. The nurses noticed that his mind was starting to wander and his condition worsened as the bronchitis developed into pneumonia. Early on the morning of 14 March the night nurse woke Daphne to say that she had become seriously concerned about Boy's condition and had sent for the doctor. Daphne dashed to his room, but when she bent down she was unable to hear any breathing. The nurse attempted to revive him, but it was too late. A blood clot had reached his heart.

Chapter 31

Postscript (1965–1989)

Boy's death was announced on the BBC news and produced a flood of obituaries in the Press. Almost immediately telegrams and letters began to pour in to Menabilly. The Queen and the Duke of Edinburgh led the condolences from the Royal Family, whilst the great and the good were represented by Eisenhower, Mountbatten and a number of others. Messages of sympathy and moving tributes from friends and relatives, former Grenadiers, old comrades from the Airborne Forces, Palace courtiers and the representatives of the many organizations with which Boy had been associated were not unexpected, but there were also a large number of letters from people of whom Daphne had never heard – old soldiers, royal servants and others to whom Boy had meant something important and who now wished to convey their feelings.

Daphne needed to know that he had been held in such high regard, as she was heartbroken. All the difficulties of the last few years and the strange life they had led for the two preceding decades, her dismay at his infidelities and the irritation she had felt over his depressions and frequent illnesses, were put aside as she realized what he had really meant to her. She missed their 'routes' and the good times they had had on their boats and she mourned not only the person, but all the wasted years. She wore only black and white for the next twelve months.

Just like the wedding, there was no grand funeral. The coffin was taken to a chapel of rest at Charlestown, where it was covered with flowers, prior to the cremation in Truro, which was attended by the immediate family and Ken Spence, but not by Daphne. She made it very clear in the notice placed in *The Times*, that there was also to be no memorial service. Although Boy had had to attend many in the past, she believed that he had disliked them. Once the cremation was over, Daphne was able to look ahead and as the months passed she found to her surprise that the immense strain under which she had been living had lifted and that she was free to move forward. There was a big gap in her life but she still had Menabilly – and when the lease came to an end she had been promised Kilmarth, the dower house of the estate – she had the family and was deriving increasing pleasure from her grandchildren, and she had her writing. Increasingly she chose to remember not the sad invalid of the last few months, but the dashing Guards officer who had wooed her so romantically.

Boy's reputation at the time of his death was still high. Few people outside the close circle of family and friends knew of his breakdown or the difficulties he had experienced during his last years. Even those with whom he had come into close contact, such as his colleagues at Civil Defence or fellow parishioners at the church, had seen a different person to those who lived with him. He had not yet attracted serious criticism over the part he had played in 'Market Garden' and was, if anything, the beneficiary of the admiration which the man in the street felt for the airborne forces as a whole. He was remembered with respect in the Army – Jock Colville wrote to Daphne that on the day Boy's death was announced he had been having lunch with four generals, including the newly appointed Chief of the General Staff, Sir James Cassels,[1] and that she would have been very proud of what they had to say about him.

This regard was demonstrated very visibly just over three years later when the Parachute Regiment decided to name its newly built regimental headquarters and depot in Aldershot the Browning Barracks.[2] Daphne, accompanied by Tessa, Kits and Hacker, unveiled the plaque commemorating the event on 6 June 1968. Her host was the Deputy Colonel Commandant of the regiment, Major General Napier Crookenden, who had served in 6 Airborne Division. Also present were a number of Boy's former wartime comrades, including John Frost, Mark Henniker, Freddie Gough and James Hill, together with Jock Pearson, the founder of the Airborne Forces Security Fund, and Leslie Hollinghurst. The unveiling ceremony was followed by a parachute drop, one of the parachutists presenting a statuette of an airborne soldier to Daphne.

Interest in 'Market Garden', far from diminishing after what was now more than twenty years since the events themselves, continued to grow. Roy Urquhart had published his own account of the Arnhem battle in 1958, including the first attribution of the 'bridge too far' comment to Boy. Serious historians, notably Christopher Hibbert in 1962, also began to provide much deeper analysis and just two years after Boy's death the Irish-American author and journalist Cornelius Ryan started work on a major new account of the whole operation. Ryan had already established a considerable reputation following the publication of his books on the Normandy landings and the fall of Berlin in 1959 and 1966 respectively. *The Longest Day* and *The Last Battle* were the product of meticulous research, written in an attractive style which owed much to his background as a war correspondent.

In March 1967 Daphne was approached by Frederic Kelly, Ryan's research assistant, for her recollections. She replied that she had known little or nothing about the operation at the time and that Boy had not talked about it subsequently, but she was helpful in recommending other potential sources of information. In a further letter she emphasized that Boy had felt deeply about the losses of men, but had never, as far as she was aware, regretted what had been done from a strategic or tactical point of view. She also went out of her way to mention the regard which Boy had entertained for Gavin.

A Bridge Too Far was eventually published in 1974 and Daphne was sent a copy. As far as she could tell, the description and assessment of Boy's role was balanced and fair, and she took no exception to it. Two months after publication the author succumbed to the cancer from which he had been suffering for four years, but before he died, he extracted a promise from the legendary American film producer Joseph E. Levine that he would make a film of the book.

Levine was an independent producer, with a number of highly successful films to his name, including *The Graduate* and *The Lion in Winter*. He was enthralled by Ryan's work and determined to bring it to the screen, so much so that he put a substantial amount of his own money into the project. He immediately set about assembling the production team, making two key decisions. To write the screenplay he chose William Goldman, who had built up a considerable reputation as one of Hollywood's finest scriptwriters, among other things winning an Academy Award for *Butch Cassidy and the Sundance Kid*. Goldman read Ryan's book and was not deterred by the enormous scope of the operation, believing that the essence of it could be distilled into a powerful narrative. To him it would be an anti-war film, in his own words 'a chance to say that war sucks'.

As the director, Levine made a more surprising choice. Richard Attenborough had made a name for himself as an actor in a career of more than thirty years, but he had only directed two films, *Oh! What a Lovely War* and *Young Winston*. He, too, relished the challenge of the enormous project. He concurred with another of Levine's decisions, which was to assemble a stellar cast of top American, British and German actors. Heading the list was Dirk Bogarde, who was to play Boy. Bogarde was a friend of Attenborough's and one of his neighbours in France, but he was there on his merits, with a fine career in films to his credit. He had served in the army during the war and claimed to have met Boy,[3] whom he had not liked, thinking him conceited and arrogant, a not unusual reaction from someone who had known him only from a distance.

The news of the film worried Daphne, whose experience of the transfer to celluloid of her own books had not always been a happy one. She was particularly distrustful of scriptwriters, a number of whom had taken liberties with her texts, and she wrote to Attenborough requesting sight of the screenplay. In the spring of 1976 he sent her the outline and she was horrified by what she read, as it was apparent that Boy would be cast in a very unflattering role. Goldman had written out of the story all the top commanders, notably Eisenhower, Montgomery (except in a newsreel sequence at the beginning and in a passing comment at the end), Dempsey and Brereton, leaving Boy and Horrocks as the most senior officers represented. Horrocks was in the event to be sympathetically portrayed by Edward Fox, as were the two American divisional commanders by the actors concerned, notably Ryan O'Neal as Gavin, but Adair and Thomas were nowhere to be seen. Even without them, it was clear that it was the British who were going to be portrayed as the bunglers. As Goldman was to say subsequently, 'The Americans did pretty well', and whilst this was unquestionably true of 82 and 101 Airborne Divisions, it was also convenient for the box office in the country with the largest audience. It would certainly not have looked good to have included a scene showing Brereton's obduracy over the timing of the lifts or the location of the drop zones, both of which had a far greater adverse impact on the operation than any decision of Boy's.

Of the key characters in the line of command, this left Boy and Roy Urquhart. The latter was to be the main victim in the film, beset by problems, including the distance of the drop and landing sites from the objective, the failure of the signals equipment and, worst of all, the apparent lack of any knowledge of the existence in the Arnhem area of German armour. Much was made of the last of these, the key sequence being the presentation by Brian Urquhart (called Major Fuller in the film so as not to confuse the audience) to Boy of the aerial photos of the tanks and his subsequent despatch on sick leave on the grounds of nervous exhaustion.

Daphne wrote immediately to Attenborough, raising a number of serious reservations, including directions on Boy's appearance which gave the impression that he would be portrayed as something of a dandy. Attenborough replied to reassure her that he would deal with these. One matter to which she attached great importance was Boy's association with the title of the film, which, she pointed out quite reasonably, demonstrated clearly that he had entertained serious doubts about the plan. The line was amended very simply by changing Bogarde's words in the original script from, 'We just went a bridge too far' to 'Well, as you know, I've always thought that we tried to go a bridge too far.' Although the new version did show Boy in a better light than the old, its inclusion in the penultimate scene would still make it appear to the viewer that he was being wise after the event. Clearly the more truthful approach would have been to put the words in his mouth close to the beginning, where they belonged. However, this would have spoilt the storyline being developed by Goldman, which cast Boy as the villain.

Bogarde later claimed that he had been concerned about the character that he was asked to portray. In a 1983 letter to Geoffrey Powell, who had been a company commander in the 156th Parachute Battalion at Arnhem and was engaged in writing what would be one of the best accounts of 'Market Garden', *The Devil's Highway*, he wrote about Boy: 'I did my very best to honour the man, because it was clear to me then that the U.S. Makers were determined to have a 'fall guy'... and it was to be Browning.' Colonel John Waddy, one of Powell's fellow company commanders and the British Military Advisor on the film, recalled that, during the rehearsal for the scene between Boy and Major Fuller, Bogarde was accused by Attenborough of departing too much from the script, and responded immediately: 'I won't have a British general made to look a fool.' Waddy had been shown the script himself on his appointment and was told by Attenborough: 'I can't change it and neither can you.' He was instructed to confine himself to ensuring the accuracy of how the airborne soldiers fought.

About a month before the film was due to be premiered in London, Daphne received a tip-off from a journalist that it would not show Boy in a good light. In desperation she wrote to Jim Orr and Mountbatten to see if they could intercede in some way, and both sent letters to Attenborough. In his reply to Mountbatten, the director told him of his attempt to satisfy Daphne's concerns, particularly about the 'bridge too far' remark, but emphasized that in many people's view the operation had been a failure and that there must therefore be some implied criticism of both Montgomery and Boy, which although true was a gross oversimplification of the complex reasons for failure. By now in any event the horse had well and truly bolted, so there was little point in attempting to shut the stable door. Mountbatten, who was asked by Daphne to boycott the premiere, was in a particularly difficult position. He and the Duchess of Kent had been invited to be the guests of honour and the proceeds from the premiere were to benefit charities with which they were associated. He had been a friend of Attenborough's for many years, having first met him on the set of *In Which We Serve*, Noël Coward's 1942 film based on Mountbatten's career as a destroyer captain, in which Attenborough had played a minor but important role. Finally, his grandson Norton Knatchbull had been in the production team as location manager. He was unlikely to do anything to rock the boat, even had it been possible.

The film premiered in London on 23 June 1977. It was generally well received by the critics, few of whom realized that it was littered with historical inaccuracies, although for the most part these did not detract from the action, which conveyed the sense of the battle very well. A few of the inaccuracies did cause great offence, notably the depiction of the taking of the Nijmegen road bridge by 82 Airborne Division before the tanks of the Grenadier Guards had started rolling across and the suggestion that those same tanks had without good reason failed to press on to Arnhem. The Grenadiers themselves were extremely upset about these two episodes, the one seemingly designed to flatter American audiences, the other putting the blame firmly on the regiment for the failure to relieve Frost at the Arnhem bridge. The editor of the *Guards Magazine* also expressed the anger of the regiment at the 'inaccurate and derogatory' portrayal of Boy.

Mountbatten, on the other hand, wrote to Daphne on the day after the premiere: 'Candidly, neither I nor the 'Royal Party', nor several friends and, above all, soldiers with whom I discussed the film, could find anything really detrimental to Boy in the film. I think perhaps they made a mistake in casting Dirk Bogarde in the role, for although Dirk is a fine actor, he is not the personality one would wish to see reflected in Boy.' In finding nothing detrimental to him, Mountbatten was in a minority amongst those who knew Boy well, but he put his finger on the more important issue, the characterization by Bogarde.

The newspaper critics, whilst praising the film in general, seized on this. Patrick Gibbs in the *Daily Telegraph* wrote: 'As portrayed by Dirk Bogarde and, of course by the script-writer, who is William Goldman, this general is not one I would have trusted to run a cocktail party' and wondered if the depiction might not be actionable. Penelope Gilliatt in *The New Yorker* saw the character as 'a suave lieutenant-general looking out for himself.' The interpretation of the character by a combination of Attenborough, Goldman and Bogarde was indeed totally at odds with the evidence of most of those who knew him well. He was portrayed as a languid and complacent officer, determined to get the operation started regardless of risk and, once on the ground, leading a life of comfort in his luxurious quarters. Given the evidence of his frequent presence at the HQs of XXX Corps, Guards Armoured Division and various subordinate units and the fact that he wrote to Daphne on D+5 that he had not washed more than his face and neck since landing, this last was a travesty of the truth.

The reaction was immediate and came largely through the correspondence columns of *The Times*. Daphne had lined up Shan Hackett to write a letter to the editor in the event that the film turned out as she feared. Hackett was a good choice, as he was not numbered among the most devoted supporters of Boy and was known to have harboured serious doubts about the operation. His letter, published on 25 June, was scathing:

Sir, It would be difficult to imagine Sir Richard Attenborough unkind, unthinkable to find him lacking in regard for the truth. It must be said, however, that the portrayal of Sir Frederick Browning in the film *A Bridge Too Far* is both untruthful and unkind.

It is untruthful because it shows a superficial, heartless, shallow person who is uncaring – even almost flippant – about the fate of brave men committed to his charge and displays, instead of strength of character, a petulant obstinacy born of weakness. He was not like that at all and could not have commanded such widespread loyalty if he had been.

It is unkind because it will affront very many men who knew Browning well and, though some might say he had his faults (and who has not?), gave him their admiration and respect, but also, though he is dead, there are those still living who were closer to him still and knew him even better, and these will be deeply and unnecessarily wounded … .

The fault, I am sure, lies in the writing of the script. I was shown this before shooting and Sir Richard was kind enough to listen to some observations from me on the caricature of Boy Browning it contained. I was grateful to see, in the outcome, he had offered a picture of this brave, austere, dedicated professional officer, who will be remembered as both stern and charming, considerably less cruel than that imagined by the script-writer. It still goes much too far.

I suppose that a script-writer needed a character like that for structural purposes in telling the story as he saw it, and that a director should probably not stray too far from what he is given. The pity is that a tragic conflict in a high-minded man, of a kind that carries an echo of Racine, might have provided for an actor as good as Bogarde under the sensitive direction he could expect from Attenborough a memorable and moving role. A great opportunity was missed here too.

Others weighed in subsequently, including Daphne's son-in-law Alastair Tower and Freddie Gough. Cyril Ray,[4] who had been a war correspondent attached to 82 Airborne Division and who met Boy during the operation, wrote: 'I do not recognize the man I knew in battle and in peacetime in the Browning of the film … Boy Browning was debonair in manner, dapper in appearance … the dapper and debonair is one all the easier to caricature by anyone wishing to please a box office, and easier still if he is dead, which Browning is, and which other generals who took part in the operation are not.'

One letter came not to *The Times*, but directly to Daphne some three months after the film had been released. It read:

Dear Lady Browning

I have now seen the film of Cornelius Ryan's book 'A Bridge Too Far' and was appalled at the portrayal of General Browning. Of course it is too late, but I have written to the Director expressing my feelings, and I understand that there was a considerable correspondence in The London Times.

I remember your late husband with great affection and find it monstrous that a man so talented, so responsible, so magnetic and so full of imagination and vitality should be portrayed as Dirk Bogarde portrayed him in the film. I was also distressed by the account of his relationship with me during the preparations for Operation Market Garden. Although we did not always agree, and I, at the time, had no idea of the appalling pressure he was under and the tragic dilemma he was in, he always treated me with the utmost kindness and friendliness. Indeed it would have been odd if he had not, since I had been working for him for some three years and we knew each other well.

I can imagine that this film must have been most distressing to you, and this particular aspect of it certainly disgusted me. I suppose it is some consolation that enough people know the truth, all those who worked with General Browning and those who knew him, but I wish there was something more one could do about it. If you feel there is anything that I could do, I would be most glad to do it.

With all best wishes
Yours sincerely
Brian Urquhart.

Many others also expressed their views directly to Daphne, including Angela Fox, a personal friend and also the mother of Edward Fox. She saw the press preview and wrote that she was 'stunned by the lies, & totally inaccurate portrayal by Dirk Bogarde. It is pretty clear to me that, having read the script, he should simply have turned it down.' As it happened, Bogarde was soon afterwards to be completely taken aback by the outpouring of criticism. In some distress he wrote a letter to Attenborough which was couched, in the words of his biographer John Coldstream, 'in venomous terms'. He felt strongly that he had been betrayed by the director and one rather sad outcome to the affair was that the relationship between them, hitherto one of the friendliest, was never to be the same again.

Attenborough himself recognized very clearly the controversy that had been stirred up, addressing the issue in a subsequent interview: 'Of course it is a tremendous responsibility, a daunting responsibility and the chances are you get it wrong because the degree of potential error, as in the battle itself, is enormous.' But he then went on to say: 'Provided you are not cheap, provided you are not meretricious, provided that you are not crude in the search for effect, then you can hold your head up and say "In my judgement, in my knowledge, what I presented was true." [5] In this case the portrayal was not true and, whilst Attenborough cannot be accused of being cheap or crude, if it was being done for the purposes of box office success then 'meretricious' might not be an inappropriate description.

A Bridge Too Far did lasting damage to Boy's reputation, since it will be how he is remembered to all except the dwindling number of people who actually knew him, or who are keenly interested in either military history or the life of Daphne herself. The damage cannot easily be undone. Daphne always refused to see the film and would not even discuss it once the immediate furore had died down.

Daphne lived for just over twenty-four years after Boy's death, becoming a Dame of the British Empire, continuing her successful writing career in Kilmarth and having the pleasure of seeing her grandchildren grow up. She never thought of marrying again. Whilst she had never been a religious person, she always felt that she and Boy would be reunited. In 1979 she wrote to his cousin Denys, who had been living for many years in New Zealand: 'I can tell you that I always believe that I shall be met by my beloved Tommy in a celestial boat of his own design, who will lean over to pull me aboard, saying "Come on, darling, what a time you have taken, I've been waiting for ages!" And off we will sail into a heavenly sunrise, not sunset.'[6]

Chapter 32

Retrospective

As a soldier, sportsman, courtier and the husband of one of the twentieth century's most popular novelists, Boy's reputation stood high in his lifetime and for a while at least he was a household name. History, however, has increasingly judged him on the back of one short episode which went badly wrong and has tended to ignore his qualities and achievements, which were considerable.

Boy was born to be a soldier. From the time he entered Sandhurst at the end of 1914 he excelled in his profession, developing into an outstanding regimental officer in both war and peace, widely respected by his subordinates and highly regarded by his superiors for setting and maintaining the highest standards. Whilst he was terrifying to those who failed to achieve his own standards – his flashes of temper were legendary, but they were just that, as swift to subside as to flare up – he would never ask anyone to do something which he himself could not. He was a strong team builder, with the knack of inspiring great personal loyalty and even affection: John Davies, who served as his Adjutant in the 1930s and went on to command the 4th Battalion of the Grenadier Guards in North-West Europe, said later that his two years with Boy were the happiest in his army life, and similar sentiments were echoed by his staffs at every formation he commanded during the War and at SEAC. He was certainly ambitious, but his ambition was on the whole a facet of his desire that every unit or formation in which he was involved should be the best. His sense of duty was unerring.

Throughout his army career Boy presented one face to his immediate friends and colleagues and another to the wider world. The latter sometimes interpreted the seemingly effortless ease with which he conducted himself as arrogance and his attention to dress as vanity. There were elements of both in his personality, but the first was unintentional, a product of his education and his membership of a famous regiment, and the second the consequence not only of a pride in his personal appearance, but also of adherence to his own high standards. Because of this veneer he could seem intimidating to his subordinates, pushy to his peer group and patronizing to his allies, notably the Americans. Those who were allowed beneath the veneer spoke subsequently of his kindness and generosity: Brian Urquhart said that he found his loyalty and friendship, especially when one was in difficulties, both touching and extremely effective.

The monument to Boy's achievement is Britain's Airborne Forces. Those who assert that these were already in existence when he was appointed to command the Airborne Division in 1941, and that he does not therefore deserve the title 'Father of the Airborne Forces', are missing the point: without him, those forces might well have had a very short life. He has been derided by some as a political general, whose only value was in the high level contacts he had made before the War. It was just these contacts which, in the face of opposition from some of the Army establishment and outright hostility from the RAF, enabled Boy to marshal the support necessary to keep the young but fragile organization alive until it could be deployed in force. He had the enormously valuable backing of Brooke, the most influential soldier of the day, but he had to work for this. At the end of 1942 there was a real possibility that the whole airborne project would be severely truncated, but Boy hung on sufficiently long for it to be not only saved but enlarged. The beret of the Parachute Regiment and the wings of the Army Air Corps remain the visible symbols of his achievement.

Boy was no intellectual soldier in the manner of Ridgway or Taylor, both of whom went on to reach the highest position in the US Army. He was, however, not totally lacking in imagination. There is a remarkable document in the Imperial War Museum, dating from 1942, in which Boy uses the device of an Airborne Division medical officer's dream to set out his thoughts for the future of airborne warfare. In the dream, the officer hears a noise far above his head and, looking up, sees strange machines hovering above him, 'big streamlined things, like very large tanks, with hardly any wings.' He climbs aboard one of them and it takes off, rising rapidly from the ground, propelled by horizontal propellers. He also sees inside another of the machines, with stretchers along one side of it and a mobile operating theatre on board. He hears one of the commanders talking about the antiquated Horsas, now museum pieces: ' "Why on earth they did not design a machine so that a motor car or a gun could be driven in or out of it beats me," said the voice, "the first Airborne Commander must have been a slow sort of fellow. That original loading ramp can never have worked." ' This is an extraordinary glimpse of the future, with Boy predicting the use of helicopters, which hardly existed at the time and were certainly not being used for warfare. It is also nicely self-deprecating.

Back in the real world, it all went wrong for Boy when he and the other airborne leaders overreached themselves. They were carried away by the success of the landings in Normandy, believing that they could deploy in ever larger numbers. In so doing they forgot some of the basic principles of airborne warfare, particularly that the biggest possible force should be landed in the shortest possible time as close as possible to its objectives and that, once the surprise which was their hallmark had been achieved, the lightly armed soldiers should be assured of artillery or air support and relieved as quickly as possible. Operation 'Market Garden' was a bridge too far in metaphorical as well as literal terms.

It was also the beginning of the end for Boy as a soldier. Whilst he never saw the operation as a failure for the airborne troops, maintaining for the rest of his life that they had done all that was asked of them, he was deeply affected by the fate of 1 Airborne Division and realized that he was at least partially responsible for it. From that time on, his appetite for command ebbed away, with the result that his career in the post-War Army could go little further. For the next three years, important though his appointments might have been, he was in fact just marking time.

The counterpoint to Boy's career was his marriage to Daphne, but from 1940 onwards the two spheres of career and marriage barely touched. From the outset this was a different Boy, one who would probably have astonished those who knew him in his other life. When in good form, he could be relaxed, casual and very funny. On the other hand, this was a weaker man than the public one, a man who used his wife from the outset as something of an emotional prop, who needed comfort after his nightmares and soothing over his frustrations. Because they did not live together, there was little real friction between career and marriage until the breakdown in 1957, which came as much of a shock to her as to him, but in spite of their physical separation, underneath it all their family and friends were convinced that Boy and Daphne adored one another. Moreover, she was extremely proud of him and he was her greatest fan.

Boy's reputation has taken a serious turn for the worse over the last twenty-five years. Successive historians have included him amongst the villains of 'Market Garden', whilst *A Bridge Too Far* dealt a major and largely unjustified blow. Few if any historians have taken the trouble to evaluate his part in the operation analytically, indeed there has been a general acceptance of criticisms which have been often repeated but which do not always stand up to scrutiny. He certainly cannot be absolved from a significant level of responsibility, but he does not deserve to be castigated above all others.

There was an element of pathos about the end of Boy's life, but those who knew him well have always preferred to remember him in his prime. After his death Mark Henniker wrote a letter to the editor of the *Guards Magazine*, in which he described his arrival at Storey's Gate in November 1941 to join the 'Dungeon Party':

> At that time the fortunes of Britain were at a low ebb. Everywhere our forces seemed to meet with reverses. There seemed to be nothing that we in Britain could do about it. The threat of invasion had not passed; Commanders were inclined to be defensively minded; and a great body of the Forces were fed-up, ill-equipped and badly turned out.
>
> Here, however, I found a man who at our first meeting spoke of the attack; and the prominent part that Airborne Forces would take in it. Here he was: tall, erect, immaculately dressed, looking you straight in the eye; he was filled with fire, enthusiasm, energy and a magical charm that cast its spell over everyone ...
>
> If ever there were a man *sans peur et sans reproche*, 'Boy' Browning was that man.

Appendix 1

Letter from Lieut.-General F. A. M. BROWNING C.B., D.S.O.
26th September, 1944
To:-
Major-General R. E. Urquhart, D.S.O., Commander, 1st. Airborne Division.

Commander, 30 Corps is sending you a letter from himself and his Corps expressing their unstinted admiration and gratitude for the gallant part played by the 1st Airborne Division in the 2nd Army's drive to cross the Rhine.

He will explain to you, and in his expression of opinion I absolutely concur, that without the action of the 1st Airborne Division in tying up, pinning down, and destroying in large numbers the German forces in the ARNHEM area, the crossing of the Waal, the capture of the bridges at Nijmegen and, above all, the advance from the bridgehead, would have been quite impossible.

I am intensely proud of the magnificent fight put up by your Division. With you, I deeply regret the sacrifice that has been entailed in the Division which I had the honour to raise originally.

I do not hesitate to say that the operation, taken as a whole, has done more to speed up the war and further disrupt the already disorganized German Army than any other action up to date. In fact, none other than an Airborne Operation could possibly have achieved the result.

(Sgd.) F. A. M. Browning,
Lieut.-General, Commander, British Airborne Corps

Appendix 2

Letter of 24 November, 1944 to Lieutenant-General Sir Ronald Weeks, Deputy
Chief of the Imperial General Staff

Sir,

I have the honour to bring the following facts to your notice with regard to Major-
General St. Sosabowski, Commander 1st Polish Parachute Brigade Group during
operation 'MARKET.'

During the weeks previous to operation 'MARKET,' a period which entailed
detailed planning for three other possible operations, the 1st Polish Parachute
Brigade Group formed part of the force envisaged.

Both during this period and, in fact, ever since the 1st Polish Parachute
Brigade Group was mobilised in July, Major-General Sosabowski proved himself
to be extremely difficult to work with. The 'difficulty' was apparent not only to
commanders under whom he was planning but also to staff officers of the other
airborne formations concerned.

During this period he gave me the very distinct impression that he was raising
objections and causing difficulties as he did not feel that his brigade was fully ready
for battle. When the brigade was first mobilised I made it absolutely clear to this
officer, and in no uncertain terms, that I was the sole judge of the efficiency of his
brigade and it was merely his duty to get them ready and train them with all the
determination of which he was capable.

It became apparent during this training period that, capable soldier as this officer
undoubtedly is, he was unable to adapt himself to the level of a parachute brigade
commander, which requires intimate and direct command of his battalions. He left
too much to his Chief of Staff and attempted to treat his parachute brigade as if it
were a much higher and bigger formation.

During operation 'MARKET' the brigade was unfortunate in being dropped in
parts owing to the weather. However, during this period of operation 'MARKET'
great difficulties were being overcome hourly by all formations of the Second Army
in their efforts to reach the 1st Airborne Division at Arnhem. This officer proved
himself to be quite incapable of appreciating the urgent nature of the operation, and
continually showed himself to be both argumentative and loathe to play his full part
in the operation unless everything was done for him and his brigade.

Subsequently, when the 1st Airborne Division had been withdrawn, and the
Polish Parachute Brigade Group reverted to my command South of the R. Waal,

this officer worried both me and my staff (who were at that time fighting a very difficult battle to keep the corridor open from inclusive Nijmegen to Eindhoven) about such things as two or three lorries to supplement his transport. I was forced finally to be extremely curt to this officer, and ordered him to carry out his orders from then on without query or obstruction.

Both Commander 30 Corps and Commander 43 Division will bear out my criticism of the attitude of this officer throughout the operation.

Major-General Sosabowski has undoubtedly, during the three years in which I have been connected with him, done a very great amount for the 1st Polish Parachute Brigade Group under disappointing circumstances. He was mainly responsible for the whole of the raising, organization and training of the brigade. However, this good record cannot be allowed to interfere with the present and future efficiency of the brigade.

I am forced, therefore, to recommend that General Sosabowski be employed elsewhere, and that a younger, more flexibly minded and cooperative officer be made available to succeed him.

There are, to my knowledge, two possible candidates now serving with the brigade. The first is Lieut-Col. S. Jachnik, who is at present Deputy Commander. This officer has had practically no opportunity to display his powers owing to the somewhat overbearing nature of General Sosabowski's personality. The appointment of this officer would, in my opinion, be essentially in the nature of an experiment.

The second candidate is Major M. Tonn, who commands 1 Parachute Battalion. This officer has trained his battalion well and, in my opinion and in the opinion of the G.S.O.1. Liaison (Airborne) Lieut-Col. Stevens, he possesses the requisite drive and administrative ability to fulfill the appointment.

However, this appointment must remain largely a matter for the Polish Army to make, and it will probably be better in the long run if new blood be brought in.

Finally, I wish to emphasise again that I consider Major-General Sosabowski is a knowledgeable and efficient soldier and up to the average of his rank, but owing to his outlook, temperament and inability to cooperate he should be given a change of employment.

I have the honour to be, Sir,
Your obedient Servant,

(Sgd) F. A. M. Browning
Commander Airborne Corps.

Abbreviations

AA	Anti-Aircraft
AAA	Amateur Athletics Association
AA&QMG	Assistant Adjutant and Quartermaster-General
ABDACOM	American British Dutch & Australian Command
ADC	Aide-de-Camp
ADMS	Assistant Director of Medical Services
ADOS	Assistant Director of Ordnance Services
AFDAG	Airborne Forward Delivery Airfield Group
AFHQ	Allied Forces Headquarters
AFS	Auxiliary Fire Service
ALFSEA	Allied Land Forces South-East Asia
AOC	Air Officer Commanding
AOC-in-C	Air Officer Commanding-in-Chief
ATS	Auxiliary Territorial Service
BEF	British Expeditionary Force
BGS	Brigadier General Staff
BOA	British Olympic Association
CAS	Chief of the Air Staff
CAS(B)	Civil Affairs Service (Burma)
CB	Companion of the Order of the Bath
CBE	Commander of the Order of the British Empire
CDC	Civil Defence Corps
CIGS	Chief of the Imperial General Staff
C-in-C	Commander-in-Chief
CLE	Central Landing Establishment
CO	Commanding Officer
COS	Chief of Staff
COSSAC	Chief of Staff to the Supreme Allied Commander (Designate)
CRE	Chief Royal Engineer
DAAG	Deputy Assistant Adjutant-General
DA&QMG	Deputy Adjutant & Quartermaster-General
DADOS	Deputy Assistant Director of Ordnance Services
DAQMG	Deputy Assistant Quartermaster-General
DCIGS	Deputy Chief of the Imperial General Staff
DDME	Deputy Director of Mechanical Engineering

DDOS	Deputy Director of Ordnance Services
DSD	Director of Staff Duties
DSO	Distinguished Service Order
FAAA	First Allied Airborne Army
GC	Gentleman Cadet
GCB	Knight Grand Cross of the Order of the Bath
GCMG	Knight Grand Cross of the Order of St Michael and St George
GCVO	Knight Grand Cross of the Royal Victorian Order
GHQ	General Headquarters
GOC	General Officer Commanding
GOC-in-C	General Officer Commanding-in-Chief
GSO1	General Staff Officer Grade 1
GSO2	General Staff Officer Grade 2
GSO3	General Staff Officer Grade 3
HQ	Headquarters
KCB	Knight Commander of the Order of the Bath
KBE	Knight Commander of the Order of the British Empire
LAA	Light Anti-Aircraft
MBE	Member of the Order of the British Empire
MC	Military Cross
MCC	Marylebone Cricket Club
MFV	Motor Fishing Vessel
MI	Military Intelligence – as in MI1(C) or MI6
NEI	Netherlands East Indies
NPFA	National Playing Fields Association
OSS	Office of Strategic Services
OTC	Officers Training Corps
NCAC	Northern Combat Area Command
NCO	Non-Commissioned Officer
NSL	National Service League
PTS	Parachute Training School
RA	Royal Artillery
RAF	Royal Air Force
RAMC	Royal Army Medical Corps
RAOC	Royal Army Ordnance Corps
RAPWI	Repatriation of Prisoners of War & Internees
RASC	Royal Army Service Corps
REME	Royal Electrical & Mechanical Engineers
RMC	Royal Military College
RN	Royal Navy
RNAS	Royal Naval Air Station
RYFC	Royal Fowey Yacht Club
SACSEA	Supreme Allied Commander South-East Asia

SAS	Special Air Service
SEAC	South-East Asia Command
SHAEF	Supreme Headquarters Allied Expeditionary Force
SIS	Secret Intelligence Service (also MI6)
SO	Staff Officer
SOE	Special Operations Executive
VCIGS	Vice-Chief of the Imperial General Staff
USAAF	United States Army Air Force
VE-Day	Victory in Europe Day

Notes

Chapter 1: Family (1335–1896)
1. John Maynard Keynes, the British Treasury representative at the Peace Conference and deeply involved with reparations, was apparently very critical of Montague Browning's tough stance.
2. The Vice-Admiral of the United Kingdom is the deputy to the Lord High Admiral. From the seventeenth century the latter office was held simultaneously by the First Lord of the Admiralty: since 1964, when the office of First Lord was abolished, that of Lord High Admiral has been vested in the monarch.
3. The arms can be seen on Browning family memorials in the parish churches of both Melbury Sampford and Coaley.
4. The Alt House still survives: whilst damaged by the atomic bomb in 1945, it was refurbished and is now part of Glover Garden, a tourist attraction in Nagasaki.

Chapter 2: Tommy (1896–1914)
1. At Eton houses are named after the incumbent housemaster.
2. His original preference was to follow his uncle into the Royal Navy, but it turned out that he was colour blind, which made him unacceptable.
3. His grandfather, Montague Charles Browning, had been President of Pop in his day.
4. Later 1st Viscount Chandos: he was the nephew of the headmaster.

Chapter 3: Boy (1914–1916)
1. It would not be until January 1916 that the Military Service Act introduced conscription.
2. In 1939, these institutions were closed in their old form and immediately reopened as Officer Cadet Training Units, whose graduates only received Emergency Commissions.
3. Collie Knox *People of Quality*, p. 76.
4. Later Field Marshal the Earl of Cavan, Field Marshal the Viscount Gort, General Sir Andrew Thorne and Lieutenant General the Lord Freyberg.
5. Notes written for the author prior to an interview in 2008.
6. Churchill admired Jeffreys greatly and was instrumental in having a barony conferred on him in 1952: having retired from the Army in 1938, Jeffreys served as Conservative MP for Petersfield from 1941 to 1951.
7. Some forty years later it was the first thing he mentioned when Boy's eldest daughter, Tessa, was introduced to him.
8. On the strength of this attachment, it was the 2nd Battalion Grenadier Guards which provided the pallbearers at Churchill's funeral in 1965.

Chapter 4: Trenches (1916–1918)
1. By this time, companies went into action with a maximum of 3 officers and with only 32 other ranks per platoon: this was a reaction to the wholesale losses of the early battles, in which whole battalions had been nearly wiped out.
2. Tanks were first used at the Somme, but in small numbers and not to great effect.
3. The 18th Bengal Lancers became the 19th King George V's Own Lancers on amalgamation with another Indian cavalry regiment in 1922: it remains the 19th Lancers in the Army of

Pakistan and retains the battle honour of Cambrai 1917. To commemorate the action the Grenadiers presented to the Lancers an inscribed bugle, receiving in return a silver statuette of a mounted Bengal Lancer.

4. Westmacott later wrote: 'I think that Boy deserved his award far more than I did mine, because he had to cope with all the very nasty fighting and sniping that was going on in the wood for five hours, while I was digging in the outside.' (Westmacott, *Memories*, p.48)
5. Wigram was promoted to Private Secretary in 1931 and created the 1st Baron Wigram in 1935; both his son, Neville, and his grandson, Andrew, served in the Grenadiers.
6. Shortly before this, Boy went on a short leave to England to receive his DSO from the King.
7. Letter to Grace Browning 13.10.18.
8. Later the 3rd Lord Glanusk.
9. Gort won the VC in this action.

Chapter 5: Peace (1918–1924)
1. As a result of his association with the SIS, he was involved in the leaking of the 'Zinoviev Letter' to the *Daily Mail*, purportedly written from the President of the Comintern to the Communist Party of Great Britain, advocating agitation. Freddie believed it was genuine, but it was subsequently revealed as a forgery. It was nevertheless probably instrumental in Ramsay MacDonald's defeat and the Conservative victory in the General Election of 1924.
2. It had been held in Hyde Park in each of the two previous years, when the King and all ranks wore service dress.
3. *Royal Military College Magazine & Record* Easter Term 1925.
4. Ibid.
5. The younger brother of Harold Alexander, later Field Marshal Earl Alexander of Tunis.
6. Later Honorary Secretary of the International Amateur Athletics Federation.
7. One of the other team members was his cousin, George Browning, son of Bertie, who had been commissioned into the Grenadiers in 1921: he was to transfer into the Welsh Guards in 1938. George was the closest to Boy of all his various cousins and they saw a lot of one another in the 1920s. Boy also proposed George for membership of the South London Harriers.
8. In 1924 Burghley was still up at Cambridge, where he famously ran round the Great Court at Trinity College within the chiming of the noonday clock. He later joined the Grenadiers himself, becoming a close friend of Boy's, but resigned his commission in 1929.

Chapter 6: Sandhurst (1924–1928)
1. M. Henniker, *An Image of War*, p.71.
2. Ruth Farquhar's son, Colonel David Fanshawe, was himself Adjutant at Sandhurst and commanded thirteen Sovereign's Parades in that capacity, without being at any time aware of his mother's story!
3. Later Field Marshal Lord Milne of Salonika.
4. Later Field Marshal Sir James Cassels.

Chapter 7: Hiatus (1928–1931)
1. Jan was a rather tragic figure. She married in 1937, but committed suicide during the Second World War by throwing herself under a train. Her mother had also committed suicide.
2. Twiss, Browning & Hallowes became a significant part of International Distillers & Vintners when that company was created in the 1960s. In 1972 IDV was acquired by Grand Metropolitan, which in due course became Diageo.
3. Flaxley Abbey was originally founded in the 12th century but was dissolved by Henry VIII. That part which survived became the manor house, which was much changed in the 17th and 18th centuries, particularly after a fire in 1777. It remains a private residence.

Chapter 8: Daphne (1931–1932)
1. More properly known in the Brigade of Guards as 'soldier-servant', the original term, but 'batman' is widely understood and thus used throughout.
2. Daphne du Maurier, *Myself When Young*, p.192.
3. Arthur Llewelyn Davies, Sylvia's husband, died of cancer in 1907 and she succumbed to the same disease three years later, upon which Barrie adopted the Llewelyn Davies children.
4. Reed would go on to be a great film director, with a number of films to his credit before and during the Second World War, although his major successes, such as *The Third Man*, *Our Man in Havana* and *Oliver!*, came later.
5. Daphne letter to Maud Waddell, undated 1932.
6. According to Lord Carrington, it was rumoured that Boy had been saved from having to resign his commission by the King, who expressed the view that it would be a complete nonsense.
7. Gerald volunteered in 1918 at the age of 45 and joined the Irish Guards. He was a hopeless soldier and both he and the Army were relieved when the Armistice came.

Chapter 9: Marriage (1932–1939)
1. Daphne letter to Maud Waddell ?.7.32.
2. It seems that at one time she thought that the wedding present might be Ferryside, and was doubtless disappointed when this turned out not to be the case.
3. Richards was devoted to Boy, who spent time teaching his batman the skills and social graces which would go well beyond those demanded of a soldier and valet and equip him for a successful life in domestic service after the Army. The regard was mutual, Boy considering that Richards epitomized the best qualities of a Guardsman.
4. Daphne letter to Maud Waddell 14.5.35.
5. From 1928 onwards it had been War Office policy to station two Foot Guards battalions at a time in Egypt and Boy's battalion was the last one from his regiment to go.
6. The battalion found a Guard of Honour when the coffin arrived in London from Sandringham and lined the streets for the funeral. Boy, like the other officers, stood watch over the coffin during the Lying-in-State.
7. Daphne letter to Maud Waddell 12.9.36.
8. Lord Carrington remembered being grateful that one of the other subalterns was so incompetent that he attracted most of Boy's considerable wrath!

Chapter 10: Brigadier (1939–1941)
1. By a coincidence, Boy was sleeping in exactly the same street in Arras where he had been billeted at the time of the first day of the Hindenburg offensive in March 1918, being awakened by the sound of bombs where once he had heard shells.
2. Papers of Captain L. C. R. Balding in the Imperial War Museum.
3. Richards had left the Army in 1934 at the conclusion of seven years service, but he and Lily stayed on with the Brownings until they left for Egypt: Richards was recalled from the Regular Reserve in August 1939, but was injured in France in 1940: later in the War he served in North Africa.
4. Brian Urquhart, *A Life in Peace and War*, p.48.
5. Letter to Daphne 24.4.65.
6. The GOC was John Swayne, who had been a fellow battalion commander of Boy's in Egypt.
7. Alex Danchev & Daniel Todman (eds), *War Diaries 1939–1945: Field Marshal Lord Alanbrooke*, p.193. Larking, who was standing next door to Boy when this news was delivered, said subsequently that it was believed by some that Boy had been disappointed not to get command of the Guards Armoured Division when this was formed in June 1941: however,

Oliver Leese was senior to Boy in the Brigade of Guards and already had experience of commanding a division, so was the most obvious candidate for the job.

8. 24 Brigade survived in a number of incarnations, latterly as 24 Airmobile Brigade, but continued to use the same sign throughout its existence: at the end of the 1990s it was merged with elements of 5 Airborne Brigade to form 16 Air Assault Brigade.

Chapter 11: Pegasus (1941–1942)

1. Although numbered as 1 Airborne Division at an early stage, it seems to have been invariably referred to by all as 'The Airborne Division' until the formation of 6 Airborne Division in May 1943.
2. A long established practice in the Household Division, which continues to this day.
3. Brian Urquhart, *A Life in Peace and War*, p.48.
4. Contrary to myth, the choice of colour had nothing whatever to do with Daphne.
5. It was probably not a coincidence that claret and light blue were the colours of Boy's racing silks when point-to-pointing between the wars.
6. Senior officers tended not to jump frequently in practice, as they were regarded as too valuable to lose. When Maxwell Taylor of US 101 Airborne Division landed in Holland during Operation 'Market Garden', it was only his fifth or sixth jump, one of the others being on D-Day in Normandy. There were exceptions, such as K. N. Crawford, Director of Air at the War Office, who seemed to relish every opportunity to leap out of an aeroplane.
7. It was reported subsequently that Boy had learnt to fly in about 1930 which may well be true, although he had clearly not kept it up since. The Civil Aviation Authority has no record of a licence, but he may have gained one through the Household Brigade Flying Club, which was active at that time. Unfortunately, the club's records have all been lost.
8. Boy's forty-sixth birthday was in December 1942, so Chatterton must have meant forty-five.
9. George Chatterton, *The Wings of Pegasus*, p.27.
10. To the disappointment of both Boy and Norman, the RAF insisted on using a Bomber Command squadron, No 51, instead of 297 Squadron.

Chapter 12: Expansion (1942)

1. Jacob had been Brigade Major of the Canal Brigade during Boy's time in Egypt.
2. Later redesignated 2nd Battalion, 509 Infantry Regiment.
3. Brian Urquhart *A Life in Peace and War*, p.54.

Chapter 13: Setbacks (1942–1943)

1. 7th Battalion The Cameron Highlanders and 10th Battalion The Royal Welch Fusiliers.
2. In fact the casualties had been so high for the Germans that Hitler had issued an order effectively ending large-scale airborne operations.
3. Brooke was Commandant of the School of Artillery at Larkhill from 1929 to 1932.
4. Alex Danchev & Daniel Todman (eds), *War Diaries 1939–1945: Field Marshal Lord Alanbrook,'* p. 337.
5. Subsequently SOE took over responsibility for the project. Operation 'Gunnerside', carried out in February 1943 by a party of Norwegians who parachuted in, was completely successful.
6. 10th Battalion The Somerset Light Infantry, 13th Battalion The Royal Warwickshire Regiment and 10th Battalion The Essex Regiment.
7. He might have been referring to the Ismay letter, but more probably to some additional lobbying. Boy later confessed to have been quite shaken by this dressing-down, as were all those who suffered a lashing from Brooke's tongue.

Chapter 14: Adviser (1943)
1. His appointment actually took effect on 5 April.
2. Leaving Lathbury in temporary command of the division.
3. 156 Parachute Battalion hung on to its Indian traditions for some time: when it eventually arrived in Tunisia, Hopkinson had to order the men to wear red berets, as they much preferred their slouch hats.
4. This was typical of Boy. On 2 August 1944, he flew in a Stirling over France, on a mission dropping supplies to the Resistance, to familiarize himself with the aircraft.
5. Letter to Daphne 19.5.43.
6. Brian Urquhart, *A Life in Peace and War*, p.60.
7. Matthew B. Ridgway, *Soldier*, p.67.
8. Notwithstanding his unwarlike, even saintly, character and hopeless timekeeping, Denys was very highly regarded by the Grenadiers for his devotion to duty throughout the campaigns in Tunisia and Italy, being awarded the honour of wearing the regiment's shoulder flashes.
9. A devout Anglican himself, Boy was largely responsible for the introduction throughout the Army of 'the Padre's Hour' a weekly informal meeting at platoon level, where the padre would give a brief talk, followed by a question and answer session.
10. Walch and the others were captured, but later escaped in the confusion.
11. John Waddy, who was a member of Hackett's brigade HQ at the time, believes that the two brigadiers approached Boy to suggest this. (Interview 18.2.09)

Chapter 15: Corps (December 1943–June 1944)
1. This is the date in 1 Airborne Division's war diary. The war diary of HQ Airborne Troops gives it as 10 December 1943, which is possibly when the announcement was made, whilst Urquhart's promotion to acting major general dated from 10 January 1944.
2. Down went out to India in early 1944, but his only formation, 50 Indian Airborne Brigade, was withdrawn to participate in the Kohima/Imphal battle, followed by most of his HQ and divisional troops. He returned to England that April and helped with training and equipping the Poles, going back to India in the late summer. 44 Indian Airborne Division was duly raised, but never used as a complete formation.
3. Roy Urquhart, *Arnhem*, p.14.
4. It was said that Boy took his 'personal' chef and doctor with him later to Nijmegen. Brian Urquhart can remember neither of these positions, although the Corps HQ mess cook would have gone, as did a medical officer, Captain Louis. Boy, in any event, was never particularly interested in food.
5. Richard Gale, *With the Sixth Airborne Division in Normandy*, p.33.
6. Letter to Daphne from Geoffrey Loring 15.3.65.
7. James Gavin, *On to Berlin*, p.82.
8. Ibid. p.83.
9. Richard Gale, *With the Sixth Airborne Division in Normandy* p.61.
10. Ibid. p.66.

Chapter 16: Frustration (6 June–9 September 1944)
1. Larger and smaller numbers are given by various authors and Brereton mentions in his diary no less than ten operations still under consideration on 11 September: my figure derives from Terence Otway's authoritative, *Airborne Forces*.
2. Thomas Firbank, *I Bought a Star*, p.174.
3. Brian Urquhart, *A Life in Peace and War*, p.66.
4. Stanislaw Sosabowski, *Freely I Served*, p.133.
5. Boy had seen Sosabowski himself on a number of occasions, the latest in March 1945.
6. Brereton was not the first choice of the US Army Air Force Chief of Staff, 'Hap' Arnold, who preferred Lieutenant General John K. Cannon, then Commanding General of the

Mediterranean Allied Tactical Air Force: with experience of a combined US/British HQ, he would probably have been a good choice.

7. Henry Pownall, later to be Boy's predecessor at SEAC, described him whilst at ABDACOM as 'a grim, humourless little creature' but conceded that he was efficient, *Diaries – Volume Two 1940–1944*, p.81.
8. Terence Otway, *Airborne Forces*, p.202.
9. Patton was reputed to have said that, if any 'Limey paratroopers' got in the way of his armour, he would shoot them!
10. It would have been a risky move by Brereton: Ridgway was having some difficulty putting together his new HQ with sufficient and suitably experienced staff and, like Boy, was particularly deficient in signals.
11. Daphne letter to Maud Waddell 23.7.44.
12. Letter to Daphne 26.7.44.
13. Roy Urquhart, *Arnhem*, p.18.
14. Letter to Daphne 7.9.44.
15. Le Havre was not taken until 12 September, Calais and Boulogne not until the end of the month.

Chapter 17: Sixteen (10–16 September 1944)
1. Papers of Field Marshal Montgomery in the Imperial War Museum.
2. Charles Richardson, *Flashback*, p.186.
3. Roy Urquhart, *Arnhem*, p.4.
4. Papers of Brigadier Gordon Walch in the Imperial War Museum.
5. These words were first recorded by Chester Wilmot in *The Struggle for Europe*, following an interview with Major General Sir Miles Graham, Montgomery's Principal Administrative Officer, who was present at the meeting.
6. Not according to his Naval Aide, who wrote in his diary on 13 September: 'Ike has decided that a northern thrust toward the Ruhr under Montgomery is not at the moment to have priority over other operations.' Harry Butcher, *Three Years With Eisenhower*, p.567.
7. Papers of Field Marshal Montgomery in the Imperial War Museum.
8. Some thirty officers attended the conference.
9. Matthew Ridgway, *Soldier*, p.108.
10. IX Troop Carrier Command, which would carry into action not only the American, but also the British and Polish paratroopers, had been substantially expanded in terms of planes and pilots in the period before the operation, but this had not been matched by additional ground staff, which provided strong support to Williams's case.
11. Chatterton volunteered to fly in to this piece of ground himself, but was turned down: he appealed to Boy, but was told that the decision was to stand.
12. There is no written evidence of this, the source being a conversation many years later between Gale and the then curator of the Airborne Museum, Geoffrey Norton: Gale asked that the information, given only verbally, should not be revealed during the lifetimes of those involved.
13. SHAEF Intelligence Summaries had limited distribution and Boy may not have seen them, but FAAA was on the list.
14. Letter to Daphne 9.9.44.
15. Brian Urquhart, *A Life in Peace and War*, p.71.
16. The Dutch Resistance had been seriously compromised in an SOE operation between 1942 and 1944 in which all the agents had been turned by the Germans; information from this source therefore tended to be viewed with great suspicion by the Allies.
17. The relationship appears to have improved somewhat after Linnet II, possibly because Brereton had been 'much struck' with the design of Boy's proposed new boat, *Fanny Rosa*.

Chapter 18: Market (17–20 September 1944)

1. According to Brian Urquhart, this caused a certain amount of hilarity among his fellow senior officers. It could only have been worn by someone with Boy's slim figure and was in keeping with the 'harmless vanity' which Urquhart recalled.
2. This might seem strange to anyone who knew Boy for his almost obsessive tidiness. However, Parks was not an airborne soldier himself and probably failed to recognise organized chaos when he saw it!
3. Lewis Brereton, *The Brereton Diaries*, p.344n.
4. Letter to Daphne 16.9.44.
5. He was later well known in cricketing circles as Secretary for many years of the MCC.
6. It is a nice story and not apocryphal, as it was mentioned in Walchs's memoirs, but from the map reference and from aerial photos which identify the Corps gliders clearly, it is certain that the wood was still in the Netherlands and that the German frontier was actually over a mile away. In any event, American soldiers had entered Germany for the first time near Aachen on September 11, although whether or not they had relieved themselves is not known!
7. Known as the Mechelen Incident.
8. During the early afternoon of 19 September, for instance, one caller from Arnhem said that the bridge had been lost, whilst another reported 100 tanks entering the town from the north. Neither was true.
9. According to Chatterton, Boy also met Taylor at the bridge, but there is no confirmation of this from the Airborne Corps war diary.
10. Interview with Lord Carrington 10.6.08.
11. Brian Horrocks, *Corps Commander*, p.110.
12. Allan Adair, *A Guards General*, p.165.
13. Von Tettau was responsible for all training in the Netherlands, but had commanded an infantry division on the Eastern Front.
14. At this stage of the War, Germany was so short of manpower that many men were drafted into the armed forces with a lower than normally acceptable level of physical fitness. They included those suffering from deafness and a wide range of chronic stomach complaints.
15. He meant Colonel Reuben H. Tucker, the commander of 504 Parachute Infantry Regiment.
16. George Chatterton, *The Wings of Pegasus*, p.178.
17. Gavin's engineers had been hard at work collecting small boats on the Maas-Waal Canal for use in any crossing: however, their efforts were foiled by the Germans destroying the lock gates leading on to the Waal.
18. It is sometimes forgotten, and invariably ignored in American accounts, that the boats were also manned by men from 615 Field Squadron of the Guards Armoured Division, who brought them back across the river for subsequent trips.
19. There has been considerable controversy over whether the Americans had taken the north end of the bridge. Carrington saw none until nearly a mile further on and Lieutenant A. G. C. Jones, the engineer charged with removing the demolition charges, remembered only the considerable number of Germans still in the girders. American accounts insist that a group from 3/504 Parachute Infantry were there to greet the British tanks. The truth is probably that both arrived at the northern end at much the same time.

Chapter 19: Garden (21–24 September 1944)

1. Letter to Daphne 15.3.65.
2. Letter to Daphne 19.9.44.
3. They became separated during an air raid on Eindhoven.
4. Lewis Brereton, *The Brereton Diaries*, p.354n.

5. This was the name given by the Allies: its local name is Betuwe or, more properly for that part where the fighting was taking place, Overbetuwe.

6. The 'Seaborne Tail' of 1 Airborne Division also arrived. More than 2,000 strong, it comprised mostly supporting troops – RAOC, REME and, most substantial in number, RASC – and carried ammunition, rations and personal kit, which proved very useful after the withdrawal.

7. Papers of Brigadier Gordon Walch in the Imperial War Museum.

8. Papers of Field Marshal Viscount Montgomery in the Imperial War Museum.

9. He was widely known, in his division and outside, as 'The Butcher' for his readiness to take objectives at any cost, not an attitude commonly associated with the British Army at this time, keen as it was to preserve its fast depleting human resources.

10. Hubert Essame, *The 43rd Wessex Division at War 1943–1945*, p.132.

11. Some writers on 'Market Garden' have said that Boy was also present, but there is no mention of this in Dempsey's personal war diary, nor those of I Airborne Corps or XXX Corps. The fact that he was having lunch with and then meeting Sosabowski reinforces this.

Chapter 20: Tragedy (24 September–9 October 1944)

1. Roy Urquhart, *Arnhem*, p.204.
2. Letter to Daphne 24.9.44.
3. No letter was enclosed.
4. Roy Urquhart, *Arnhem*, pp.179–80.
5. Letter to Daphne 28.9.44.
6. Michael Packe, *First Airborne*, p.1.
7. Letter from Daphne to Frederic Kelly 29.3.67.
8. Stanislaw Sosabowski, *Freely I Served*, p.189.
9. Brian Urquhart, *A Life in Peace and War*, p.75.
10. Ibid.
11. Bernard Montgomery, *The Memoirs of Field-Marshal Montgomery*, p.298.
12. Matthew Ridgway, *Soldier: The Memoirs of Matthew B Ridgway*, p.110.
13. Roy Urquhart, *Arnhem*, p.203.
14. Brian Horrocks, *A Full Life*, p.231.
15. James Gavin, *On to Berlin*, p.170.
16. Papers of Air Chief Marshal Sir Leslie Hollinghurst in the Imperial War Museum.

Chapter 21: Verdict (10 September–26 October 1944)

1. Roy Urquhart, *Arnhem*, p.14.
2. James Gavin, *Airborne Warfare*, p.75.
3. Stanislaw Sosabowski, *Freely I Served*, p.183.

Chapter 22: Aftermath (October–December 1944)

1. Including O'Connor, Horrocks, Ritchie, Adair, Thomas and Gale.
2. Stanislaw Sosabowski, *Freely I Served*, p.199.
3. Essame was particularly close to Horrocks, who later employed him as one of his two co-authors in his book 'Corps Commander'.
4. Hubert Essame, *The 43rd Wessex Division at War, 1943–1945*, pp.131,132.
5. In 1947, somewhat bizarrely given his attitude towards the Poles, Thomas was appointed Administrator, Polish Forces under British Command.
6. It cost £140 and Daphne paid!
7. Papers of Field Marshal Viscount Montgomery in the Imperial War Museum.
8. O'Connor left VIII Corps at the end of November 1944 to take up the appointment of GOC-in-C Eastern Command, India.
9. Henry Pownall, (ed. Brian Bond), *Chief of Staff*, p.193.
10. Alex Danchev & Daniel Todman (eds), *War Diaries 1939–1945: Field Marshal Lord Alanbrooke*, p.627.

11. Letter to Daphne 26.10.44.
12. Letter to Daphne 8.12.44.
13. Lewis Brereton, *The Brereton Diaries*, p.371.
14. It was also reported that Boy and Urquhart were invested with the CB. Urquhart had actually received his from the King nearly two months earlier, but handed it back so that it could be presented again. The date of Boy's investiture is not recorded, but it was nearly two years since he had been gazetted, so it must have been much earlier. Like Urquhart, he possibly went through the motions again.

Chapter 23: Kandy (December 1944–May 1945)

1. Henry Pownall, (ed. Brian Bond), *Chief of Staff*, p.198.
2. Letter to Daphne 27.12.44.
3. Letter to Daphne 2.1.45.
4. Ibid.
5. Letter to Brooke 25.12.44.
6. Rowland Ryder, *Oliver Leese*, p.211.
7. Daphne letter to Maud Waddell 18.2.45.
8. Letter to Daphne 14.2.45.
9. Letter to Daphne 18.3.45.
10. Not so, her interest in clothes was nearly non-existent. If his uniforms diverged from the official issue, it was of his own doing. None of the photos of him during this period show him in anything other than authorized dress.
11. Maureen Baker-Munton (née Lushwitz) thought that his sterness was bluff and that it may have disguised the fact that, in some ways, he was unsure of himself. (Interview 22 June 2009)
12. Papers of Major J. H. Money in the Imperial War Museum. (By kind permission of the Provost and Scholars of King's College, Cambridge 2010)
13. Letter to Daphne 4.3.45.
14. So called because it had been presented to him by 'Hap' Arnold, the USAAF Chief of Staff.
15. Letter from Mountbatten to Boy 11.3.45.
16. Letter to Daphne 28.2.45.

Chapter 24: Victory (May–November 1945)

1. Mountbatten, (ed., Philip Ziegler), *Personal Diary*, p.205.
2. Danchev & Todman, *War Diaries 1939–1945*, p.692.
3. The brother of Boy's friend, 'Chink' Dorman-Smith.
4. Aung San led the Burma National Army, which had been collaborating hitherto with the Japanese, but which turned against them in a rising on 28 March.
5. Mountbatten, (ed., Philip Ziegler), *Personal Diary*, p.218.
6. It is easy to have some sympathy with Leese, whose career came to an effective end, without even the promotion to full general which his record and recent responsibilities would usually have justified. He was, however, naïve in his dealings with Slim, whilst his attitude – almost one of condescension – towards Mountbatten was certain to lead to disaster in the end.
7. Letter to Daphne 10.6.45.
8. Ibid.
9. Letter to Daphne 18.1.46.
10. Daphne letter to Maud Waddell 27.7.45.
11. In accordance with Mountbatten's instructions that all Japanese officers should surrender their ceremonial swords to their opposite numbers, Boy received Numata's. In a gesture of reconciliation he returned it to Numata many years later.
12. Letter to Daphne 28.9.45.
13. Letter to Daphne 13.11.45.

Chapter 25: Singapore (November 1945–July 1946)

1. One of Boy's Wren 'writers', Joan Ward, recalled being very self-conscious about having to walk the length of the room in order to take dictation.
2. Letter to Daphne 15.12.45.
3. The Indian Parachute Regiment was to prove short lived, being disbanded in November 1946 as part of the immediate post-war reorganization of the Indian Army. A new Parachute Regiment was formed in India in 1952, which retained the maroon beret, but changed the badges, Pegasus and Bellerephon becoming Shatrujeet, a figure from Hindu mythology, half-man and half horse, although the colours of maroon and blue were retained. The new regiment, however, does not regard the old one as its predecessor. Its battle honours are those of the former infantry regiments from which it was formed, but these do not include 'Sangshak'.
4. During his stay he found himself under fire for the first time since Nijmegen, when his party became the target of an insurgent sniper.
5. Letter to Daphne 16.2.46.
6. Letter to Mountbatten 6.3.46.
7. Mountbatten letter to Boy 9.3.46.
8. Bernard Hailstone. The painting is in the Imperial War Museum.
9. 'Q' Quiller-Couch was a friend of the du Mauriers and something of a mentor to Daphne: his daughter, Foy, was one of her best friends.
10. Letter to Daphne 21.2.46.
11. Letter to Daphne 13.3.46.
12. Later Lord Inverchapel. He had been British Ambassador in Moscow and was due to take up the same position in Washington.
13. Mountbatten letter to Boy 30.5.46.
14. Letter to Mountbatten 1.6.46.
15. Text of talk on 12.6.46.
16. Letter to Daphne 7.6.46.
17. Pirie letter to Mountbatten 15.7.46.

Chapter 26: Return (July 1946–December 1947)

1. She was 23 at the time.
2. At this time brigadier was not a substantive rank in the Army, but was only an acting or temporary appointment. The substantive rank immediately below major general was colonel.
3. There were two other selection boards, one for colonels and brigadiers, the other for more junior staff appointments: their secretaries were one or other of the two Deputy Military Secretaries.
4. Shinwell was an Eastender of Jewish-Polish extraction who had been a trades union leader of pronounced left-wing views before being elected an MP.
5. This had not been the case with Gort, who was brought in by the then Secretary of State, Leslie Hore-Belisha, over the head of the CIGS, with the express intent of clearing the logjam of generals which excessive patronage and a late retirement age had produced in the inter-war years.
6. After working tirelessly for the Girl Guides, latterly as Assistant County Commissioner for North London, Grace had chaired the National Association of Training Corps for Girls. She was awarded the OBE.
7. Boy himself remained devoted to Nancy, but saw her relatively infrequently. Nancy and Grace both moved to Downderry in Cornwall in 1953, living there until the former's death in 1959.
8. Now called the Chief Executive.
9. Although born a Prince of Greece, Philip had given up his title on becoming a British citizen in 1947. Whilst created both Duke of Edinburgh and a Royal Highness, he did not in fact become a Prince of the United Kingdom until 1957.

10. There appears to be more than a suggestion of Mountbatten's earlier comments about Boy's political judgement in this statement.
11. Broadlands Archives E 23.

Chapter 27: Princess (1948–1952)

1. One of whom was Edward Ford, who had been on Boy's staff at 24 Guards Brigade Group. The other was Michael Adeane, who was to succeed Alan Lascelles as Private Secretary.
2. Norman Gwatkin, formerly commander of 5 Guards Armoured Brigade during Market Garden.
3. Boy gave the Princess his full dress sash to wear on the occasions on which she 'went into scarlet'. He gave the Duke his bearskin.
4. Letter to Daphne 15.3.65.
5. The son of King George V's Private Secretary, who had written to Freddie after Gauche Wood.
6. It is now called Fields in Trust and the Duke is still the President, over sixty years later.
7. Letter to Daphne 3.10.48.
8. Eisenhower had recently retired as Chief of Staff of the US Army and was now President of Columbia University.
9. Colonel C. F. H. Gough. He was much closer to Boy in age than his wartime rank of major might suggest. He commanded the 1 Airborne Reconnaissance Squadron during Market Garden and took over command at the Arnhem road bridge when John Frost was wounded.
10. Now the Royal Academy of Dance.
11. Letter to Boy 30.1.51.
12. *The Kipling Journal*, December 1950.
13. Letter to Lieutenant General E.A.B. Miller 15.5.51.
14. Ridgway subsequently described himself and Boy as having become 'staunch friends': *Soldier: The Memoirs of Matthew B Ridgway*, p.68.

Chapter 28: Duke (1952–1956)

1. The Equerry is more formally called the Equerry-in-Waiting, a role held by a relatively junior officer (lieutenant commander, major or squadron leader) of the armed services on attachment, usually for two years. There are also three or four Extra Equerries, who are not permanently employed but are available as required.
2. She also used to do private work for him at weekends.
3. Now the Cutty Sark Trust.
4. The party flew back in a BOAC Comet 1, the first commercial jet airliner, which had entered service only two months before. It was piloted by Group Captain John Cunningham, one of the most famous test pilots of the day.
5. The three men were commonly known in the Palace as 'The Duke's Beasts', equating them with 'The Queen's Beasts' – the Lion of England, the Unicorn of Scotland, the Red Dragon of Wales, the White Horse of Hanover and other heraldic animals.
6. The second son of King George III and C-in-C of the British Army 1795–1809 and 1811–27. He resigned in 1809 following a case against him for accepting bribes for commissions at which Clarke was a prosecution witness. It was subsequently revealed that she had been paid by his chief accuser and he was exonerated and reinstated.
7. Dame Anne Griffiths is now the Duke's Librarian and Archivist.
8. Boy himself had given time to Wilmot, although he is not included among the list of interviewees.
9. Letter to Horrocks 4 3.52.
10. Chester Wilmot, *The Struggle for Europe*, p.523.
11. Horrocks letter to Boy 5.3.52.
12. It was the Sherwood Rangers Yeomanry from this brigade which provided Gavin with his armoured support.

13. Letter Prior-Palmer to Boy 24.2.55.
14. Letter to Prior-Palmer 25.1.55.

Chapter 29: Breakdown (1956–1959)

1. Horace Evans had also been Physician to King George VI and was regarded as a friend by the Royal Family. He was also the doctor for many establishment figures, including the former Prime Minister, Anthony Eden. He had only just been made a Baron, on 1 July 1957.
2. In the tale, Kay has his heart frozen by the Snow Queen and a piece of glass from a troll's mirror is lodged in his eye. It is only the warm tears of his friend Gerda which can melt the ice and cause the glass to fall out. 'Snow Queen' became an alternative codeword for 'Covent Garden'.
3. One of the five children who had been adopted by J. M. Barrie and possibly himself the model for Peter Pan.
4. Oriel Malet, *Letters from Menabilly*, p.102.
5. Daphne letter to Williams 23.10.57. Evie had been Gertrude Lawrence's secretary.
6. He had been the Queen's Colour Officer in Malta when the Duke, as its Captain-General, presented new colours to the Corps in 1952, and the Officer Commanding Royal Marines in HMS *Surprise* when the Queen carried out the Coronation Review from the ship in 1953.
7. Boy admired Reed, but delighted in telling the story of taking him up in a plane and seeing him turn from pink to yellow to green!
8. In one famous scene in *The Big Country*, Ives walks out alone shouting 'Hold your fire' to his opponents; during the filming of *Our Man in Havana*, Boy would frequently ask Kits 'And how's old "hold your fire?"'
9. This entitled him to have supporters for his coat of arms. He chose a golden eagle on one side and, very appropriately, 'an English Archer of ancient times' on the other.
10. Daphne letter to Williams 14.5.59.

Chapter 30: Finale (1959–1965)

1. Letter to Grace Browning 20.10.60.
2. They had known each other for more than thirty-five years, from the pre-war period during which Carew-Pole had served with the Coldstream Guards.
3. Letter to Grace Browning 15.7.63.
4. Oriel Malet, *Letters from Menabilly*, p.184.

Chapter 31: Postscript (1965–1989)

1. After winning the Sword of Honour at Sandhurst on the day on which Boy had first ridden his horse up the steps into the Old Building, Cassels had come across Boy frequently in 1942, when he had worked closely with the Airborne Division as an army liaison officer at the Air Ministry.
2. The Regimental Depot remained at the Browning Barracks until 1993, when it moved to Colchester. The site continued to house the Airborne Forces Museum until this was closed at the end of 2007, to be reopened as the Airborne Assault Museum at Duxford in 2009.
3. He was attached to an aerial photography interpretation unit, but was certainly not involved with 'Market Garden', although he may have met Boy in Normandy. Immediately after the War he served on the staff of 23 Indian Division in the Netherlands East Indies, and an alternative possibility is that he may have come across Boy there.
4. Ray subsequently became a well-known writer on wine, with books such as *The Complete Imbiber* to his name.
5. Richard Attenborough: 'A Filmmaker Remembers' – Featurette from the DVD Special Edition of *A Bridge Too Far*.
6. Daphne letter to Denys Browning 18.3.79.

Acknowledgements

I must start by expressing my gratitude to His Royal Highness The Duke of Edinburgh, both for honouring me with a Foreword and for giving me some of his valuable time during my research. Boy Browning worked for Princess Elizabeth and the Duke jointly for four years, and then for Prince Philip alone for another seven years, following Her Majesty's accession to the Throne. Moreover, His Royal Highness has, for some thirty-five years, been Colonel of the regiment in which Boy served from 1915 to 1939. He is thus uniquely qualified to offer a view on my subject.

I could not have written a full biography without the support of Boy's family. Tessa, Viscountess Montgomery of Alamein, is the expert on family history, and as the oldest of his children, has the longest standing recollection of him. She has been consistently encouraging and helpful far beyond my expectations, allowing me full access to Boy's letters and other papers and providing me with a number of valuable introductions. Her husband, David, was able to add some colour to Boy's relationship with his own father, from whose papers I am grateful for permission to quote and her son, Paul de Zulueta, gave me yet another view from the perspective of a grandchild. Flavia, Lady Leng, shared her memories with me, whilst her charming book on her mother includes some valuable insights into her father. Flavia's son, Rupert Tower, produced some documents which I would not otherwise have seen. Kits Browning gave very generously of his time when I visited him at Ferryside, the old du Maurier house in Cornwall, and he and his wife, Hacker, were most hospitable. The photos in the book were substantially provided by Tessa and Flavia.

My other acknowledgements fall roughly into the chronological order of Boy's life. For the detail of and background to the Browning coat of arms, I am grateful to William Hunt, Windsor Herald of Arms. Nick Hodson, the Secretary of the Old West Downs Society, pointed me towards the background to Boy's early schooldays and Penny Hatfield, the College Archivist at Eton, put the resources of the College Library at my disposal.

My research into Boy's long career with the Grenadier Guards was assisted enormously by Lieutenant Colonel Conway Seymour, the Regimental Archivist. He arranged for me to use the Library at Wellington Barracks, where I worked under a three-quarter length portrait of Boy, painted in the 1920s by Sir Gerald Kelly and on loan from the family. By a coincidence, Colonel Seymour received at just this time a letter from Jake Whitehouse, whose father had served under

Boy in the 2nd Battalion during the Great War, and to whom I am grateful for the latter's reminiscences. Other former Grenadiers who helped me included Major General Bernard Gordon Lennox, the late Colonel Oliver Lindsay, then editor of the *Guards Magazine*, and Lieutenant Colonel Henry Hanning, the author of an excellent history of the regiment. I had the privilege of meeting two pre-war Grenadiers, Lord Carrington, who had served under Boy in the 2nd Battalion, and Lord Wigram, who first met the recently engaged Boy and Daphne when out from school to tea with Admiral Sir Montague Browning, Boy's uncle and a friend of Lord Wigram's father.

Major General David Rutherford Jones, then the Commandant of the Royal Military Academy, assisted by his ADC, Captain Will Jelf, arranged for my visit there. Andrew Orgill, the Librarian, provided some most useful information, Anthony Morton, the Archivist, followed up a number of my queries, and Peter Thwaites, the Curator of the Sandhurst Collection, gave me the benefit of his thoughts. Major Marcus Elmhirst, the Adjutant, explained the technicalities of riding up the steps of the Old Building and he and his wife were kind enough to let me look round Lake House, still the Adjutant's residence. Shortly before my visit, Major Elmhirst had received a letter from Colonel David Fanshawe, himself late of the Grenadier Guards and a former Adjutant of the RMA, enclosing his mother's account of Boy's first ride up the steps. I am most grateful to Colonel Fanshawe for allowing me to use this.

As far as Boy's athletic career in the 1920s was concerned, I had a most useful correspondence with Peter Emery, the Chairman of the South London Harriers. Tessa Pollack, the daughter of Boy's batman in the 1930s, Guardsman Richards, let me have her father's recollections. I gathered my information on the Small Arms School from a visit to the Corps Museum at Warminster, where Major Norman Benson was very helpful.

To many readers the most interesting part of Boy's career will be the period with the Airborne Forces. Sir Brian Urquhart was on Boy's staff from the earliest days of the Airborne Division. He was, of course, a critical witness on the question of Intelligence prior to Operation 'Market Garden', but his proximity to Boy over a much longer time made his recollections uniquely valuable and I am most grateful for his ready cooperation. Roy Urquhart's daughter, Judith, has been consistently interested in my progress and has helped with introductions. Through her and Frank Newhouse, the Treasurer of the Arnhem 1944 Veterans Club, I was able to talk to a number of veterans, including David Eastwood, Bill Bloys and Maurice Herridge. I had a spirited correspondence with Major Tony Hibbert and a long interview with Colonel John Waddy. Colonel Waddy also told me of his experiences as an adviser on the film *A Bridge Too Far*, whilst John Coldstream, Dirk Bogarde's biographer, was immensely helpful on the same subject.

My research on the airborne forces was further helped by Jon Baker, Curator of the Airborne Assault Museum, Susan Lindsay, Curator of the Museum of Army Flying, and her colleague Keith Male, Major Steve Elsey of the Army Air Corps,

Mike Collins of the Parachute Regimental Association, and Nicholas Humphrey of the Airborne Forces Security Fund. I should also mention Jon Moore, the Chief Executive of Moor Park Golf Club, and Maz O'Brien, who showed me round Boy's 1944 HQ.

In the Netherlands I had two meetings with Adrian Groeneweg and Wybo Boersma, both former directors of the Airborne Museum 'Hartenstein' in Oosterbeek and the undoubted experts on the Arnhem battle. I also met Frank van den Bergh of the National Liberation Museum at Groesbeek, who has an encyclopaedic knowledge of the whole of 'Market Garden' and who was able to correct some misconceptions. Arie-Jan van Hees was extremely helpful on the use of gliders during the operation and a number of other matters.

My particular thanks are due to Peter Harclerode and Neil Powell, both of whom read a draft of the section on 'Market Garden' and offered their own views on my description of the operation and my conclusions. Whilst I did not necessarily agree with them on everything, their criticism was most constructive and added value to what will be, for many people, the most important, but also the most controversial part of the book.

Maureen Baker-Munton (née Luschwitz), Boy's Personal Assistant at SEAC, contributed considerably to my understanding of Boy's time there and Joan Ward also sent me some of her recollections. Mrs Baker-Munton was also very helpful on the post-war period as were Julie Burt (née Parker), Laila Embelton (formerly Spence), and Oriel Malet. I am grateful to Mrs Burt for allowing me to use a photo of Boy and her father with the Queen and the Duke of Edinburgh. Lieutenant General Sir Alistair Irwin, himself a former Military Secretary, helped me to understand that role. At Buckingham Palace, in addition to the Duke of Edinburgh, I was able to meet Brigadier Sir Miles Hunt-Davis, the Duke's current Private Secretary and Treasurer, and one of his predecessors, Sir Brian McGrath, whilst Dame Anne Griffiths, the Duke's Librarian and Archivist, had worked for Boy and was the most valuable source of information on his career there. Major General David Alexander told me how he had stood in for Boy as the Duke's Treasurer.

For information about some of Boy's extramural activities, I am obliged to Peter Carpenter (Kurt Hahn Trust), Simon Clegg (British Olympic Association), Deborah Dowdell (The Duke of Edinburgh's Award), Jane Keskar (The Kipling Society), Luke Rittner (The Royal Academy of Dance), Gail Smith (Cutty Sark Trust) and Major General John Sutherell (The Officer's Association), all of whom responded readily to my request for information, as did Lady Mary Holborow, the Lord Lieutenant of Cornwall. Tim Essex-Lopresti of the Civil Defence Association and Robin Woolven of the Mountbatten Centre for International Studies filled me in on the Civil Defence issues of the 1960s.

I am most appreciative for their help to Helen Taylor, Professor of English at Exeter University, and the acknowledged expert on Daphne du Maurier's works, to Jessica Gardner and Christine Faunch, Professor Taylor's colleagues at the University's Special Collections, where the du Maurier papers are deposited, and to the Chichester Partnership for permission to quote from them. Others who assisted me during visits to their institutions were Karen Robson of the Hartley Library at the University of Southampton, where the Mountbatten Papers are housed, and Katherine Godfrey of the Liddell Hart Centre for Military Archives at King's College, London. I thank the Trustees of the Broadland Archives for permission to quote from the Mountbatten Papers and the Trustees of the Liddell Hart Centre for permission to quote from the papers of Field Marshal Alanbrooke. Roderick Suddaby and the staff at the Imperial War Museum were invariably helpful and I am grateful to the Trustees for allowing me access to its collections and to each of the copyright holders who gave me permission to use extracts. I never failed to be impressed by the efficiency of the National Archives.

I would like to thank Henry Wilson of Pen & Sword for his enthusiastic support throughout the process and my editor, Jan Chamier, for her professionalism and good humour.

Finally, I could not have written this book without the encouragement of my wife, Sheelagh, and my two sons, Tim and Rupert. Rupert was a most valuable sounding board throughout the project, correcting the drafts of each chapter as they emerged and acting as my companion and chauffeur on my two visits to the Netherlands.

Sources and Bibliography

Interviews

His Royal Highness The Duke of Edinburgh
Major General David Alexander
Mrs Maureen Baker-Munton
Mr Bill Bloys
Mr Wybo Boersma
Mr Christian Browning
Mrs Julie Burt
Lord Carrington
Mr Paul de Zulueta
Mr David Eastwood
Mrs Laila Embleton
Dame Anne Griffiths
Mr Adrian Groeneweg
Lady Leng
Mr Maurice Herridge
Lady Oriel Malet
Viscount Montgomery of Alamein
Viscountess Montgomery of Alamein
Sir Brian Urquhart
Mr Frank Van den Bergh
Colonel John Waddy
Lieutenant Colonel The Lord Wigram

Primary Sources

The National Archives

AIR/1026	US XVIII Corps, 82 & 101 US Airborne Divisions reports on Market Garden
AIR 37/1214	I Airborne Corps report on Market Garden
AIR 37/1249	XXX Corps summary on Market Garden
CAB 121/97 & 98	Cabinet papers re Airborne Forces January 1941- August 1944
CSC 104034 & 4066	Royal Military College Exam Lists
DEFE 3 220-7	Ultra Decrypts 31 August–18 September 1944

WO 32/10927	Establishment of FAAA
WO 32/12322	Division of duties between Adjutant-General and Military Secretary
WO 95/1215	2nd Battalion Grenadier Guards War Diaries August 1915–January 1919
WO 165/82	Directorate of Air 1942
WO 166/978	128 Brigade War Diary
WO 166/927	24 Guards Brigade War Diary
WO 166/6547	1 Airborne Division War Diary December 1941–December 1942
WO 166/10464	1 Airborne Division War Diary January–April 1943
WO 166/10465	HQ Airborne Troops AQ December 1943
WO 166/10472	HQ Airborne Troops War Diary December 1943
WO 169/392	1 Airborne Division War Diary January–June 1944
WO 169/8666	1 Airborne Division War Diary July–December 1943
WO 171/133	HQ 21st Army Group intelligence summaries September–October 1944
WO 171/223	HQ Second Army G(I) War Diary September 1944
WO 171/366	I Airborne Corps War Diary 17–30 September 1944
WO 171/367	I Airborne Corps (Rear) War Diary 9–29 September 1944
WO 171/368	HQ Airborne Troops January–May 44 (Documents)
WO 171/369	HQ Airborne Troops War Diary January–July 1944
WO 171/370	HQ Airborne Troops War Diary August & October–December 1944
WO 171/376	Guards Armoured Division War Diary September 1944
WO 171 393	1 Airborne Division intelligence summaries September 1944
WO 171/594	Browning address re morale 17 August 1944
WO 171/605	5 Guards Armoured Brigade War Diary September 1944
WO 171/638	32 Guards Brigade War Diary September 1944
WO 204/10504	1 Airborne Division in Italy
WO 203/518	Formation & Training of 44 Indian Airborne Division
WO 205/313 & 314	21st Army Group re Market Garden
WO 205/432	Orders for Operation 'Comet'
WO 205/433	VIII Corps War Diary September 1944
WO 205/693	21st Army Group lessons of Market Garden
WO 205/872	21st Army Group report on Market Garden
WO 205/1125	Capture of Nijmegen Bridge
WO 205/1126	XXX Corps report on Market Garden
WO 205/1341	XXX Corps Operational Order for Market Garden
WO 208/5562	G2 SHAEF intelligence summaries September 1944
WO 219/552 & 2860	Formation of FAAA

WO 219/5167   SHAEF weekly intelligence summaries August–October 1944

WO 285/3 & 4   Second Army Intelligence Summaries 24 May–31 December 1944

WO 285/9 & 10   Diary of General Sir Miles Dempsey 6 June–9 October 1944

Imperial War Museum
Montgomery Collection
BLM 108, 109, 115, 119, 120, 126, 128 & 130
LMD 59, 62 & 63

Papers of Captain L. C. R. Balding, Air Chief Marshal Sir Leslie Hollinghurst, Major J. H. Money, Lieutenant-Colonel G. Tilly, Major-General R. E. Urquhart, Brigadier A. G. Walch

Liddell-Hart Centre, King's College, London
Papers of Field Marshal Viscount Alanbrooke, Captain Sir Basil Liddell-Hart, General Sir Richard O'Connor, Major-General Sir Ronald Penney, General Sir Harold Pyman

National Army Museum
Army Lists

Hartley Library, University of Southampton
Mountbatten Papers MB1/C1, 32, 47, 50, 64, 120, 125, 129, 132, 144, 145, 146, 148, 150, 152, 153 & E23

Special Collections, University of Exeter
Du Maurier Collection

Airborne Assault Museum, Duxford
Papers of General Sir Richard Gale
Various letters, minutes and other papers

Museum of Army Flying, Middle Wallop
Various letters, minutes and other papers

Archives of the Grenadier Guards
Various letters, minutes and other papers

Eton College Library
Term calendars and school lists

Private Browning Papers
Letters from Boy to Daphne, Grace Browning and Helen Browning
Letters to Boy on his retirement
Letters to Daphne following Boy's death
Sundry letters written by and to Boy
Description of the voyage of *Ygdrasil* to Fowey in 1931
Outline for ballet *Jeanne d'Arc*
Boy's Army Service Record and Confidential Reports
Browning and Alt family trees
Sundry other papers

Other Sources

Dictionary of National Biography
Eton College Chronicle
First Guards Club Handbook
London Gazette
Royal Military College Magazine & Record
The Times Digital Archive
The Guards Magazine
Who's Who

Books

Adair, Allan (ed. Oliver Lindsay), *A Guard's General – The Memoirs of Major General Sir Allan Adair*, London 1986
Asher, Michael, *The Regiment – The Real Story of the SAS*, London 2007
Badsey, Stephen, *Arnhem 1944 – Operation Market Garden*, Oxford 1993
Baynes, John, *The Forgotten Victor – General Sir Richard O'Connor*, London 1989
Baynes, John, *Urquhart of Arnhem*, London 1993
Belchem, David, *All In A Day's March*, London 1978
Bennett, David, *A Magnificent Disaster – The Failure of Market Garden, The Arnhem Operation, September 1944*, Newbury 2008
Blake, George, *Mountain and Flood – The History of the 52nd (Lowland) Division 1939–1946*, Glasgow 1950
Bond, Brian (ed.), *Chief of Staff – The Diaries of Lieutenant-General Sir Henry Pownall – Volume Two 1940–1944*, London 1974
Boothroyd, Basil, *Philip – An Informal Biography*, London 1971
Brandreth, Gyles, *Philip & Elizabeth – Portrait of a Marriage*, London 2004
Brereton, Lewis H., *The Brereton Diaries*, New York 1946
Browning, Denys, *Why The Grenadiers? – A Chaplain's Memoirs of the 5th Battalion Grenadier Guards 1942–1945*, Privately Published 1986
Bryant, Arthur, *The Turn of the Tide – 1939–1943*, London 1957
Bryant, Arthur, *Triumph in the West – 1943–1946*, London 1959
Buckingham, William F., *Arnhem 1944*, Stroud 2002

Butcher, Harry C., *Three Years with Eisenhower*, London 1946

Carton de Wiart, Adrian, *Happy Odyssey*, London 1950

Chatterton, George, *The Wings Of Pegasus – The Story of the Glider Pilot Regiment*, London 1962

Churchill, Winston S., *The Second World War, Volumes II to VI*, London, 1949–1954

Clark, Lloyd, *Arnhem – Jumping the Rhine 1944 and 1945 – The Greatest Airborne Battle in History*, London 2008

Coldstream, John, *Dirk Bogarde – The Authorised Biography*, London 2004

Colville, John, *Man of Valour – Field-Marshal Lord Gort VC*, London 1972

Danchev, Alex & Todman, Daniel (eds), *War Diaries 1939–1945 – Field Marshal Lord Alanbrooke*, London 2001 & 2003 (paperback)

Davies, Brian L., *British Army Uniforms & Insignia of World War II*, London 1983

D'Este, Carlo, *Bitter Victory – The Battle for Sicily 1943*, London 1988

D'Este, Carlo, *Eisenhower – Allied Supreme Commander*, London 2002

De Guingand, Francis, *Operation Victory*, London 1947

Dover, Victor, *The Sky Generals*, London 1981

Du Maurier, Daphne, *Myself When Young* (originally published as *Growing Pains: The Shaping of a Writer*), London 1977

Du Maurier, Daphne (ed. Oriel Malet), *Letters from Menabilly – Portrait of a Friendship*, London 1993

Eisenhower, Dwight D, *Crusade in Europe*, London 1948

Essame, Hubert, *The 43rd Wessex Division at War 1944–1945*, London 1952

Firbank, Thomas, *I Bought a Star*, London 1951

Forster, Margaret, *Daphne du Maurier*, London 1993

Fraser, David, *Alanbrooke*, London 1982

Fraser, David, *And We Shall Shock Them – The British Army in the Second World War*, London 1983

Fraser, David, *Wars and Shadows – Memoirs of General Sir David Fraser*, London 2002

Fullick, Roy, *Shan Hackett – The Pursuit of Exactitude*, Barnsley 2003

Gale, Richard, *With the Sixth Airborne Division in Normandy*, London 1948

Gale, Richard, *Call To Arms – an Autobiography*, London 1968

Gavin, James M., *Airborne Warfare*, Washington DC 1947

Gavin, James M., *On to Berlin – Battles of an Airborne Commander 1943–46*, New York 1978

Greacen, Lavinia, *Chink – A Biography*, London 1989

Hamilton, Nigel, *Monty – Master of the Battlefield 1942–1944*, London 1983

Hamilton, Nigel, *Monty – The Field-Marshal 1944–1976*, London 1986

Harclerode, Peter, *Go To It! – The Illustrated History of The 6th Airborne Division*, London 1990

Harclerode, Peter, *Arnhem – A Tragedy of Errors*, London 1994

Hanning, Henry, *The British Grenadiers – Three Hundred and Fifty Years of the First Regiment of Foot Guards 1656–2006*, Barnsley 2006

Hastings, Max, *Armageddon – The Battle for Germany 1944–45*, London 2004

Heald, Tim, *The Duke – A Portrait of Prince Philip*, London 1991

Henniker, Mark, *An Image of War*, London 1987

Hibbert, Christopher, *Arnhem*, London 1962

Horrocks, Brian, *A Full Life*, London 1960

Horrocks, Brian, (with Eversley Bellfield & Hubert Essame), *Corps Commander*, London 1977

Joslin, H. F., *Orders of Battle – Second World War 1939–1945*, London 1960

Judd, Alan, *The Quest for Mansfield Cumming and the Founding of the Secret Service*, London 1999

Kemp, Anthony, *The SAS at War 1941–1945*, London 1991

Kempson, Chris, *'Loyalty & Honour' – The Indian Army September 1939–August 1947*, Milton Keynes 2003

Kershaw, Robert J., *It Never Snows in September*, Shepperton 1994

Knox, Collie, *People of Quality*, London 1947

Koskodan, Kenneth K., *No Greater Ally – The Untold Story of Poland's Forces in World War II*, Oxford 2009

Lamb, Richard, *Montgomery in Europe 1943–45 – Success or Failure?*, London 1983

Leng, Flavia, *Daphne du Maurier – A Daughter's Memoir*, Edinburgh 1994

Lewin, Ronald, *Slim: The Standardbearer*, London 1976

Lewin, Ronald, *Ultra Goes To War – The Secret Story*, London 1978

Lovat, The Lord, *March Past – A Memoir*, London 1978

Lindsay, Donald, *Forgotten General – A Life of Andrew Thorne*, Salisbury 1987

Lyman, Robert, *Slim, Master of War – Burma and the Birth of Modern Warfare*, London 2004

Macmillan, Harold, *Winds of Change*, London 1966

Margry, Karel (Ed.), *Operation Market Garden Then and Now*, Harlow 2002

Melvin, Ronald (Ed.), *The Guards and Caterham – The Soldiers' Story*, Coulsdon 1999

Middlebrook, Martin, *Arnhem 1944 – The Airborne Battle*, London 1994

Mollo, Boris, *The Armed Forces of World War II*, London 1981

Montgomery of Alamein, The Viscount, *Normandy to the Baltic*, Germany 1946

Montgomery of Alamein, The Viscount, *The Memoirs of Field-Marshal Montgomery*, London 1958

Mountbatten of Burma, The Earl, *Report to the Combined Chiefs of Staff by the Supreme Allied Commander South-East Asia 1943–1945*, London 1951

Neillands, Robin, *The Battle for the Rhine 1944 – Arnhem and the Ardennes: the Campaign in Europe*, London 2005

Newnham, Maurice, *Prelude to Glory – The Story of the Creation of Britain's Parachute Army*, London 1947

Nordyke, Phil, *All American – All the Way – The Combat History of the 82nd Airborne Division in World War II*, St Paul, Minnesota 2005

Norton, G. G., *The Red Devils – The Story of The British Airborne Forces*, London 1971

Otway, Terence, *Airborne Forces*, London 1990

Packe, Michael, *First Airborne*, London 1948

Parlour, Andy & Sue, *Phantom at War – The British Army's Secret Intelligence & Communications Regiment of WWII*, Bristol 2003

Powell, Geoffrey, *The Devil's Birthday – The Bridges to Arnhem 1944*, London 1984

Place, Timothy Harrison, *Military Training in the British Army, 1940–1944 – From Dunkirk to D-Day*, London 2000

Parker, Eileen, *Step Aside for Royalty*, Maidstone 1982

Picardie, Justine, *Daphne*, London 2008

Ponsonby, Frederick, *The Grenadier Guards in the Great War of 1914–1919*, London 1920

Pyman, Harold, *Call to Arms – The Memoirs of General Sir Harold Pyman*, London 1971

Richardson, Charles, *Flashback – A Soldier's Story*, London 1985

Richardson, Charles, *Send for Freddie – The Story of Montgomery's Chief of Staff, Major-General Sir Francis de Guingand*, London 1987

Ridgway, Matthew B., *Soldier – The Memoirs of Matthew B Ridgway*, New York 1956

Ryan, Cornelius, *A Bridge Too Far*, London 1974

Ryder, Rowland, *Oliver Leese*, London 1987

Seth, Ronald, *Lion with Blue Wings – The Story of the Glider Pilot Regiment 1942–1945*, London 1955

Sosabowski, Stanislaw, *Freely I Served*, London 1960

Strong, Kenneth, *Intelligence at the Top – The Recollections of an Intelligence Officer*, London 1968

Taylor, Helen (Ed.), *The Daphne du Maurier Companion*, London 2007

Taylor, John M., *An American Soldier – The Wars of General Maxwell Taylor*, Novato, California 1989

Taylor, Maxwell D., *Swords and Ploughshares*, New York 1972

Thompson, R. W., *Montgomery: The Field Marshal – The Campaign in North-West Europe 1944–5*, London 1969

Urquhart, Brian, *A Life in Peace and War*, London 1987

Urquhart, Roy (with Wilfred Greatorex), *Arnhem*, London 1958

Van Hees, Arie-Jan, *Tugs and Gliders to Arnhem*, Eijsden, The Netherlands, 2000

Verney, Gerald, *The Guards Armoured Division – A Short History*, London 1955

Waddy, John, *A Tour of the Arnhem Battlefields*, Barnsley 1999

Warner, Philip, *Horrocks – The General Who Led From The Front*, London 1984

Warren, John C., *Airborne Operations in World War II, European Theatre*, Maxwell, Alabama 1956

Westmacott, Guy, *Memories*, Privately Published 1978

Wilmot, Chester, *The Struggle for Europe*, London 1952

Ziegler, Philip, *Mountbatten – The Official Biography*, London 1985

Ziegler, Philip (Ed.), *Personal Diary of Admiral The Lord Louis Mountbatten – Supreme Allied Commander South-East Asia 1943–1946*, London 1988

Index